Financing Education

Finance Management and Planning in Education: Lessons from the U.K. System

Financing Education

Finance Management and Planning in Education: Lessons from the U.K. System

Vol. I

D.K. GHOSH
Registrar, Indian Institute of Technology, Bombay

Foreword by

PROFESSOR JOHN SIZER, CBE

Chief Executive,
Scottish Higher Education Funding Council,
Edinburgh, Scotland, U.K.

COSMO PUBLICATIONS
INDIA 1997

First Published 1997

FINANCING EDUCATION (2 Volumes)

ISBN 81-7020-768-1 (Vol. I)

ISBN 81-7020-736-3 (Set)

Published by:

MRS. RANI KAPOOR
COSMO PUBLICATIONS
for GENESIS PUBLISHING PVT. LTD.
24-B, Ansari Road,
Darya Ganj,
New Delhi-110002, INDIA

Typeset by:
Manav Computer House

Printed at :
Mehra Offset Press

Contents

For

Shri Bimal Chandra Basu

Foreword

Two successive changes in British Government policy followed a period of expansion of the university sector of higher education until May 1979. The first, made in Autumn 1979, was a decision to withdraw subsidy progressively from overseas students coupled with the policy of 'level funding' for home students. The second, in the period December 1982-March 1981, was a decision to reduce annual expenditure on home students by amounts totalling 8½% by 1983-84. These two aspects of policy were cumulative and the University Grants Committee considered they were likely to produce an overall loss of recurrent resources between 1979-80 and 1983-84 in the range 11% (minimum estimate by the UGC) and 15% (suggested by the Committee for Vice-Chancellors and Principals) by 1983-84.

The impact of the two successive changes varied considerably between institutions. Firstly, the number and percentage of overseas undergraduate and post-graduate students in universities in 1979-80 varied considerably between institutions. Secondly, the UGC adopted a highly selective approach in implementing the reductions in grant, and also decided to reduce home and European community student numbers by 5% from 1979-80 levels by 1984-85, representing a reduction of 7½% on the 1980-81 total. There were significant variations in the advice given by the UGC to individual institutions. For example, the University of Salford faced a 30% reduction in student numbers and a 44% reduction in recurrent grant, the University of Sheffield faced a 0% change in student numbers and a 40% reduction in recurrent grant, and the University of Bath was allocated an extra 2% student numbers but faced 7% reduction in recurrent grant.

I directed a project which examined the responses of nine universities both to events leading up to, and to the UGC's 1 July 1981 grant letters; their impact upon the organisational structures, management style, planning resource allocation processes, etc. and upon the teaching, research, academic and administrative services, and related activities of institutions. Nine universities participated in the study and each prepared a detailed case study in four parts:

Part 1	Background Information.
Part 2	Build up to receipt of the UGC's grant letter for 1981-82, dated 1 July 1981.
Part 3	Responses to the UGCs grant letter for 1981-82.
Part 4	Impacts of the UGC's grant letter for 1981-82.

In a comparative analysis of the nine case studies the responses of, and differential impacts on, institutions which faced substantially different percentage cuts in recurrent grants and/or student numbers were considered and summarised, together with the implications for the future policy formulation by the Department for Education, the University Grants Committee and the Committee for Vice-Chancellors and Principals, and for the effective and efficient management of universities. In particular, a set of managerial guidelines for managing financial reductions was drawn from the analysis.

Since completing the study there has been a period of substantial expansion with a significant shift from an elite higher education system towards a mass higher education system. Nevertheless, economy and efficiency and effectiveness, value for money, performance indicators, executive styles of management, devolved budgeting and accountability within institutions, and departmental and individual performance assessment have remained high on the agendas of Government, funding bodies and institutions. As in many other countries, the government has been committed, not only to reducing public expenditure and encouraging a market economy in higher education, and, therefore, requiring institutions to seek additional non-Government funding, but also to institutions justifying their activities and accounting for their use of resources and their performance in terms of economy in the acquisition in the use of resources, efficiency in the use of resources, and effectiveness in the achievement of institutional, departmental and individual objectives, through the successful implementation of strategies and action plans. Therefore institutions of higher education in the United Kingdom have faced a period of continual change and uncertainty against the background of continuing requirements of efficiency gains by Governments. There have been significant reductions over the last decade in the unit of resource provided for teaching of students. We have now entered a period of consolidation but also with a requirement of continuing efficiency gains. Therefore, many of the lessons derived from study of managing the cuts in grants and student numbers imposed by the University Grants Committee in 1981 are still very relevant today. They are also relevant to many of the developments taking place in other countries that are faced with continuing pressures to reduce public expenditure against the background of expanding higher education systems.

The award of an Association of Commonwealth University Scholarship to D.K. Ghosh to visit the United Kingdom in June and July 1991 provided him with the opportunity to examine developments since my study was completed and to examine the implications of these developments. I have no doubt that the results of his study will be of value to those responsible for developing higher education policy and managing higher education institutions in India and in other countries that are facing the world-wide problems of managing expanding institutions against the background of continuing squeezes on public expenditure and greater demands for public accountability.

Through my close involvement with the institution of Management of Higher Education programme of the OECD for some 10 years and also my other international activities, I have benefitted considerably from participating in and learning lessons from international comparative studies of developments in higher.education and I therefore welcome D.K. Ghosh's valuable contribution to the literature of resource management in higher education.

— John Sizer CBE

Scottish Higher Education Funding Council
Edinburgh
Scotland

Preface

At the outset, I must clarify why I decided to write this book on the 'Finance Management and Planning in Education. Lessons from the U.K. System', rather than, my country, India.

Primarily, two reasons prompted me to write on this important area. First: UK and India have, for historical reasons, a deep and sustained century-old relationship and an important relevant reason is that the educational system of both the countries have still a number of things which are common. That also again is because of the historical reasons for the structure and organisation of the University System in India were designed and shaped by the British rule in India when in 1857, the first three universities at Calcutta, Bombay and Madras, along the lines of the then University of London, were established. Second: the unprecedented resource crunch that the universities of UK faced in 1980s, we, in the higher education system in India, have started facing the same more acutely than ever before in the past and therefore that being inevitable, it would be to our advantage to know what had happened in a more or less similar situation which may provide some guideline to meet the crisis and get over it. What India is facing is also equally true elsewhere in the developing countries. For historical reason, many developing countries have British model of higher education and therefore the experience of UK is of special significance and importance to all the universities of the developing countries.

The problems that the universities of UK faced in 1980s, the pains that they suffered in the process of restructuring and ultimately how they succeeded to overcome the difficulties would really help the universities of the developing countries in meeting and getting over the crisis and again how the universities of UK are doing now. The idea is not to suggest that what the universities of UK did in their critical hours should be adopted. The universities of the developing countries can gain a good deal from the experiences of the UK system.

The resource crunch and the need to generate income are now facts of life. But it need be appreciated and accepted by the various segments of the university community. Besides the event and episodes that took place in the university system in UK during the late seventies and early eighties, the universities have had many changes later following the various legislations in the last few years as also the impact of the Jarratt Committee, which made excellent recommendations to make the system efficient. These will provide excellent opportunities to the universities of the developing countries including, of course, India, whose higher education size is huge having more than two hundred and twenty universities and other institutions of higher education with a total higher education student number of more than five million.

Inspirations for writing this book basically came

to me after reading the Research Project of the Department of Education and Science of the Government of UK, called 'Institutional Responses to the Financial Reductions of the University Sector'. The Project was undertaken by Professor John Sizer, currently, Chief Executive, Scottish Higher Education Funding Council, Edinburgh, when he was the Head of the Business School of the Loughborough University.

I am grateful to the Association of Commonwealth Universities for the Fellowship that was awarded to me in 1991-92 which enabled me to visit UK to study the happenings during 1980s and the subsequent developments in the university system. I am also grateful to the British Council to provide some additional support in this venture and of course, my own Institute which encouraged me and also extended partial financial assistance.

My visit to UK, again in 1994 enabled me to meet Professor John Sizer and discuss with him about the treatise. I also visited most of the universities that were covered by the Research Project of DES. I had opportunities to meet the Officers of the Association of Commonwealth Universities and the Committee of Vice-Chancellors and Principals (CVCP) of UK. A new organisation that came into being for the training of non-teaching and teaching staff as also for academic audit, is the "University Staff Development and Training" (USDT). I gained sufficiently through detailed discussions that I had with the Director, Dr. Patricia Partington, about the objectives and functioning of the USDT.

I must confess here that writing a book on a complex university system of the United Kingdom which has a history of university system of about 800 years was a difficult job. But I am very happy to place on record the cooperation that I received particularly from Professor Sizer and a number of university Officers who also helped me by providing a lot of information without which I could not have accomplished the job. I have heavily drawn from the DES Research Project which provided me a lot of information and analysis. I am grateful to the DES for this excellent material that was made available to me through Professor Sizer. I am also grateful to him for writing the Foreword for this book.

The book has seven Chapters, the last being the Conclusion and what would be the position and needs of higher education in the 21st century and the Chapter 1 about the University Development in the United Kingdom.

The book has been so designed that while the thrust is on the position of the universities following the 1981 cuts of grants by the Thatcher Government, Chapter 1 would enable the readers to understand the complex university system of the United Kingdom particularly of the Oxford, Cambridge and the University of London. This chapter also speaks about the growth of universities, post-war scenario and the unprecedented expansion of 1960s when-in one decade alone, 22 new universities came into being. The Robbins Committee was so far the first National Committee on Higher Education in UK. This chapter discusses the various recommendations that it made including the creation of binary system which was a landmark in the history of higher education in UK. However binary system has been abolished in 1992. This chapter also speaks about the distinctive features of the new universities of 1960s which also marked new approach and experimentation in higher education.

Chapter 2 narrates and analyses the various incidents and happenings including the policy led expenditures. It also discusses the famous suggestions (rather warnings) of Mrs. Sharley Williams, the then State Minister for Education and Science, that the universities should initiate certain steps to reduce cost. Impact of the oil crisis was leading to the gathering clouds for the 1981 cuts. The pressing demand on the public exchequer was also visible. Another important aspect of the chapter is the decision of the Government for full cost recovery from the overseas students.

Frequent changes of the Government policy relating to the student number and the demise of the quinquennial system of funding had their toll on the universities in their planning system. Funding of the University Grants Committee as a buffer body between the Government and the Universities was far from satisfactory. However, it demonstrated its respect and concern for the autonomy of the universities.

Chapter 3 begins with the end of the Labour Government and coming into power of the Conservative Government. Pressure on the public exchequer were already building up, and the new government took it up on a priority basis to reduce the public expenditure. On one hand, the government had its own compulsion to reduce public expenditure, on the other hand, as a result of the announcement of the cuts in the grants of the universities by a minimum of 6% to a maximum of 44% on a selective basis, averaging out 17%. for all the universities, created a 'traumas' for the universities and to some it was a question of "bankruptcy". The University Grants Committee apparently could not play its role effectively; it only implemented the decisiòn of the government disregarding the damages caused to the university system. Even the 'dialogue meetings' that it had arranged separately with the universities failed to indicate the impending difficult time. In fact, some universities got optimistic indications, not knowing what was shortly in the store for them.

As for the universities, they did their best to meet the crisis. However, for a variety of reasons the process of internal restructuring had different story, results and pains, which depended on a few factors, eg. leadership, preparations, etc.

Chapter 4 is fully devoted to research funding, for

this aspect has always been a matter of great concern throughout, and there were debates at various forums across the country. In this chapter, the 'dual support system' for research activities in the UK has been discussed at reasonable length including the divergent views on research funding. The White Paper on Higher Education, 1991, in so far as research funding is concerned and the policy of 'selectivity' and its merits and demerits have also been discussed.

Is it only the funds that determine the level of research? This has been discussed reasonably with relevant data. While selectivity is a *sine-qua-non* for quality research, there should be built-in flexibility in the total mechanism so that the procedures of selectivity may not deprive the academic world from a possible high quality research activity.

Chapter 5 is primarily about the conditions of the universities after the cuts were announced in July 1981, when they had to face the realities and challenges, and work for restructuring the system which itself was a very painful process, to meet the crisis. In retrospect, the role played by (i) the government in general, and the Department of Education and Science in particular, (ii) University Grants Committee as the buffer body, and (iii} the Committee of Vice-Chancellors and Principals (CVCP) have been discussed. Performance of the universities before and after the communication from the UGC dated 1st July, 1981 including the role played by the Vice-Chancellors as leaders of the system have also been discussed. A good deal of discussions took place across the system about the performance of the universities. However, it was clear that because of the frequent changes in the policy of the government, an optimistic past history of expansion of 1960s and the not-so-clear indications from the government, the universities were unable to make preparations. Even the suggestions of Mrs. Sherley Williams were not taken seriously by the government and UGC also. It has, however, to be admitted that universities are forward looking organisations and therefore unless there were definite restrains from the buffer body, it could not have prepared itself for any eventuality, of its own to reduce expenditure which meant activities.

Chapter 6 discusses various actions and situations of the universities at the end of the restructuring period of 1981-82 to 1983-84. Of the various actions for future, the appointment of Jarratt Committee and its recommendations covering the various areas of functioning of the university system have far-reaching impact on the efficiency of the universities, viz. the roles of Council and Senate, Heads of Departments, planning and resources and budget delegation and more importantly, the performance indicators and cost awareness, have all brought new dimensions to the university system.

The last Chapter 7 discusses briefly conclusions and importantly what would be the position of higher education in the 21st century with special reference to the needs and preparations. Inescapably, the needs will be very different and to meet the needs of the pressures, re-engineering is the answer to the university system.

I am particularly grateful to Dr. R.M. Mawditt, Director, International Centre for Higher Education Management, University of Bath, who had readily accepted my request to go through the manuscripts and made valuable suggestions.

I must also put on record that this book has been written with the financial support of the Curriculum Development Programme (CDP), Government of India, at IIT Bombay.

I cannot forget the labour that my colleague Anil Kumar has put in, to complete the work, with usual promptness without which, I would have found it hard to accomplish the work.

At home, I must mention the facility and environment provided by my wife Lily to complete the work along with my daughter Rinki. My son Rahul was of real help to me in finalising many data and conclusions.

Finally, I place the treatise in the hands of my worthy readers for their suggestions and guidance which I shall value greatly.

— D.K. Ghosh

Mumbai,
15th January, 1997

1

University Development in The United Kingdom

Role of Church

In his famous work, 'The Universities of Europe in the Middle Ages', Hastings Rashdall maintained that the true concept of a university structure and system began to appear only in the twelfth and thirteenth century. According to him, it was not correct to call the Schools of Athens, Rome and Alexandria as University for they did not have the essential characters and features of a University, eg. Teaching corporation. courses of study, examinations, degrees and licences to teach. Based on these essentials, the origin of the university system of today could be traced to the twelfth-thirteenth century Europe, when the role of Church as a religious institution was significant, particularly the struggle against the high handedness of the Church Authorities.

Schools at the Cathedrals came into being in 1179 following a decree issued by the Third Lateran Council that all Cathedrals should have a Master to teach Clerks and poor scholars.[1] Persons who were thus trained were entitled to be sanctioned 'licence' by the Bishop so that they could teach within the Cathedral precints. But the Chancellor, as an Officer of the Bishop, who was empowered to sanction licence 'to teach' grew so strong that he could exert the power of 'veto' and sometimes be 'venal' and at times, would even refuse to issue licence to anyone he considered 'unorthodox'.[2]

Birth of the University System

Such high handedness of the Chancellor gradually germinated discontent and frustration among the Masters and a stage came when the teachers (or masters) in such great Cathedral School as Notre Dame in Paris organised themselves with a self-protecting guild or 'Universitas.'[3] Came thus into being the 'universitas of masters'. Paris is therefore considered as the examplar of Oxford and also to Cambridge.

Bologna, a free city in northern Italy, was the other originator of the idea of university which had the 'universitas of students'. These two originators of university ideas had distinctive features. For example, while Paris had its 'guild of masters', Bologna had the 'guild of students'. Further, while Paris had the high reputation for studies in theology, Bologna was preeminent in both Civil and Canon Law. Bologna which had its guild of students, appointed their own Rector, hired and paid their teachers and also decided their courses of studies. In Italy, in course of time, more Universities grew up at Naples, Reggio, Padua, Siena etc. Over about a period of three or four centuries, the rule of students was replaced by the control of masters.

Through the combination of a number of factors such as growth of the Cathedrals, the initiative of the city state, the welcoming charity of monasteries, the brilliance and reputation of teachers like Aberald and John of Salisbury, the interest of the Pope and the King, the universities could establish themselves.

First Universities of England

Remarkable in the world history of univercity system, are the first two Universities of England, namely, the University of Oxford and the University of Cambridge which came into being in the twelfth century as examples of excellence right from their early days. They have not only kept up the reputation as centres of excellence throughout, they have incredibly established as being capable of retaining the best of the past and at the same time prove to be the best of the modern needs and challenges. Oxford is about 800 years old while Cambridge about 700 years. Both are predominantly based on collegiate system and that is unique by itself. Without a little more mention about the two Universities which are even today the 'pride' of the Great Britain and good models for the World, the history of the university system of U.K. will appear to be incomplete.

Without any formal foundation, about eight hundred years ago, the University of Oxford came into existence in Oxford, a city which lies at the confluence of rivers Thames and Cherwell, 56 miles west of London. Until the fifteenth century, the University passed through many hurdles both academic and in the area of physical facilities. It had to arrange lectures in hired rooms or in churches. In 1571, the University was incorporated by an Act of Parliament which resulted in a lot of reorganisation. The University extended its support to the King during the period of civil war and the King made Oxford his headquarters and Parliament met there.

The University is essentially a conglomeration of colleges. While the colleges are corporate bodies distinct from the university, manage their affairs, they are subject to the university statutes in respect of certain matters, eg. presentation and audit of accounts, contributions for university purposes and election to professional fellowships. Finally, all who are persons of colleges are also members of the University and therefore come under the University rules. Interestingly, teaching is carried out partly by way of lectures and classes held by the University Professors, Readers and Lecturers and partly by way of individual tutors by college tutors and lecturers. A number of these tutors and lecturers should work both in the colleges and in the university.

There are 35 independent, self-contained, self-governing colleges, and six permanent private Halls. Twenty-eight of the thirty-five colleges admit students for undergraduate degrees, about 9800 in all in a total student body of 13900.[4] The teaching at Oxford combines the standard methods of University educators - lectures, classes and (in the science) laboratory work - with a systematic and intensive use of tutorials. Lectures, classes and laboratory courses are provided by the University tutorials by the colleges. A college is thus not just a hall of residence but a place where social life and learning are combined.[5]

For the first time, the University received Treasury Grant in 1923, following the work of a Royal Commission and changes in the constitutional arrangements.

The University of Cambridge is the name of another centre of excellence from its inception and goes together with the name and fame of the University of Oxford to denote age, excellence and also character. In 1209, a number of scholars moved out of Oxford due to disturbances there and joined the community of scholars at Cambridge. The City of Cambridge lies on the river Cam, or Granta, 51 miles north of London and is the county town of Cambridge.

The origin of the University of Cambridge is estimated from 1209. However, according to another source it '... is known to have been in existence from 1226[6] and although certain important privileges were given to the University by King Henry II, it received formal recognition as a studium generale from Pope John XXII in 1318. The first college, Peterhouse, was founded in 1284 and now there are 31 Cambridge colleges of which 29 accept undergraduates. Similar to Oxford, in order to belong to the University, all undergraduates must first belong to a College.[7] The University which was already in financial difficulties faced aggravated situation by 1914-18 i.e. during the World War I. In 1919, for the first time, the University received a Treasury Grant on the condition that there should be an enquiry into its resources and organization. Following the recommendation of the Royal Commission, the University started getting annual grant from 1920 subject to fulfillment of certain conditions.[8]

Senior members of the Colleges most of whom are also lecturers in the University are called Fellows. They include: The Master, Mistress, Principal, Provost or President of the College. Colleges provide various facilities for the students, eg. accommodation, meals, individual tuition, library and social and cultural facilities. The University had about 13,920 full-time students and 1583 part-time students during 1991-92.

First Universities of Scotland

For about a long period of over five hundred years, until the early nineteenth century, England had only these two universities. In Scotland, in the fifteenth century itself, three Universities came into being namely, St. Andrews (1411), Glasgow (1451) and Aberdeen (1495). St. Andrews, although the oldest in Scotland

and third oldest in the Great Britain, is relatively small in size. It is basically a university town and holiday centre on the coast of Fife, fifty miles north-east of Edinburgh and thirteen miles south-east of Dundee. In 1583, the University of Edinburgh was founded as the fourth university of Scotland.

Glasgow is an industrial and commercial centre and sea port on the river Clyde. The University of Glasgow was established, by a Bull of Pope Nicholas V, as a *studium generale*, with the privileges of Bologna of Italy 9, one of the proginators of the university system. In 1577, the university was reconstituted by the *nova erectio*, a charter of King James VI which was the foundation of the Statutes of the University until the Universities (Scotland) Act, 1858,[10] as modified by the acts of 1889 and 1966.

Under an Authority of a Papal Bull obtained in 1494-95 with the initiative of King James IV, the University of Aberdeen was founded, and in 1505, the College of St. Mary was founded which was later called Kings College. This was the first foundation and the other one was the Marischal College founded in 1593 by George Keith. Both these foundations were later reconstituted in 1860 as 'The University of Aberdeen' which is incorporated under the Universities (Scotland) Act of 1889.

The City of Aberdeen is a University town and a beautiful holiday centre which is situated on south-east coast Aberdeenshire in the north-eastern part of Scotland.

Fourth in Scotland and sixth in Great Britain is the University of Edinburgh, which came into being almost after ninety years of the last University established in Scotland, namely the University of Aberdeen (1495). The

University of Edinburgh was originally 'the Tounis College' founded in 1583 by the Town Council of Edinburgh under the general powers granted by a charter of King James VI dated April 14, 1582. From the inception, the college had the authority of conferring degrees. This power was later ratified by the 'act of confirmation' passed in 1621 "which secured to the 'Coll of James VI' (as it had come to be called)" all the rights and immunities of other universities of Scotland".[11] Over the years, "in acts of the general assembly, of the Town Council, and of parliament, the 'Coll, of James VI' came to be styled the University of Edinburgh".[12]

Referring to the tradition of the Scottish Universities of St. Andrews, Glasgow, Aberdeen and Edinburgh, the Robbins Committee said, 'founded in the fifteenth and sixteenth centuries, these have always had a standing of their own and many of their traditions are more like those of the continent than of England and Wales'.[13]

According to Dr. Tress, 'England in the industrial revolution of the nineteenth century was heavily reliant on the products of the Scottish Universities for the scientists, engineers and medical men who were needed. The Scottish Universities, though more democratic, shared both the meritocratic outlook of the German and the German's willingness to enter into the new sciences and technologies: That universities should be concerned with servicing the professional needs of society was not a new idea and was indeed present during the early days of the universities at Bologna and Padua, but the Germans reaffirmed this function and extended the definition of 'professional' needs to include the economic and industrial requirements of a technologically based society.[14]

GROWTH OF UNIVERSITIES

University of London

Idea of a University in London was mooted in order to co-ordinate and manage as well, the colleges of different specialisations in London.

Characteristically different and functionally diverse is the University of London which came into being in 1836. It is unique in the British system of higher education initiated through private efforts established mainly as an examining and degree giving body for the students of the University College, London and the Kings College. While Kings College was founded in 1829, the University College of London was founded in 1826. The University of London "until the end of the nineteenth century it remained largely an examining and degree giving body".[15]

The Kings College was founded by a royal charter for instructions in the various branches of literatures and sciences and the doctrine and duties of Christianity. Over the years, the college added many branches including Medical Sciences and Engineering. The University College, London having been founded in 1826, was incorporated as University College, London, by a royal charter in 1836. A few other institutions which were in existence from before the birth of the University of London, became part of the University later from time to time.

With the character of the University of London that it was then, simultaneously more colleges and schools came into being in the metropolis including a Womens College. The University of London is today a federation of colleges and schools, and has a unique character and functions for, on one hand, it is the head of the Colleges and Schools, on the other hand, some of the Colleges have grown to be bigger than some of the Universities in size, and established themselves as centres of excellence, eg. the Imperial College of Science, Technology and Medicine (1891); University College, London (UCL) (1926), and the London School of Economics and Political Science (1895). Today, the University of London is a federal form, which has a number of colleges and schools, separate Institutions and Institutions having recognised teachers. The university had 51,392 full-time and 13,352 part-time students in 1991-92.[16] Before war, it had 13,010 students and after war, in 1962-63, it had 23,000[17] students which was more than the total of any two universities in UK. That position is maintained even now.

While by 1583, Scotland had four Universities, England had only two, namely the University of Oxford and the University of Cambridge. The Universities of Scotland have always had a standing of their own and many of their traditions are more like those of the continent than of England and Wales. For example, except at St. Andrews, relatively few of the students live in halls of residence provided by their Universities. Even in terms of the system of governance of the University, as contrast to the Universities of England, the universities of Scotland included a substantial lay element in the governance of the Universities.

Other Universities

For two reasons, the University of Durham-founded in 1832 and, granted charter in 1837, is different from others. First, it has a collegiate system in some respects similar to that of Oxford and Cambridge. Second, it is the first of the older civic universities of England and even women were admitted to the University as early as in 1896 and non-collegiate students from 1871. In one more respect, the university is different from the other English civic universities. While nearly all of them owe their origins to the civic pride of their citizens especially rich business and professional men of the Victorian age and early twentieth century "the University of Durham was '... founded by the Church (strictly by the rich Dean and Chapter of Durham Cathedral)'".[18]

Until the creation of an independent University in Newcastle upon Tyne in 1963, the College of Medicine (origin - 1834) as The New Castle Upon Tyne School of Medicine and Surgery was associated with the University - first in 1852 and more closely in 1870. The renamed Armstrong College (1904) was originally founded in 1871 as the University of Durham College of Physical Science. In 1937, the two colleges were merged into one as King's College, Newcastle Upon Tyne and finally became the new University of New Castle Upon Tyne, separating the colleges at New Castle Upon Tyne from the University of Durham.

The last two Universities established in the nineteenth century in Great Britain were one in England, i.e. the Victoria University of Manchester and the other in Wales, as the University of Wales.

With its origin in the Owens College (1851), named after a Merchant of Manchester who bequeathed 96000 Pounds for its establishment in 1851, the Victoria University was founded by the charter of 1880 incorporating federal constitution and making Owens College as a constituent college of the University as also the Manchester School of Medicine merging in the University. The new charter of 1903 reconstituted the University as the Victoria University of Manchester.

The establishment of the University also marks the

industrial revolution. In 1905, with the addition of the Faculty of Technology,the Municipal School of Technology (later College) became part of the University and under a charter of 1955, the College of Technology was established in 1956. In 1966, the College was granted permission to adopt the title of the 'University of Manchester Institute of Science and Technology'.

The first University founded in Wales was the University of Wales in 1893. This was also the last University that came into being in Great Britain in the nineteenth century. The University was granted charter in 1893. Prior to the establishment of the University, there were three colleges. Consequent to the successive charter of 1920 and 1931, a number of important structural changes were introduced. Today, it functions as a strong federal University having a number of established colleges.

The University of Wales is another unique system of higher education. It is the only University in Wales, and through its federative character and functions, university education is provided to 20,000 students registered in various faculties. At the time of the University's coming into force, in 1893, three university colleges were already existing in Wales which were made part of the university system. Following a supplemental charter of 1920, a number of changes were introduced of which the most important was the establishment of a fourth constituent college at Swansea. The second supplemental charter of 1931 provided among others for the Welsh National School of Medicine (later the University of Wales College of Medicine) and to allow establishment of Schools of theology which resulted into three schools. A third supplemental charter of 1967 was introduced providing among others, for the incorporation of the former Welsh College of Advanced Technology as a constituent institution of the university, namely 'The University of Wales Institute of Science and Technology'. Importantly, provisions were made for the reconstitution of the governing and executive bodies, with more academic representation and redeployment of the powers of the various bodies of the university giving authority to the academic body in all academic matters as the ultimate authority.[19]

Twentieth century marked its beginning with the establishment of the University of Birmingham in 1900. Nucleous of the university was in the Mason Science College founded in 1875 and opened in 1880, and later merged with the medical faculty of the Queens College in 1892. In 1894, the Birmingham Training College for teachers was transferred to the Mason College. Later, the college was incorporated by an act of Parliament as 'The Mason University College'. In 1900, the University of Birmingham was established by the Royal charter merging the Mason University College.

After the establishment of the University of Birmingham in 1900, the other universities that came into quick succession were Liverpool (1903), Leeds (1904) and Sheffield (1905), Belfast (1908) and Bristol (1909). Then followed the period of first World War (1914-1919) during which time, no university came up. One important factor that led to the development of institutes into universities was the industrial revolution in UK's big industrial cities, namely Birmingham, Liverpool, Leeds, Sheffield, Bristol and Manchester.

The University of Liverpool was founded in 1903 absorbing in it the University College, Liverpool, founded by Royal Charter in 1881 which was admitted to the privileges of the Victoria University, Manchester, in 1884.

Like the nucleous of the University of Liverpool, the nucleous of the University of Leeds was also part of the Victoria University, Manchester. In 1904, the University of Leeds was established following a Royal Charter.

The University of Sheffield was established as a result of a Royal Charter in 1905, merging the University College, Sheffield, in it.

The Queen's College, Belfast (1845), became a constituent college in 1879 of the Royal University of Ireland. This ultimately became the Queen's University of Belfast in 1908, with the Royal University of Ireland being dissolved in 1909.

Realizing the need of financial support from the government, an ad-hoc committee was appointed by the Treasury in 1889 when for the first time general grant of 15,000 pounds per-annum was sanctioned to the University Colleges of Great Britain. In 1906, a permanent committee was appointed when the size of the grant was revised to 133,000 pounds.[20]

POST-WAR SCENARIO

Until the turn of the twentieth century, expansion of higher education was sluggish. Changing attitude was noticed after the two World Wars, in particular towards the role of higher education in the social, economic and political areas. Manifold expansion of higher education took place all over the world following the World Wars particularly the World War II.

Recognizing the impact of higher education on the society in various areas and different measures, the Government of United Kingdom had generally demonstrated priority for funding of higher education. It is also known for its respect to the traditions of universities which have played important role in science, art and literature and the prestige that many of the universities of Great Britain have brought to the country.

The 1943 white paper on Educational Reconstruction and importantly the Education Act, 1944 followed by a number of Reports, White Papers and Education Act, 1979 and Education Act, 1980 as also the Act of 1988 and the latest Act of 1992 clearly established the importance attached by the Government to education at all levels and sectors for social and economic objectives of the country. Although subsequent to the 1944 Act, there have been more Education Acts, the 1944 Act despite modification remains the basic framework. In fact this Act "... has to be seen partly as a product of post-war reconstruction when, for the first time, social policy measures were being welded together into a more coherent whole which could legitimately be referred to as a Welfare State".[21]

Despite '... negative effects of the balance of payments deficits mainly created by responsibilities' that the British Government shared as "... second only to USA in power and responsibility in 1945" on the economic front of the country, it had to '... sustain welfare-oriented social democratic policies in the context of an open and unplanned international economic system'.[22] In 1945, social democracy meant the central planning of domestic resources to ensure full employment and a dramatic extension in the provision of health, education and social service".

In 1948, Sir Stafford Cripps in a message to the Universities Quarterly said:

> "The darkness of the economic outlook gives no ground for economy in the sphere of university grants. The universities have a great contribution

to make towards national economic recovery. We look to them to continue with unabated vigour, the search for new knowledge and the education of increased numbers of young men and women from all classes of the community. For it is on the energy, initiative, directive capacity and courage of these young graduates that the economic future of the country will largely depend".

Despite financial constraints, the Parliament of Great Britain had allotted Rs.12.5 million pounds to the 19 universities then in existence and the Minister in charge assured that if there was a demand for a further increase in grants, he would not hesitate to approach the Parliament in the interest of higher education. This precisely spoke about the approach to higher education and the concern that its health cannot remain vigour without investment and such support.

British economy was passing through a continued period of crisis. This was primarily because of its international commitments *vis-a-vis* the internal developmental requirements pertaining to the social services. on the balance of payments front "on current account remained in surplus in 1953 and 1954, but without creating a margin sufficient to build up reserves. In 1955, it was again in deficit".[23] It '... ran serious deficits on the current balance of payments in 1951, 1955 and 1960 and if the account is divided into its components, it is seen that these were attributable to large visible deficits in these years together with a continuous decline over the whole period from 1950, of most serious proportions, in invisible earnings". On the whole, the economy was far from being stable, the annual growth of industrial production during 1953-55 through 1964-66 was one of expansion and stagnation too, while in terms of percentage, it was 5.68 in 1953-55, it came down to 1.5 in 1964-66.[24]

Reason for the change in attitude towards the higher education could be attributed to the realization of the superiority through science and technology and better training of mind which only Universities and Colleges could provide. What would have been the higher education scenario without the socio-economic consequences of the World Wars is difficult to say today. But what it has been so far and what it is now today is well-known. It is now fast changing.

In Great Britain, there was the coincidence of another important factor for the demand of expansion of higher education facilities in the post-World War II. The School leaving age was raised to fifteen and free education of all type was made available to all. This was as a result of a number of successive important legislations in England, Scotland and Wales, namely, the Forster Act of 1870, the corresponding measure of 1872 in Scotland for free and universal education and the Welsh Intermediate Education Act of 1889, the Scottish Act of 1892, the Education Acts of 1902, 1944, and 1945. All these steps resulted in improving the situations in Schools creating demand to increased higher education facilities. In 1938, only about 3 per cent of those aged nineteen, were receiving full-time education.[25] In terms of numbers, in 1938-39, there were 69,000 full-time higher education students. But in 1961-62, the number rose to 1,93,000 when unprecedented expansion started to find more place for the growing school leavers.

Going by the pattern of higher education in Great Britain - both full-time and otherwise there were the following three sectors:

Sector One	:	Universities
Sector Two	:	Training Colleges and the Scottish Colleges of Education.

Sector Three : Further Education System, i.e. Colleges of Advanced Technology, Technical Colleges of various kinds, Colleges of Commerce and Schools of Art and the Scottish Central Institute.

However, at the turn of the Century, all full-time higher education was provided by the Universities. Standard of education in Sector two, i.e. in Training Colleges and Scottish Colleges of Education was correspondingly restricted. While the sector one had a small number of part-time students, sector two had hardly any, and most of part-time higher education was provided in Institutions of sector three. The number of students in the various sectors of higher education during 1938-39, 1962-63 and in 1982-83 were as given in Table-1.1.

Table 1.1[26]

Period	*Universities*	*Other Sectors*	*Total*
1938-39	50,000	19,000	69,000
1962-63	1,18,000	98,000	2,16,000
1982-83	2,73,000	2,49,000	5,22,000

Growth of higher education has always have natural force behind it, generated out of the needs of the society. The same is true for the kind of education that the society looks for. For example, 'The great medieval universities prepared their students for the professions of the Law and the Church. Many of the American land-grant colleges had their origin in the labour needs, especially in Agriculture, of the developing States.[27]

In the post-World War-II period, "An increasing

demand has been placed on academic institutions to produce relevant, useful contributions to the wealth and growth prospects for society, and this they have clearly achieved in the developed world."[28] This is true for "in Japan, for example, an almost universal linking of industrial needs to the output of higher education has been created, while Amrica and Europe have seen a very close correspondence between industrial growth in consumer society and educational norms".[29]

No new University came into being in UK during 1910 and 1925. Even the sluggish expansion had stopped. One strong reason for that was the involvement of England in the World War-I (1914-1919). Preparation prior to the war and the time needed for recovering from the impact of the war perhaps diverted the resources, attention and energy for expansion of higher education.

However, it has to be admitted that in the post World War first period, recognising the need and impact of higher education in meeting the national aspirations, the permanent committee appointed in 1906 to distribute government grants was replaced by the structured University Grants Committee in 1919. Despite financial constraints the decision of the government for larger grants in higher education as a long-term investment demonstrated the vision of the far reaching impact on the country's all round progress. The UGC was charged with the responsibility "to enquire into the financial needs of University education in the United Kingdom and to advise the government as to the application of any grants that may be made by parliament towards meeting them.[30] It was reorganised in 1934 and in 1946, and its terms of reference were enlarged by the addition of "to collect, examine and make available information on matters relating to University education at home and abroad, and to assist, in consultation with the universities and other bodies concerned, the preparation and execution of such plans for the development of the Universities as may from time to time be required in order to ensure that they are fully adequate to natural needs".

After the World War-I, the first University that was established was the University of Reading in the year 1926. As has been the history of most of the Universities, the nucleous of the University existed in the University Extension College (1892) based upon the local Oxford university Extension Centre and the local schools of science and art. This became the Reading College in 1898 and in 1902, it became a University College and it received state grant. Since then, it continued to improve its position through endowments of land, money and buildings from benefactors. In 1911, Pounds 200,000 was raised and the university was established in March 1926.

The gap for the next new university was still more for between 1927 and 1947 no new university came into being. The next university to come into force was the University of Nottingham in 1948. The University College, Nottingham (1881) emerged as the University of Nottingham. Prior to its becoming the University College, its origin was in the Adult School (1798), the Mechanics Institute, the People's College and first Cambridge University extension lectures of 1873. In 1875, an anonymous gift of Pounds 10,000 provided an impetus to the corporation of Nottingham to erect a building and to maintain it. In 1881, the said building was opened as the University College incorporated by the Royal Charter in 1903.[31]

Universities of 1950s

The period that followed the establishment of the University of Nottingham was one of having new Universities rather fast in 1950s and 1960's are of-course too well known for having the largest number of Universities in UK with 8 universities in one single year i.e. 1966.

Next to the University of Nottingham, came the University of Southampton in 1952. Origin of the University lies in the Hartley Institute (1862) which was established from a bequest by H.R. Hartley. It was incorporated in 1902 as the Hartley University College at Southampton. Since then, till the coming into being of the University, students of the College studied for the external degrees of the University of London, the former being situated 80 miles south-west of London. In 1953, the college was merged in the University of Southampton, constituted by the Royal Charter in 1952.[32]

With a gap of only one year, came the University of Hull in 1954. The city grew into an educational centre with a donation of Pounds 250,000 from a leading industrialist of the city of Hull for a University College. This encouraged the corporation of Kingston upon Hull to pay Pounds 150,000 for buildings and equipment together with an annual grant for maintenance. Another industrialist also donated Pounds 100,000. The University Grants Committee recognised the college for state grants in 1945 and in 1954 it was merged in the University of Hull on being granted a royal charter.[33]

In 1955, came into being the next University, i.e. the University of Exeter. Ground for a University at Exeter was prepared with the establishment of a School of Art in 1855 followed by a building in 1865 for a museum library and school of art as a memorial to the

Prince Consort. Later, University extension lectures were organised and candidates were prepared for South Kensington science and arts examinations. In 1893, classes were extended and Exeter Technical and University Extension Cell were established which became in 1899 the Royal Albert Memorial College.

In 1901, students were prepared for the external degrees of the University of London and in 1922, the College became a University College of the south-west of England and it received its first treasury grant as a recognised university institution. In 1955, royal charter was granted for the University of Exeter to merge the University College.[34]

The last University of the fifties was the University of Leceister founded in 1957. It's nucleous lies in the University College of Leceister founded in 1918. However, the original site and buildings which date back to 1837 were donated in 1919 and an endowment was created by the Citizens. The college was recognised by the University Grants Committee in 1945 entitling it for grants. In 1950, it received the royal charter of incorporation as a University College and in 1957, it became part of the University of Leceister under a royal charter.[35] It is situated only 98 miles north of London and is an industrial city in the east Midlands.

EXPANSION OF 1960s

Consequences of the Second World War led to a number of actions perceived through the experiences of the war and the most important of which was the realization of the superiority of science and technology and impact of professionally qualified men '... needed for economic and technological advance'.[36] In UK, that was the position which influenced the planning for expansion of higher education with new thrust to meet the challenges of the future. Recognising the need of expansion of higher education, a number of committees were appointed at the end of the war of which the Barlow Committee (1946), one of the important Committees on Scientific Manpower, had recommended a doubling of the output of scientists within ten years.[37]

The UGC had forecast in its 1953 Report that in order to meet the sudden swollen number coming out of the schools into higher education, "... a marked increase in student number will be required from about 1960 onwards if the proportions of new age group which reaches the University is to be maintained". The Zuckerman Committee on Scientific Manpower (1952) opined that "if our institution of higher education fail to grow, they will not be able to keep pace with the growth in the demand for scientists necessary to promote industrial efficiency and productivity".

Primary of all reasons for the unprecedented coming into being of the New Universities of 1960s, except Keele, was the need to accommodate the fast increasing number of new students coming out from the schools. The need to accommodate more places in higher education was further accentuated by the immediate aim of accommodating the thousands of demobilized servicemen who had earned the academic and moral right to a degree course.

During the period 1961 and 1969, twenty four new Universities were established. The first one was the University of Sussex and the last one was the Open University, the latter broke a new ground in the world of learning and made its impact all over the World.

Whatever be the deeper and underlying contributing force to the creation of new universities in 1960s, the dominating factor was the pressure of the numbers for new places for higher education. Added to this was also the urgent expansion rather than slow expansion which has been the history of the then existing universities as also the need of experimentation strongly felt in the fast changing scientific and technical advancement. Lord Murray, Chairman of the Sub-Committee appointed by the UGC to report on the application for new Universities had told Dr. H.J. Perkin on being asked by the latter as to the relative emphasis on number and experimentation, that "it was one-third numbers and the two-thirds new ideas". It has been mentioned that the nation had to plan to accommodate thousands of demobilised service men and women. But greater pressure was the school leavers aspiring for higher education and it was found that "The 18 year old age-group is at present growing larger with each year".[38] In terms of the percentage of increase due to population bulge, it was '28 per cent increase in births which took place between 1954 and 1964'.[39] This population increase was a major factor for establishment of the new Universities.

The University Grants Committee which was keen to have more universities to meet the growing demand for places in higher education however, "... recognized that new universities could do little to relieve the critical situation that was developing in the second-half of the sixties, and would make a significant contribution only in the early 1970's, when indeed their own estimates showed a slackening in the growth of the demand for places".[40] The apprehension relating to a decline in the demand of higher education at later years was also in the minds of others like G.T. Fowler, M.P., when he observed that "the 18 year-old age group is at present growing larger with each year, but from 1983 it declines in size. Unless qualified demand from 18-year-olds again increases sharply, as it did in the sixties, there must be excess capacity of some 30 per cent in higher education institution by the early nineties".[41]

In order to meet the challenges behind the superiority of science and technology that the world was striving to achieve, it was recognized that experimentation was the need and this was considered as the other important reason for creation of new universities. This is supported by Dr. H.J. Perkin when he observed that while as the public case expansion due to the number of student was true, '... there is reason to believe that in the minds of those most responsible, educational experiment may have been uppermost'.[42]

To sum up as to the reasons of coming into being a large number of universities in 1960, they were two: one was to accommodate more number of students and the other was to make them experiment oriented from the beginning itself. These two reasons precisely meet all that have been mentioned earlier.

Universities of 1960s

The first University of 1960s is the University of Sussex. Although local civic demand for a University College at Brighton as a constituent part of the University of London was originally made in 1911 and later revived in 1947 and 1954, the success came when it was projected as a national need and "In 1957, the Government authorised the UGC to support the project provided they were satisfied with the plans and the public support for it, and in February 1958, the Chancellor of the Exchequer announced that one million and a half pounds of the new capital grant of 60 million pounds for the Universities in 1960-63 was provisionally reserved for building the University College of Sussex. The

UGC gave its formal Royal approval to the scheme on 1st July, 1958.[43] In 1961, the royal charter was granted and thus came into force, on the 16th August 1961, the University of Sussex. It opened in October, 1961 when the first batch of students were admitted.[44]

The University of Sussex being the first University of the series of new Universities of 1960s could be credited with a number of norms that evolved out of discussion, consideration and decisions which became the guiding factor for the new Universities. For example, it was decided that the University of Sussex should have an enrolment of not less than 3000 within a period of ten years of establishment, with an increased capacity, the capital grant for building was raised from one and a half million pounds to six million pounds.

It may be mentioned that the University achieved the minimum target of 3000 students within seven years as against the ten years.

For a variety of reasons, the University of Sussex became the model, and paved the way, for new Universities. The "... greatest contribution made by Sussex was the dialogue which it conducted with the UGC in the five years before it opened, which established both the needs of New Universities and the practical designs, their size, rate of growth, methods of establishment and of guaranteeing their academic standards, and complete freedom to experiment with their curriculum and methods of teaching and examination".[45] These are very important norms that would contribute to achieve success in achieving the objectives of higher education. The University of Sussex attracted both the staff as well as students. Its success "... created an image in the public mind of a New University as an exciting and stimulating place for young people to go, both to learn and enjoy themselves, which has greatly benefitted the other New Universities and given them a flying star".[46] Encouraged by the success story of the University of Sussex both in becoming a University as also in moving to the right direction of achieving the objectives, twenty eight requests for new Universities were received by the UGC - twenty in England and eight in Scotland. Further assessment of the demand for more places in higher education by the UGC led to the revision of the figures from an estimated 124,000 (1958) with a temporary rise to 135,000 (1965-70) to new figures of 165,000 rising to 200,000 in 1968 and 229,400 in 1976. In order to meet the increasing demand the UGC persuaded the Government for a target of 170,000 - 175,000 places by the late 1960 which, it clarified to the government, would lead to creation of additional Universities. Finally, a decision was taken by the government to establish six new Universities.

However, in April 1959, the UGC appointed a Subcommittee on New Universities "to examine and report on proposals received by the University Grants Committee for new University institutions".

The second new University of 1960's that came into being with the Royal Charter, was the University of Keele. The University College of North Staffordshire which was founded in August 1949 became the University of Keele in January, 1962. This University too, like the University of Sussex, has, to its credit the experimentation that it conducted as will be evident from the statement of a former Vice-Chancellor of Eas Anglia "As a historian, it is difficult for me to conceive of the Norwich 'experiment' without the precedents of Keele and Sussex. We have benefited greatly from the detonation with which they have cleared the air".[47]

Growth of new Universities continued for the pressing need to accommodate more students and to seriously provide more centres for innovation and experiments. Although the forecast was that the demand for more places would decline with the birth rate coming down, in reality the pressure did not reduce, the reason being explained as follows:

> "What the UGC did not, and could not at that time, foresee was that the post-bulge decline in the birth rate in the 1950's would be succeeded by a further rise to a higher and more permanent 'plateu' from about 1960 onwards, and that meanwhile the trend to stay on at school and qualify for university entrance would soon begin to accelerate so as to pile the bulge of university applicants in the mid-1960's even higher than the mere natural increase led them to expect. The proportion of 17 year olds remaining at school rose from 6.6% in 1950 and 1952 to 7.9% in 1954 and to 12.0% in 1962, when the Robbins Committee and the Ministry of Education were to agree that it was likely at a conservative estimate to reach 18% by 1973 and about 22% by 1980.[48]

From the preceeding assessment, the necessity for more places in higher education as a pressing need, continued and the earlier forecast proved incorrect. The other new Universities established during 1960s are as follows - the distribution being seventeen in England, four in Scotland and only one (Ulster) in northern Ireland:

1. University of Essex
2. University of York
3. University of New Castle upon Tyne

4. University of East Anglia
5. University of Lancaster
6. University of Kent at Canterbury
7. University of Warwick
8. University of Aston
9. University of Surrey
10. University of Bath
11. University of Bradford
12. University of Brunel
13. City University
14. University of Louborough
15. University of Salford
16. Buckingham University
17. Ulster University (Northern Ireland)
18. Open University
19. University of Strathclyde
20. University of Stirling
21. University of Heriot-Watt
22. University of Dundee

THE ROBBINS COMMITTEE

For more than one reason, 1960s are important years in the history of higher education in UK. For the first time in 1961, in the history of UK, an official body was appointed to report on the higher education.

By the Treasury Minute dated 8th February 1961, a Committee was constituted with Professor Lord Robbins, as its Chairman:

'to review the pattern of full-time higher education in Great Britain and in the light of national needs and resources to advise Her Majesty's Government on what principles its long-term development should be based. In particular, to advise, in the light of these principles, whether there should be any changes in that pattern, whether any new types of institution are desirable and whether any modifications should be made in the present arrangements for planning and co-ordinating the development of the various types of institution'.[49]

In the history of higher education of UK, the Robbins Committee was the first one to 'consider the pattern of full-time higher education in Great Britain'. In the words of the Committee Report:

'We believe that no such instructions have been given to any committee or commission in the past. There have been Royal Commissions on the affairs of particular universities and committees on various aspects of technical education and the training of teachers. There has never been a comprehensive survey of the field of higher education in the sense in which we have decided to use that term'.[50]

For the first time, the nation had the opportunity to look into a comprehensive authorised official document covering all aspects of higher education which made excellent surveys and important recommendations. This Report submitted by the Committee on the 23rd September 1963, was presented to the British Parliament in October, 1963. Besides its 335 pages main Report, there are the following Appendices containing useful data and analyses:

Appendix One (342 pages)	: The demand for places in Higher Education.
Appendix Two (342+622 pages)	: Vol. A: Students and their educa tion Vol.B: Educational and Social Background.
Appendix Three (259 pages)	: Teachers in Higher Education.
Appendix Four (165 pages)	: Administrative, Financial and Eonomic Aspects of Higher Education.
Appendix Five (306 pages)	: Higher Education in Other Countries.

It is interesting that while the government had appointed the Robbins Committee in 1961 to review the pattern of higher education, it continued to grant charters to the creation of new Universities without waiting for the recommendations of the Committee obviously because of the pressures and the fact that the cases of many new Universities were pending for quite some time. Out of twenty four new Universities of 1960, it is only the University of Sterling in Scotland that owes its establishment to the Robbins Committee recommendations.

However, there was no dispute on the basic reason for creation of new universities, for the Robbins Committee not only expressed its opinion that there should be expansion of higher education facilities, it showed great concern to create additional places for the increasing demand. This will be clear from the following observations of the Committee under the title 'The short-term emergency':

"807: Before we come to our final chapter we must turn to an immediate problem which, although it is not strictly within our terms of reference, we cannot ignore. Our terms of reference concern the long-term development of higher education; but in the years from 1965/66 to 1967/68 we are faced with an emergency which, if it is not adequately met, may well frustrate our recommendations for the more distant future.

808: In these years, the nature of the crisis, the very large numbers of boys and girls who were born just after the war will reach the age of entry to higher education. Their numbers are so great as to make it certain that those qualified and wanting to enter higher education will far outnumber the places that, on present plans, will be available for them: institutions will suddenly be faced with pressures almost different in kind from those that they have faced hitherto".[51]

The Committee felt great concern about the need to provide higher education facilities to the children born in the post-war period. There was no difference of opinion that unless expanded higher education facilities are provided, it would not be possible to meet the new social and political problems and pressures which the community never faced before. The concern of the Robbins Committee is clearly expressed in the following words:

"810: The young people who will be seeking to enter higher education in the years 1965/66 to 1967/68 were born in the period when the population of this country was beginning to return to normal life after the upheavals and separations inevitable in war. The trials that their parents had to undergo are in themselves sufficient reason for the country to exert itself to meet the needs of their children. Moreover, if great numbers of these young people are qualified and eager to enter higher education it would be gravely unjust that, simply because so many were born at the same time, a smaller proportion of those qualified should receive higher education than in the age groups coming immediately before or after them. If they are denied the opportunity of higher education they will have good reason to feel frustrated and dissatisfied. Further, a chance will have been lost to make good some of the shortages of qualified people, including the acute shortage of teachers for the schools".[52]

The concern is heightened when the summary of the Report concluded with the following words:

"The Report concludes by drawing attention to an educational emergency now confronting higher education because of the arrival at the ages of seventeen and eighteen of the very large numbers of children born immediately after the Second World War. In our judgement, this is an emergency of the same importance as the emergency produced by demobilisation after the last war and demanding the same type of extraordinary measures to meet it. If the needs of the situation are not adequately met by immediate government action, many of our plans for long-term expansion will be seriously endangered".[53]

From the preceeding paragraphs, it is clear that the Robbins Committee made strong and positive recommendations for new places in higher education. The Committee provided estimates of the number upto 1980-81. When the Committee concluded its work, the number of full-time higher education enrolment in GB was 216,000 (62-63).[54] It estimated that over eight years, the increase will be by 117,000, to 133,000 in 1970-71 and over the next one decade by a further 195,000, to 507,000 in 1980-81. These figures took into account the entire higher education area. By 1982-83, the total higher education enrolment touched 522,000.

Although not a conceptual university, based on the recommendation of the Robbins Committee (1962-63), the Royal College of Art which has its origin in 1837 as a School of Design and later reorganised in 1901 into four schools with further addition in 1912 of professional training in TV and Film areas, was brought within the purview of the University Grants system. A Royal charter was granted to the College in 1967.

The Cranefield Institute of Technology which has its origin as a College of Aeronautics founded in 1946, was granted a Royal Charter in December 1969, as a national and International Centre for Advanced Teaching and Applied Research in Science, Technology and Management.

One special feature of the new Universities was that quite a few advanced Colleges of Technology were upgraded into Universities, eg., Aston, Bath, Bradford, City, Louborough, Salford, Surrey, Heriot-Watt etc. The Robbins Committee observed that "while there has been much initiative from the centre, all the new Universities owe their origin to local enterprise".[55]

Breaking new ground, the establishment of the Open University has provided a model to the whole-world to cater to the needs of those aspirants for higher education who for various reasons in life, were or are unable to pursue higher education through the formal channel of collegiate education.

Idea for an 'Open University' was mooted in 1963 for providing teaching through TV and Radio. In a White Paper published in 1966, the project was known as 'The University of the 'Air'. On the recommendation of a Committee appointed under the Chairmanship of the then Vice-Chancellor of the Aston University, which suggested change of the title of the University to 'The Open University' and recommended that broadcast media would be only one of the various means by which the University would perform its teaching role.

The University which began its activities from 1969 on being granted a Royal Charter the same year, prepared the initial courses for undergraduate teaching from June, 1971.

With the great potentiality that the University has had and the mandate that the charter provided, it expanded its activities and on the recommendation of a committee appointed in 1976, on continuing education, a centre was established in 1980 for Continuing Education, with a view to bringing together and expand the University's programme for associated students. As a result of the abolition of the Council for National Academic Awards by the Further and Higher Education Act 1992, "... the university embarked on a major new development by offering a nationwide validation service to other educational institutions which do not have degree awarding status".[56]

Creation of Binary System

By the time, the Robbins Report was submitted in 1963 many new Universities came into being with different historical background. These universities were established for more places to meet the needs of the rising population in general and the number of school leavers then and the estimated ones in near future. Following the Robbin's Report, more universities were to be established. However, keeping in view the Robbin's recommendations to create more places for students involving expansion, the government introduced the new 'binary system' under which Polytechnics were established by the Labour Government as public sector highest level institutions controlled and financed by the local authorities with sizable funds from the Central Government.

The Government considered that these polytechnics will meet the needs of more places for higher education and of industry. These polytechnics were to have close links with the further education sector, industry, commerce, the professions and public services. They were also to cater to the needs of part time students.

During 1969 to 1973 alone, thirty polytechnics were formed. Besides the total thirty four polytechnics in England and Wales, there are five technological central institutions in Scotland, of which two are polytechnics.

A number of these have had long history, e.g. the Polytechnic of Central London, which was originally the Polytechnic Institution. Polytechnics have contributed significantly to the development of the higher education system in Great Britain and some of them have established reputation both within and outside Britain.

Their record of achievements in terms of status, growth and efficiency has earned them the reputation of 'the higher education success story'.

The Education Reform Act, 1988 took away Polytechnics and most other higher education colleges in England and Wales from the local authority control and financing and created a separate Funding Council called Polytechnics and Colleges Funding Council (PCFC). However, the binary line was abolished following the Further and Higher Education Act, 1992. This will be discussed later in the Chapter Five.

CONCLUSION

Admittedly, in the world history of university education, Great Britain has played a significant role. The University of Oxford and the University of Cambridge have served as great sources of inspiration to the rest of the world and also as models for a very long time. These universities have been dreams of many a bright young minds both at home and all over the world.

There are other Institutions too in Great Britain that have also ranked high in the world of higher education. For example, the Imperial College of Science, Engineering and Medicine, University College, London, University of Manchester Institute of Science and Technology.

From the very beginning, the universities of Scotland have been known for their own tradition and standing. England, in fact, in the industrial revolution was "heavily relient on the products of the Scottish universities for the scientists, engineers and medical men".

New universities were born out of the social and economic needs as also the need to meet the new challenges through technological advancement. In many cases, pressures for new universities were pending for quite some years. Universities of Great Britain are known for their own traditions, structures and approaches. The new universities marked special characteristics and they are the following:

(i) The new universities were founded, unlike the earlier universities, by the state with the flow of funds from the beginning both for infrastructural facilities as also for maintenance. Additionally, they raised funds through appeals to public.

(ii) They have had the power of conferring degrees from the beginning, including determining their own curricula and methods of teaching and examinations.

(iii) All these universities are 'Campus' Universities on large and self-contained sites. Buildings have been constructed with comparatively new methods of industrialised buildings with pre-fabricated or factory-made components.

(iv) Most important characteristic of these universities are the readiness to experiment in the areas of courses, combination, methods of teaching and assessment. However, it must be noted that not all that appear in the new universities are their own innovation. Some are those which were successfully experimented elsewhere in the world and accepted.

The Binary System also marked a new concept to meet the rising demand of higher education which turned out to be a success story. This was, however, abolished in 1992-93 following the White Paper of 1991 and the 1992 legislature. This would be discussed later.

The Robbins Report is the first classic document on higher education in U.K. The Open University has served as the first formal model of non-formal education system and it must be admitted that it was a timely adventurous innovation which has helped millions of people all over the world to fulfill their aspirations in life, for the system is now so popular internationally that large number of Open Universities are now functioning all over the world.

References

1. Steward, Campell: The place of higher education in a changing society, *In The American College: A Psychological and Social Interpretation of the Higher Learning.* ed. by Nevitt Sanford. Stanford, California, 1961, p-908.
2. *Ibid.*, p. 908.
3. *Op. Cit.*, p. 909.
4. U.K., University of Oxford, Under-Graduate Prospectus, 1991-93, p. 9.
5. *Ibid.*, p. 10.
6. U.K., University of Cambridge, *Information for Students from Overseas*, Cambridge, 1992-93, p. 1.
7. U.K., University of Cambridge, *Admission Prospectus*, 1991-92, p. 6.
8. Association of Commonwealth Universities, Commonwealth Universities Year Book 1992. London, p. 2291.
9. *Ibid.*, p. 2295.
10. *Op. Cit.*, p. 2388.
11. *Op. Cit.*, p. 2359.
12. Ibid.
13. U.K., Committee on Higher Education, Report (Robbins Report) London, HMSO, 1963, p. 22.
14. Tress, Ronald, C., Higher Education Alternatives *In Universities Alternatives in Quarternary Educatiom*, ed. by Michael D. Stephens and Gorden W. Roderick, London, Longman, 1978, p. 16.
15. U.K., Committee on Higher Education, Report (Robbins Report) London, HMSO, 1963, p. 23.

16. Association of Commonwealth Universities, Commonwealth Universities Year Book 1993, London, p. 2508.

17. U.K., Committee on Higher Education Report (Robbins Report) London, HMSO, 1963, p. 23.

18. Perkin, H.J., New Universities in the United Kingdom (Case Studies on Innovation in Higher Education). London, Organisation for Economic Cooperation and Development, 1969, p. 39.

19. Association of Commonwealth Universities. Commonwealth Universities Year Book 1993, London, pp. 2858-59.

20. Perkin, H.J., New Universities in the UK (Case Studies in Innovation in Higher Education). London, Organisation for Economic Cooperation and Development, 1969, p. 38.

21. Finch, Janet. Education as Social Policy. pp. 10-11.

22. Brett, E.A., The World Economy since the War: the Politics of Uneven Development, Hampshire, MacMillan, 1985, pp. 1321-34.

23. *Ibid*, p. 150.

24. Lomax, K.S. Growth and Productivity in UK, *In Economic Growth in Twentieth Century Briton*' ed. by Derek H. Aldcroft, London, MacMillan, 1969, p. 19.

25. *Ibid.*, p. 12.

26. U.K., Committee on Higher Education, Report (Robbins Report) London, HMSO, 1963, p.15 (Figure for 1982-83 taken from Table A-2 of the document "The Development of Higher Education into 1990s", UGC, p. 43).

27. Fowler, G.T. Conclusion: Present Trends and Future Policies, *In Higher Education Alternatives*. ed. by Michael D. Stephens and Gordon W. Roderick, London, Longman, 1978, p. 156.

28. Holroyd, P. and Loveridge, D.J. Industry and Higher Education Alternatives. *In Higher Education Alternatives*, ed. by Michael D. Stephens and Gorden W. Roderick, London, Longman, 1978, p. 68.

29. *Ibid.*, p. 68.
30. Parkin, H.J. New Universities in the UK. (Case Studies in Innovation in Higher Education). London, Organisation for Economic Co-operation and Development, 1969, p. 36.
31. Association of Commonwealth Universities. Commonwealth Universities Year Book, 1993, London, p. 2673.
32. *Ibid.*, p. 2793.
33. *Op. Cit.*, p. 2423.
34. *Op. Cit.*, p. 2369.
35. Op. Cit., p. 2498.
36. Perkin, H.J., New Universities in the UK, London, (Case Studies in Innovation in Higher Education). Organisation for Economic Cooperation and Development, 1969, p. 55.
37. *Ibid.*, p. 55.
38. Fowler, G.T. Conclusion: Present Trends and Future Policies, *In Higher Education Alternatives*, ed. by Michael D. Stephens and Gordon W. Rodrick, London, Longman, 1978, p.160.
39. The International Encyclopedia of Education, Research and Studies, V.3 (D-E), ed. by Torsten Husein and T.N. Postlethwater, Oxford, Pergamon, 1985, p. 5351.
40. Perkin, H.J., New Universities in the United Kingdom. (Case Studies in Innovation in Higher Education), London, Organisation for Economic Co-operation and Development, 1969, p. 69.
41. Fowler, G.T., Conclusion: Present Trends and Future Policies. *In Hiqher Education Alternatives*, ed. by Michael D. Stephens and Gordon ~~W.~~ Roderick, London, Longman, 1978, p. 160-61.
42. Perkin, H.J. New Universities in the UK. (Case Studies in Innovation in Higher Education). London, Organisation for Economic Cooperation and Development, 1969, p. 61.

43. *Ibid.*, p. 165.

44. Association of Commonwealth Universities. Commonwealth Universities Year Book 1993, p. 2840.

45. Perkin, H.J., New Universities in the United Kingdom. (Case Studies in Innovation in Higher Education). London, Organisation for Economic Cooperation and Development, 1969, p. 68

46. *Ibid.*, p. 68.

47. *Op. Cit.*, p. 68.

48. *Op. Cit.*, p. 62.

49. U.K., Committee on Higher Education Report (Robbins Report), London, HMSO, 1968, p. iii.

50. *Ibid.*, p. 4., Robbins Report

51. *Op. Cit.*, p. 257, Robbins Report

52. *Op. Cit.*, p. 257, Robbins Report

53. *Op. Cit.*, p. 276, Robbins Report.

54. *Op. Cit.*, p. 15, Robbins Report.

55. *Op. Cit.*, p. 24, Robbins Report.

56. Association of Commonwealth Universities, Commonwealth Universities Year Book 1993. London, p. 2696.

2

Changing Scenario

INCREASING EXCHEQUER BURDEN

Driven by the pressing need of creating more places in higher education for the fast increasing population who would like to go in for higher education as also the needs of economic and technological advance of the country which was so necessary to catch up with the new trends of technological development meaning thereby competition at the international level, an unprecedented number of new Universities came into being in 1960s with an increasing dependence on the government funding for them right from the inception. The additional growing burden of funding the new universities - both for capital and for recurring expenses, was making a dent on the public exchequer.

The post-second world war period witnessed a number of changes in various aspects of all walks of life. In the pre-war period, the major part of income of the university (about 57%) came from fees, endowments and local authority grants as also from research contracts. As against this the government grants was 35.8% in 1938-39. Due to the post-war internal developments that the Government of U.K. undertook, commitments were fast growing resulting in financial constraints.

Besides, on account of the additional funds that the government was required to make available for new universities of 1960s, the share of the government was fast increasing for the universities, rising from 69.6% in 1952-53 to 70.9% in 1962-63 and 76.4% in 1972-73. There was a general impression both within the government as well as in some section of the public that the growing pressure on the public exchequer needed to be checked.

SUGGESTIONS OF MRS. SHIRLEY WILLIAMS

In the late 1960s, the then Minister of State for Education and Science (Mrs. Shirley Williams) had made several suggestions to the universities to the need of adopting new approaches so that efficiency could be increased through reorganisation and restructurisation in a few areas, eg. increasing student-staff ratios from around 7:1 to about 10:1 or 11:1, to encourage more students to study near their home so that residential needs is reduced, making more effective and efficient use of buildings and equipment, avoiding duplication of facilities, sharing of facilities between universities and polytechnics, changes in student support formula including loans, introduction of new academic year and expansion of distance education, etc. However, the repeated suggestions of the Minister were not taken seriously by the Universities.

In retrospect, the suggestions of Mrs. Williams were not considered unreasonable. However, it should also be admitted that while some of the suggestions could have been taken seriously by the universities, some were for the UGC and government to act. It is true that the universities did not take the suggestions seriously, but the government too did not do so for otherwise it would have announced its policy covering these suggestions. However, in the course of debate in the House of Commons, replying to the Labour Opposition after the UGC's letter of 1st July, 1981 was issued. Dr. Rhodes Boyson, the Under Secretary of State for Education and Science, referred to the letter of Mrs. Williams which came handy to the government.

THE FUNDING STRUCTURE

Genesis of Funding for Higher Education

For the first time in 1889, the government had sanctioned a general grant of Pounds 15,000 per-annum to the university colleges of Great Britain. Realizing that payment of grants to the Universities and colleges would be a permanent activity, the government planned for an organised structure for this purpose and with that end in view, it had appointed a number of ad-hoc committees from 1889, and in 1906, a permanent committee was created when the size of the government grant grew to Pounds 133,000. This Committee was made accountable to the then Board of Education.

The first world war broke out in 1914 and during the war "... the student numbers at universities were depleted, income from fees had become negligible, inflation had considerably lessened the value of income from endowment, local authority contributions had dropped, buildings were run down and in need of extensive maintenance and repair (many had been requisitioned during the War) and all-in-all the financial situation of the universities was seriously threatened".[1]

Emergence of University Grants Committee

After the war, realization of the impact of superior scientific and technological advancement both for political superiority and economic development and stability paved the way for expansion of higher education and the government decided to provide more funds and better organised structure for funding higher education. Came thus into being the University Grants Committee as a Standing Committee of the Treasury "to... distribute among the Universities the grant of Pounds 692,000 per-annum, which was allocated for the post-war expansion". The term of reference of the UGC as amended in 1946 was as follows:

> "To enquire into the financial needs of university education in Great Britain - to advise the Government as to the application of any grants made by Parliament towards meeting them; to collect, examine and make available information relating to University education throughout the United Kingdom; to assist, in consultation with the universities and other bodies concerned, the preparation and execution of such plans for the development of the Universities as may from time to time be required in order to ensure that they are fully adequate to national needs".

Although the University Grants Committee was created as a body between the Universities and Government, the bureaucratic control was inevitable. The UGC was responsible for the 7 Universities in England, 4 in Scotland and 1 in Northern Ireland. Additional 10 university colleges (4 in England, 3 in Wales and 3 in Ireland) as also the colleges of technology in Manchester and Glasgow came under the UGC (19 institutions in all)".[2] Till about 1922-23, the UGC did not have its jurisdiction over Oxford and Cambridge which were managing their affairs without government grants. At this time, the Irish Institutions were transferred to the Irish Government.

The University Grants Committee consisted of a full-time Chairman with eighteen members. Of this:

(i) two were concerned only with salary question;

(ii) ten were persons active in the service of Universities (excluding Vice-Chancellors and other administrators);

(iii) two were connected with other forms of education;

(iv) three were from Industry; and

(v) one was from a Research Establishment.

Depending on the needs, personnel from the Ministry of Agriculture, Fisheries and Food, the Education and Health Departments, the Research Councils and the Office of the Minister for Science were ".. represented by assessors, either on the Committee or on one of its sub-Committees".[3]

The members were appointed by "the Chancellor of the Exchequer, after consultation with the Minister of Education and Secretary of State for Scotland, normally for five years" with possibility of re-appointment which of late became almost routine.[4]

While the government showed its interest and concern for the all-round development of higher education with more funds and support, in 1946, the universities on their part assured the government and the Chancellor of the Exchequer in particular that they "... entirely accept the view that the government has not only the right but the duty to satisfy itself that every field of study which in the national interest output to be cultivated in Great Britain is in fact being cultivated in the university system and that the resources which are placed at the disposal of the university are being used with full regard to efficiency and to economy".[5]

However, increasing dependences on government funding led to consequential pressures on the autonomy of the universities including freedom in the academic affairs and how the block grant should be spent. This perhaps was the natural outcome.

Funding System

The UGC had a dual task of advising the Treasury on the total grants to be paid to the Universities on the basis of the government_sanction and in turn to allocate funds to the universities. Broadly, two kinds of grants recurring and non-recurring were assessed by UGC through structural visitation to the universities. Recurring grants mainly meant 'Block Grants' to meet the recurring expenditure of the universities and the non-recurring grants meant for capital development to cover expenditure, eg. erection and renovation of buildings, purchase of equipment and furniture for new buildings, payment of professional fees and purchase of sites and properties. The non-recurring grants were paid on annual basis, but estimates prepared for a few years in advance. Recurring grants which was assessed as block grants for a period of five years was also paid annually. It is true that the total amount for each of the five years was decided by the government on the advice of the University Grants Committee, but the actual allocation and payment of grant of the total approved funds by the government between universities was the responsibility and discretion of the Committee. The grants for each of the five academic financial years were calculated on a growing scale for each of the quinquennium. However, fixation of the amount did not preclude review of the amounts during the course of the five years.[6]

One speciality of the recurring grants was that the

UGC could earmark part of the already announced recurring grant for a earmarked purpose of recurring nature, say, introduction of a specific programme/ course. At times, depending on the nature of the need, additional recurring grant could also be given for purposes, say, increased intake of medical students.[7] In addition, special grants could also be made for recurring expenditure to meet any particular needs of recurring nature.[8]

The Robbins Committee after examining and analysing the function and status of the University Grants Committee had suggested that the committee should be made 'Commission' with minor change in the membership to make it broad base. The Robbins Committee felt that with re-organised and expanded higher education system for greater attention and better co-ordination that would be needed particularly after bringing the colleges under the umbrella of the grants committee system it would be prudent that —

> "... the universities and the Colleges of Advanced Technology, and with the universities the associated Schools of Education, together with the Scottish Colleges of Education, should be placed in the hands of a Grants Commission. This body, which would be the lineal successor of the University Grants Committee, would have the duty of advising the government on the magnitude of the grants and assessing the correct allocations to the different institutions concerned. The main body of the Commission would be constituted on the same principles as the University Grants Committee, with a suitably augmented staff. Much of its detailed work would, however, be conducted by a structure of committees, whose membership need not be restricted to members of the main Commmission. In this way we

believe that the intimate contacts characteristic of the operations of the University Grants Committee will be retained, although the scope of the Commission will be considerably wider".[9]

Although the government finally did not elevate the Grants Committee to that of the 'Commission', it "... transferred the government's responsibility for the UGC in 1963 from the Treasury to a new Minister of State for civil science and the universities, who in turn was absorbed into the Department of Education and Science which replaced the Ministry of Education in 1964".[10] This saw the beginning of closer government control for the UGC was required to work 'in liaison with the Department of Education and Science! With new decision (1967-68) under which it became necessary to make the accounts of the universities available to the authority of the Comptroller and Auditor General on behalf of the Parliamentary Committee of Public Accounts, the Permanent Secretary of DES became the accounting officer responsible for ensuring that the accounts are maintained properly and that deficiencies if any, are made up.

For the government it was necessary to ensure that more and more students eligible for higher education are placed in the universities and for the University Grants Committee, it was obligatory to implement the national policy and in that process, student number driven funding policy became the basis for allocation of grants to different universities. Firstly, due to the 'policy led expenditure programme followed by the UGC following the Robbins Report and secondly, due to the unprecedented number of growth of universities in 1960s, more and more students found places in the universities which also contributed to increasing university enrolment.

The following Table-2.1 shows the rising student population in full time university education.

Table 2.1[11]

Year	Student Number *In Thousand*	Percentage of increase
1961-62	113	--
1965-66	173	53.1%
1966-67	189	9.25
1968-69	217	14.8
1969-70	226	4.15

During 1960s, twenty-four new universities came into being and although a number of them had existed as colleges/centres of an already existing University having some student population, but for obvious reasons with the infrastructure facilities of new universities and new subjects etc., more students were attracted to the universities.

Demographic Phenomenon

Demographic factor has multiple implications for its impact has varied consequences on the social, political and economic fronts of the country. According to the UN Report on the Social Situation (1961). "Since economic growth is ordinarily defined as growth in per capita national income, which in turn is defined as the ratio of production to population, it is obvious that trends in population can, mathematically speaking, play as large a role in economic growth as trends in production. In fact, some observers maintain that, for a number of countries, from a purely economic point of view, the most efficient investment to promote economic growth would be investment, not in economic production, but in reduction of birth rates".[12] The annual increase in world population around 1960-61 was between 45 and 55 million registering '... the rate of increase from about 1 per cent in the years before the Second World War to a value between 1.6 and 1.9 per cent, and is still rising'.[13] Precisely, population factor is crucial to decide the magnitude of investments needed for various social services as measuring all the developmental activities.

Why expansion of education in general was a common social welfare and national economic development programme almost in all the countries has been well expressed in the UN Report on the World Sociai Situation (1961) which runs as follows:

> "... almost everywhere educational budgets have risen steadily (by 12 to 14 per cent a year as an unweighted average). In some countries more than 5 per cent of the national income now goes to education, and the percentage is expected to rise still higher. The conception of education as a productive investment as well as a form of social consumption continues to gain ground, and the debates over educational methods and purposes also continue. One of the most widespread trends thus relates to the future; both the heavy cost of education and the developmental tasks assigned to it have led to a rapid increase in the number of educational plans, regional as well as national; to long-term forecasts of costs and teacher requirements; and to studies of the relationships of different levels of education to each other and to the national economy".

The United Kingdom was no exception. It was due to the population increase that a large number of universities came into being in 1960s.

With the accepted and desired target of a new university to reach a 'minimum viable size' of at least 3000 students within 10 years, it was clear that the 'number of students' was a crucial factor as part of the expansion programme of higher education. By 1967-68, most of the new universities had achieved the originally proposed student numbers.

Due to population increase growth of higher education was not peculiar to UK only. For identical reasons, in some countries also, student number increased fast as would be clear from the following Table 2.2.

POLICY LED EXPENDITURE

With the acceptance of the Robbins Committee Report (1963) by the Government, the 'policy led' expenditure for higher education expansion programme was followed during 1960s and early 1970s when the University Grants Committee paid grants to the Universities on the basis of the number of students. This led to a situation that the Universities were bidding to UGC for higher student numbers and in turn, the Deans and Heads within the Universities demanded their share on the basis of the projected numbers. This policy aimed at doubling the number of full-time higher education students making it 453,000 in 1971-72, from 184,000 during 1962-67 registering a 63% increase. It was 235,000 during 1967-72 quinquennium. The consequences of unhealthy competition among universities and within the same university for more number of students reflected well in the following observations of Dr. A. Christodulu, Secretary General, Association of Commonwealth Universities, London:

Table 2.2[14]

Country	In thousands			
	1950	*1960*	*1965*	*1970*
Austria	22.5	38.9	50.1	62.5
France	185.4	256.0	527.0	778.8
Italy	240.7	284.3	424.7	694.2
Japan	240.0	712.0	1093.0	1685.6
Sweden	27.3	47.9	83.5	145.7
Denmark	19.5	32.3	53.2	77.1
Australia	34.9	70.7	131.7	175.4
Canada	2297.0	3610.0	5570.0	7608.0

> "Speaking from the experience some years ago in Leeds University, in the heady days of expansion, what struck me more and more as the years went by from 1963 onwards was that the criteria for a department to get more staff, to get more resources at the time, were increasingly based on student numbers, particularly undergraduates and the departments fell over themselves to try to admit more and more students to keep their competitiveness within the university. In many instances they were prepared to lower standards of entry in pursuit of expansion. And the UGC seemed to reflect this more and more allocating resources according to student numbers, and evolving formulae for funding based primarily on unit costs per student".[15]

Nothing sustains in a democracy without political will, for when the party in power running the government decides an approach that becomes the policy of the country in whatever area it may be. The *modus-operandi* for implementation of the policy are incidental, once the policy is decided. The need to provide more places in higher education due to the rising population of the 18 years plus, had, in general wide acceptance in the political level irrespective of the party, which implied expansion of higher education.

1972 WHITE PAPER - CONTINUED EXPANSION

The programme of expansion of higher education continued as evidenced by the 1972 White Paper 'Education; A Frame-work for Expansion' projected further expansion. The White Paper proposed that by 1981, 200,000 annual entrants would be accommodated within Great Britain aged under 21 which would represent about 22 per cent of the age group then 18, as against 7% in 1961 and 15% in 1971. This meant a jump of 7%. In terms of the total number of students in the higher education sector, it was expected that the rise would be from 463,000 in 1971-72 to 750,000 in 1981, that is, a quantum jump of 74%. This estimate included sandwich students also in higher education.

Coming to the university sector, the 1972 White Paper had estimated that over 1972-77 quinquennium, there would be a 30% growth in full-time student numbers. It also estimated a reduction in recurrent grant by 2% in real terms per-student as it had calculated to reduce the unit cost while maintaining academic standards by tightening student-staff ratios for it had projected change in the arts-science ratio from 45:55 in 1971-72 to 47:53 in 1976-77. However, the 1972 White Paper announced a sizable capital works for buildings and residents so that planned growth could be accommodated.

For the first time, after the continued expansion

programme of about a decade initiated following the Robbins Committee Report, one could see the beginning of a discreet changing tone for the White Paper also envisaged that while the Government would fully compensate the salary increases, the universities were expected to reduce the proportion of post-graduate students from 19% in 1971, to 17% in 1976 besides a 10:1 student-staff ratio by 1982 from 8:1.

The 1972 White Paper also assumed that in view of the changing arts-science ratio, the arts numbers would rise by 36% while science by 26%. It also assumed that the growth of the GB entrants would be more than the overseas students. It is interesting that the 1972 White Paper was prepared by Mrs. Margarat Thatcher when she was Minister of State at the Department of Education and Science.

QUINQUENNIUM 1972-77

Primarily in the backdrop of 1972 White Paper on Education, the University Grants Committee had to do its homework for the quinquennium 1972-77. Taking the hint from the White Paper, the Committee issued letters to the Universities in January 1973 communicating the recurrent and equipment grants. For the first time, the UGC also issued, with the letter, a Memorandum of General Guidance which it was perhaps designed to help the universities prepare for the changing environment that the White Paper envisaged, although that did not in reality happen.

It was indicated by the Committee that from 243,000 in 1972-73, by 1976-77, the number of students in Universities would be 306,000 full-time and 15,500 full-time equivalent part-time students. In terms of percentage of increase over the previous year in the number of full time students and the year-to-year increase, from 1972-73 to 1976-77 the estimates were as shown in Table 2.3.

Table 2.3[16]

Year	*Percentage*	*Numbers*
1972-73	3.3%	(243,000)
1973-74	3.5%	(251,500)
1974-75	5.2%	(264,500)
1975-76	7.0%	(283,000)
1976-77	8.01%	(306,000)

As regards the recurring grants, it was expected that the yearly increase from year to year for the period 1972-73 to 1976-77 would be as shown in the Table-2.4.

Table 2.4[17]

Year	*Percentage*	*Amount*
1972-73	—	(295.5 million pounds)
1973-74	5.4%	(311.50 million pounds)
1974-75	5.2%	(327.75 million pounds)
1975-76	5.8%	(346.75 million pounds)
1976-77	5.8%	(367.00 million pounds)

For Equipment grants also, the Committee worked out estimates of grants on year-to-year increase for the aforesaid period as shown in the Table-2.5.

The memorandum aimed at achieving an economy in expenditure per student from 100 in 1971-72 to 98 in 1976-77 which meant a change from an "improvement factor" to an "economy factor" approach. However, the universities were assured of full compensation for any inflation during the period for academic salaries

Table 2.5[18]

Year	*Percentage*	*Amount*
1972-73	—	(25.50 million pounds)
1973-74	5.9%	(27.0 million pounds)
1974-75	3.7%	(28.0 million pounds)
1975-76	5.4%	(29.5 million pounds)
1976-77	8.5%	(32.0 million pounds)

adding that for about the 50% of future cost increases of other items, there would be uncertainity.

It also contained a few other points, eg. an overall increase in library expenditure within the assumed fall in central expenditure per student in 1976-77, dangers of student number driven resource allocation formulae affecting the research activity of the Departments and effectiveness and efficiency of small departments.

Inflationary impact on the fiscal position of the universities and the consequential difficulties that they were facing forced the government to new procedure for being introduced in Spring 1973 to reassess the grant on the basis of the current prices and to pay supplementary grants to neutralise 100% rise for recurring expenditure and 50% for equipment grants. The public expenditure constraint having already on the priority agenda of the government, the UGC had to ask the universities to defer building programmes till June 1974 and it even indicated that in 1974-75 (July, 1974 to June, 1975) allocation for building programmes would be much reduced. Gradually, the strong quinquennial system was getting eroded. In fact, those were some of the first visible impacts of the inflationary pressures which led to the breakdowns of the quinquennial system.[19]

Although one can argue that there were reasonable hints to the UGC and the universities to tighten their belts on the financial front, none of the universities really did so, or even took the same seriously. Even UGC which was the buffer body between government and the university either did not realise the magnitude of the difficult time lying ahead or did not think it proper to create panic at that stage without definite direction from the government.

Slowly but surely the situation was leading to a breakdown of the quinquennium system. However, despite the not so comfortable picture, neither the government nor the UGC came forward to warn the universities even of the likelyhood of a crunch. Who is to be blamed for this? Rather, can the universities who are the ultimate sufferers be blamed on the ground that they should have analysed the various developments from time to time including the general pressure on the public expenditure and review the position? These questions are but natural to come to fore. These are difficult questions to be answered easily, but they will surely be discussed and analysed later.

GATHERING CLOUDS - IMPACT OF OIL CRISIS

The academic year 1973-74 was in fact the beginning of the process of end of expansion period which began in the early sixties. The adverse impact on the economy of the country due to the oil producing nations' decision to a 25% minimum cut in oil supplies to the West, engulfed all alike and universities were no exception. As a result of the 25% cut in oil supplies, there was 66% rise in the price of oil in October 1973 and 5% cumulative cut back in oil production the same month. Consequently, in January 1974, oil prices were doubled. In a chain impact of this, price escalation took place all over the world. In UK, prices of raw material, whole sale prices and weekly wage rates increased sizeably; the wage rate increase was 28.5%. Added to this was the major miners strike, three-day working week in the first half of 1974 and the government had to present three Budgets in order to balance the economy. In fact, the '... oil price explosion marked the end of the post-war Golden Age of growth and full employment'.[20] The damage to economy caused by this oil prise rice was so serious that "The partial collapse of oil prices in the mid-1980s certainly did not restore earlier conditions of trouble free growth.[21]

In order to meet the unexpected situation of inflation the government had to take hard decisions on public expenditure. In December 1973, the White Paper on Public expenditure announced the following actions for the universities to reduce the burden on the public expenditure:

(i) Fifty per cent withholding the additional (supplementary) recurrent expenditures for the academic year 1974-75 and the remaining year of the quinquennium i.e. upto 1976-77.

(ii) Not to pay any additional (supplementary) grant for the equipment expenditure for one year's increases in prices.

Still favouring the growth in higher education as planned, the government made it clear that the adjustments and reduction should be made without allowing the planned growth suffer during the whole period of quinquennium. However, the already grim situation turned grave with the announcement of the Chancellor of the Exchequer the same month that further economies were unavoidable and directed the following actions for the universities:

(i) Withholding from recurrent grant for the academic year 1974-75 the remaining 50% of the additional grant otherwise payable on account of one year's price rise; and

(ii) Reduction by 15 million pounds furniture and equipment grants to 23 million pounds from 38 million pounds with stipulation that the savings should be achieved in full during the financial year 1974-75 itself.

While it is true that individual universities had suddenly to face difficult time, the University Grants Committee had greater difficulties to listen to the problems of the universities and take decisions to make adjustments. In order to provide some relief to the universities, the Committee decided to provide the 2.8 million pounds unassigned grants for 1974-75, which was kept separately for important developments in particular fields in certain selected universities between 1973-74 and 1974-75.

At a time when the tempo of expansion was in full swing, such a situation which was so unexpected, came as a serious set back, rather the first one of its type since the initiation of the expansion programme. On one hand the government did not announce a 'halt' to the expansion programme, and on the other hand the reduction seriously affected the expansion programme and the enthusiasm of the academics.

In its efforts to do its best, the government provided a further 4 million pounds to help the universities fight the inflation which was found to be more than initially estimated. The Committee after deliberation decided to add to it an amount of 1.5 million pounds from the earmarked grant for furniture and equipment and distributed 5.1 million pounds to universities in

September 1974, retaining 0.4 million pounds as a reserve. It also used an unallocated reserve of equipment and furniture grant of 2.5 million pounds to reduce the 14 million the economies to be faced for 1974-75.[22] These exercise meant "... a reduction of about 40% in each university's equipment and furniture grant at a time when expansion was taking place and new technologies emerging".[23]

All these efforts also could not provide the relief needed by the universities as would be evident from page 18 of the Annual Survey of the University Grants Committee for the academic year 1973-74:

> "The additional sums thus made available fell very substantially short of the increase in salaries, wages and prices registered during the year, and all the universities therefore intensified the programmes of severe economy which they had instituted earlier. While different universities adopted different measures, steps reported to the Committee included restrictions (in some cases an absolute prohibition) in the filling of posts falling vacant among teaching and non-teaching staff; deferment of repairs and maintenance; reduction of library expenditure; and restrictions on the use of heating and lighting, and on general departmental expenditure. Many of these economies, while practicable in the short term, cannot be continued in the longer term without impairing the work of the universities and their capacity to accommodate their planned intakes of students".

The picture was gradually changing from a rosy, mighty and growing one to a dismal, difficult and disappointing one for on one hand the year 1973-74 failed to register the level of the planned growth for though the number of the students rose by 1.6% over the previous year, there were 6,772 less than the quinquennial settlement figure. What appeared to be worrying was that as against the aforesaid position of the lower students growth, the full-time teaching and research staff paid fully from the university funds had grown by 2.3% for the induction of the staff was done in anticipation of the future growth of the student number. This was widening the gap.

The quenquinnium 1972-77, except the first year 1972-73 when the higher education age participation rate peaked at 14.2% registered diminishing growth rate of students. It was clear to UGC that a review and reassessment of the situation was but essential before it was late so that the requirements of funding could be known. With that end in view, in July 1974, all the universities were invited to inform UGC by the end of October, 1974 about their latest estimates for undergraduate growth of student numbers in 1976-77 keeping in view the student enrolment pattern in the first three years of the period 1972-77. The analysed position showed that for the entire country, 'the probable total full-time university student population would be between 8 and 11 per cent below the original target for 1976-77 of 306,000 full time students". Based on this and the staff recruitment trend, the UGC decided the new provisional figures for 1976-77.

THE END OF QUINQUENNIAL SYSTEM

The academic year 1974-75 turned out to be the last year of the quinquennial system. Keeping in view its limitations to rescue the universities in 1973-74 on account of the sudden and serious financial difficulties that they were left to face and make adjustments within the university, the University Grants Committee realized well that it was necessary to project the autonomy of the universities *vis-a-vis* the role of the UGC as the national body to interact with the universities. Accordingly, the committee explained the purpose of the block grants distribution and the full discretion that the universities have to adjust and balance between education and research as they may deem fit including rearranging the priorities at a time of economic stringency. The Committee also explained in the Survey Report (para-6) that "... the principle that the universities with whom we deal are autonomous and responsible for their own decision and their own management" and that it has 'to exercise influence on the shape and size of the growth of the system as a whole so that it correspond to national needs'.

The attitude and approach of the UGC having been made clear, and also the Committee having realised the difficulties of the universities in the previous year, distributed pounds 5.1 million in September, 1974 which it found was inadequate and therefore advocated for more funds from the government. In view of the continuing inflation and the government finally sanctioned 15 million pounds for recurrent expenditure for 1974-75. The government also announced that when the grants for the remaining two years of the quinquennium are fixed, the growth position of the student numbers would be taken into account.

One of the difficulties that the universities were facing despite the fact that UGC was providing some additional grants to meet the escalating prices as a result of inflation, that the actual grant was being received later. This posed two major problems. One: the universities were unable in a situation of continuing and rising inflation, to decide their long-term financial planning. Two: in the absence of any prior commitment or guarantee from the UGC, even the short-term planning became difficult. As part of the planning, intake of students could not in such a situation of uncertainty be decided. By the time the quantum of grant is known, the universities had already committed to increased intake. Thus, they could not safeguard by regulating the intake of students and consequently, their real income per FTE through review.

Operationally, the additional grant of 1974-75 was based on the 1973 inflation rate 1973 which was 10.1% while in 1974, it was 29.4% leaving a gap of 19.3% which was taken care next year. While it was true that the universities had to face difficulties due to the aforesaid situation, it has also to be admitted that there was perhaps no better workable formula by which the whole year's inflation rate could be known on the basis of which supplementation could be done during the year itself.

What would have worked satisfactorily on both sides was a clear cut policy declaration by the government/UGC announcing clearly which are the items of expenditure for which the universities would be compensated to neutralize the impact of inflation. That would have, on the strength of the declared policy, lessened, but not removed fully, the constraint. It is for this reason that the CUA's Resource Allocation Group observed that:

> "In practice perhaps the most serious consequence of the breakdowns of the quinquinnial system for the internal management of universities lay in the uncertainty created by the timing of grant announcements for the annual financial settlement".

On their part, the universities had to do their exercises of adjustments howsoever difficult and painful they were. This was admitted by the UGC when it reported that 1974-75 was "one of severe strain for both - the universities and the committee". In reality, the universities had "reduced real costs over the years of severe inflation by 8%".[24] Of the various steps taken by the universities, freezing of about 500 academic posts could be mentioned besides serious reduction in services, and compression of the potential for scholarship and research. Despite all these, "... the prospect for the end of the academic year 1974-75 was one of insolvency for some institutions and great financial uncertainty for the system as a whole".[25] However, the university grants committee accepted the fact that whatever steps taken were not adequate to meet the gap created by the inflationary cost increase of 29.4% in 1974.

Carrying the serious financial stringency of the previous years, in to the academic year 1975-76, the position turned out still more difficult. In its four-page printed statement entitled "Universities in a period of Economic Crisis", the Committee of Vice-Chancellors and College Principals reaffirmed its views of last year that it must bear its share of cuts in public expenditure. At the same time it requested the Government as follows:[26]

(i) To promote a more efficient use of resources by establishing a system of university grants which departs from the ad-hoc arrangements of the present and immediate past, and which provides a planning perspective and a real terms funding commitment extending beyond a year.

(ii) To give firmest possible assurance to the universities that, at the end of this period, they will be able to resume their programmes of development with financial support at a level

in keeping with their national and international standing and commensurate with the burdens they have shouldered.

(iii) To give a clear commitment that effective long-term planning and financing arrangements will be restored so that preparations - including consideration of the necessary capital programmes to meet expansion after 1977 - can be made in the intervening period.

However, there was no impact of the aforesaid request to the Government. The UGC made the following observations in its Annual Review for 1975-76:

"The year under review marked a conclusive downturn in a process of growth of resources which has continued for about twenty years, and is unlikely soon to be resumed. Universities are now conscious not only of difficult but of novel problems which cannot be solved by improvisation. At the same time the financial system which permitted and encouraged forward planning has been seriously damaged by successive short-term decisions related to changing national pressures. As a result there is a deep and damaging sense of uncertainty which can only be removed by the restoration of a longer planning horizon".

During the year, the value of the recurrent grant and fee income had dropped by 6% as against 2% originally estimated in the quinquennial system. Savings were all in the non-salary areas. The number of students however increased by 10,693 (4.3%) and the full-time teaching and research staff paid from university funds by only 43 (i.e. 0.14%).

QUINQUENNIAL SYSTEM BROKE DOWN

For a variety of reasons, the year 1976-77 was important. First: it was the last year not only of the 1972-77 quinquennium but the end of the quinquennial system. Second: with effect from this year, with a view to restricting the spending by the various Departments the Government introduced a new discipline through its White Paper cash limits on Public Expenditure under which it was obligatory to function within the cash limits which in the case of the universities was the UGC's recurrent grant and equipment grant allocations. No supplementary grant was payable whether for academic salary increases or otherwise. However, the cash limits scheme tried to cover some of the anticipated increases, eg. a pre-determined allowance (grant) for increases in pay and prices. Third: a new pattern of government announcements in March and UGC distribution in May/June came in practice which left very little time for the universities for student intake adjustments and internal resources allocations.

The new cash limits created a number of problems for the universities. The CUA's* Resource Allocation Group had observed as follows:

> "This began to set a pattern of government announcements in March and UGC distributions in May/June, leaving very little of the academic year left for universities' own internal allocation of resources, and no opportunity to gear student intakes to recurrent grant fluctuations in the same year. Moreover, a further problem was created by the cash limits policy, because the grant reflected the inflation level of the previous year. If inflation

---

* CUA: Conference of University Administration now Association of University Administration (AUA).

rose in the following year the grant was in theory supplemented. In practice, whether or not inflation had risen could only be determined late in the Government's financial year (April-March), so that each year the UGC and subsequently the universities began to receive inflation supplements for the university financial year (August to July) towards the end of the year in question. The effect of this was that the year began in an atmosphere of grave austerity and ended with a UGC hand-out which sometimes made a mockery of past economy decisions. Psychologically this was distinctly unhelpful to the establishment of a satisfactory environment within universities where planning and resource allocation could go hand in hand. Moreover, large cash sums arriving late in the year were difficult to anticipate and plan for and difficult to allocate to best effect. If placed in a reserve fund they were in danger of fuelling a government complaint that universities held too much in their reserves. It was undoubtedly an inefficient method of university funding, it discouraged rational planning and encouraged adhocery".

However, 1976-77 was, as compared to the previous years, better from the angle of financial performance particularly the various figures of students growth, staff induction and cost rises. The full-time students number increased by 4.0% to 271,779 as compared with 306,000 originally estimated at the beginning of the quinquennial settlement. Less numbers of full time teaching and research staff were inducted and paid from the university fund which was 28 as against 43 in the previous year. The furniture and equipment grants were also according to the earlier indication. While reviewing the unstable situation of the quinquennium, in its Annual

Survey for 1976-77, the University Grants Committee made the following observations:[27]

> "Although the combined unit of resource (including that earmarked for equipment and furniture) rose somewhat in real terms at the beginning of the Quinquennium, over the Quinquennium as a whole it has fallen by 6.9 per cent against an intended decline of only 1.2 per cent. In making this comparison it should be noted that the level of the first year of the Quinquennium (1972-73) was preceded by a lower unit of resource which on recurrent grant alone was in fact only a little below that reached in 1976-77, but this had been depressed below intentions by the university system having admitted considerably more students than had originally been budgeted for; and even on this comparison, the combined unit of resource in 1976-77 was 5 per cent below what it was in the last year of the previous Quinquennium".

The UGC survey also provided a number of graphs and tables showing the declining 'average unit of resource' available to the universities since 1971-72. of this, the fiqure-2.1 is relating to the movement of the combined unit of resource for recurring grant including the grant for equipment. Figure-2.2 shows unit of resource for recurrent grant alone.

The UGC made further comments on the status of the deterioration of the 'unit of resource'. In the analysis, it was felt that if the committee had "... acknowledged the simplistic nature of the 'average unit of resource', it might have concluded that, although there had been a greater than planned deterioration in the 'average unit of resource', in retrospect, the planned decline of 1.2% in the 'unweighted average unit of

INDEX OF UNIT OF RECURRENT GRANT ONLY PLUS FEES
REVALUED TO 1976-77 PRICES (1971-72 = 100)

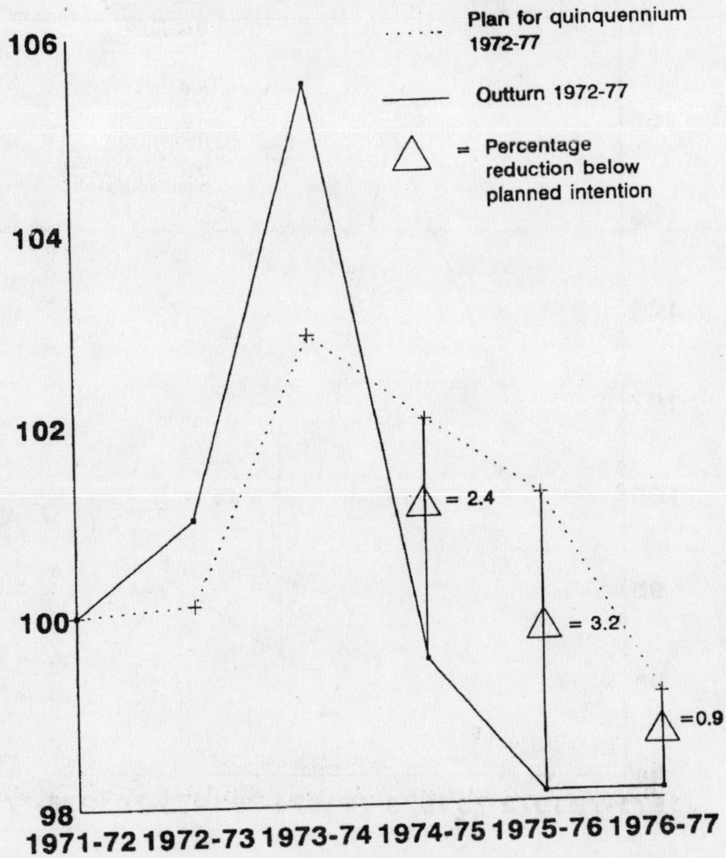

Source: UGC Annual Survey, Academic Year 1976-77, Cmnd. 7119, Appendix-I (i)

Change in the Average Unit of Resource

Fig. 2.1

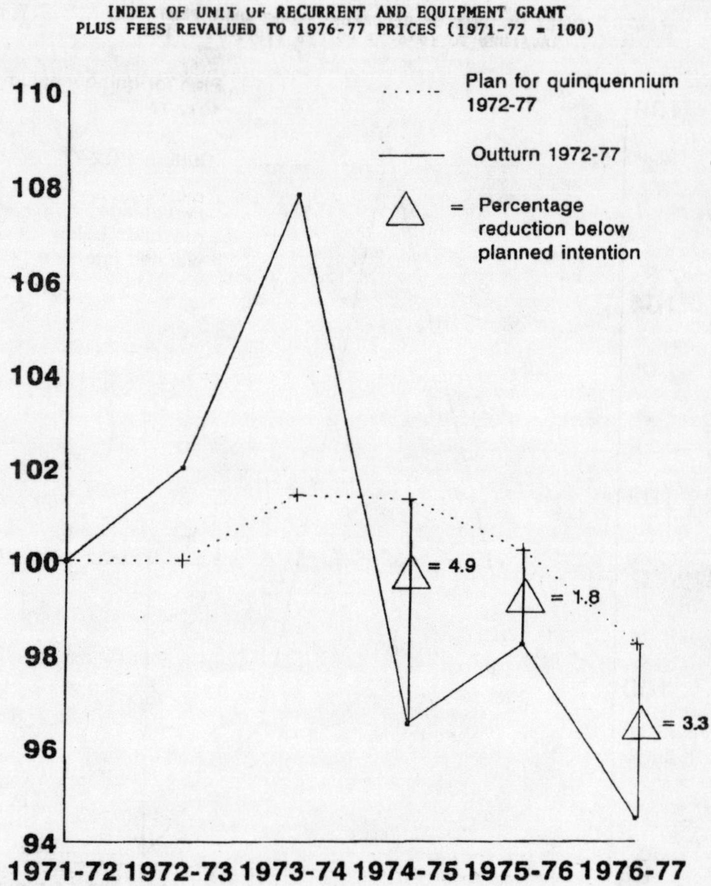

Source: **UGC Annual Survey, Academic Year 1976-77, Cmnd. 7119, Appendix-I (ii)**

Change in the Average Unit of Resource

Fig. 2.2

resource' at the time of the quinquennial settlement may have been too generous".[28]

Although the quinquennial system was getting eroded over the years mainly due to the unexpected pressure on the public expenditure and in consequence 'economies' effected all over including universities and the impact of unpredicted inflation, by the end of the year 1976-77, it ultimately collapsed.

Undeniably, the uncertainty in respect of the commitment for grants and rather frequent changes in policies for funding the universities, they faced unprecedented problems in academic planning as also in the general management in order to keep up the academic standard. The UGC considered that the 'over ambitious numerical expansion would be a disservice to both the universities and those who aspire to study in them'.[29]

As given in the figure-2.1, the erosion of the average unit of resource from 1974-75 to 1976-77 was constantly downward which kept the universities on their toes to meet all their educational needs. Figure-2.2 which shows the change in the Average Unit of Resource with equipment grant also proves similar position of steep fall from 1973-74 to 1976-77 in relation to the plans for the quinquennium 1972-77.

Relatively better was the year 1977-78 with the recurrent grant, for that year, having already been settled in March, 1976, after taking into account the substantial increase in tuition fees for home as well as oversees students. It was expected that the fees increase should in future be of the order of about 25% of total income of the university. The furniture and equipment grant was 3.4 million pounds as settled earlier. But for building activities, it was reduced to 3.4 million pounds in 1977-78. However, later an additional 2.0 million pounds was sanctioned for short term projects in July, 1977.

ALTERNATIVE PROJECTIONS FOR HIGHER EDUCATION DEMAND

Three alternative projections for higher education demand were made in the Joint Discussion Document - Higher Education into the 1990s, of the DES and Scottish Education Department published in February 1978, which examined the possible demographic trends as might influence the pattern of higher education between 1981 and 1994. The projections made in the Document based on three variant assumption - "a high variant" assumed growth to 21%, "a central projection" estimated a growth of 18% and "a low variant" considered a moderate growth from about the 14% that had been over the previous seven years to 15%. The Document also provided the following models for 1992 broadly along the lines of 1978 system, inviting interested parties to offer views:[30]

Model A: which might involve first expanding and then contracting the full-time and sandwich higher education system to the full extent postulated in the central projection, which would imply acquiring and then disposing of unwanted buildings and of building up and then releasing staff no longer required - a very difficult process.

Model B: which might involve reducing the scale of the projected expansion after 1981, and therefore the need for so much contraction after 1990, on the basis of the "low variant" projection, which to many appeared the most realistic in relation to the recent trands in age participation rates. To freeze the system at the 1981 level of 560,000 students would not involve reduced opportunities, but for the "central projection" it would mean a break (if only temporary) with the Robbins principle.

Model C: which might involve adopting a policy of catering fully for projected student numbers (even if in the event they rose above "low variant" projections) but to do so more economically in terms of both recurrent costs and long term resource commitments. Such a policy might involve renting of short-term accommodation, and appointing temporary staff so as to make it easier to shed staff and buildings as student numbers fell at the end of the 1980's. Significantly, in elaborating on Model C, the discussion document also identified another possible policy, "tunnelling through the hump":

> "A more drastic approach would be to adopt a deliberate policy of not adding either to accommodation or to staff numbers beyond those necessary to provide for, say, 560,000 students at current accommodation and staffing standards. On this basis, accommodating an extra 40,000 students in each year of peak numbers (assuming the "central projection") would require a 7% squeeze in accommodation standards and unit teaching costs".

Two more Models - 'D' and 'E' were also provided in the Joint Discussion Document as stated below:

Model D: suggested it might be possible to cater for all students seeking entry to higher education in the 1980's without needing to allocate resources to the full extent implied by the peak levels of the "central projection". This might mean interpreting the Robbins principle in a new way, by for example, a combination of encouraging provision and take up of two-year rather than three-year higher education courses; diverting students from full-time to part-time courses and deferring initial entry to higher education for a period after leaving school.

Model E: which might involve a policy designed to change the pattern and composition of the higher education student body and thereby maintain demand by encouraging participation by children of manual workers and by providing more systematic opportunities for recurrent education for mature students, those who had missed higher education at normal entry age as well as providing systematic continuing education opportunities at an advanced level.

Divergent views were expressed by the interested parties on the alternative models that the discussion document provided. However, models C and E were the ones that came under focus. The Treasury considered the Model C attractive for to it, this model appeared to be catering fully for the projected student numbers and at the same time appeared economic particularly in respect of the items of recurrent costs and long-term resource commitments.

Sizer's study believed that "Thus in the 'drastic approach' version of Model C lay the seeds of the events leading up to the letter of July 1981, but it is doubtful whether the Discussion Document, particularly given the focus of the discussion on Model E, helped to concentrate minds and prepare the ground for events to come".[31]

As against this, Model E looked forward for a student body providing opportunities of participation by children of manual workers as also to a sizable number of mature students who also needed to be given their share in higher education. This model had the support of the UGC and was considered that it offered "... at least stability and at best further growth".[32]

Commenting on the Document,the UGC held that "Whilst some eventual decline in full-time student numbers is probably inevitable, the right conclusions about timing and extent cannot be reached 10 to 15 years in advance, and must depend upon regular and sensitive review between D.E.S. and U.G.C. (so far as universities are concerned) taking into account the latest statistical and any other relevant evidence.[33]

Later, it was found that the recurrent grant for 1977-78 (553 million pounds) had included only 5% increase in pay and 12% for other items of expenditure, while the actual pay settlements involved increase of 10% for a considerable part of the said year. A supplementary recurrent grant of 11.2 million pounds was therefore released to the universities in April, 1978 to bridge the gap on account of pay increase and for other increased costs.

Consequently, the recurrent grant for 1978-79 reflected the care that was ultimately taken for 1977-78, and a firm grant for 1978-79 was announced by the Government in April, 1978 to be 619 million pounds. Again in May, the UGC announced a small increase in the total grant in real terms over that for 1977-78. A further increase was provided by UGC to accommodate increased number of students. At the same time, the Government also indicated grants for 1979-80 through to 1981-82 based on projected student numbers of 310,000 at 1978-79 prices, the indicated grant levels were as shown in the table-2.6.

Table 2.6[34]

1979-80	—	635 million pounds
1980-81	—	648 million pounds
1981-82	—	670 million pounds

Believing that there was a reasonable financial stability and a modest growth of student numbers as reflected in the Circular letter 9/78 of 5th July 1978, the universities seemed to be complacent. Sizer opined that "The universities' subsequent responses to the various events that occured during the period 1st August, 1979 to 1st July 1981 have to be considered in the context of the decisions and guidance that were contained in this letter, as well as the individual guidance received through main and sub-committee visits and informal discussion with the Chairman of the UGC".[35]

Growing constraint on the public expenditure was building pressure on the Labour Government and the modest growth scheme as contained in the letter of July 1978 should have been reviewed in the backdrop of the national mood. Following the Public Expenditure Survey and the publication of the Public Expenditure White Paper in January 1979, the growth programme was revised as shown in the table-2.7.

Table 2.7[36]

1979-80	:	292,000
1980-81	:	301,000
1981-82	:	308,000
1982-83	:	310,000

From the beginning of the 1961-62 i.e. the time since when the university sector expanded unprecedentally, till the end of eighties, the growth of the student population showing the change over the previous years is given in the table-2.8.

From table 2.8, the growth pattern reveals that till

1967-68, the growth was highest. During 1968-69 and 1972-73, the rate varied between 5.34% to 2.06% after which it fell to 1.62% in 1973-74. It again rose to 2.79% next year (1974-75) touching a little higher in the next three years, and again came down to 2.78% in 1978-79 and later gradually to 0.98% in 1981-82.

For two years (1982-83 and 1983-84), there was a fall in the number but the growth resumed from 1984-85 at 1.67% touching 4% in 1988-89.

The combined figures of higher education enrolment (Universities and PSHE) for 1965-66 to 1987-88 are given in the table-2.9.

The government informed the Chairman, UGC that the 2000 reduction of the number by 2000 from the earlier target for 1981-82 should be achieved by reducing the target for Oversees students from 31,000 to 29,000.

The increased fees for the overseas students effected from 1977-78 from an average of 420 pounds to 650 pounds for UG and 850 pounds for PG level did not check the inflow of such students. In fact, fears were expressed that that overseas students were crowding out the well qualified home students. In the background of this situation, the Public Expenditure White Paper published in January, 1978 aimed at reducing the total number of overseas students for 1978-79 onwards to 67,000 by 1980-81. The UGC in turn advised the universities to plan for '... a shift of atleast 3% in favour of home undergraduates'[39] and provided the following overseas student number targets as given in table-2.10.

Table 2.8[37]

Year-wise Full-time Students in University Section (1961-62 to 1988-89)

Year	No. of students (in thousands)	Difference (in thousands)	% change (+) (-)
1961-62	113	-	-
1965-66	173	-	-
1966-67	189	+ 16	9.2
1967-68	206	+ 17	9.0
1968-69	217	+ 11	5.34
1969-70	226	+ 9	4.14
1970-71	235	+ 9	3.98
1971-72	242	+ 7	2.97
1972-73	247	+ 5	2.06
1973-74	251	+ 4	1.62
1974-75	258	+ 7	2.79
1975-76	269	+ 11	4.26
1976-77	279	+ 10	3.71
1977-78	288	+ 9	3.2
1978-79	296	+ 8	2.78
1979-80	301	+ 5	1.68
1980-81	306	+ 5	1.66
1981-82	309	+ 3	0.98
1982-83	304	- 5	- 1.618
1983-84	300	- 4	- 1.315
1984-85	305	+ 5	1.67
1985-86	310	+ 5	1.64
1986-87	316	+ 6	1.93
1987-88	321	+ 5	1.58
1988-89	334	+ 3	4.00

Table 2.9[38]

Enrolment *(in thousands)*

Year	*Universities*	*PSHE*	*Total*	*% change*
1965-66	173	136	309	-
1970-71	235	221	456	+ 47.5
1975-76	269	246	515	+ 12.9
1980-81	307	228	535	+ 3.9
1985-86	310	290	600	+ 12.15
1987-88	321	305	626	+ 4.34

Table 2.10[40]

Year	*UG*	*PG*	*Total*
1977-78	17,100	17,700	34,800
1981-82	14,000	17,000	31,000

However, it was found that in the absence of the UGC not having given target number for each university, the advice was not properly understood and according to the information from UCCA for 1979 showed that the demand for overseas students was constantly rising. Giving definite instruction to the universities to reduce the number of overseas students, the UGC informed them in February, 1979 that "Universities with significant number of overseas students should therefore aim to achieve a total for that group in 1981-82 which is 7% below their 1975-76 figure".[41] Resultantly, overseas student numebrs fell in 1979-80 by 4.6% compared to 1978-79. Nevertheless, the demand continued to rise. This encouraged the UGC to discourage the overseas students by raising the fees further.

A review of the situation of 1970s particularly the later half of 70's point out to a few weaknesses in the overall policy framing for the universities by the Government. Although to the universities, UGC was the proper authority both to get the funds as well as guidance on the national policy, but it was more than clear that UGC had hardly any voice in the ultimate policies relating to the funds and expansion programme. On one hand, UGC had to ensure that the national policies were executed through the universities and on the other hand, it had to demonstrate due respect for autonomy of the universities and on the whole, it seemed at times that it failed to provide the universities with definite guidance in the form of firm instruction. How much, the UGC could throw weight on the government and what was its state in 1979, was expressed by Shattock and Berdahl in the following words:

> "By 1979 the UGC system was in serious disrepair. Its planning mechanisms were in tatters, with the Chairman being able to do little more than react to the twists and turns of the Government's counter inflation policy. It had sought with some success to keep universities informed of developments but there could be little pretence that it remained a body which carried weight with the DES or Whitehall".[42]

It appeared that long before the above remarks were made, as early as in the late 1960s it's image was gradually moving "... from being a 'buffer' between the universities and government towards becoming a central strategic planning agency, but with the breakdown of the quinquennial planning system increasingly became the 'messenger boy' for governmental short-term decrementalism".

However, there is a good deal that can be put

forward in favour of the UGC keeping in view the limitations that it as a Committee had had, and the respect for the autonomy of the universities that it showed and therefore perhaps it deliberately did not want to force the universities to act in a way that would have impaired the freedom and flexibility of the university system as would be clear from the following. contained in its letter dated the 28th November, 1978:[43]

> "6. The Committee have no wish to interfere with universities' selection procedures. They would also wish to emphasise the great importance which they attach to the presence of overseas students in the universities. However, they had hoped that universities would have been able to reconcile their policies with those of the Government without any question of laying down sectorial student targets for individual universities. Nevertheless it is the Committee's expectation that the serious financial effects which I have described will occur to the extent to which overseas student numbers exceed the levels of 1975-76.
>
> "7. The Committee are well aware of the problems arising from the devolved nature of admissions procedures but it is clear from the returns that some universities have been able to exercise more restraint in this area than others and if overseas numbers at your university are above those for 1975-76 the Committee would be glad if you would examine very carefully what you could do to return to the total for that year in terms of undergraduates and postgraduates taken together, although not necessarily for each category separately".

As for the performance of the universities, it must be admitted that in view of the traditions and structures of the university system, the freedom, flexibility and autonomy that they have been enjoying and the practical difficulties that are involved in bringing restrictions and limitations in the different departments and centres in the universities most of whom are not used to appreciate and abide by such constraints, they could not have been expected to start advance planning to cut their own activities particularly in the absence of compelling circumstances. Therefore, it will be uncharitable to comment that the universities too, on their part, failed to prepare for the various constraints that were lying ahead. It was more so because they had seen and implemented the expansion programmes which injected a sense of optimism that not only higher education should expand, greater resources would be invested for better results for stronger economy of the country.

DUAL SUPPORT SYSTEM

The Dual support system which was introduced during 1970s was under severe criticism for it was felt that it was gradually deteriorating and failing to serve the purpose of funding for the fundamental research which was so vital for providing incentives and facilities to the researchers.

The Report of the Joint Working Committee on the support of the University Scientific Research established in 1980 by the Advisory Board for the Research Councils (ABRC) and the UGC strongly advocated the availability of continued and smooth support for fundamental research so that as the initial work recognised, additional external funds start flowing for without the former, the latter could not happen.

The Report which examined and compared the

resources that were available between 1971-72 and 1978-79 made several important observations on the deteriorating student: staff ratios for while between 1971-72 and 1978-79, the student number grew by 24% from 250.8 thousand to 310.1 thousand, the full-time academic staff number growth was by only 13% from 29.4 thousand to 33.3 thousand.

The Report also made observations on the rising External funded temporary research appointments and the deteriorating technical staff and support staff. On the situation of the Research students number during 1971-72 and 1978-79, although it increased from 24,057 to 24,721, the home student numbers fell from 16,897 to 15,169.[44]

The chapter four covers exclusively Research Funding where greater details are given and various aspects of Research Funding have been discussed.

CONCLUSION

No Government can sustain the fast increasing financial burden on the public funds for the pressures on other welfare sectors' demand keep growing, which sometimes occupy higher priorities on their own right and merit for social and economic needs and at other times for political reasons. The unprecedented growth of the number of universities in 1960s resulted in the inevitable action on the part of the government which was inevitable. From the later-half of 1970s, situation changed and it was strongly believed that "The turning point in macro-economic policy, if not politically, was as much as in 1976, as in 1978 or 1981".[45] According to Peter Scott, "When the conservatives came to power in 1979, they had no settled policy on universities and polytechnics, but they were determined to curb public expenditure.[46]

Crucial to the Government's approach of the higher education is what the policy of the Government is and the policy of the Government depends on how it perceives the role of higher education to the direction of raising the quality of life of the people and the nation as a whole.

While it is true that unlimited funds cannot be provided to the universities, it is also true that prospect of economy can be, and actually is, brightened through the higher education itself. So the importance lies in the perception and vision in planning.

While higher fees for overseas students is understandable, the forced decision for 'full cost' recovery from them and also to reduce the number of such students as a national policy might have been jusitified by the Government from financial angle, but not from the angles of the universities and the academic interest. Initially, this "... led to serious financial instability in many universities (polytechnics and colleges were better protected from the turbulance because they were sheltered by local government)".[47]

Admittedly, it is necessary to plan the needed growth of higher education enrolment. It is commendable that the successive governments of UK have shown enormous interest in higher education. But it has also to be conceded that frequent changes of the Government plan relating to the student number and the demise of the quinquennial system of funding had their toll on the universities in their internal planning system. Lately, short-term grants allocation also created untold problems to the universities. All such vital factors led to affect adversely the functioning of the system as a whole.

As regards the universities, while there are

instances to show that they had been given hints from time to time beginning from the suggestions by Mrs. Shirly Williams, to tighten their belts, it is also true that at times signals of stability and long-term planning were given by the Government and UGC. The universities as agents of developments, always saw more optimism than pessimism. Besides, the liberal funding of the 1960s and also of the first-half of 1970s, although the British economy was not in good shape had the lingering impact on the universities. Another important point cannot be lost sight of and that was the absence of definite instructions from the Government and the UGC to implement an economy package. Without such instructions, it must be admitted that it was not possible for any Vice-Chancellor to go ahead of his own to effect economy in selected areas.

Turning to the role of the University Grants Committee, a dispassionate view would be that as a body responsible primarily to the Treasury and essentially required to sell the Government's policies could not perform better in the given circumstances from time to time. At the same time, it has demonstrated its respect and concern for the autonomy of the universities. More discussion on the role and performance of the UGC will be made later in the subsequent chapters.

References

1. Perkin, H.J., New Universities in the United Kingdom. (Case Studies on Innovation in Higher Education). London, Organisation for Economic Co-operation and Development, 1969, p. 36.
2. Mawditt, Richard, M., Higher Education: Cost or Investment?, the author, University of Bath, 1990, pp. 4-5.

3. U.K., Committee on Higher Education (Robbins Report) Appendix Four: Administrative, Financial and Economic Aspects of Higher Education, London, HMSO, 1969, p. 5.
4. *Ibid.*, p. 5.
5. *Op. Cit.*, p. 6.
6. *Op. Cit.*, p. 9.
7. *Op. Cit.*, p. ll.
8. *Op. Cit.*, p. ll
9. *Op. Cit.*, p. 275.
10. Perkin, H.J., New Universities in the United Kingdom. (Case Studies on Innovation in Higher Education) London, Organisation for Economic Cooperation and Development, 1969, p. 37.
11. Johnes, Jill and Taylor, Jim. Performance Indicators in Higher Education. Buckingham, SRHE and Open University Press, 1990, p.15. (Source: University Statistics Vols 1&3. Various issues. 1961-62 figures taken from Robbins Report, p. 26).
12. UN Report on the World Social Situation. 1961, p. 25.
13. *Ibid.*, p. l.
14. Perkin, H.J., New Universities in the United Kingdom (Case Studies on Innovation in Higher Education), London, organisation for Economic Cooperation and Development, 1969, p. 81.
15. U.K., Department of Education and Science. Institutional Responses to the Financial Reductions in the University Sector John Sizer (1987), Background Paper No.1, P. 3 (unpublished.
16. *Ibid.*, Table-1.
17. *Op. Cit.*, Table-1.
18. *Op. Cit.*, Table-1.
19. *Op. Cit.*, p. 13.

20. Brittan, Samuel. The Thatcher Government's Economic Policy. *In the Thatcher Effect*, ed. by Dennis Kavanagh and Antony Seldon, Oxford, Clarendon, 1989, p. 9.
21. *Ibid.*, p. 10.
22. U.K., Department of Education and Science, Institutional Responses to the Financial Reduction in the University Sector, John Sizer (1987), Background Paper No.1, p. 15 (unpublished).
23. *Ibid*, p. 15.
24. *Op. Cit.*, p. 19.
25. *Op. Cit.*, p. 20.
26. *Op. Cit.*, p. 20.
27. *Op. Cit.*, p. 23.
28. *Op. Cit.*, p. 24.
29. *Op. Cit.*, p. 26.
30. *Op. Cit.*, pp. 27-28.
31. *Op. Cit.*, p. 29.
32. *Op. Cit.*, p. 28.
33. A Strategy for Higher Education into the 1990s: The University Grants Committee's advice, final report submitted by UGC Chairman to Secretary of State, Letter dated 16-8-1984, p. 7.
34. U.K., Department of Education and Science, Institutional Responses to the Financial Reduction in the University Sector, John Sizer (1987), Background Paper No.1, pp. 31-32 (unpublished).
35. *Ibid*, p. 34.
36. *Op. Cit.*, p. 34.
37. Jones, Jill and Taylor, Jim: Performance Indicators in Higher Education, Buckingham, SRHE and Open University, 1990, p.15 (figure for 1961-62 taken from the Robbins Report, p. 26).

38. *Ibid*, p.14 (in respect of student number).
39. U.K., Department of Education and Science. Institutional Responses to Financial Reductions in the University Sector, John Sizer (1987) Background Paper No.1, p. 38 (unpublished).
40. *Ibid*, p. 38.
41. *Op. Cit.*, p. 40.
42. *Op. Cit.*, p. 37.
43. *Op. Cit.*, p. 39.
44. *Op. Cit.*, p. 41.
45. Ridell, Peter. The Thatcher Effect and its Legacy. Oxford, Blackwell, 1991, p. 16.
46. Scott, Peter. Higher Education, *In The Thatcher Effect*. Ed. by Dennis Kavanagh and Anthony Seldon, Oxford, Clarendon Press, 1989, p. 198.
47. *Ibid*, p. 199.

3

Towards the Traumatic Cuts

END OF THE LABOUR GOVERNMENT

Undeniably, the developments - sometimes optimistic and at other times gloomy though - that took place during 1970s provided, on the whole, reasonable hints of the difficult time that lay ahead which could have been absorbed by the universities in making at least some preparation to face the future adverse situation. It has, however, to be admitted at the same time that the events of 1970s as they happened from time to time, were one of hide and seek as also of light and shade between the universities on the one hand and the UGC and the Government on the other, for neither the former nor the latter made any statement to make the message clear enough.

The recurrent grant for the academic year 1979-80 was originally fixed in April 1978 at 635 million pounds which was refixed at 714 million pounds after revaluation based on the pay and price rise. In doing so, 9% increase on fees over the previous year, was kept in view.

The growth in the number of students, was expected to be about 292,000 in 1979-80. The grant for furniture and equipments in 1979-80 was fixed at 51.1

million pounds which was higher by over 9 million pounds taking into account the cost increase of about 8.9% in 1979-80 following an increase in real terms of 10.1% in 1978-79.

While the General Election was scheduled in the laterhalf of May 1979, the Labour Government not only revised the grant for 1979-80, in April, 1979, it had also announced, through the University Grants Committee, the revised allocations of the recurrent grant and fees for the period from 1979-80 to 1981-82. The Secretary of States announced the recurrent and equipment grants for 1982-83 as conveyed by the Chairman of the UGC in his letter dated 3rd May 1979, which also contained the following optimistic picture, viz.:

> "The Committee has asked me to stress that the greater degree of certainty implied by the indication of grants beyond 1979-80 should enable universities to plan the provision and replacement of equipment with reasonable confidence and to eliminate uncommitted balances of grant".[1]

NEW GOVERNMENT - REDUCTION ON PUBLIC EXPENDITURE

Much as was expected, the new Government of the Conservative Party came in power in the later-half of May, 1979 which had promised to bring down the public expenditure of the country. Accordingly, formal announcement was made, and the provisional grants for 1979-80 were reduced by 9 million pounds when the budget of June 1979 was prepared. The grant stood further reduced by 5.5 million pounds as a result of the decision of increase of about 20%, against 9%, in fees of the overseas students. Although the furniture and equipment grant was not reduced, but a lumpsum cut of 1.5 million was imposed on the capital allocations. The UGC formally informed the universities on the 25th June, 1979 about the aforesaid reduc-tions. The said letter while indicated about the availability of additional grant for further salary and wage settlements which was expected shortly, cautioned the universities stating that "It would be prudent to assume that extra sums necessary for payment of these settlements will not in every case be compensated in full by additional grant".[2] To meet the additional liability on account of pay and price increases for the full year, the recurrent grant was increased three times and finally the total grant stood at 801.9 million pounds. The letter also suggested that the universities should "... examine very carefully all recurrent expenditure to which you are not irretrievably committed".[3] It was thus clear that black clouds which perhaps had some element of uncertainty until then, were gathering in the horizon of the universities. But neither the Government nor the UGC did provide any more indications of a thunder in the store for the universities which would prove "traumatic".

VISIBLE CLOUDS - CRUCIAL 1980-81

Slowly, but steadily, the inevitable 'storm' was approaching as the government was determined of its plan to reduce public expenditure and the nation was aware of the same.

A number of events preceeded the final blow to the universities and in that direction the first definite indication started flowing from the UGCs letter dated 15th August, 1979 (13/79) restricting, by advice, the number of home undergraduates in October, 1980 to 94% of the number admitted in October, 1979. This followed another letter of UGC dated the 15th October, 1979 (16/79) which was more crucial, from which it was clear that although the government was yet to announce the future level of expenditures for the purpose of recurrent grant, the level of the home students was not likely to be higher in real terms than that for 1979-80.[4]

With this end in view, it adviced the universities to reduce the number of home students admission in 1980-81 so that it was possible for the universities to ensure that the total home student population did not substantially exceed the 1979-80 level.

OVERSEAS STUDENTS

Fundamentally, the component of the overseas students in the composition of the total students population in any university of any country is considered both desirable and favourable student mix. The Robbins Committee even after thirty years, is a valuable document and considered to be relevant in a number of areas despite the vast change in the situation since then held that "The presence here in institution of higher education of students from abroad is widely regarded as valuable, and rightly so in our judgement. It fosters a sense of international community on both sides. It encourages a valuable give and take".[5]

The policy of charging higher fees from the overseas students than from the home and European community students was first introduced by Mr. Wilson's Labour Government in December 1966 along with the university grants for 1967-72 quinquennium. It was announced that fees for overseas students other than those already enrolled for full-time courses would be charged from an average of 80 pounds, to 250 pounds. At that point of time no revision of fees was announced for the home students.

In 1961-62, in the university sector the total overseas students in GB in relation to the entire student population was 12%.[6] During 1966-67 and 1975-76, the increase was 84.6%. In 1966-67, the percentage of overseas students was 16.9 and in 1975-76, it rose to 31.2 as given in the following Table-1.

Table 3.1[7]

Year	*Overseas students in GB as percentage of total*
1966-67	16.9
1967-68	15.2
1968-69	15.7
1969-70	16.5
1970-71	18.0
1971-72	19.7
1972-73	21.8
1973-74	24.7
1974-75	27.8
1975-76	31.2

After about a period of over 9 years, in July 1976, further revision was made in the rates of tuition fees but this time the revision took place for both the home as well as overseas students from 1977-78 as shown in the following Table-2.

Table 3.2[8]

Category	UG level (pounds)	PG level (pounds)
Oveaseas Students	650	850
Home Students	500	750

FULL COST RECOVERY FROM OVERSEAS STUDENTS

In 1978-79, there was a further revision by about 9%. However, demand from overseas students continued despite steep increase in fees which posed a simmering fear that the overseas students were elbowing out well qualified home students.

By its letter dated the 15th October 1979, the UGC clearly indicated the likely decision of the government to recover full cost of their overseas students which would reflect in the UGC grant from 1980-81 onwards. In view of this, the restrictions earlier imposed on the number of overseas students contained in the UGC letters of 28th February, 1978 and l9th February, 1979 during the regime of the previous government were removed.

This brought a new turn in the policy of funding as this conveyed the decision of the government that it will no longer subsidise students from overseas beginning from September 1980, other than the earmarked funds available for aid to overseas students. The UGC also advised the universities the following scales of fees recoverable from the overseas students from 1980-81 academic year adding that while these scales were the minimum ones, if need be, the universities could charge higher fees in order to receive the full cost of tuition;

although it was not clear whether the full cost was linked to teaching only or teaching and research:

Arts courses	Pounds 2000
Science Courses	Pounds 3000
Clinical Courses in Medicine, Dentistry and Veterinary Science	Pounds 5000

During 1979-80, the overseas students at the postgraduate level was 36.6% of the total post-graduate students of Great Britain and for undergraduate level, it was 7.1%.[9]

The following Table-3 shows the picture of the registration of overseas students (new entrants) from 1979-80 to 1983-84 from which it is clear that even by 1983-84, the figure of 1979-80 in respect of new entrants could not be touched. Clearly, the aspirants from overseas for admission to UK Universities had not recovered from the shock of steep increase.

Table 3.3[10]

Overseas Students

Year	*Undergraduates* *Overseas Students (New entrants)* *Number*	*% of total entrants*	*Postgraduates* *Overseas students (New entrants)* *Number*	*% of total entrants*	*Total Number*
1979-80	5410	8.3	9369	36.2	14,779
1980-81	4101	6.8	8111	32.1	12,212
1981-82	3940	6.2	7734	30.4	11,674
1982-83	4091	6.7	7861	31.2	11,952
1983-84	4316	7.2	8663	32.4	12,979

Two aspects were thus clear. One: in view of the full cost fees recovery from overseas students, the restriction on the number of admission of such students was removed obviously because that would now not be a burden to the universities and in turn, to the nation. Two: Income from fees will increase and will help the universities.

The new policy of withdrawing subsidy progressively posed another dimension to the problem of funds the universities were already in. However, this problem was not uniformly the same in its magnitude in all the universities. According to the Annual Survey of UGC for 1979-80, the estimated income needed to be made good in making adjustments to the recurrent grant for 1980-81 "... on account of the expectation that new overseas students would pay 'economic' fees plus income that would have arisen from the previous rates of fee, was 53.8 million poundse."[11]

With the varied number of overseas students in the different universities ranging from as high as 7331 (UG + PG) in the University of London and as low as 155 in the University of Keele with an overall 36.6% of all post-graduate students of Great Britain, and 7.1% for undergraduate level of all undergraduate students of Great Britain (as on 31.12.1979)[12] the magnitude of the problem was bound to be different in different universities.

The Universities which had lower number of overseas students had the advantage of attracting more number by making their courses attractive and publicising them abroad and thereby generate more income. As against such universities, the universities which had large number of overseas students had the problem of maintaining the number in view of the hike in the tuition fees. This also created a situation of aggresive competion among the universities.

However, obviously due to high fees, less number of students took admission from 1980-81 and that happened both at undergraduate level (except 1982-83) and at the post-graduate level. From 1983-84, the change started taking place, but it could not touch the figure of 1979-80.

After 1983-84, the trend changed and growth resumed upward movement. The Figure-3.1 shows the position of overseas students number for the period from 1974-75 to 1988-89.[13]

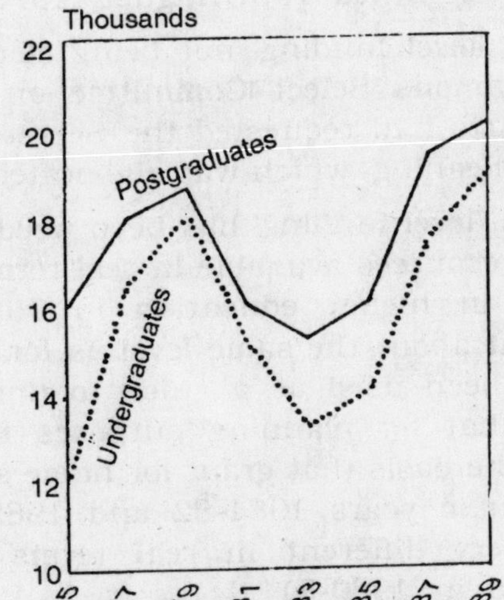

Source: USR
Non-EC Students

Fig. 3.1

LEVEL FUNDING

In November 1979, the government published the Public Expenditure White Paper which confirmed the indication of UGC, given a month ago, that the resources for home students in higher education would be about the same as in 1979-80 bringing about a system of 'level funding'. In respect of the overseas students, it mentioned that they would be expected to meet the full cost of their tuition.

Although the White Paper did not state the target for the home students but by introducing the 'level funding' formula, the universities were forced to control the number of home students as was adviced by the UGC in its letter dated 15th August, 1979.

The term 'level funding' not being clear to it, the House of Commons Select Committee on Education, Science and Arts had requested the Secretary of State to clarify the meaning, which was elaborated as follows:

> "The term 'level funding' has been used to indicate that the resources available in real terms for home students in higher education in 1980-81 were planned at about the same level as for 1979-80. It has also been used as a guide to universities to indicate that for planning purposes they should work on the basis that grant for home students for the academic years 1981-82 and 1982-83 would not be yery different in real terms from that announced in 1980-81".

The Select Committee found the definition 'disappointing' as that would neither help the universities for planning student numbers nor would relate realistically to student numbers.

The decision of full cost recovery from the overseas

students (other than European countries who are treated at par with home students) created sharp reaction in many quarters for before the decision was taken prior consultation at different level did not take place. Even the Committee of Vice-Chancellors and Principals (CVCP) which played crucial role in all matters of policies affecting the universities in any respects, was not consulted as mentioned by Sir Alec Merrison in his evidence to the Select Committee that "... it would be true to say there was no consultation with us whatsoever".[15]

THREE HYPOTHESES OF UGC

For the purpose of ascertaining both the position and the plan and programme of the universities particularly keeping in view the new policies, the UGC in its wisdom decided to give the three hypotheses for allocation of grants. The implications of the three hypothesis were explained by UGC as follows:[16]

> "Allocation *(a)* is included not in any expectation that total resources will enable these figures to be made good generally, but because at individual universities the Committee may consider such an allocation desirable; *(b)* represents the continuation of the 1979-80 figure modified only in respect of overseas students; *(c)* represents a position in which the financial situation could be worse, for some or for all universities".

Later, by way of explanation, the UGC informed the universities that "hypothesis" *(a)* represented a 2% increase in grant, while *(b)* represented the level funding and *(c)* meant a 5% reduction in grant. The Committee decided to hold dialogues with individual universities during the first half of 1980 for advising the government in allocating resources for the remainder of the quadrennium and in order to do so, with relevant data from the universities, it requested the universities to respond as a preliminary view as to how the university might be influenced by each projection. The universities were also requested to send the estimate of student numbers for the quadrennium 1980-81 to 1983-84 in a given format. They were also requested to inform the UGC by July 1980, a more detailed and considered statement in another format. The view was needed for UGC's consideration for 1980-81 allocation and also for the proposed dialogue meetings with the universities.

Behind the emergence of the third hypothesis given by the UGC to the universities by its letter of the 15th October, 1979, there lay some unknown fact at the end of the Department of Education and Science for on one hand in July 1979, the UGC was invited by the DES to advise it on the different effects of grants based on new policies upto the year 1982-83 and on the other, in October, the same year, the UGC communicated of its own, as the government had not yet taken decision on the levels of expenditure in future, to the universities that, it, according to its '... best judgement of the situation was the probability that total recurrent grant for home students would be held for a number of years at no higher level in real terms than that for 1979-80".

What role the UGC played in advising the DES was not coming to surface in the absence of which mistery shrouded on this issue. Even the Select Committee on Science and Arts was keen to know the truth. In the course of the question and answers before the Select Committee, it revealed that in view of the earlier discussion that took place between UGC and DES, no fresh advice was given to DES by UGC as to what would happen to the universities in a situation of allocation of grants smaller than their need. However, the UGC had apprised the DES of the difficulties that the universities would have in the event of smaller allocation of grants. It also became clear that the UGC had hints from the discussions with DES that the grant position could vary from a small improvement to even a slightly worse than the announced ones.

Sir Edward Parkes (the then Chairman, UGC) also mentioned that the period of level funding' was to be for one year and not "for a few years" and would follow a cutback as is evident from his evidence before the Select Committee, as stated below:

> "We ourselves in our inquiries to universities thought it probable that the period of level funding would be followed by a cutback and therefore, we did to the universities set scenarios which included cutback in funding and asked them what they would do if certain levels of cutback occurred".[17]

In the process of its efforts to reduce recurrent expenditure of the universities, the UGC, based on the recommendation of its sub-committee and finally by the main committee, had desired that they should either discontinue, restrict or gradually phase out teaching of Russian at about 20 universities. However, the recommendations or guidelines of UGC in this regard was 'defied' by senates of some universities and made no impact on the universities as a whole. However, it was realized by the UGC Chairman as is evident from his evidence in Select Committee that the impact of the Russian studies in terms of cost, was insignificant. But at the same time it was realized that the UGC should be more dirigiste. The UGC had also communicated to the Select Committee in its January 1980 memorandum that "... there will have to be a reduction in the provisions of resources in some areas or to some institutions in order to provide for innovation and growth in others".[18] This indicated that UGC could be selective in the matter of grants in future. This development was important at a time when the dialogue meeting of UGC with the individual universities on the three hypotheses was about to take place.

DIALOGUE MEETINGS WITH UNIVERSITIES

In order to assess the strengths and weaknesses of the different universities in the event any of the three hypotheses being the ultimate situation which the UGC had given to them in November 1979, it had informed that during January and May, 1980 meetings will be held with each university based on the statements that they would submit to UGC a fortnight in advance, explaining the plans for the quadrennium together with the necessary supporting material. The idca of UGC was to find out what contingency plans the universities could prepare to meet three different situations.

According to the case studies of the nine universities conducted by Prof. John Sizer, the impression on the whole was that adequate time was not given to the universities for an indepth deliberations, within the individual university system with the various constituents whose participation in the management of the university affairs was important. Besides, the universities were not given any indication, not even indirectly about the "traumatic" grant letter dated the 1st July, 1981. At the same time, how much importance the UGC had attached to these meetings are evident from the following contained in the enclosure to the UGC Chairman's letter dated 2nd November, 1981 to the Select Committee.

> "The dialogues were unique in the history of the U.G.C. Taken together, they provided the base for the whole of the Committee's work over the

subsequent 12 to 18 months and the material provided by each university and the points which emerged in discussion influenced the Committee's consideration of individual institutions at all stages of its deliberations".

It took about a month for the University of Hull to prepare the draft text of a submission to UGC by its Development Committee and meet the UGC representatives within about a fortnight. The University was told "to examine very carefully the full cost and feasibility of its proposed developments, including science subjects".[19] Another message conveyed through the meeting was "Level funding was the best that could be hoped for, and developments must come from existing resources".[20] The Hariot-Watt University's experience, as reported by the Principal to the Senate and Court was that 'the UGC had concentrated on the positive aspects of the statements' for which he was reasonably pleased with the way the meeting had gone'.[21] However, there was not even the slightest indication of a disastrous situation that was in store from July, 1981. The University of Bath was the third one to have similar meeting with UGC and its "... representatives felt sufficiently encouraged by the meeting to hope for more equitable funding in future years".[22] However, the university had taken no specific action on return from the meeting.

The other universities covered by the Project Studies included Aston, Sussex, Salford, Stirling, Sheffield and Aberdeen. Meeting for Aston and Sussex took place in February, for Salford and Stirling in April and in May for Sheffield and Aberdeen.

It may not be wrong to conclude that while the UGC considered the meetings very important as part of the procedure leading to the 1981-82 grant distribution, some of the case writers of the case studies felt them "... both surprising and disturbing".[23] What was more surprising that when UGC attached so much importance to the meetings it appeared that 'A number of the meetings left false impressions and, rather than leading universities to recognise the need to develop contingency plans, appeared to have created a false sense of security'.[24]

What really went wrong in the entire affair? On one hand the UGC attached considerable importance to the meetings for it '... regarded the four meetings as a very important and part of the procedure leading to the 1981-82 grant distribution'[25] and on the other hand, very little time was available to the universities to understand the various implications of the letter and formats and to apprise, consult and reach a consensus or at least a general agreement to face possible situations as envisaged in the three hypotheses.

According to UGC, "the dialogues were unique in the history of the UGC. Taken together, they provided the base for the whole of the Committee's work over the subsequent 12 to 18 months and the material provided by each university and the points which emerged in discussion influenced the Committee's consideration of individual institutions at all stages of its deliberations".[26] How important the UGC thought the meetings were to assess different aspects of the future grant distribution would be more clear from the following explanation of Dr. Edward Parkes, Chairman, UGC to the Select Committee on 23.1.1980:

> "Part of the purpose of this very intensive dialogue which we are engaged in with every university and every university college at the moment is to try to determine the amount of flexibility in the system,

so that we can see to what extent we can encourage certain areas and assume that natural wastage will enable the others to decline somewhat, and see to what extent we will actually have to put additional funds into this exercise, either because we want to encourage people to early retirement or want people to move to other places, and so on".

Against the claims of the UGC, Kogan and Kogan in their critical assessment of these meetings observed "The discussion took place between Vice-Chancellors and the UGC, and entailed no detailed process of assessment of departments and other components of the institutions, consultation with universities was variable. Yet it was upon these discussions that many key judgements were made which were later to determine policies".[27]

According to one of the authors and former head of the department of one of the universities, "The UGC claim to have made a thorough assessment of the universities during this period of negotiation is therefore untenable. At most it could have formed an assessment of the thinking of the Vice-Chancellors and of their quality".[28]

The role of the Committee of Vice-Chancellors and Principals (CVCP) was a difficult and delicate one. Visualising the picture that was likely to emerge, although they advised the universities to "... face more boldly the prospect of inter-institutional arrangements", how much they played the role to 'encourage and facilitate such arrangements'[29] was not clear.

RECURRENT GRANT 1980-81

It is interesting to note that on one hand, the UGC, by inviting the universities to offer their views as to how they might be affected by each financial projections and by asking for the estimate of student numbers for the quadrennium 1980-81 to 1983-84 to be followed by the dialogue meetings in the first part of 1980, gave the impression that the grant for 1980-81 would be decided only after the dialogue meetings are over, on the other hand, although the dialogue meetings had started in January, long before, the Recurrent Grant for 1980-81 was announced in March 1980, which gave the impression that nothing arising out of the dialogue meetings was taken into account in deciding the grant for 1980-81.

For 1980-81, the grant was announced as a cash limit of 987 million pounds which included components for home students and also for those overseas students who were admitted in 1979-80 or earlier at almost the same level in real terms, as for the year 1979-80. This was in March 1980, which was in fact within the dialogue meetings period.

In retrospect, when a severe cut was in the offing, announcement of the level of grant for 1980-81, with a supplimentary grant of Pounds 62.4 million for 1979-80 reinforced the impression of at least some of the universities that the practice of payment of grant would be continued as before. The grant for 1979-80 was to compensate the inflation. The Equipment grant was increased by 9 per cent in real terms over the previous year at 71.59 million pounds.

In the background of a difficult time that lay ahead, such a policy could and actually did create a different impression on the part of the universities in general, far from the need to prepare for the adverse situation. The CUAs Resource Allocation Group felt "... it persuaded the university community that severe cuts would not be made in higher education and Vice-Chancellors and other such university figures who had 'cried wolf' every year since 1975 could safely be discarded".[30] By its letter of the 28th May, 1980 of the UGC, it clarified firstly that the grant had been fixed without knowing the effect on admission of the policy on overseas students fees and secondly, before the completion of the dialogue meetings. It therefore, clarified that the distribution of grant did not convey to the individual universities, the government's intention on level funding.

The universities were also told that the grant had no relationship to the three hypotheses. Nor was it indicated that in arriving at the figure of the grant, specific academic developments of the universities were taken into consideration. However, in the aforesaid letter, the Committee mentioned that "... for 1980-81, universities would be wise to exercise caution on proposals for academic developments to which they are not committed and for which counter railing savings have not been found". With regard to the number of students' entry for 1980-81, the following portion of the letter is confusing with reference to the advices of UGC earlier committed:

> "For 1980-81 the Committee has decided to announce grants, rather than allocations in terms of income from grant and fees. The Committee considers that in 1980 most universities should be able to admit about the same number of home undergraduates as in 1979. For some universities this will mean a constant population of home students; for others it will mean a small increase. The Committee is satisfied that this is feasible within the total resources likely to be available, even granted the uncertainty about overseas

students' fee income, and has made some allowance for increases in home student numbers (and the effect on fee income) in the grants for the universities concerned".

The confusion and contradiction between the above advice of UGC and those given earlier in regard to the students' entry would be evident from the fact that in August, 1979 (letter 13/79) the UGC had adviced the universities "... so to arrange their admissions procedure that the number of home undergraduates admitted in October 1980 can if necessary be restricted to 94 per cent of the number being admitted in October 1979; universities should not for the present make firm offers which would be likely to result in that 94 per cent figure being exceeded". Again in its subsequent letter dated 15th October, 1979 (letter 16/79), UGC stated as follows:

"A reduction of entry in 1980-81 and subsequent years to a level below that expected in 1979-80 will be necessary, over the system as a whole, if the roll-on effect of the entries of earlier years is not to produce a total population of home undergraduate students substantially in excess of that expected for 1979-80".

In reality, the home undergraduates entry increased by 3.7% in October 1980 over the number in October, 1979. Universities on their part failed to control the admission which ultimately caused further erosion in the 'unit of resource' which they were complaining earlier. Dr. Parkes, Chairman, UGC also made the following observation in this regard:

The government stated that grant for 1980-81 was based on the assumption that home undergraduate admissions would be the same in the previous year, but in spite of advance warning from the U.G.C., universities did not succeed in holding intakes to the previous year's figures, and, combined with the effect of 'roll on', this meant that home student numbers increased by 3.7% between the two years. So the first result of the new government's policies was a worsening of the unit of resource by 3.7% or, as it was probably regarded, an improvement in efficiency of 3.7%".

Although the universities were requested by UGC in October 1979, to submit by July 1980, detailed and considered statement on Table-B (sent with the letter), the UGC asked them in June 1980 to bifurcate the information and submit the first part in July and the second part in November with a revised forecast of home student numbers only, assuming the relationship between numbers and load is the same in 1979-80, together with information about the continuing education.

For obvious reasons, quite a few universities submitted information for 'hypothesis (b)' which was as stated by UGC, soon after its letter dated the 15th October, 1979 to represent 'level funding', while, hypothesis (a) represented a 2% increase in grant and (c) envisaged a 5% reduction in grant. Besides, keeping in view the possibilities of acceptance of the two hypotheses (a) and (b), the latter was considered more practical while (a) was not considered a possibility in a situation of rising pressure on the Public Expenditure. As regards (c), since it implied a reduction by 5% which involved deliberation at the university level with the relevant functionaries and heads meaning thereby dealing with question of reduction of expenditure in certain areas and levels which were certainly not pleasant exercises, serious attempt to examine the same was not made.

However, in October 1980, Dr. Parkes addressed the Committee of Vice-Chancellors and Principals when he firmly stated that UGC intended to be more 'interventionist' than in the past and expressed his doubt about the continuity of the 'level funding' basis. He said that "... I have said that it is our hope that level funding will be maintained, and we shall urge the Secretary of State to sustain this position. We have to recognize, however, that the pressures to cut the education vote in favour of other forms of government spending are very high, and we may not in the end be entirely unscathed". Even if 'level funding' is agreed to, Dr. Parkes expressed his doubt as to 'for how long'?[31]

Two indications were thus clear. One: that UGC would in future be more 'inteventionist' and two: that the 'level funding' was uncertain.

In retrospect, it could be said that in view of the resource crunch that was in store for the universities the caution and advices of Dr. Parkes were of sufficient significance. Visualising the changing needs, he observed that "I think it likely that both you and we may wish to start new departments and to close existing ones, and the latter may involve litigation. I think that except in very rare cases, it is unlikely that either of us will want to open or close complete facilities. I see nothing at present which would suggest the closure of a complete university".[32]

While the above observation was by way of caution and mental preparation, Dr. Parkes also emphasised on the need to work in strong collaboration between universities, CVCP and UGC for he felt that was the need of the hour. He felt that "During the coming years, the universities, the CVCP as a body and the UGC must not only work together to reshape the system to meet new needs and new opportunities, but must be seen to be doing so, and to be seen to be effective in doing so".[33] In case the togetherness fails, Dr. Parkes cautioned "... we shall cease to control our own destiny, because it is at any rate my own view that the greatest threat to the United Kingdom universities today is not a financial one". The latter part seems to be hinting at fighting together in the competitive situations.

Around the end of November, 1980 based on a communication received by CVCP from the UGC it was clear that sizable cuts were imminent in the financial years 1981-82, 1982-83 and 1983-84. However, the magnitude of the cuts was expected to be known only around the end of December, 1980. From the development that were taking during this period, it was almost certain that funding may not continue any longer on 'level funding' basis.

FEARS COME TRUE

A new chapter began on the 16th December, 1980 when the Secretary of State announced in Parliament, a 3.5% reduction in the recurrent grant amounting to 30 million pounds, for the fiscal year 1981-82. The UGC informed the universities of the implications of the reduction of grant when it estimated that taking into the loss on account of other factors, notably the possible loss of income from less number of overseas students, the total reduction for the year 1981 might be of the order of 5 to 6 per cent. When the universities considered reduction, with reference to the different hypothetical figures, they found that even the worst hypothesis "... did not represent so poor a financial prospect as the system must now face".

The situation threw new challenge to the UGC for it became necessary to provide new rationale and guidance in the matter of distribution of grants to the universities. As the first step, the UGC asked the universities by its letter dated the 30th December 1980, (letter 24/80) to plan and decide the activities for the year 1981-82. The UGC indicated that for many universities the reduced grants would not be sufficient even to keep up all the current commitments which eventually would mean that some reduction in the existing activities would be necessary. Although, the UGC was aware of the likely pecentage and cuts, it gave no indication to the universities. However, it informed the universities that the grant allocation for many universities would be inadequate even to maintain the existing commitments which would necessitate reduction in the current level of activity.

In retrospect, it is felt that if the UGC had given definite indications, rather than giving three hypotheses, it would have helped the universities to prepare the contingency plans to meet the unexpected situations. For the universities, in their financial management, it was important to know what would be the home students target for the three years in question. In view of this, the UGC informed the universities that while issuing the letters of grant allocation, guidance on home student numbers for arts, science, technology and medicine would be given. It also indicated that they were "... likely to imply a total home university population in 1983-84 not very different from that in 1980-81" and that as compared to 1980-81, some reduction was on the cards.

By no means, it was a comfortable job for the UGC to work out the details of distribution of reduced grants to the universities. The committee was seized throughout the first-half of 1981, in this task. It had to examine the various data that the universities had submitted which included the form B returns, details of research grants and studentships awards by the Research Councils and by DES as also other government departments. Information of other sources of research income, reserves funds of the universities etc. was also kept in view. The committee also looked into the various statistical data received from the universities as also those published by the Universities Statistical Record.

According to the Annual Survey Report of the UGC for the academic year 1980-81, the Committee examined *inter-alia* the following:[34]

"*(a)* the results of the 1980 dialogues, which provided the starting point for the whole of the Committee's work over the subsequent months; these supplemented and complemented the Committee's knowledge of institutions gained from information supplied by the universities themselves, from external agencies of various kinds, from visits and from main and sub-committee members' contacts in the course of their own academic work;

(b) evidence on the immediate and possible future supply of suitably qualified and willing candidates from the schools, particularly in "numerate" skills which are not only required for increasing ranges of courses in science, technology and medicine, but are becoming relevant to studies within the arts;

(c) the physical facilities and the intensity of their use within individual institutions;

(d) staffing resources - including information about rates of renewal, age structures and subject balances;

(e) the available information and opinions about the long-term patterns of employment of graduates;

(f) the views of our specialist sub-committees on the scale and strength of each subject, and on the problems of expensive facilities, including libraries, and their effective utilisation;

(g) the strength of research activity including the facilities available and the pattern of support from outside (both from Research Councils, and from elsewhere in the public sector and from industry and commerce); and

(h) special institutional, regional or national factors, including the differenent structures of courses (4-year, sandwich, combined etc.) and the special requirements in the Welsh Colleges for teaching through the medium of Welsh".

The first definite indication of the size of reductions to 1983-84 appeared in the 1982 Public Expenditure White Paper published in March, 1981 following which the UGC informed the universities in its letter dated 15th May, 1981 (8/81). The committee made rather clear that it would not distribute the cuts in resources equally between universities and fields of study and that it would allot a given student target for each university for 1983-84. However, it did not warn that between 1979-80 and 1983-84 home student numbers would have to be reduced by 5%.

It may be recalled that Dr. Parkes had earlier indicated in his address to CVCP about the need to support more to strong areas than weak ones. The decision of UGC not to equally distribute the cuts among universities confirms the underlying meaning of the aforesaid statement of Dr. Parkes.

Primarily, with two objectives before it, namely, to keep up the output of the "well qualified graduates" and "to maintain an adequate research base", the UGC examined indepth the subjects of study and the planned reduction of home student numbers in 1983-84. While deciding subject areas, priority was attached to such subjects as would have direct relation to help '... contribute to the solution of the problems of an advanced industrial society'. This led to the selection of universities for different subjects based on their strengths and weaknesses of the past. For the first time indications were given by UGC by its letter dated the 15th May, 1981 when it was made clear that cuts would be on selective basis. It also cautioned the universities in the following words:

> "... savings of the order required must involve reducing the range of subjects taught at some universities, and this will involve recommendations for the closure or radical reduction of some departments with the likelihood of consequent redundancies of staff, both academic and non-academic. There will also be implications for the continued ability to conduct post-graduate teaching and research in some areas of study in some institutions".[35]

REACTIONS OF THE CRUNCH

What were the reactions of the nine universities covered under the Research Project Studies of the Department of Education and Science conducted by Professor John Sizer, would precisely present a representative picture of the university system affected by the decision of the government as conveyed by the UGC letter dated the 30th December, 1980 (24/80). The nine universities in question are Hull, Aberdeen, Aston, Stirling, Sussex, Salford, Heriot-Watt, Sheffield and Bath.

The University of Hull was already facing financial difficulties and was relying on fees of a large number of undergraduates. The Vice-Chancellor who felt greatly concerned, wrote to UGC about the actual loss of income. He also warned the university constituents and established in February 1981, the Development Committee of a Working Group on Economies with a Pro-Vice-Chancellor, a few administrative and the senior academics. The Committee foresaw sizable cuts during 1981-82 to 1983-84. The committee examined the following possible steps to control the situation:

(a) possibilities for augmenting income,

(b) transferring costs to consumers,

(c) possibilities of raising additional income,

(d) scope to reduce expenditure through better budgetary control,

(e) reduction in services,

(f) increased operational efficiency,

(g) individual savings, and

(h) short-term savings.

However, the Development Committee postponed decisions until the receipt of the grant allocation letter which was 1.7.1981. The Vice-Chancellor on his part apprised the Senate in June and his statement was circulated to all staff. Precisely, on 1.7.1981, the university was ready with a proposal, but did not draw up any action plan to reduce expenditure and/or supplement income. It also did not review and evaluate its academic profile.

The University of Aberdeen was already in financial difficulty and therefore, the UGC letters brought new dimensions to its problems. The Planning Committee of the University had anticipated a loss in real terms of 8% by 1983 and a recurrent deficit in 1981-82 between 1.00 and 1.5 million pounds and therefore it recommended to effect all possible economies in the current year itself. Except for Engineering which needed some additional resources and to maintain the existing staff in Medicine, the Committee recommended to increase savings targets from 100,000 pounds to 300,000 pounds for academic and academic ralated staff. For non-academic staff, it wanted to increase savings target from 75,000 pounds to 175,000 pounds. Various aspects and means of achieving savings including redundancies were discussed in the Senate. Finally, the Senate decided that no action be taken until the receipt of the grant letter in July. In reality, however, the university went ahead with the savings target, but did not finalise the contingency plan.

No different was the financial condition of the University of Aston in December, 1980. But it had drawn up a contingency plan for the likely adverse situation that might come up through the UGC grant allocation letter of July, 1981.

Anticipating a budget deficit of the order of 1.6 million pounds for 1981-82, the Senate recognised certain areas which were important to tide over the difficulty, eg.:

(a) to increase earnings,

(b) to achieve short-term expenditure reductions by freezing vacant posts, and

(c) to introduce schemes for early retirement and redeployment of staff.

The University also recognised the need to review the academic profile and to encourage academic schemes for early retirement and redeployment of staff.

With the initiative of the Vice-Chancellor the university identified likely savings of 1 million pounds. It even prepared itself for a cut of upto 30%. He was able to communicate successfully with the university constituent through questionnaires, etc. and placed a paper on the objectives of the university, financial and academic opportunities as also constraints and organisational structure.

Against a revised deficit projection of 2.2 million pounds for 1981-82, reduction in expenditure was estimated of the order of 1.7 million. Aston was thus ready with a contingency plan in place on 1st July 1981, particularly for a review of the academic profile.

Unlike other universities, the University of Stirling, the youngest of all, had a new Principal in February 1981 who anticipated a cut between 11-15% and visualised the need to freeze all vacant academic posts. He circulated the UGC letter 8/81 widely within the university and planned to submit proposals to the Court so that it could consult the Academic Council. Of the three hypotheses the Principal favoured (a). Although the university initiated steps to prepare contingency plan in March 1981, but no concrete proposal was submitted before the 1st July, 1981.

In the University of Sussex, although deliberations on the future financial positions in view of the fall in income which it anticipated to be of the order of 20% for 1980-81 base line by 1983-84, ultimately, no definite contingency plan was drawn up by July, 1981. Except temporary and arbitrary reduction in expenditure, the university did not come up with any contingency plan in place on the 1st July, 1981.

Despite good deal of deliberations at different levels, nothing concrete emerged out for a contingency plan. However, in the process, a paper was prepared wherein 0.5 million pounds (2.5% of budget) was projected as deficit for 1980-81 and a target reduction of 1.2 million pounds (8%) for 1981-82. Suggestions were made for temporary and arbitrary methods for achieving reductions. No action plan was finalised before the receipt of UGC grant letter of 1.7.1981. Review of Academic Profile was also slow.

Although the University of Salford swung into action to examine and presumably to come out with the plan of actions to meet the new situation, on the plea that there was no definite indication about the likely level of grant for 1981-82, ultimately no contingency plan was prepared from July, 1981. In fact, in January 1981 itself, it started taking proper stock of the situation by examining the address of Dr. Parkes to CVCP together with the UGC letter 24/80.

The Vice-Chancellor on his part had warned the Council for a possible cut of atleast 11% by 1983-84, and suggested redundancies as the best and sure way to achieve meaningful savings. It was true that certain short-term and short-sighted decisions were taken for reductions in expenditure, but no planned and well thought decisions were taken to meet the uncertain and difficult situation. Even no review of the academic profile was undertaken.

Despite the fact that the University of Heriot-Watt had assessed the difficult time that lay ahead, it too had not drawn up any contingency plan from July, 1981. It had initiated review of the academic profile in December, 1980 itself, but made no proposal for any change. Even no formal cost reduction programme was implemented.

Unlike the aforesaid universities, the University of

Sheffield had initiated well planned actions to tide over the cut in store. The Senate, the Academic Development Committee and various sub-committees charged with different responsibilities had worked hard to find out the right way to go about and:

(a) examined alternative models;

(b) considered different survival strategies; and

(c) assessed the academic and financial considerations or different courses of action.

It had initiated review of the academic profile and identified potential savings from over provision of staff in some areas. In view of the legal difficulties, compulsory redundancy was not favoured. Through exercises at various levels including the Finance Committee, it projected savings of 1.119 million pounds for 1981-82 based on a likely UGC grant of 23.5 to 24.5 million pounds for that year and an initial savings target of 1.745 million pounds (at 1981 prices) for 1983-84. The university had thus contingency plan in hand from July, 1981.

From the beginning, the University of Bath was confident of favourable treatment by UGC. The presence of a strong leadership in the university proved helpful in the comfortable management of the University both before and after the UGC letter dated 1st July, 1981. Although no formal cost reduction took place, the university had done the necessary exercises by the Finance Committee and it was agreed that in case of need, labour cost would be reduced. The Vice-Chancellor had made his strong pleadings to UGC to protect the university cuts. At the same time, it was decided by academic planning not to fill the already frozen academic position. In order to augment income, the Senate was impressed upon the need to attract overseas students.

However, it prepared no formal contingency plan for July 1981 letter of UGC not knowing what was in store.

GAINS OF THE EXERCISES

While it is true that of the nine universities excepting the University of Aston and the University of Sheffield, no other university had prepared any formal contingency plan from July, 1981, even though they had made exercises at various levels within the individual university system, but undeniably certain gains could be identified which have left their impact in their own ways on each individual university and there is no doubt that in varying degrees they were of help and guidance to act faster than otherwise they would have without such exercise. Such invisible impacts had their contribution for future gains of the system particularly when analysed in a systematic way.

The need for an effective management not only to take precautionary measures during the difficult times due to change of policy or programmes, was recognised. It's role to create a culture in the system itself to respond boldly and ably to change is another important aspect of the management. Another gain was that the universities had realized that the end of the golden period had come and that inescapably they should effect economies in every possible ways and so also generate income. Although the degree of savings differed from university to university depending on a number of factors such as scope, seriousness of efforts, readiness of the various functionaries in the individual university system to co-operate, identification of items etc. and finally how ably handled the affairs, nevertheless every university succeeded in achieving some savings.

For a better and effective financial control, the University of Heriot-Watt introduced the system of feeding EPC with relevant statistical data on a regular basis. In the University of Aberdeen, the jurisdiction of the Planning Committee was extended to include consideration of the estimates and forward budgetting. In Aston, it was recognised that better allocation procedures should be devised. A distinct gain was in the University Salford where driven by the need and visualizing the gains, the Academic Policy and Development and the Estimate Committee functioned effectively which brought together the academic planning and resources allocation auguring well as an ideal and effective mechanism to achieve the objectives.

FINAL BLOW AND NEW ERA OF FUNDING

Finally, the 1st July 1981, came imposing the crunch which was so much talked about for quite some time not only in the UGC and the university system but in public too.

Although the UGC letter was dated 1st July, 1981 to all the universities it was not one and the same to all. While the general approach and certain guidance were common, in respect of quantum of grants and subject groups and number of students, each university got a separate letter. Some of the important points that the UGC communicated to the Universities in the matter of allocation of grants and the subject groups and numbers given to each university, were as follows:

1. The Committee had met every university on its grant list, taken into account the 'dialogue meetings' it had with different universities and of course the responses of the universities to the three hypotheses.
2. Additional detailed academic information that the university had submitted to UGC covering

full-time home student numbers (undergraduate and post-graduate) and student loads for 1979-80 distributed among 17 subject groups, forecasts of full time student numbers in 1983-84 on the three hypotheses; and forecasts of numbers of continuing education students, on the said hypothesis.

3. The Committee worked out the reduced allocation basis throughout the first-half of 1981 and was "drawing on the advice of its sub-committees and other subordinate bodies" which on their part had worked "intensely in their respective areas over most of the period".

4. The committee had before it the data input of "demographic trends, qualified school leavers, new entrants to universities, undergraduate and post-graduate student numbers, students attainments and first employment, short courses in continuing education, and data on university staff and finance together with analyses by universities as appropriate". The Committee had also details of research grants and various studentships. It also had information on the university reserves.

5. The Committee had made in-depth studies of the reviews done by the various sub-committees including the implication for each institution. It had considered various options including "the possibility of reducing the number of institutions in receipt of grants; the idea of a tiered system of institution with a top tier liberally funded and staffed for substantial research, with others to be financed principally as teaching organisations and the application

of the same percentage cut to every institution. Finally, the selective approach was decided with the provision of student places within each subject group.

6. In order that the universities are able to manage the affairs in a situation of likely reduction between 11 per cent and 15 per cent with a forced additional 10 per cent deterioration in the unit of resource, a 5 per cent reduction in the number of students was concurred by the committee, together with a cut in staff numbers of about 15 per cent.

7. The Committee had also kept in mind the various relevant factors, eg. students demand, employment prospect, national needs of personnel in different areas, cost involvement for teaching different subjects, current research activity, potential of each institutions. It's objective '... was to define and seek to establish an effective university system of the size which it would be feasible to maintain adequately at the level of resource planned by the Government for 1983/84".

8. The Committee decided that within the reduced total number of students in view of the demand for science and technology and positive role and need for national economic interest, "advantage should be taken of the existing investment in the university departments concerned" and "student numbers in physical sciences and technology should be increased as should numbers in mathematics and computer science, business studies and some aspects of biology". The committee realised that "A heavy price had to

be paid for this in terms of studies in other fields". While arts and social sciences suffered more, even medicine suffered for a different reason and that was cost. It was estimated that in terms of cost, one student of medicine was equal to six students in arts and sciences while the comparison with science and technology was between two and three.

9 The Committee worked out the allocation of grants based on the distribution of the reduced number of students places among 17 subject groups and the student load among subjects and institutions. "By working student loads rather than student numbers, account was automatically taken of the teaching load in each institution, including the specialized service teaching across departments. Modification- were made to take account of adjustments to the unit of resource, the subjects and for institutions considered by the Committee to be appropriate in the light of local circumstances, to take account of other factors such as research activity (which is not closely related to student numbers) and having regard to the consequences of the overall reduction in Exchequer grant decided upon by the Government'. The number of students for the continuing education as proposed by the universities under hypothesis (b) was also added.

10. Finally, "allocations" relating to 1983/84 were converted to a provisional grant distribution for that year by deducting estimated free income and adjusting pro-ratas to the total grant provisionally indicated by Government for 1983-84.

STATE OF WOUNDS

The grants and the student number reductions announced on the 1st July, 1981 for the different universities are shown in Appendix-1.[36] As against the total number of home and EC students of 260,970 in 1979-80, the target fixed for 1983-84 (or 1984-85) which was the last year of restructuring the universities was 248,720 i.e. a reduction of 4.7%.

In relation to the 1980-81 target, number of students for 1983-84 (or 1984-85), estimated and allowed by UGC with its grant letter of 1st July, 1981 was less by 18,510 which worked out 7% below the level of 1980-81. The university-wise position is shown in the Appendix-II.[37]

What was the state of wounds of each of the nine universities covered by the DES Research Project following the announcements of grants and fixation of the number of students with effect from the year 1981-82.

The university of Bath was the only university which received relatively better treatment. Although the recurrent grant was reduced by 7%, the number of students based on 1979-80 level was not reduced but increased by 2%; it was by 1% compared to 1980-81. Of the remaining eight universites, while three, namely, University of Sheffield, University of Sussex and University of Heriot-Watt - received 'middle range' treatment, the remaining five universities - University of Aberdeen, University of Hull, University of Stirling, University of Aston and the University of Salford were relatively 'harshly' treated. The number of these nine universities showing the home and EC students of 1979-80 and 1983-84 (or 1984-85) which was the last year of restructurisation as also the grants for 1980-81 and 1983-84 with percentage of change, indicating the percentage of overseas students are also mentioned in the Appendix.

Based on the inputs given by various sub-committees and the home work that it did for each university, the UGC had prepared and sent separate letters to each of the universities including the advice that it deemed necessary for each one. This meant that the UGC was highly selective in its decision for grants, number of students and the subjects or group of subjects. It also decided the subject areas including whether or not a university should cease to provide facilities for a subject or group of subject and decrease or increase the student numbers. It even focussed and adviced on the need relating to merger with or transfer to or collaborate with another university or maintain student numbers currently they had. All these efforts however indicated the approach of avoiding duplication and making the system cost effective.

As an example of giving advice by UGC to different universities differently in respect of subjects, student numbers need of collaboration, the following may be quoted from the letters that UGC issued which were published by THES:

> "*Bradford:* The University should concentrate on languages and on maintaining European Studies and interdisciplinary human studies. The Committee recommends a small increase in business studies and invites the university to consider discontinuing courses in education. It recommends a substantial reduction in student numbers in other subjects (in the arts) and invited the university to explore with Leeds the possibility of increased collaboration in social studies.
>
> "The Committee suggests that the university should

concentrate on its activities in engineering and technology, for which no reduction in student numbers is suggested. It invites the university to consider phasing out biological sciences and the course in medical sciences. The Committee recommends a substantial reduction in student numbers in physical sciences, in those specialising in mathematical sciences, and in pharmacy.

"*Nottingham*: The Committee recommends a decrease in student numbers in social sciences but within the reduced total the Committee hopes it will maintain numbers in Law. It suggests an increase in student numbers in the physical sciences, particularly in physics, but a decrease in the numbers specialising in the mathematical sciences and a substantial reduction in pharmacy numbers.

"The Committee also invites the university to consider collaboration with other institutions in planning studies. A greater than average reduction in the level of funding in clinical medicine is assumed.

"*Newcastle:* The Committee recommends a decrease in numbers in arts and social studies. It wishes to see Russian phased out and invites the university to explore with Durham the possibility of increased collaboration, particularly in psychology and sociology.

"A significant increase in student numbers in physical sciences, and an increase in those specialising in mathematical sciences is recommended. A small increase in numbers in biological sciences and a significant decrease in architecture but with the maintenance of town and country planning are suggested.

Medicine: the general policy applies."[38]

In the case of the University of Bath, the student number for 1980-81 (3234) was more by 44 than the 1979-80 (3190) constituting (+) 1.36% for 1984-85, which was the last year of restructering, the target was fixed at 3260 i.e. 70 more students than 1979-80 which worked out + 2%.

The University of Bath was relatively treated well but in that case too, while in respect of student number, it was on the plus side, the recurrent grant for 1983-84 which was fixed as the last year of restructurisation, was fixed at 7% below the level of 1980-81 estimate. The loss of grant was least in the case of the University of Bath, out of the nine universities, and second lowest out of all the universities. The University of York had the lowest cut (6%) out of all universities of Great Britain. Of the remaining eight, the position of the three universities which received 'middle range' treatment, was as shown in the Table-3.4.

Table 3.4[39]

University	<u>*Student Numbers*</u>			*Recurrent Grant* <u>*(m. pounds)*</u>		*Approx. change (80-81 vs. 83-84)*
	79-80	80-81	83-84 or 84-85	80-81	83-84	
(1) University of Sheffield	6860	7441	6860	25.40	21.72	-14%
(2) University of Sussex	3890	3971	3710	11.67	9.21	-21%
(3) University of Heriot-Watt	2430	2820	2120	8.16	7.09	-13%

The remaining four universities were treated 'harshly' and in their cases the position was as shown in the Table-3.5.

Table 3.5[40]

University	*Student Numbers*			*Recurrent Grant (m. pounds)*		*Approx. change (80-81 vs. 83-84)*
	79-80	80-81	83-84 or 84-85	80-81	83-84	
1. University of Salford	3940	3928	2750	15.31	8.59	-44%
2. University of Hull	5070	5120	4200	11.44	9.19	-20%
3. University of Stirling	2470	2716	2020	6.99	5.08	-27%
4. University of Aberdeen	5140	5195	4940	19.75	15.19	-23%
5. University of Aston	4670	4438	3640	14.39	9.86	-3.1%

REDUNDANCY - NEW BLOOD SCHEME AND INFORMATION TECHNOLOGY INITIATIVE

Following the Public Expenditure White Paper, 1981-82, the Secretary of State of DES and the Chairman of the UGC, in their evidence to the Public Accounts Committee in March 1981 explained the need to introduce the Redundancy Scheme. According to the UGC, the scheme was necessary to reach to the rescue of the universities so that they were able to contain their expenditure within the reduced allocation. Without the redundancy scheme, the Chairman, UGC, feared that even if the universities decided not to fill up the vacant posts and effect economies in non-staff areas, they would not be able to achieve the targets. The scheme was much more necessary for those universities which received harsh treatments.

The redundancy scheme involved considerable money and therefore without sizable support from the Government, it was not possible to implement the same. Steps to implement the scheme without government support meant leading to bankruptcy.

According to the estimate of the Chairman, UGC, about 3000 academic staff would have to be covered over a period of three years besides about 4000 non-academic staff.[41] In terms of the financial implication for the above redundancies, it was estimated to be between 100-200 million pounds. However, he made it clear that part of the amount would have to be found by effecting economies.

The task involved difficult exercises and decisions for it was found that in a normal course, only about 390 staff members would retire by 1983, by which time the restructuring was to be complete. It was unfortunate on the part of the universities and a failure on the part of the UGC and the Government, that although the UGC was convinced that the universities would have enormous difficulties to achieve the targets without the redundancy scheme being implemented, it did not announce the scheme on the 1st July, 1981. It made a beginning by its letter dated 15th May 1981, *inter-alia* asking the universities to work out redundancy proposal and inform UGC by January, 1982 the likely annual implication. It only informed that 20 million pounds would be used during 1981-82 for restructuring the same and part of the money could be used for early retirements.

It was only in December 1981 that the Government formally announced for being reimbursed by UGC an additional amount of 50 million pounds for the financial year April 1982 to March 1983 specifically for, restructuring the university system including the cost of compensation for staff redundancies. It was also indicated that further sums would be provided for the financial year 1983-84.

REDUNDANCY SCHEME

In January 1982, the terms of compensation was announced by the government for the academic and academic related staff. The redundancy scheme was implemented mainly on voluntary retirement basis. During 1981-82 claims for reimbursement of compensation were settled by UGC for about 1600 academic and academic related staff most of whom took premature retirement after 50 years of age. Those included in the number were mainly professors, senior lecturers and readers.[42]

By the end of the academic year 1983-84, the UGC settled claims for 3700 academic and academic related staff at a cost of 96 million pounds and an additional amount of 24 million pounds was reimbursed for 2200 non-academic staff.[43] The UGC also reimbursed 75% of the salary costs towards part-time teaching arrangements as part of the restructuring efforts.

How far the objective of savings was achieved from the capital investment by the government for redundancy claims, was a question which needed assessment. But due to the inherent problem of comparing the projected saving at 1980 survey prices with actual outturn, it was difficult to reach a realistic figure. However, it was estimated that "In very general terms the continuing annual savings were of the order of 140 million pounds at 1986 prices and were secured by the capital investment of 153 million pounds paid out under the redundancy arrangements".[44] However, later when calculated at the projected net savings for 1986-87 it was of the order of 159 million pounds.[45] This was considered as "... a very satisfactory financial return on its investment, i.e. a one year pay back period".[46] According to the published Report of the National Audit Office, despite "... the difficulties caused by the size and pace of the required contraction DES the UGC and the universities achieved the overall financial objectives imposed".[47]

Coming to the assessments of the UGC on the progress of the restructuring, the following are the important observations[48] viz.:

(a) Some universities had overshot their desired staff losses in some academic areas and would have to start recruiting again when they still had to make further reductions in other areas (particularly in the arts and social sciences); this might cause severe management problems.

(b) In engineering, technology, mathematics and computer science and certain other areas the percentage of posts shed in 1981-82 was much higher than average. This was not unexpected, since the staff in these subjects found it easier to obtain other employment.

(c) The present evidence about the prospects for 1984-85 was generally consistent with the changed balance between arts, science and medicine and with the shifts in student/staff ratios which the Committee had in mind.

NEW BLOOD AND INFORMATION TECHNOLOGY

In addition to the redundancy scheme, in December 1982, the Government announced separately that it will provide additional funds in the academic year 1983-84 for "New Blood" and "Information Technology".

Under the "New Blood" scheme, extra funds were assured to pay for additional 230 lecturers in the natural sciences (including technology and medicine and the remainder in the arts). It was also expected to provide for almost the same number in 1984-85 and 1985-86 as in 1983-84. The purpose of the new blood lecturers was primarily to contribute to research in addition to teaching duties in the early years. While such appointees would hold the posts in the normal way, but induction age limit was 35 years.

However, in relation to the large number of staff members that took voluntary retirement the recruitment under the new blood scheme was disproportionately very low which created an imbalance in the structure of academic staff that existed. The imbalance was mentioned by UGC as follows:[49]

(i) Less than 30% of all non-technical academic staff are aged 50 or over and in a dozen institutions the figure is below 20 per cent. This is mainly the result of the contraction of the past three years: between August 1981 and March 1984 about 2000 staff over the age of 50 took voluntary retirement. The substantial further number of voluntary retirements which is expected this September can only make things worse.

(ii) Less than 15 per cent of staff are under 35 because recruitment in the early 1980s was well below the levels of the 1970s. This has

been only partially offset by the new blood scheme.

(iii) About 60 per cent of staff are aged between 35 and 49. This is the result of high recruitment in the late 1960s and early 1970s. Most of the members of this large group will not reach retirement age until the first decade of the twenty-first century.

For comparison, a university system with a balanced age structure would have about 40 per cent of staff over 50, about 20 per cent under 35 and about 40 per cent between 35 and 49".

The 'Information Technology' scheme too like the New Blood Scheme was primarily intended to strengthen research. In March 1983, allocation of 70 posts (or the part-time equivalent) were announced and Pounds 20,000 additional grant was allocated per post. Later, the universities were supported for such posts upto 1985-86.[50]

It was envisaged that 30 posts would be deployed to strengthen research and the remaining 40 "... would be associated with the provision of 400 additional post-graduate advanced 'conversion' studentships".[51] In the case of these appointments, no upper age limit was prescribed.

The Salford University stated that "... without the compensation schemes and redundancy funds, the run down of the university system would have been more divisive, disorderly and disjointed than it actually was".[52] It felt that "The most disturbing aspect was the great delay in introducing them".[53] According to the Salford University, "The 'new blood' and 'IT' posts were not at all useful in implementing the university's plans; the outcomes being entirely unpredictable and a university's own preferance and rank orders being totally ignored".[54] Primarily based on the UGC letter, the universities had to explore and implement the redundancy scheme before the UGC came out formally with the national scheme. The approach of the scheme being sensitive, the universities had to hold series of consultations across the university.

In the case of the University of Aston which had a strong tenure position and a negligible reserve, it had conceived the redundancy scheme to be essential for survival and rational restructuring and a voluntary severance scheme was provided before 31st July, 1981 which directly helped the restructuring process. However, while the university had to commit to the voluntary severance payments for more than 3 million pounds, it could get reimbursement of only 1.5 million pounds.[55]

This scheme proved more successful at the University of Heriot Watt but some of the best academics left. Perhaps the situation was inevitable in a process where redundancy scheme was offered on voluntary basis. In the said university, the new blood scheme helped recruit good young researchers. In the University of Sheffield the new blood and IT initiatives were introduced but were not as successful as expected. But the redundancy scheme was extremely helpful in the restructuring process of the university.

CONCLUSION

The events and episodes that took place in the University System in UK during 1970s and the new situation created in 1981 due to the new government's public expenditure policy adversely affected unprecedentally that important sector of the society which has played and would always continue to play crucial and dominant role in the social, cultural, industrial and economic life of thc country provide forewarning to the governments, educationists, academics and administrators concerned with higher education management of all countries to pause, introspect, review and then revamp through restructurisation that the time may demand.

In order to understand the impact of the various stray decisions imposed on the university system by the university grants committee, it is necessary to recall thcm and examine the propriety of various decisions. Compulsions of the government and in turn of the UGC also need be discussed. In a democratic set-up decisions of expansion and reduction are always stated by the government to be related to the public interest. But how much is it really in the ultimate interest of public and how much due to the approach of the party in power of the government is a valid question that the people of any country should certainly debate.

Role of the UGC that is expected by the government on one hand and the public on the other importantly the expectations of the system for which the UGC primarily exists, is another aspect of the story that calls for discussion. However, despite its limitations and the delicate job of functioning between the government and the universities there was relative openness on the part of the UGC particularly its Chairman. How closely the government interacted with UGC in real sense, and how much did it confide in UGC, also need discussion. Despite the fact that the UGC and the Government were convinced of the need to provide the redundancy scheme and financial support therefor, there was delay in announcing the national scheme. In fact, this should have been announced along with the letter of the 1st July, 1981.

Performance of the universities both in responding to the need to share the difficult economic condition of the country and in restructuring and in a sense reshaping certain areas in the process of meaningful response to the call of adjustments, would throw new lights and would serve as pointers to all concerned.

Appendix-1

Grant and Student Number Reductions announced on 1st July, 1981

Universities ranked according to % loss of home students	*Home & EEC students 79-80*	*83-84 or 84-85*	*% change*	*Grant (m. pounds) 80-81 (est.)*	*83-84*	*approx. % change*	*% overseas students 79-80*
(1)	(2)	(3)	(4)	(5)	(6)	(7)	(8)
Salford	3,940	2,750	-30	15.31	8.59	-44	14
Aston	4,670	3,640	-22	14.39	9.86	-31	17
Bradford	4,360	3,530	-19	14.45	9.64	-33	13
Stirling	2,470	2,020	-18	6.99	5.08	-27	8
Keele	2,680	2,230	-17	8.57	5.64	-34	5
Hull	5,070	4,200	-17	11.44	9.19	-20	7
Surrey	2,880	2,470	-14	11.81	8.78	-26	12
Heriot-Watt	2,430	2,120	-13	8.16	7.09	-13	12
Kent	3,430	3,180	- 7	8.44	6.64	-21	10
St. Andrews	3,110	2,880	- 7	9.24	7.51	-19	9
Lancaster	4,210	3,920	- 7	10.32	8.68	-16	9
Sussex	3,890	3,710	- 5	11.67	9.21	-21	12
City	2,130	2,020	- 5	10.31	8.24	-20	20
Reading	5.030	4,770	- 5	15.00	12.66	-16	12

(1)	(2)	(3)	(4)	(5)	(6)	(7)	(8)
Aberdeen	5,140	4,940	- 4	19.75	15.19	-23	7
Essex	2,240	2,150	- 4	6.88	5.47	-20	22
Strathclyde	5,790	5,540	- 4	17.90	14.69	-18	12
London	33,510	32,220	- 4	200.00	165.03	-17	16
Bristol	6,650	6,390	- 4	23.05	19.43	-16	4
Nottingham	6,380	6,150	- 4	21.39	18.36	-14	7
Newcastle	6,880	6,600	- 4	23.97	20.85	-13	11
Durham	4,530	4,360	- 4	12.93	11.60	-10	4
Oxford	10,700	10,410	- 3	34.00	29.74	-13	10
Glasgow	9,100	8,810	- 3	33.08	29.56	-11	6
East Anglia	3,760	3,640	- 3	11.25	10.28	- 9	8
Leicester	4,340	4,200	- 3	13.12	11.95	- 9	4
Lough borough	4,670	4,550	- 3	13.06	11.98	- 8	10
Exeter	4,690	4,600	- 2	12.21	9.69	-21	6
Manchester	9,930	9,710	- 2	38.20	31.93	-16	11
Liverpool	7,060	6,910	- 2	31.18	26.13	-16	6
Leeds	9,430	9,270	- 2	33.93	28.72	-15	12
Cambridge	10,490	10,280	- 2	32.27	28.91	-10	8
Warwick	4,600	4,550	- 1	13.17	11.23	-15	6
Brunel	2,460	2,470	0	11.14	8.9	-19	11
Birmingham	7,750	7,770	0	30.81	25.69	-17	13
Wales	17,330	16,130	0	57.20	47.67	-17	12
Dundee	2,490	2,480	0	12.64	10.53	-17	11
Sheffield	6,860	6,860	0	25.40	21.72	-14	11
Southampton	5,690	5,660	0	18.91	16.60	-12	9
Edinburgh	8,830	8,840	0	33.81	30.20	-11	7
York	3,100	3,090	0	7.48	7.02	- 6	5

(1)	(2)	(3)	(4)	(5)	(6)	(7)	(8)
Bath	3,190	3,260	+ 2	9.38	8.69	- 7	8
UMIST	2,790	2,980	+ 7	15.94	11.08	-30	27
Manchester Busi. School	120	170	+42	1.14	0.87	-24	21
London Busi. School	170	290	+70	1.13	1.49	+11	26
Total GB	260,970	248,720	-4.7	971.85	808.07	-17	11

Appendix-II

Changes in Full-time Home and EC Student Numbers by 1983-84 (or 1984-85)

	Home & EC Students 80-81	79-80	Total Home & EC Students/Increase (+)/Decrease (-) 83-84 (or 84-85 v. 79-80 Number	1983-84 80-81 v. 79-80 Number	(or 1984-85) v. 80-81 % change Number	%
(1)	(2)	(3)	(4)	(5)	(6)	(7)
Aston	4,438	4,670	(-) 1,030	(-) 232	(-) 798	(-) 18
Bath	3,234	3,190	(+) 70	(+) 44	(+) 26	(+) 1
Birmingham	7,974	7,750	(+) 20	(+) 224	(-) 204	(-) 3
Bradford	4,488	4,360	(-) 830	(+) 128	(-) 958	(-) 21
Bristol	6,745	6,650	(-) 260	(+) 95	(-) 355	(-) 5
Brunel	2,576	2,460	(+) 10	(+) 116	(-) 106	(-) 4
Cambridge	10,680	10,490	(-) 210	(+) 190	(-) 400	(-) 4
City	2,219	2,130	(-) 110	(+) 89	(-) 199	(-) 9
Durham	4,570	4,530	(-) 170	(+) 40	(-) 210	(-) 5
East Anglia	3,892	3,760	(-) 120	(+) 132	(-) 252	(-) 6
Essex	2,311	2,240	(-) 90	(+) 71	(-) 161	(-) 7

(1)	(2)	(3)	(4)	(5)	(6)	(7)
Exeter	4,814	4,690	(-) 90	(+) 124	(-) 214	(-) 4
Hull	5,120	5,070	(-) 870	(+) 50	(-) 920	(-) 18
Keele	2,687	2,680	(-) 450	(+) 7	(-) 457	(-) 17
Kent	3,489	3,430	(-) 250	(+) 59	(-) 309	(-) 9
Lancaster	4,262	4,210	(-) 290	(+) 52	(-) 342	(-) 8
Leeds	9,665	9,430	(-) 160	(+) 235	(-) 395	(-) 4
Leicester	4,581	4,340	(-) 140	(+) 241	(-) 381	(-) 8
Liverpool	7,337	7,060	(-) 150	(+) 277	(-) 427	(-) 6
London Bus.School	161	170	(+) 120	(-) 9	(+) 129	(+) 80
LondonUniv.	33,956	33,510	(-) 1290	(+) 446	(-)1,736	(-) 5
Loughborough	4,810	4,670	(-) 120	(+) 140	(-) 260	(-) 5
Manchester Busi. School	139	120	(+) 50	(+) 19	(+) 31	(+) 22
Manchester University	10,197	9,930	(-) 210	(+) 267	(-) 477	(-) 5
Manchester Inst. of S & T	3,116	2,790	(+) 190	(+) 326	(-) 136	(-) 4
Newcastle-upon-Tyne	6,883	6,880	(-) 280	(+) 3	(-) 283	(-) 4
Nottingham	6,632	6,380	(-) 230	(+) 252	(-) 482	(-) 7
Oxford	10,702	10,700	(-) 290	(+) 2	(-) 292	(-) 3
Reading	5,068	5,030	(-) 260	(+) 38	(-) 298	(-) 6
Salford	3,928	3,940	(-) 1,190	(-) 12	(-)1,178	(-) 30
Sheffield	7,441	6,860	-	(+) 581	(-) 581	(-) 8
Southampton	5,649	5,690	(-) 30	(-) 41	(+) 11	
Surrey	2,898	2,880	(-) 410	(+) 18	(-) 428	(-) 15
Sussex	3,971	3,890	(-) 180	(+) 81	(-) 261	(-) 7
Warwick	4,734	4,600	(-) 50	(+) 134	(-) 184	(-) 4

(1)	(2)	(3)	(4)	(5)	(6)	(7)
York	3,225	3,100	(-) 10	(+) 125	(-) 135	(-) 4
Aberystwyth UnivCollege	3,005	2,940	(-) 230	(+) 115	(-) 345	(-) 11
Bangor Univ. College	2,720	2,580	(-) 310	(+) 140	(-) 450	(-) 17
Cardiff Univ. College	4,878	4,680	(-) 300	(+) 198	(-) 498	(-) 10
St. David's Lampeter	764	710	(-) 40	(+) 54	(-) 74	(-) 10
Swansea Univ. College	3,491	3,340	(-) 110	(+)151	(-) 261	(-) 7
Univ. of Wales Inst. of S&T	2,446	2,400	(-) 240	(+) 46	(-) 286	(-) 12
Welsh National School of Medicine	693	680	(+) 10	(+) 13	(-) 3	-
Aberdeen	5,195	5,140	(-) 200	(+) 55	(-) 255	(-) 5
Dundee	2,737	2,490	(-) 10	(+) 247	(-) 257	(-) 9
Edinburgh	9,090	8,830	(+) 10	(+) 260	(-) 250	(-) 3
Glasgow	9,233	9,100	(-) 290	(+) 133	(-) 423	(-) 5
Heriot-Watt	2,540	2,430	(-) 310	(+) 110	(-) 420	(-) 17
St. Andrews	3,148	3,110	(-) 230	(+) 38	(-) 268	(-) 9
Stirling	2,716	2,470	(-) 450	(+) 246	(-) 696	(-) 26
Stratchclyde	5,934	5,790	(-) 250	(+) 144	(-) 394	(-) 7
Total G.B.	267,232	260,970	(-) 12250	(+)6262	(-)18510	(-) 7

References

1. U.K., Department of Education and Science, Institutional Responses to Financial Reductions in the University Sector, John Sizer (1987), Background Paper No.2, p. 4 (unpublished).
2. *Ibid*, p. 5.
3. *Op. Cit.*, p.16.
4. *Op. Cit.*, p. 6.
5. U.K., Committee on Higher Education, Report (Robbins Report), London, HMSO, 1963, p. 66.
6. *Ibid.*
7. U.K., Department of Education and Science, Institutional Responses to Financial Reduction in the University Sector, John Sizer (1987), Background Paper-l, Table-3 (unpublished).
8. *Ibid*, p. 38.
9. *Op. Cit.*, Background Paper No. 2, Table-7.
10. *Op. Cit.*, Background Paper No. 3, Table-4.
11. *Op. Cit.*, Background Paper No. 2, p. 16.
12. *Op. Cit.*, Background Paper No. 2, Table-7.
13. Higher Education in Britain: the Universities, Information Pack, British Council and the Committee of Vice-Chancellors and Principals of U.K., London (1991).
14. U.K., Department of Education and Science, Institutional Responses to Financial Reductions in the University Sector, John Sizer (1987), Background Paper No. 2, p. 7. (unpublished).
15. *Ibid.*
16. *Op. Cit.*, p. 8.
17. *Op. Cit.*, p. 12.
18. *Op. Cit.*, p. l9.

19. U.K., Department of Education and Science, Institutional Responses to Financial Reductions in the University Sector, Comparative Analyses of Universities Case Studies John Sizer (1987), p.19 (unpublished).
20. *Ibid.*
21. *Op. Cit.*, p. 19.
22. *Op. Cit.*, p. 22.
23. *Op. Cit.*, p. 22.
24. *Op. Cit.*
25. *Op. Cit.*, B.P. No. 2, p. 20.
26. UGC Chairman's Letter dated 2.11.1981 to the Select Committee, Para-3 of Appendix-B (unpublished).
27. Kogan, M., Kogan, D., The Attack on higher education, Kogan Page, 1983, pp. 45 and 100. Extract from the Background Paper No. 2, p. 21.
28. U.K., Department of Education and Science, Institutional Responses to Financial Reductions in the University Sector, John Sizer (1987), Background Paper No. 2. p. 21 (unpublished).
29. *Op. Cit.*
30. *Op. Cit.*, Background Paper No. 2, p. 23.
31. *Op. Cit.*, Background Paper No. 2, p.27, Extract.
32. *Op. Cit.*, Background Paper No. 2, p. 28.
33. *Ibid.*
34. *Op. Cit.*, Background Paper No. 2, p. 30, Extract.
35. *Op. Cit.*, Background Paper No. 2, p. 34.
36. *Op. Cit.*, Background Paper No. 2, Table-11.
37. *Op. Cit.*, Background Paper No. 2, Table-12.
38. *Op. Cit.*, Background Paper No. 2, p. 39, Extract.
39. *Op. Cit.*, Background Paper No. 2, Tables 11 and 12.
40. *Ibid.*

41. *Op. Cit.*, Background Paper No. 2, p. 33.
42. *Op. Cit.*, Background Paper No. 3, p. 6.
43. *Op. Cit.*
44. *Op. Cit.*, p. 9.
45. *Op. Cit.*
46. *Op. Cit.*, pp. 9-10.
47. *Op. Cit.*, p. 8.
48. *Op. Cit.*, p. 6.
49. *Op. Cit.*, Background Paper No. 3, p. 12, Extract.
50. *Op. Cit.*, p. 11.
51. *Ibid.*
52. *Op. Cit.*, Comparative Analysis of Universities Case Studies, p. 81.
53. *Op. Cit.*, Comparative Analysis of Universities' Case Studies, P.181.
54. *Ibid.*

4

Research Funding

ARE UNIVERSITIES FOR TEACHING OR RESEARCH?

Conceptually and functionally too, universities are both - Teaching and Research - for really speaking they are inseparable - integral part of each other. No university is known anywhere in the world which is designed to carry out only research. And there is no university in any part of the world which does not teach undergraduates and/or post-graduates. All universities have the basic function of teaching with invariably at least some research activities which may vary from very significant to even rather insignificant - both in terms of actual output and extent - but some reasonable research activities would surely be carried out in all the universities. Fundamentally, however, a university is for teaching and therefore it has the predominance of the teaching function. This function "... is privileged in two ways: the financial needs determine the number of students and university organisations is determined according to disciplines; in both cases it is a matter of 'modules', financing of facilities is determined by the number of students and the internal organisations of universities is defined by the discipline of which, in the end, it is merely the institutional projects".[1]

The Robbins Committee while observing that "on the one hand, it has been strongly argued that more and better opportunities for research are needed, and that a main factor in the attractiveness of the universities in the United States is the superior research facilities they offer, on the other hand, it has been argued that the exphasis on research in the universities is excessive and that university teachers devote too much time and energy to their personal research to the detriment of their teaching".[2] The Committee firmly held that[3]:

> "We are in total disagreement with the extreme view that would remove reserch altogether from the universities and concentrate it in reserch institutes, leaving the universities to devote themselves wholly to teaching, and we are confident that the experience of the world is against such a separation. We would not dispute that at times a university teacher is confronted with conflicting claims on his time and attention; but the need to reconcile differing professional obligations is not peculiar to the university teacher. We would not dispute either that some students could be better taught. But the remedy for this is to be sought in improved arrangements for teaching and these need not be made at the expense of research".

Deliberating on the question of a balance between teaching and research, the Robbins Committee had conducted a joint survey with the committee on University Teaching Methods, and it revealed that during the term period, teachers spend on an average one third of their working time on teaching (including preparation and correction of students' work), generally less than a third on research. Rest of the time they spend for private study, administration, other work within the university and some work outside the university.

Grade-wise the time spent for teaching and research in terms of percentage was as shown in the following Table-4.1.[4]

Table 4.1

Grade	*Teaching (percentage)*	*Research (percentage)*
Professors	26	18
Readers	30	29
Senior Lecturers	35	23
Lecturers	37	26
Asstt. Lecturers	42	32
Demonstrators	36	41
Research staff	12	62

Faculty-wise, the time spent for teaching and research in terms of percentage was as shown in the Table-4.2[5]

Table 4.2

Faculty	*Teaching (percentage)*	*Research (percentage)*
Humanities	40	22
Social Sciences	32	20
Sciences	34	34
Applied Sciences	38	22
Pre-clinical Medicine	25	40
Clinical Medicine	19	29

It is also interesting that the survey found that as university groups, the time spent on teaching and research considerably varied as mentioned in Table-4.3[6]

Table-4.3

University Group	*Teaching*	*Research*
Oxford and Cambridge	30	30
London	31	32
Larger Civic	34	28
Smaller Civic	39	23
Wales	40	23
Scotland	34	27

DUAL SUPPORT SYSTEM - HOW EFFECTIVE FOR RESEARCH FUNDING

From 1970s, the dual support system came into operation in UK which faced strong criticism for its failure to provide smooth, efficient and sharp funding mechanism for research activities and therefore does not as the general impression of the academic world is, enthuse the researchers. Under the dual support system, initial funding for research comes from the general funds in the form of Block Grants from the University Funding Council (UFC) and as the research work gets recognised, additional funds are sought in the form of external specific grants from the Research Councils as also from Contracts Research. However, there is a brighter side of the system for it, "... gave the universities considerable advantages as research establishments, since they could undertake research at lower cost to their sponsors than research institutes, which had to cover all their costs out of research income".[7]

With a view to encouraging research and to specify a portion of block grant for research activities, a new model of funding was developed in 1985 for the period from 1986-87 to 1989-90 which consisted of three components[8]:

(i) teaching,

(ii) reserch, and

(iii) special factors.

While teaching component was to be of the range of sixty per cent of the total allocation (may vary between subjects), the research component was to be for about thirty five per cent. However, the exact amount varied from university to university for research and depended on a number of criteria[9]:

(i) Student numbers,

(ii) Income from research grants awarded by research councils,

(iii) Income from research contracts, and

(iv) Selectivity.

The 1989-90 breakdown of grants by UGC to the universities was as shown in the Table-4.4[10]

Table 4.4

Allocation of Resources by the UGC (1989-90)

	% of total allocation
Teaching	61.2
Research	
- student number related	14.8
- grant-related	5.2
- contract income-related	0.7
- selective	14.1
Special factors	4.0

For allocating funds within the universities, they were expected to take into account the research activities and performance thereof.

The UFC provides as the first part of the dual support system, funds "for the costs of the basic infrastructure of university research, such as laboratories and equipment as well as the salaries of academic staff".[11] This helps the universities to "undertake seedcorn research at their own discretion".[12] Funds "for specific projects (are) distributed on a competitive basis for which all universities, polytechnics and colleges are free to apply".[13] Reiterating the positive aspect of the system, the White Paper (1991) stated "The plurality of funding sources means that a much broader spread of opinion can be brought to bear on the most promising direction for future research".[14]

The first part of the dual support system which constitutes of the block grant by UFC and the publicly funded tuition fees both of which contain an allocated sum of money known as the R element (roughly 36%) calculated on research-based criteria, has the following four components:

- SR: in relation to planned student numbers - about fifteen per cent of the total block grant.
- DR: in relation to research grant income from research councils and charities - about five per cent of the total block grant.
- CR: in relation to income for research from industry and government departments - about one per cent of the total block grant.
- JR: based on the UFC's assessment of research strength and performance - about fifteen per cent of the total block grant.

The other part of the 'dual support' system of research funding flows from the Research Councils to individuals and research groups for items like research staff, equipment and various materials for research work. In terms of the percentage of total University income from Research Councils for research activities, the Jarratt Report estimated that "A typical University is likely to receive 6% of its total income from Research Councils, excluding any large special facility grants". Besides the UFC and Research Councils, "Other sources of research funding are Government department contracts and Commercial and Industrial contracts and grants from charitable foundations".[15] Research Income has been defined by the CVCP/UFC as "... income for the purpose of research receivable in the year through the University's accounts, including income attributable to a department, or an individual within a department, and is returned under the following heads (excluding income from University companies):[16]

(i) Research grant and contract income received from Research Councils covered by the Advisory Board for Reserch Councils.

(ii) Income from all UK Central Government bodies except Research Councils.

(iii) Income from UK Local Authorities.

(iv) Income from UK Public Corporations, such as the Nationalised Industries, the British Technology Group or the Ordnance Survey.

(v) Income from other UK industry and commerce.

(vi) Income from all charitable foundations, trusts etc., based in the United Kingdom.

(vii) Income from bodies operating in the European Community, outside the United Kingdom.

(viii) Income from overseas bodies.

(ix) Other sources.

The following figure-4.1 will provide a picture related to the Research income per FTE academic during 1984-85 and 1988-89.

Although expenditure is not strictly related to the research performance but that has important bearing on the research activities and performance. The research expenditure per full-time member of academic staff in respect of individual universities; for two years is given in the Table-4.5.

Fig. 4.1. Research Income per FTE academic[17]

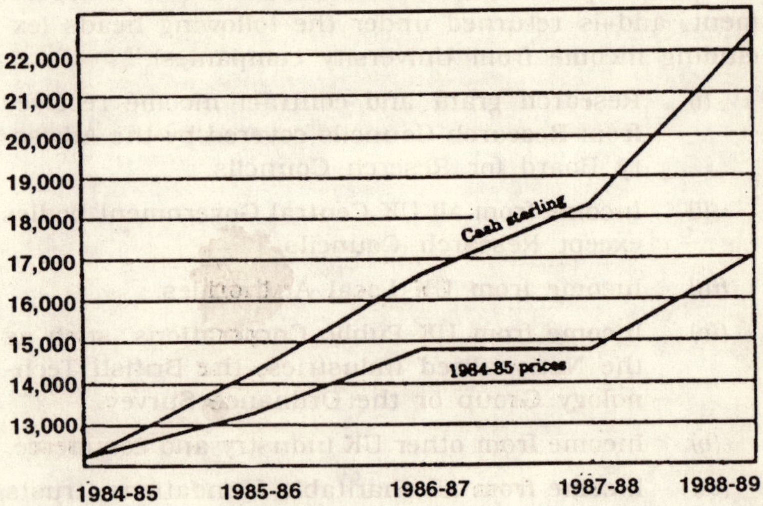

Source: UMS and Pl. vols 1-4

Table 4.5[18]

University	*Research Expenditure per full-time Academic* *1986-87*	*1987-88*
1	*2*	*3*
Aston	8393	7306
Bath	8351	8815
Birmingham	8482	9282
Bradford	5773	6133
Bristol	9390	10022
Brunel	12226	11595
Cambridge	11212	12406
City	6573	6204
Durham	6400	6693
East Anglia	5924	5691
Essex	6531	6939
Exeter	3750	5184
Hull	5677	4265
Keele	6028	6435
Kent	6184	8564
Lancaster	5164	5758
Leeds	6954	7403
Leicester	8445	8939
Liverpool	8395	9551
London	14892	16059
Loughborough	10900	11266
Manchester	7663	8142
UMIST	15020	13738
Newcastle	8286	9264

1	*2*	*3*
Nottingham	9049	9157
Oxford	13816	15746
Reading	7555	9120
Salford	6015	6936
Sheffield	7181	8522
Southampton	12297	12177
Surrey	11662	12656
Sussex	9175	9808
Warwick	9829	11405
York	9863	110061
Aberdeen	5958	6787
Dundee	11505	12077
Edinburgh	10679	11838
Glasgow	10228	11756
Heriot-Watt	11500	15724
St. Andrews	6172	6238
Stirling	5690	6414
Strathclyde	9707	9507
Queen's	4774	6138
Ulster	2636	3131
Wales	9125	8373

During 1975-87, the percentage changes in finance for specific projects in the universities in U.K. and some other countries were as shown in the figure-4.2.

The expenditure on R&D in UK by the various Departments during 1985-86 to 1987-88 was as shown in the Table-4.6

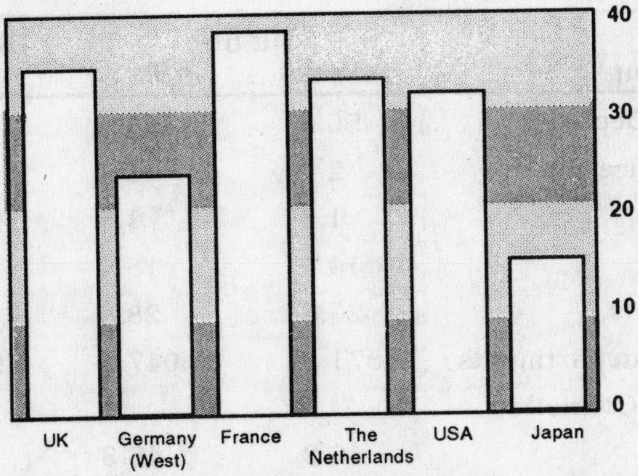

Source: SPRU (Science and Public Policy, vo. 17 No. 1, pp. 3.13)

Fig. 4.2. Percentage Change in Finance for Specific Projects in Universities (1975-87)[19]

Department wise R & D Expenditure

Table 4.6[20]

Department	Out-turn 1985-86	Out-turn 1986-87	Estimate 1987-88
Civil departments			
MAFF	122.3	118.3	109.0
DES	73.0	72.8	75.0
DEn	33.4	192.4	168.6
UKAEA	195.8	-	-
DOE	47.2	59.0	60.8
DHSS	28.1	49.4	48.5
HSC	5.5	5.4	4.9
Home Office	14.2	13.3	15.0
ODA	24.3	27.0	31.0
DTI	386.7	362.9	308.9
DTp	25.8	24.6	24.8
NI Depts.	14.2	17.0	17.3

Department	Out-turn 1985-86	1986-87	Estimate 1987-88
Scottish Depts.	55.6	53.4	51.0
Welsh Office	2.7	3.5	1.8
DEmp	1.3	1.5	1.9
MSC	14.1	18.4	24.1
Other depts.	27.8	28.5	29.7
Total civil departments	1,071.8	1,047.2	971.2
Research Councils			
AFRC	46.2	46.3	45.7
ESRC	19.0	20.0	20.0
MRC	125.3	127.6	132.4
NERC	68.3	68.0	68.1
SERC	286.5	295.9	317.1
Unallocated			
Total research councils	545.2	557.7	583.3
UGC	690.8	720.0	714.3
Total Civil R&D	2,307.8	2,324.9	2,268.8
Ministry of Defence			
Research	412.3	407.8	382.1
Development	1,927.9	1,778.3	1,852.3
Staff & Superannuation	77.0	78.2	76.5
Total defence	2,417.3	2,264.2	2,310.8
Total	4,725.1	4,589.2	4,579.7

Note: Amounts, in constant million pounds (base year 1986-87), have been rounded off.

DIVERGENT VIEWS ON RESEARCH FUNDING

Research Funding in the universities has always been an important issue. Various forums and individuals have deliberated on the mechanism of the Research Funding and made their suggestions which will be discussed here.

In 1980, the Advisory Board for the Research Councils (ABRC) and the UGC had appointed a Joint Working Party on the support of University Scientific Research (The Merrison Report) to go into the system and make recommendations. The Report of the Committee was published in 1982.

In practice, the UGC block grants to the universities includes amounts that the universities may need and decide to deploy for research also. However, it is not specifically shown as to the quantum meant for deployment for research or the areas for which allocated, in the absence of which the Joint Committee Report, observed that "they may take account of varying departmental responsibilities, student/staff ratios and the relative expense of one subject compared with another. They may be very much formula-based, or make provision for exercising discretion and judgement. They may operate at the centre, or be devolved to faculties or departments. Ideally they should be sensitive enough to enable support to be channelled to priorities within existing commitments, and to provide the necessary development and innovation, from within the sums available to them (6.5)".

The Committee fully acknowledged the difficulties on the part of the universities in a situation of fund crunch and it also observed that "In practice, it is often the case that the mechanisms used to distribute economies within universities involve a combination of "across the board" cuts, and a concentration of economies on costs which are easiest to cut such as consumeables, and posts with a fairly rapid turnover, such as research assistants and demonstrators. Universities should be more selective than this. General measures such as these, while understandable as an immediate reaction, do not take sufficient account of the needs of particular areas which may be vital to a university's long-term health and if they are prolonged will ultimately weaken the whole institution". (para 6.5).

Clearly, the universities resort to various measures to meet the exigencies of the situation through ad-hoc actions having far reaching impact which, it need hardly be said, are not in the ultimate interest of the university. Such measures might have been those accepted "across the board", but not necessarily the best ones but forced ones, by circumstances of pressures.

As revealed in the Report, during 1971-72 and 1978-79, while the student load in UK universities increased by 24% from 250.8K to 310.1K, the full time academic staff numbers grew by only 13% from 29.4K to 33.3K worsening the student/staff ratios. However, the external funded temporary research appointments grew from 4985 in 1972-73 to 7605 in 1978-79. The Committee observed that the morale of the temporary research appointees affected due to the very limited number of permanent positions becoming available in the universities.

On the question of the research students, the Report observed that during 1971-72 and 1978-79, the number rose marginally from 24,057 to 24,721. However, home student number fell from 16,897 to 15,169.[21]

For effective research activities, the Committee found that the conditions were not encouraging. The departmental and laboratory running expenditure declined in real terms between 1971-72 and 1978-79 by 19%; by 28% per member of staff. With a sizable backlog of UGC equipment grants over the period 1972-73 to 1980-81 (Pounds 22.79K), the "well founded laboratory" which is one of the important responsibilities of UGC under the dual support system, was suffering from obsolesence. Even on the library side, although the total expenditure increased from 4.14% in 1971-72 to 4.36% in 1978-79, there was a minus allocation by 1.5% on periodicals which are so crucial to researchers and on the whole, the research activities suffered.[22]

The Committee's concern was not only for the continued erosion of allocation in real terms for research activities under the dual support system, it also expressed doubt about the effective allocation and efficient utilisation of funds within the individual universities. The number-driven allocation inherently suffers from recognising the merit for if a particular department has less number of students, but otherwise doing good research, will be inadequately funded. The joint working committee made the following observations in this regard:

> "... university funds were no longer sufficient to support the reasonable research needs of staff in many disciplines and departments. Well-found laboratories had become partly-found laboratories even in universities recognised for their expertise in particular areas. Good research was still being done, but it was relying heavily on external funds. The effort of securing such funds was absorbing time and energy that would in easier circumstances have been devoted to research. Moreover some worthwhile research proposals were not gaining support". (para-7.4).

In his paper on Academic Leadership and the Management of Research", Professor Sir David Smith, Principal and Vice-Chancellor, University of Edinburgh, observed that "The government believes that British Universities are very good at basic research, but bad at translating the results into profitable applications which improve national wealth. Funding of basic research does not therefore need to be increased, but universities must be compelled to work much more closely with industry".[23]

Ostensibly, the interest of the government in allocating increased funds for research was lacking which wanted the universities to earn additional funds through interaction with industry. The Merrison Report had also advocated stronger university-industry links. In the letter dated the 15th October, 1979 (letter 16/79) of the UGC asking for responses on the alternative models of level funding of universities, the word "research" was conspicuously absent. The CVCP had cautioned in a memorandum dated 1st February 1980, on the student number-driven allocation in the matter of funding in the following words:

> "Indeed since 1974, it (the 'unit of resource') has fallen by some 13% in real terms. Our experience suggests (and this is confirmed by the UGC) that the effects are felt mostly by limitation on research rather than by economies in teaching".

The crucial letter of UGC dated the 1st July, 1981 regarding the grant for 1981-82 and guidance for the succeeding years, however, did not ignore the research funding aspect. It made it clear that in fixing the recurrent grant, it had taken into account the needs of research and equipment. Similarly, reference to the needs of library was mentioned. The letter also pointed out that there would be selectivity in the support of research and "... that the committee was continuing discussions with Research Councils and other funding bodies in order to ensure that there was some linking of policies for supporting research at a time when further concentration of research was inescapable".[25]

Although the UGC did not address the "Research" aspect specifically in its communication earlier so as to demonstrate its special interest and concern in this respect, the issues connected with research funding and research selectivity were deliberated in a number of Forums. Primarily, due to the funds constraint, the universities were under growing pressure to adopt selectivity in their internal distribution of resources.

Separately, an important seminar held under the banner of Leverhulme Programme of Study into the Future of Higher Education, recommended[26] *inter-alia* that each university should have a research policy - which policy should help to:

(i) Identify the balance of research effort within the institution that is to be devoted to each of the competing demands on that institution's research system, i.e. it would determine the balance between fundamental basic research, strategic research, the training of post-graduates, scholarship, and research directed to the solution of local, national and international problems.

(ii) Identify those departments and units whose past research performance warrants their being singled out as centres of excellence deserving special research support.

(iii) Identify mechanisms to ensure that new research, and people with exceptional research

talents have an opportunity to succeed. This is because universities should aim to select on 'promise'

- that a process of consultation between universities and between the universities research and funding bodies (including research councils and the U.G.C.) take place, in order to ascertain which institutions will be designated for research in particular disciplines.
- that a new system of university funding be introduced which distinguishes between undergraduate teaching and the support of scholarship on the one hand, and postgraduate teaching and research on the other.

The recommendation of the Seminar led to important public debate about the future of research in Great Britain for in particular it recommended that:

> "... the UGC would continue to fund both teaching and research. It would, however, use different criteria for each. The funding would be linked to designated research centres at each institution and there would be a measure of "reasonance" between the general support for research provided by the UGC and the specific funds provided by the research councils. The recommendations would mean that in consultation with the universities and research councils the UGC would become more selective in its allocation of funds".[27]

The Report of the joint UGC/ABRC working party on the Support of University Scientific Research (The Merrison Report) concluded that the dual support system "is in principle an impressive system for the support of University research and that it should be retained" (p. 3).

The Merrison Report believed that the universities should follow the policy of "concentration" of funds into broad areas of research. Turning to the mechanism for implementing "selectivity purposes, it suggested that the universities should create Research Committees, which should *inter-alia* identify the research areas on which the universities should concentrate and provide funds. Payment of separate grants by the UGC for teaching and research was not recommended by the Report, as suggested by Durham and Oldham. It also did not recommend 'extensive earmarked addition to the Block Grants for research support'.[28]

While endorsing and commending the Merrison Report to the Universities, inviting comments, the UGC had asked in July, 1982 for its information of any action that the universities proposed on the recommendation of the Report. The CVCP's reaction to the report was as follows:

> "It is widely felt among the universities that the establishment of special Research Committees along the lines recommended by the Working Party is not necessarily the most effective method for determining reserch priorities and allocating resources. It all depends upon whether the present structures of academic development and planning committees which deal with the general distribution of recurrent funds to departments can take account of research priorities. Universities are considering this point in the light of their individual circumstances. They believe in any case that it would be wasteful to separate responsibilities for the allocation of research funds from the general allocation of departmental funds".

For a variety of valid reasons, university-industry interaction was and still is accepted as the most viable activity. A joint committee which worked on "Improving Research Links between Higher Education and Industry" of ACARD/ABRC (Muir Wood Report published in June, 1983) also endorsed the conclusion of the Merrison Report that the universities should channelise proportionately more funds for research and concentrate research funds in selected areas. The Committee recommended for the following:[29]

(a) to agree an appropriate average level of research activity in universities, each university proposing the level which it wishes to adopt;

(b) to assure adequate support for research by means of an identified proportion of the U.G.C. grant;

(c) to ensure funds intended for research are used for that purpose; and

(d) to ensure that research funds are effectively managed by means of Research Committees (as advocated in the Merrison Report) or equivalent bodies. A need was identified for the provision of extra funds to provide staff time for more industrially oriented work.

Muir Wood Report suggested that action should be taken by DES, UGC, CVCP and other relevant bodies as follows:[30]

(a) the Government should establish an 'industrial seedcorn fund', initially of Pounds 10 m. per annum to support the infrastructure and basic research that will complement effective industrially financed applied research. Higher Education institutions would receive allocations

from the fund equal to 25% of the money they earned through research contracts and consultancies with industry; and

(b) there should be a 'pump-priming fund' of a minimum of Pounds 5 m. per annum from the Department of Industry to give active encouragement to those not yet industrially aware.

Prior to the publication of the Merrison Report, the Leverhulme seminar on Resources and their allocation which was chaired by Sir Kenneth Berril and convened by Alfred Moris and John Sizer had considered the funding of research in the universities and allocation of funds for research purposes within the universities. In particular, the seminar considered whether:

(a) the UGC should continue to provide a single block grant for teaching, scholarship and research;

(b) the UGC should keep a separate grant for research; or

(c) the research money should be given to the research councils with the UGC concentrating open funding, teaching and research scholarship.

The issues debated in the seminar coverd the various divergent views that have been expressed from time to time relating to funding of research. The seminar's general view was against UGC's resources being moved to the Research Councils. It advocated for a separate research grant with guidance to universities on specific plans and proposals.[31]

Turning to the mechanism for allocation of resources within the university, the seminar recommended that there should be a separate research budget in each university and the university should identify its departments and units based on the past performance and future potential and then decide about the internal allocation. Broadly while these recommendations of the seminar are consistent with the Leverhulme research seminar they are an improvement on the Merrison Report.

Jointly, the need for greater allocation for research activities was recognised and it also emerged that more importance should be given to research funding and the procedure should be structured and made known to all concerned. Another aspect for research funding was the selectivity. In his response (dated 1st Sept. 1983) to Sir Edward Parkes' letter dated 26th July, 1983, Sir Keith Joseph, Secretary of State *inter-alia* stated that - "In view of the pressures on public expenditure, greater selectivity in the funding of research activity both within and between institutions might be necessary". Sir Joseph also conveyed in the said letter that:[32]

> "I should in particular, value the Committee's views on the proposition that the contribution through recurrent grant to the dual support system should be based on greater specificity of funding, possibly involving *inter-alia* recognition of institutions' differential success in securing research monies from outside sources, especially from industry and the Research Councils; co-ordination with the Research Councils should perhaps be stepped up, and indeed the Committee might allocate some of the funds at its disposal only after joint consideration with Research Councils of individual institutions' research plans".

In its advice, the UGC proposed "... to develop a more systematic and selective approach to allocation of funds for research. This will not be effective unless the universities make a complimentary effort to develop explicit research strategies..." (para-5.2)[33]. While strongly supporting the need for greater academic and industrial collaboration, the UGC cautioned that "... effective collaboration in applied research must be based on a firm groundwork of basic scientific research" (para-59).

Despite the fact that UGC had endorsed and commended the Merrison Report to the universities, it was unable to implement the Merrison Report's proposal of a long-term objective that a sizeable proportion of funds be diverted into research by the universities, the reason being that it did "... not propose any further shift in the plans of university activity from teaching to research".[34] Reiterating the level funding of recurrent grant it sanctioned for "... a substantial increase in equipment grant if expenditure on research is to grow".[35] It acknowledged its obligation to ensure that the allocations for research were managed to the best advantage and suggested the following general principles, viz.:

"*(i)* The UGC should be more selective in its allocation of research support among universities.

(ii) Each university should know what resources it is devoting to research and the distribution of these resources should be a matter for careful planning.

(iii) Allocation by the UGC and planning by the university should be interactive processes." (para.5.14)

The UGC agreed with the view of the Merrison Committee that "it is the essence of basic scientific reserch that its outcomes are unpredictable and that it frequently flowers in unexpected places. Its finding must therefore provide the necessary degree of flexibility" (para-5.16).

The Secretary of State in his guidance letter dated 30th January, 1985 welcomed the UGC's approach of selectivity in its allocation of research support. Referring to the general claim that the cuts in university budgets had mainly affected on research, the government pointed out that the income from research grants and contracts had nevertheless been rising in real terms in the universities in the past few years. While observing that there was no evidence to accept the argument that all academic staff must engage in research, it agreed to the need to keep up the scholarship. The government also suggested that "... some departments or even whole universities might lose research funding from the UGC. Universities will still have discretion over the funds at their disposal and be able to seek research funds from other sources" (para-5.7). The UGC in its strategy advice mentioned that "we believe that each institution on our list should have a substantial commitment to reserch though not equal in each field and with a change in the balance between fields over time" (para-5.16).

In the higher education policy document of UK "Development of Higher Education into the 1990s", presented to the Parliament in May 1985, it was clearly recognised that "Higher education institutions exist for scholarship and research - in all disciplines - as well as for teaching. The universities have, and will retain the chief role within the higher education in basic or fundamental research and undertake applied research directed towards industry, commerce and public services".[36] "All institutions" the document mentioned "may seek research council money for specific projects".[37] It also clarified again that the "dual support system" to the universities provides an element of research within the block grant made by the UGC.[38]

THE WHITE PAPER ON HIGHER EDUCATION, 1991

In May 1991, the White Paper "Higher Education - A New Framework" was presented to the Parliament which categorically restated that "The quality of research in the United Kingdom has achieved worldwide recognition. The government remains committed to maintaining the international competitive research base through higher education institutions and the research councils".[39] This statement clearly brings out the commitment of the government and therefore its responsibility to provide funds for research. The document also spelt out the different categories of funding of research as stated below:[40]

- basic research - concerned with the advancement of knoweldge;
- strategic research - speculative but with clear potential for application; and
- applied research - directed primarily towards practical aims and objectives.

Having spelt out the categories of funding of research, the document clarified that the following two key policies for the purpose of research in UK, have been "underpinned".[41]

(i) The operation of the "dual support"; and

(ii) The selective allocation of funds by reference to assessment of quality.

Until the year 1991-92, the Research Council grants covered not all, but only certain additional costs of the projects submitted by the universities while some costs were made by the universities which led to some confusion as regards the "boundary between those costs". In order to solve the problem and also to improve accountability, the document provides new arrangements from 1992-93. It is stated in the document that the Research Council "... will become responsible for meeting of the costs of their projects except for academic salaries and premises which will continue to be made from institution's general funds".[42]

Under the title "The Way Forward", the White Paper stated the following principle for public funding of research in higher education, viz.:

- Plurality: there should be two channels of public funding for research:

  general funds, to be used at institutions' discretion; and funds tied to specific projects.
- Competition: to promote further the most effective use of resources within higher education, all institutions should be able to compete for research funds.
- Selectivity: research funds should be distributed selectively, as now, on the basis of assessment of reserch quality. This will continue to reward quality, encourage innovation and make the best use of scarce resource.
- Accountability: the principle of accountability must apply to all higher education institutions receiving general research funding, in the same way as for other bodies receiving substantial public funds. The Government is determined to ensure greater transparency in the planning and use of general research funds, as well as clearer funding arrangements for Research Council Projects.[43]

To achieve these objectives, new mechanisms will be required for distributing the general research funds which are now distributed through the UFC. This could be done by either:

- funding teaching and research separately, with general research funding routed either through the existing Research Councils, or through a new research funding agency building on the existing Advisory Board for the Research Councils (ABRC) arrangements; or
- a single channel - on the lines of the UFC - for the general funding of research alongside funding for teaching.[44]

One of the main reasons of criticism of the "dual support system" was that the allocation of grants to the universities was related to the student numbers and in the case of a department having smaller number of students, but stronger research track record and potential, was suffering from the formula. In order to avoid the negative part of this, the policy document declared that, "The element of research funding currently allocated by reference to student numbers will need to be phased out".[45] It also said that "The Government does not expect there to be an abrupt change in the broad research missions of present universities, polytechnics and colleges, and it wishes to see continuing emphasis on applied and strategic research. It accepts, however, that the location of high-quality basic research will evolve and need to be reflected in the distribution of general funds for research".[46]

SELECTIVITY - MERITS AND DEMERITS

For obvious reasons, funds are always limited for research activities as are they for other sectors or areas. In situation where part of the Block Grant was to be used for research activities, there could not be any option but to be selective. Even otherwise, utmost care should be taken to utilise the public money for any purpose, more particularly the purposes which are uncertain as regards the return from the investments. Research is navigation in an unknown area which basically begins with hopes but not infrequently ends with partial success or disappointments. The element of 'risk' is mostly involved in research activities. These arguments precisely make the selectivity the right appearance for research funding.

In his speech to CVCP (on 29.9.1991), the Education Secretary, Sir Kenneth Clarke, while emphasising on the imperative need of increasing efficiency in the university system held that the increased selectivity and concentration of funding, "... should lead to still more effective use of the public funds available for research. As part of the greater selectivity, universities may need to make increasing use of teaching only contracts in some departments while building up the research capability in others".

While selectivity cannot be avoided, evolving of a smooth mechanism to be selective, poses perennial problem. However, '... practices for allocating research resources selectively, particularly within departments'[47] is considered to be better developed than the departmental research plans. The UGC Report (1988) held that on the whole since 1985, there was considerable progress in research planning and selective use of resources for research and that further development was expected in this direction". Prof. Sizer observed that "However in many institutions selectivity within departments and subject areas did not appear to have been fully integrated into mechanisms which brought planning, resource allocation and accountability into one linking academic, financial and physical aspects with the objective of ensuring the economical, efficient and effective use of resources devoted to research".[48]

Contrary to the general belief that only larger investments are capable to contribute to quality research, evidences show that not only such impression is illusive, even lower investments also can show high quality research results. Undeniably, however, there are instances that larger investments also have shown quality results. Really speaking, there cannot be any definite norm in this regard. For quality research, quite a few factors are involved, eg. committed high level of academics, the time that they can devote for research, physical facilities, conducive environment for carrying out research activities etc.

While resources are essential prerequisites for carrying out research, they are not everything. In his foreword to the book "fundamental research and the universities", Dr. Alexander King, Director for Scientific Affairs, OECD (1968) observed that "... the provision of greater financial resources for fundamental research will not by itself guarantee that Europe regains and maintains its place in international competition: most of the obstacles are structural and not financial". Even "A low level of research income does not necessarily mean a low level (or low quality) of research".[49]

The Research performance ratings of the universities calculated from the UFC's 1989 research ratings of each cost centre were as shown in the Table 4.7.

Table 4.7[50]

University	*Average research ratings*	*Weighted average research ratings*
1	2	3
Aston	2.6	2.5
Bath	2.8	2.9
Birmingham	3.1	3.3
Bradford	2.4	2.6
Bristol	3.8	3.8
Brunel	2.1	2.3
Cambridge	4.7	4.8
City	2.0	2.1
Durham	3.2	3.2
East Anglia	3.1	3.3
Essex	3.4	3.7
Exeter	2.9	3.1
Hull	2.5	2.7
Keele	2.0	2.1
Kent	2.7	2.9
Lancaster	3.2	3.3
Leeds	3.1	3.1
Leicester	2.8	2.9
Liverpool	3.3	3.2
London	3.5	3.4
Loughborough	2.6	2.7
Manchester	3.6	3.6
UMIST	3.7	3.7
Newcastle	3.1	3.5
Nottingham	3.1	3.4

1	2	3
Oxford	4.6	4.8
Reading	2.9	2.9
Salford	2.0	2.2
Sheffield	3.2	3.3
Southampton	3.3	3.7
Surrey	3.0	3.3
Sussex	3.4	3.4
Warwick	4.1	4.2
York	3.7	3.8
Aberdeen	2.7	2.8
Dundee	2.5	2.7
Edinburgh	3.3	3.3
Glasgow	2.9	3.3
Heriot-Watt	2.3	2.3
St. Andrews	2.9	3.1
Stirling	2.2	2.4
Strathclyde	2.4	2.9
Queen's	2.3	2.6
Ulster	2.1	2.2
Wales	2.8	2.7

SPENDING AND RANKING RELATIONSHIP

In order to find out the relationship of investments in research and the rankings, statistics of a number of universities showing their research spendings and rankings have been shown in the Appendix-1 for the years 1986-87, 1987-88 and 1988-89.[51] The statistics in the appendix are given for the following Cost Centres in a representative manner:

(i) Biological Sciences

(ii) Chemistry

(iii) Computer Science

(iv) Engineering

(v) Other Social Studies

(vi) Business Management Studies

(vii) Humanities

An analysis of the data of the seven Cost-centres in U.K. for the years 1986-87, 1987-88 and 1988-89 reveals mixed results. Within the same Cost-centre, it is found that there are examples of all types.

In Biological Sciences, Oxford spent £K 2422 in 1986-87 securing a research rank of 8; next year (1987-88), it spent £K 2912 and secured a better rank of 6 and in 1988-89, it spent the highest in these three years £K 3522 and also secured the best ranking of 3. But Surrey, with lesser investment of £K 1916 in 1986-87, it secured the 'first' rank in research in the same cost-centre area. In the next two years also, it kept up its level of "number one" when again its spendings were less than that of Oxford. In Biological Sciences, the same way, the performances of the Warwick, Dundee and Stirling were better than Oxford with lower investments.

In 1988-89, between Kent and Leicester, it was found that the former secured lower rating 6 with lower investment of £K 410 while the latter with higher investment of £K 1879 secured second position.

In Chemistry, UMIST spent £K 1283 in 1986-87 and secured the research rank 'one' while London University with more than double spending £K 2738 secured a much lower ranking 19. Similar trend continued between these two institutions in the next years too (1987-88 and 1988-89). In these two years, the UMIST spent £K 1401 and £K 1632 securing the ranks of '2' and '3' respectively while the London University spent K 3025 and £K 3827 and secured rankings '19' and '14' respectively. Southampton's spending was close to those of UMIST and it secured rankings not much lower than UMIST.

Another example of lowest spending and lowest ranking is the Sheffield University out of the seventeen universities for the Chemistry Cost Centre in the Appendix. Sheffield spent the lowest £K 254, £K 296 and £K 440 during 1986-87, 1987-88 and 1988-89 with research ratings of 38, 43 and 35 respectively which are lowest out of the seventeen universities in the Appendix, except Birmingham for 1988-89 which ranks only two points lower than Sheffield in that year.

In Computer Science, Heriot-Watt spent only £K 820, £K 644 and £K 356 in 1986-87, 1987-88 and 1988-89 and secured ranking '1' and '2' and '15' respectively. As against this, the London University spent £K 2962 £K 3560 and £K 4286 in 1986-87, 1987-88 and 1988-89 respectively, but secured the rankings of 11, 7 and '7' respectively. The Edinburgh University, however, secured better rankings with lesser investments. It spent £K 2201, £K 1629 and £K 2223 during the aforesaid years and earned the rankings of '1', '2' and '1' respectively. Reading with one of the lowest spendings £K 399, £K 607 and £K 453 in each of the three years secured research ranking 3, 1 and 2.

In the Engineering Cost-Centre, the cases of the London University and the University of Warwick are noticeable. Of the eighteen universities in the Appendix, the London University spent highest in all the three years under reference - £K 15610, £K 15280 and £K 16989 but the research ratings earned by it were '4', '3' and '3' respectively while the University of Warwick with lesser spendings in all these years £ K 3634, £K 3986 and £K 4782, it earned the 'first' rank. Southampton also secured better or close rankings to Oxford while it spent about one-third of the spending of Oxford. Even the University of Edinburgh spending only £K 1536, £K 2840 and £K 2308, earned better ratings than others particularly during 1987-88 and 1988-89. This again is the repetition of the trend mentioned earlier.

In the Cost-centre 'Other Social Studies', generally higher research ranking is found in the case of the universities which spent highest among the universities in the Appendix as shown in the table-4.8.

Table 4.8

University	*Year*	*Spending Pounds K*	*Research Ranking*
1. Birmingham	1986-87	3963	1
	1987-88	4329	1
	1988-89	4867	1
2. Brunel	1986-87	1533	2
	1987-88	1513	2
	1988-89	1540	2
3. Sussex	1986-87	1533	3
	1987-88	1836	3
	1988-89	1899	4
4. York	1986-87	1442	4
	1987-88	1421	4
	1988-89	2247	3
5. Oxford	1986-87	1551	14
	1987-88	2083	10
	1988-89	1977	13

Of the universities of the study included in the Appendix for the Cost Centre, 'Other Social Studies', the five universities mentioned below spent the highest. Excepting the University of Oxford, all the five secured highest research rankings in all the three years.

With a much lower investments, two universities, namely the University of Heriot-Watt and the University of Bangor secured relatively higher rankings as compared to other Universities. The University of Heriot-Watt spent £K 275, £K 296 and £K 282 and secured the rank of 6 in each of the three years while the University of Bangor spent £K 396 and £K 492 and secured the rank 7 in the first two years (1986-87 and 1987-88) and the rank 9 in 1988-89, the spending for that year was £K 492 and £K 525.

The Cost Centre 'Business Management Studies' also does not present any different picture. Oxford with the second lowest investment of £K 207 in 1986-87, £K 184 lowest in 1987-88 and £K 217 in 1988-89 again with second lowest investment secured high rankings of '2', '1' and '2' respectively. The highest spending was of Warwick £K 2100, £K 3397 pounds and £K 4971 securing the ranking 5, 3 and 3 in 1986-87, 1987-88 and 1988-89 respectively.

In the case of cost-centre 'Humanities', the spendings were all in three digit except the London University which having spent highest among the fourteen universities of the Appendix, £K 1040, £K 1357 and £K 1763, secured the ranks of 4, 3 and 3 in 1986-87, 1987-88 and 1988-89 respectively. New Castle, one of lowest spenders, secured the rankings 1 in 1986-87 and 1987-88 when its spendings were £K 190 and £K 183 only. In 1988-89, it spent £K 127 and secured 6 rank.

From these analyses, it is clear that it is not just

finance but other factors too that are responsible to show quality research.

The following figure-4.3 provides an indication of the trends in overall government funding of academic and academic related research (1975-87) in U.K. and some other countries.

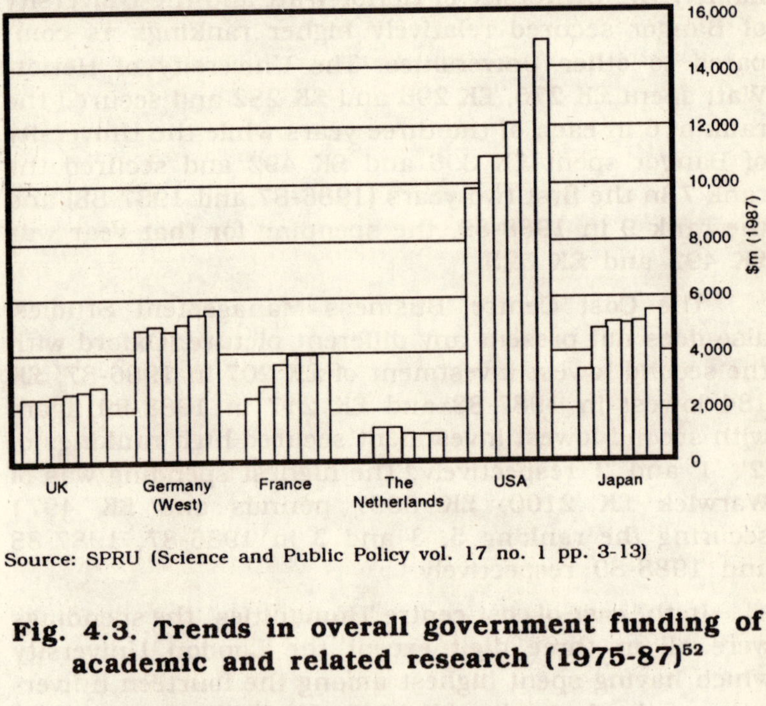

Source: SPRU (Science and Public Policy vol. 17 no. 1 pp. 3-13)

Fig. 4.3. Trends in overall government funding of academic and related research (1975-87)[52]

ASSESSMENT AT NATIONAL LEVEL

Primarily aiming at quality research, smooth funding has been a matter of concern. Various related issues have been debated and deliberated in the Universities and at different forums throughout the Great Britain. The White Paper on Education (1991) reiterated that "the Government remains committed to maintaining an internationally competitive research base through higher education/institutions and the reserch councils". Although the White Paper maintained that "the quality of research in United Kingdom has achieved world-wide recognition", the CVCP expressed its worry that "Britain, once pre-eminent after America for true research, has now fallen behind Japan and other competing nations are catching up".[53] The following figure-4.4 reflects the simmering worry of the CVCP.

Fig. 4.4 National Shares of World Publications 1986 (Pure Science)

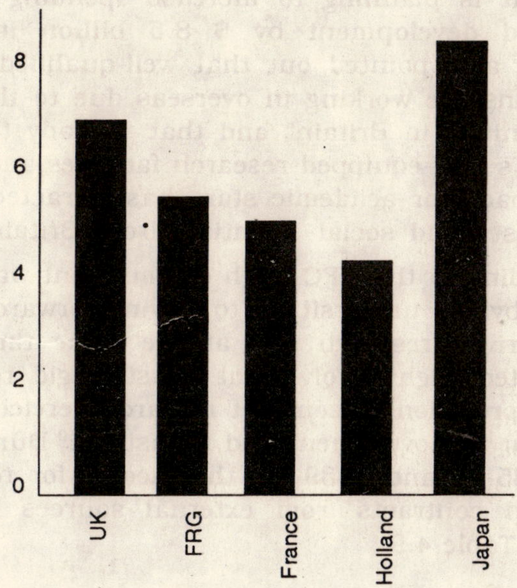

***Source:* CHI/NSF Science Learner Indictors USA not included**

For the world class research, the CVCP observed that "UK Universities must be able to compete internationally".[55] It however, realized that adequate opportunities are but prerequisites to creating excellence in research. Referring to 1980's, when expensive research was concentrated in fewer universities, so that some definite quality research is assured, the CVCP mentioned that "Discussion, designed to increase this concentration, are now going on between the Government, the Funding Council and the Research Councils".[56] It also stated that "The development of world class centres of excellence is supported by the universities but not if it is just a way of making so on too little money".[57] Acknowledging the world class research of USA, the CVCP pointed out that "The United States Federal Government is planning to increase spending on research and development by $ 8.5 billion in 1991 alone".[58] It also pointed out that well-qualified young academicians are working in overseas due to the 'lack of opportunities in Britain" and that 'Already the lure of America's well-equipped research facilities and small teaching loads for academic stars has attracted many top scientists and social scientists from Britain".

According to the UFC, high commitment was demonstrated by the universities "to driving forward basic, curiosity-driven research and at the same time they demonstrated high involvement in strategic research and their provision of contract research services (mission-driven) to Government and industry".[59] During the period 1985-86 and 1989-90, the income for research grants and contracts from external sources was as shown in Table-4.9.

Table 4.9[60]

(Million Pounds)

1985-86	535	100%
1986-87	607	114%
1987-88	604	113%
1988-89	673	126%
1989-90	762	143%

In 1989-90, the figures of the external research income including those from the Research Councils were as shown in the Table-4.10.

Table-4.10[61]

(Million Pounds)

Research Councils	265
UK based Charitable Trusts	156
UK Government Departments	106
UK Local Authorities	4
UK Public Corporations	9
UK Industry and Commerce	96
UK Health/Hospital Authorities	14
European Community Grants	38
Other Overseas	43
Other sources	31
Total External Research Income	762

Out of the above income, it is interesting that 75% of the external research income were achieved by the eighteen universities of the fifty one in the United Kingdom during the aforesaid period.

For the third research assessment exercise that the

UFC conducted in 1992-93 which was open to all UK higher education institutions, to decide new research ratings, the University Funding Council has laid down Rules as shown in the Appendix-II[62] which is "... to comply with the stipulation by the Secretary of State that new assessments should be available to contribute the allocation procedures for 1993-94".[63]

CONCLUSION

The importance of Research and the need of funding therefor, needs no justification. In fact, it is the level of the research activity that a University is known for. It is true that teaching is the basic function of any university which, in a way, is a 'taken for granted' activity. Therefore, even when quality teaching is done, it does not arouse that much excitement in the academic world as would a new research result do.

The deliberations that took place in different forums and at various levels in the government, UGC and in the university system itself confirm the concern for, and the importance of, research and so, the need of funding the same. For a variety of reasons, 'selectivity' is necessary. It is not only due to the constraint of funds, but in order to promote only deserving research projects and serious researchers that 'selectivity' is a *sine-qua-non*. There should always be built-in flexibility in the total mechanism so that the procedures of 'selectivity' may not deprive the academic world from a possible high quality research activity. The decision to phase out the linking of the student number is certainly a good and welcoming step.

The dynamism of the university system is bound to come out with better norms to promote research for there is a real concern to excel in research at the national and international level.

As a result of the further and Higher Education Act, 1992 it will be the responsibility of the Research Councils to provide for all the costs of approved research projects except for the salaries of permanent academic staff and general premises costs. Out of the UFC's block grants, some money would, for this purpose, be transferred to the Research Councils from 1992-93 onwards which ultimately will, through the procedure of competitions, find their ways back to the universities.

Appendix-I

RESEARCH EXPENDITURE AND RANKINGS[64]

University	*Expenditure and Ranking*					
	1986-87		*1987-88*		*1988-89*	
	K Exp.	*Ranking*	*K Exp.*	*Ranking*	*K Exp.*	*Ranking*
I. Cost Centre (Biological Scs.)						
1. Birmingham	1030	15	1020	20	1013	25.5
2. Cambridge	1986	11	2341	11	3410	11
3. Kent	263	4	598	2	410	6
4. Leicester	1289	3	1429	4	1879	2
5. London	5151	14	5639	15	7470	14
6. Oxford	2422	8	2912	6	3522	3
7. Surrey	1916	1	2299	1	2799	1
8. Warwick	1750	2	2026	3	1776	4
9. Dundee	619	9	818	8	857	8
10. Edinburgh	2604	6	2851	7	3214	7
11. Stirling	1136	5	1513	5	1788	5

II. Cost Centre (Chemistry)

1. Birmingham	324	37	571	3.6	541	37
2. Bristol	1014	14	1092	11	1285	15
3. Cambridge	960	13	1041	14	2019	6
4. Leeds	768	26	1094	13	1289	17
5. Liverpool	505	21	652	15.5	5801	12
6. London	2738	19	3025	19	3827	14
7. UMIST	1283	1	1401	2	1632	3
8. Oxford	1632	7	1607	10	3399	1
9. Salford	587	22	484	32	205	44
10. Sheffield	254	38	296	43	440	35
11. Sussex	559	18	528	26	756	16
12. Southampton	1207	2	1238	5	1391	5
13. Warwick	402	17	777	4	505	21
14. York	706	4	823	3	966	7
15. Aberystwyth	102	34	147	35	-	-
16. Aberdeen	344	32	370	33	500	26.5
17. Edinburgh	792	11	682	24	1385	9
18. St. Andrews	443	5	307	25	670	10

III. Cost Centre (Computer Science)

1. Aston	75	36	154	32.5	62	44
2. Bristol	20	10	67	35	238	18
3. Cambridge	494	10	474	13	348	16
4. Leicester	487	9	229	21	217	26
5. Leeds	76	34	129	39	177	39
6. London	2962	11	3560	7	4286	7
7. UMIST	587	14	365	22.5	740	12
8. Oxford	631	6	541	8	574	10
9. Sussex	469	8	478	5	422	14
10. Warwick	196	23	233	19	319	17
11. York	805	4	368	15	240	32
12. Aberystwyth	209	19	358	4	353	5
13. Swansea	25	40	79	40	159	33
14. Edinburgh	2201	1	1629	2	2223	1

15. Glasgow	189	28	295	22.5	378	22
16. Heriot-Watt	820	1	644	2	356	15
17. Reading	399	3	607	1	453	2
IV. Cost Centre (Engineering)						
1. Birmingham	2232	31	4144	10	4423	12
2. Bradford	1386	38	1391	37	1657	37
3. Bristol	1337	20	1578	15	2365	8
4. Brunel	2078	14	1969	14	2314	13
5. Cambridge	3316	15	3690	12	3148	25
6. Essex	947	4	1009	46	868	11
7. Leeds	3117	19	3433	30	3439	23
8. London	15610	4	15280	3	16989	3
9. Manchester	2095	17	1818	26	1555	36
10. UMIST	4817	8	3570	17	4203	18
11. Oxford	2600	5	2942	4	3150	5
12. Salford	1757	31	1392	38	1995	34.5
13. Sheffield	2525	19	3336	9	3670	9
14. Warwick	3634	1	3986	1	4782	1
15. Edinburgh	1536	13	2840	3	2308	7
16. Glasgow	1527	22	1834	21	2889	45
17. Heriot-Watt	2581	12	3054	8	4179	4
18. Southampton	4715	2	5009	5	5173	6
V. Cost Centre (other Social Studies)						
1. Bath	775	5	844	5	686	11
2. Birmingham	3963	1	4329	1	4867	1
3. Brunel	1533	2	1513	2	1540	2
4. Cambridge	939	12	824	16	852	24
5. Essex	251	31	289	32.5	434	31
6. Exeter	185	34	277	32.5	511	28.5
7. Lancaster	340	29	348	29	294	36
8. Leeds	499	22	539	22	639	33
9. Oxford	1551	14	2083	10	1977	13
10. Sussex	1533	3	1836	3	1899	4

11. Warwick	997	8	1059	11	1289	12
12. York	1442	4	1421	4	2247	3
13. Aberystwyth	23	40	17	46	54	44
14. Bangor	396	7	492	7	525	9
15. Edinburgh	636	20	750	17	992	16
16. Glasgow	748	17	734	19	1130	14
17. Heriot-Watt	275	6	296	6	282	6
VI. Cost Centre (Business Management Studies)						
1. Bradford	1373	9	1529	8	2239	9
2. City	2037	6	2642	5	2844	8
3. Durham	787	1	1653	9	1792	1
4. Oxford	207	2	184	1	217	2
5. Warwick	2100	5	3397	3	4971	3
6. Edinburgh	233	14	291	16	405	13
7. Glasgow	531	8	778	6	512	10
8. Heriot-Watt	173	13	191	9.6	167	22
9. Stirling	838	7	1047		1418	7
VII. Cost Centre (Humanities)						
1. Birmingham	348	2	366	2	417	1
2. Bristol	20	22	16	34	69	24
3. Cambridge	317	7	438	9	557	4
4. Leicester	104	8	80	15	118	12
5. London	1040	4	1357	3	1763	3
6. New Castle	190	1	183	1	127	6
7. Warwick	50	19	81	23	55	28.5
8. York	27	20	152	7	138	9
9. Cardiff	138	4	133	4	62	18.5
10. Edinburgh	69	21	49	30.5	57	31
11. Glasgow	104	14	96	22	180	15
12. St. Andrews	131	10	170	12	150	18.5

Appendix-II

THE NEW RESEARCH ASSESSMENT EXERCISE

Coverage

1.1 What research to assess - In assessing the quality of research being carried out, it is necessary to take into account the full range of research - basic, strategic and applied. (Appropriate definitions and guidance to follow to assessment panels). It is proposed that the panels should take into account both publicly-funded and other commissioned research but only research the outcome of which is available to those conducting the assessment.

1.2 Whether to exclude some departments from assessment - All areas of the academic arena must be eligible to participate in the exercise. However, it will be open to institutions to decide that they do not wish one or more academic units to be considered. The possibility of identifying qualifying thresholds is also being examined. These would help to make exercise manageable.

The method of Assessment

2.1 The UFC has resolved to continue to make use of peer review. It considered the use of objectively verifiable criteria but accepted that there were no agreed criteria which are sufficiently well established to be used as a major determinant in distributing resources. However, institutions will be asked to provide relevant objective data which can have a clear bearing on the judgements to be made (see below).

Definition of Quality

3.1 In the 1989 exercise, quality was not defined, other than through the definition of the rating scale, since it was assumed that the assessment panels would recognise quality when they saw it. This enabled each panel to give the relative weight it thought fit to each of the elements within its overall assessment. It is likely that the guidance will be more specific for the new exercise.

Composition of Assessment Panels

4.1 It is proposed that each subject unit should be assessed by a panel with appropriate specialist membership. The assessment panels will again consist largely of people with recent experience of academic work including research in the area to be assessed - drawn from both current sectors of higher education. They should also include, where appropriate, people not currently employed in higher education but with a valuable contribution to make. Advice will be sought on panel memberships from a wide range of sources - academic institutions, research councils and other funding bodies, professional groups, subject associations, etc.

Research Ratings

5.1 In both 1986 and 1989, the exercise yielded comparative quality judgements on a scale from 5 (high) to 1 (low). It is expected that these ratings will be used for the 1992 exercise.

Rating 5

Research quality that equates to attainable levels of international excellence in sub-areas of activity and to attainable levels of national excellence in virtually all others.

Rating 4

Research quality that equates to attainable levels of national excellence in virtually all sub-areas of activity, showing some evidence of international excellence.

Rating 3

Research quality that equates to attainable levels of national excellence in a majority of the sub-areas of activity, or to international level in some.

Rating 3

Research quality that equates to attainable levels of national excellence in a majority of the sub-areas of activity, or to international level in some.

Rating 2

Research quality that equates to attainable levels of national excellence in upto half of the sub-areas of activity.

Rating 1

Research quality that equates to attainable levels of national excellence in none, or virtually none, of the subareas of activity.

Currently a rating of 1 attracts limited JR funding. This position is under scrutiny by the Council and it is likely that there will be a move in the direction of greater selectivity.

Assuring Commonality of Approach

6.1 The assessments made must reflect as far as possible the specific characteristics of each subject area but at the same time the ratings determined must mean the same across all subjects. The assessment panels will be required to work to the same broad criteria, to consider the same basic questions and to consider identically specified data sets.

References

1. Caty A., University and Research in a Teaching Oriented Environment. *In The Research System*, V. II. Belgium, Netherlands, Norway, Sweeden, Switzerland, London, OECD, 1973, p. 68.
2. U.K., Committee on Higher Education, Report (Robbins Report), London, HMSO, 1963, p. 181.
3. *Ibid.*, p. 183.
4. *Op. Cit.*, p. 181.
5. *Op. Cit.*, p.183.
6. *Ibid.*
7. Higher Education: A New Framework. Paper presented to Parliament in May 1991, London; HMSO, pp. 16-17.
8. Jill, John and Taylor, Jim, Performance Indicators in Higher Education, UK Universities, London, SRHE and Open University, 1990, p. 147.
9. *Ibid.*
10. *Op. Cit.*, p. 147.
11. Higher Education: A New Framework. Paper presented to Parliament in May 1991, London, HMSO, pp. 16-17.
12. *Op. Cit.*
13. *Op. Cit.*, p. 17.
14. *Ibid.*
15. Report of the Steering Committee for Efficiency Studies in Universities, CVCP, March 1985 (Jarratt Report), p. 15.
16. U.K., University Management Statistics and Performance Indicators in the U.K., London, CVCP and UFC, 1990, Edn., p. 185.
17. U.K., Higher Education in Britain, The Universities: Information Pack, London, CVCP and British Council, 1991.

18. Jill, John and Taylor, Jim, Performance Indicators in Higher Education, UK Universities, London, SRHE and Open University, 1990, p. 163.

19. U.K., Higher Education in Britain, The Universities: Information Pack, London, CVCP and British Council, 1991.

20. Wilkie, Tom, The Thatcher Effect in Science *In The Thatcher Effect*, ed. by Dennis Kavanagh and Anthony Seldon, Oxford, Clarendon Press, 1989, p. 318.

21. U.K., Department of Education and Science, Institutional responses to financial reductions in the university sector, John Sizer (1987) Background Paper No. 1, pp. 41-42 (unpublished).

22. *Ibid.*, p. 42.

23. The Association of Commonwealth Universities; What can we do for our Countries?; the Contribution of Universities in National Development, the Report of Proceedings of 14th Congress at Perth, Feb. 1988, p.112.

24. U.K., Department of Education and Science, Institutional Responses to Financial Reductions in the University Sector, John Sizer (1987) Background Paper No. 1, p. 15 (unpublished).

25. *Op. Cit.*, p. 37.

26. *Op. Cit.*, Background Paper No. 3, pp. 35-36.

27. *Op. Cit.*, p. 36.

28. *Op. Cit.*, p. 37.

29. *Op. Cit.*, p. 38.

30. *Op. Cit.*, Background Paper No. 3, p. 23.

31. *Op. Cit.*, p. 39

32. *Op. Cit.*, p. 39.

33. *Op. Cit.*, p. 39.

34. *Op. Cit.*, pp. 39-40.

35. *Ibid.*
36. U.K., The Development of Higher Education into 1990s, Report submitted to Parliament in May 1985 by the Secretary of State for Education and Science, the Secretary of State for Scotland, the Secretary of State for Wales and the Secretary of State for Northern Ireland, London, HMSO, 1985, p. 20.
37. *Ibid.*, p. 20.
38. *Op. Cit.*, pp. 20.
39. Higher Education: A New Framework. Paper presented to Parliament in May, 1991, London, HMSO, pp. 16-17.
40. *Ibid.*
41. *Op. Cit.*, p. 16.
42. *Op. Cit.*, p. 17.
43. *Op. Cit.*, p. 18
44. *Op. Cit.*, p. 19.
45. *Op. Cit.*, p. 20.
46. *Ibid.*
47. The Role of the Funding Councils and Performance Indicators in Quality Assessment in the United Kingdom. Lecture delivered at the Centre for Higher Education Policy Studies, The Netherlands, John Sizer (1990), p. 12.
48. *Ibid.*
49. U.K., University Management Statistics and Performance Indicators in the U.K., 1990, CVCP and University Funding Council, London, p. 162.
50. Jill John and Taylor, Jim, Performance Indicators in Higher Education, UK Universities, London, SRHE and Open University, 1990, p. 162.
51. The University of Warwick, Academic Database 1990/91, incorporating statement of student statistics, Nov. 1990, pp. 160-181.

52. U.K., Higher Education in Britain, The Universities, information Pack, British Council and CVCP, London, August, 1991.
53. U.K., The State of the Universities, CVCP, London, 1991.
54. *Ibid.*
55. *Op. Cit.*, p. 8.
56. *Op. Cit.*
57. *Op. Cit.*, p. 8.
58. *Op. Cit.*
59. Davis, Graeme, "UFC: Present and Future Policies", Lecture at Residential Meeting of the Committee of Vice Chancellors and Principals, Warwick, 1991, p. 4.
60. *Ibid.*, p. 5.
61. *Op. Cit.*, p. 5.
62. *Op. Cit.*, pp. 7-9.
63. *Op. Cit.*, p. 6.

5

Realities, Challenges and Changing Structures

THE TEMPEST

The cuts which came to the universities as a violent storm shocked the entire university system. The high selectivity employed by the UGC in the application of cuts in grants and the size of the student population as also the subject-mix additionally disturbed the universities in general after which they were left with no alternative but to face the harsh realities and meet the challenges.

Precisely, the universities in general felt that they were cought unaware not knowing how to go about to meet the challenges. What was the preparation of the nine universities of the DES Research Project on the 1st July, 1981 is summarised and given in the Appendix-1.[1] These nine universities have been categorised in the Appendix-2[2] to show the different treatment they received following the UGC letter dated the 1st July, 1981. The categories are three-relatively well treated, middle range and relatively harsh.

It was only the University of Bath which was treated relatively well. Three universities namely, Sheffield, Sussex and Heriot-Watt came under the second category of middle range treatment. Rest of the universities of the group of nine, i.e. Aberdeen, Hull, Stirling, Aston and Salford were treated relatively harsh.

It was true that the universities had prior indications of difficult days, but the intensity of that was not clear to them as a result of which the shock that finally came was nothing less than a 'trauma'. How the shock was felt, how the same was absorbed with or without casualty and how the challenges were met will be discussed. Successes or failures of the universities both in respect of contingency plans as also in tackling the shock and how have they performed also need discussion and analyses.

What role the government and the UGC played before and after the disastrous 1st July, 1981 letter of the Committee will also be discussed. The role of the Committee of Vice-Chancellors and Principals (CVCP) also assumes importance.

The financial reductions imposed on the universities had evoked widespread reactions in the academic world which seriously felt concerned about the future of the universities. Tracing the reasons for the cuts by the government, the Editorial of the Higher Education Review[3] observed that "The crisis has arisen from the combined effect of the decleration of growth of numbers, widespread disillusion with higher education, loss of income caused by increases in overseas student fees and most importantly from the Governments rigid monetarist policy wnich had led to severe cuts in higher education in real terms". Apart from the problems of the cuts, the Editorial also observed that "For decades, they (universities) were able to plan their development for upto five years ahead under the quinquennial system. Now according to one Vice-Chancellor, they can see no further ahead than eight months".[4] This, it commented

"... prevents from intelligent planning, promotes wastes and constrains academic development."[5] Of the nine universities included in the DES Research Project, it revealed through the case writers that to the University of Stirling, it was nothing less than a shock for the cut imposed on it was 27% and the student numbers - both home and overseas were reduced pushing the university almost to the wall. The university found the cuts beyond any estimation of the dialogue meetings.

Perplexed by the precarious situation, the universities released a Press Note highlightling the intensity of the problem and the difficulties to run the university. This indicated that the university was in deep problem not knowing how to get out of it. The Principal (Vice-Chancellor) therefore addressed a letter to the UGC on the 2nd July itself expressing the serious difficulties of the university and sought for a meeting with it.

The highest cut was in the case of the University of Salford, slashing by 44% of its recurrent grant. This created disquiet in the university against the criteria and methodology employed by the UGC in deciding the cuts in grants and student numbers. Suddenly, the atmosphere of the university changed.

Since the cuts of grants and student numbers varied from university to university making them highly selective, while all the universities felt disturbed, because of 'selectivity', the degree of disturbance was not the same everywhere.

IN RETROSPECT

For a systematic study and analysis, it is necessary to discuss the policy followed and the role played by the following:

(i) Public Funding for Higher education and the role of the Conservative Government in general and the DES in particular for university system.

(ii) Role of the UGC as the buffer body - its accountability to the Government and its obligations to the university system and finally the wisdom of 'selectivity'.

(iii) The Role played by the Committee of Vice-Chancellors and Principals (CVCP) particularly before and after the 1st July, 1981 letter of UGC.

(iv) Performance of the universities before and after the UGC letter dated the 1st July, 1981 including the role played by the Vice-Chancellors as Leaders of the system.

PUBLIC FUNDING FOR HIGHER EDUCATION

Admittedly, education is not simply a welfare subject but an important investment in building, reshaping and bringing prosperity to the society through a variety of ways. The role of the universities and higher education institutions in achieving these, need hardly be debated. In a structure where the government decides either directly or through a buffer body like UGC to give directions to the universities and have the in-built responsibilities to fund the university education, what kind of role it should play does not need arguments.

During the period 1889 to 1919, payment of grants to the universities was not related to student numbers whether current or future. Although the Parliamentary grants accounted for between 20-25% of the income of the Universities, income from fees alone paid by the students without support from Local Authority or grant was between 25-30%. Income from endowments, donations, etc. was around 15-20%.[6] A sizeable part of about 40-45% was always the major source of income from Local Authorities, subscriptions, rents etc. As days went by and UGC became more structured, new norms were brought into practice. The expansion of university system during the 1960s speak about the liberal investments of the government in university education. During the 1970s also in the first-half, universities were funded relatively well. It is only during the later-half of 1970s that indications of difficult days were seen.

Public expenditure all over the world and also in UK was under great pressure for the demand was increasing in all sectors including education. Arguably the heavy investments in university education did not pay the dividend to the society. However, this is debatable for there are no norms for investments in education so as to establish that the 'X' investment has to return 'Y'.

How did the Robbins Committee consider investments in higher education? Projecting the cost of expansion that the committee suggested and giving an estimate of the public expenditure involvement from 1963-64 to 1980-81, it itself asked the question "can the country afford them? Can it afford the still bigger sum representing not only the cost to the public purse, but also the other sacrifices involved by devoting resources to higher education on this scale, rather than to other purposes?".[7] The Robbins Committee addressed not only the fundamental issue for investments in higher education but demonstrated its vision when it pointed out that - "To devote resources to the training of young people may be, au fond, as much entitled to be considered a process of investment as devoting resources to directly productive capital goods. Judged solely by the test of future productivity, a community that neglects education is as imprudent as a community that neglects material accumulation".[8] According to the Robbins Report, "... there is no means of measuring the rate of return ..."[9] It also observed that "The return on education even if it be considered solely in terms of productivity, is not something that can be estimated completely in terms of the return to individuals and of differential earnings".[10] To those who tend to measure the return from investments in earnings differentials, the Robbins Report very rightly pointed out that, "There is a further return in the shape of general adaptibility and increased capacity for technological advance which "... is probably more important than what is measured within the system of relative prices".[11]

While holding these views on the investments on higher education and how they should be looked at, the Robbins Committee did not ignore the commercial aspect. It clarified that "... we do not mean to argue that the commercial return never has relevance to any possible argument".[12] It added that "All that we are contending here is that a solution of the problem of allocating resources should not be sought on the basis of narrow notions of the nature of the economic return and of measurements which, if they are comparatively easy to make, omit elements of fundamental value".[13]

Although education is also a welfare sector, in reality, it is a long term investment for without it being strong including research activities, it is not possible to ensure that the other sectors are strong. For example, agriculture, transport, communications and health, are those sectors, which need trained man power supply from the university system. It is also not possible to build a viable economy without improved technology and research contributions. In view of this, while by a general unexplainable impression, one can comment that there is no commensurate return from the investments in university education, it is difficult to prove that statement, as there are no acceptable and definite instruments to measure the return. Yet it is possible to say that the return is visible for it is due to the return of the university education that the complex advanced and fast growing society could sustain itself.

Gone are the days when the need of higher education was felt to inject more intellect and better culture in the individuals and was limited to elites. Higher education was not considered essential either for survival or success in the career of the individual, not to talk of the nation. Gradually of course, it was realized that in order to meet new challenges and to lead the society to better quality of life, higher education was necessary. In course of time, impact of research in science and technology enhanced the utility of higher education. Countries possessing better technology have had edge over others both in war and peace.

What would have happened to the bulging population of the world if higher education had not made its contribution for higher production of food with modern technology? What messy it would have been if the technology had not contributed to innovate and increase the production of the daily necessities of today's complex life and how chaotic it would have been without new and improved technology of transport, communications, energy and even housing? How painful it would have been if advanced techniques of treatment of medical sciences had not come to our rescue through the gift of higher education and research. And how confusing it would have been if higher education had not produced economists, planners and managers to advice, plan and manage the problems of everyday with modern methods and techniques.

The role that the university education has played justifies amply that it needs more and more funding. The question is how investment in university education is viewed. In 1960s when the government realized that university education should be expanded to provide more places to the growing 18 year old citizen, it did not hesitate to invest heavily on the capital as well as recurrent expenditure to establish as many as twenty four universities and other institutions of higher education. Did the government do so because it had surplus funds for university education or it did decide to invest to meet the social needs despite the fact that the country was passing through economic problems or was that because of a political pressure?

The first word of caution to the universities came from Mrs. Shirley Williams, the Secretary of State for Education and Science in the Labour Government who had also remarked that 'the party is over for the scientists'. In 1978-79, the public spending for Education and Science was 14.3% which came down to 12.7% in 1985-86 and further to 12.1% in 1988-89.[14] A Table showing the public spending in UK by function for these years is given in the Appendix-3.[15] Not only did the public spending decline sharply, when the inflation is taken into account, the erosion was much more than what was seen besides the further gap created by the increasing needs of the universities. In fact, if government funding had been maintained at 1975 level in real terms the allocation would have been some 700 million.

Coming to the role of the Conservative government that came in power in 1979 election, although it was committed to reduce the public spending, "... when it first took office, the government was surprisingly ignorant of its own machinery for supporting science - machinery that had developed gradually since the recognition during the First World War, that modern states had to support scientific research if they were to survive".[16]

Even about the policy on the universities and polytechnics. "When the conservatives come to power in 1979 they had no settled policy on universities and polytechniques but they were determined to curb public expenditure".[17] This precisely make it amply clear that regardless of the relative importance of the different sectors, reduction was the aim, not relevance and importance. However, "their broad aims were the same as those of Mrs. Shirley Williams".[18]

Precisely, curbing the public expenditure was the package programme of the Conservative government and the reduction in grants was part of the total national programme. This also meant that university education did not receive the treatment that it deserved in the national interest again. How would one reconcile this with the following message of Sir Stafford Cripps in May 1948 to the Universities Quarterly:

> "The darkness of the economic outlook gives no ground for economy in the sphere of university grants. The universities have a great contribution to make towards national economic recovery. We look to them to continue with unabated vigour, the search for new knowledge and the education of increased numbers of young men and women from all classes of the community. For it is on the advances that we make in scientific knowledge and on the energy initiative, directive capacity and courage of these young graduates that the

economic future of the country will largely depend".

In 1948, not only the Parliament of Great Britain allotted higher grant at 12.5 million for the 19 Universities that it then had, the Minister-in-charge had assured that if there was a demand for higher grants, he would not hesitate to approach the Parliament.

Is there a change since then in the role or otherwise of the effectiveness of the universities to the national development either as a matter of fact or in the approach of the government. Perhaps, the truth is both 'yes' and 'no' on both sides. There is a strong feeling that universities have not paid the dividend of the public funds invested in them and therefore it might appear that the effectiveness got diminished. But is that true for on the other hand the UGC in its advice (1984)[19] to the Secretary of State for DES on the development of a strategy for higher education into the 1990s, stated that:

> "The universities provide the bulk of the country's science and engineering graduates and research workers, as well as qualified graduates for medicine, law, architecture and numerous other professions. They protect, develop and transmit much of our cultural heritage and carry out most of the country's fundamental research. It is from the universities that the leaders of our industries, professions and national life are predominantly recruited. The rest of the educational system largely depends on the universities for the quality of its teaching staff. Any policy that diminished the role and status of the universities would damage many aspects of our educational, cultural and industrial life".

What the UGC as the body competent to assess the performance of the universities observed is the logical conclusion that the universities are discharging their duties and performing well. As regards the approach of the Government in relation to the universities, the White Paper of 1987 asserted that: "Higher Education has a crucial role in helping the nation meet the economic and social challenges of the final decade of this century and beyond; and identified one of its aims and purposes as 'serving the economy more effectively'. This statement clarifies the approach of the Government to the higher education which means there is no change in the approach of the Government. Even the 1991 White Paper entitled "Higher Education - A New Framework recognised that "In line with the Government's aims, higher education has continued to promote the advancement of learning, and high levels of scholarship". It also acknowledged that "Higher education has also responded to the need, identified by the Government in 1987 White Paper to take increasing account of the economic requirements of the country".

Despite the well worded recognition in the national document, of the role of higher education to the national development, the universities have suffered and are still suffering due to ill-funding and there are lots of restrictions imposed on the universities. These actions tend to establish that the liberal approach of the Government has changed since the time Sir Cripps gave his message in 1948. The Jarratt Committee deliberating on the role of the government stated that "... Government must recognise the need for a university system and what it provides".[20] It also said that the Government should "... make it clear how it sees the role of universities..."[21].

ROLE OF THE DEPARTMENT OF EDUCATION AND SCIENCE (DES)

Within the entire system of the Government, what role the Department of Education and Science (DES) played for the university system, and how effective and meaningful the role requires some discussion for not infrequently, finger had been raised to the DES for it's role.

Historically in tracing the links of what happened in July 1981, one has again to refer to Mrs. Shirley William's caution. Later, the rejection or the unresponsiveness on the part of the universities to the suggestion of Mrs. Williams came handy to the successive governments to justify their unilateral action. This would be evident in the following remarks on the 8th July, 1981 of Dr. Rhodes Boyson (the Under Secretary of State for Education and Science) on the UGC's letter dated 1st July, 1981 reminding the opposition of Mrs. William's proposals:

> 'The Labour Government put out a document, but, with the exception of one point, the universities have done nothing about it. The Right Hon. member for Orkney and Shetland (Mr. Grimond) said recently at Kent University:
>
> "It was a pity that these proposals, were not treated more seriously at the time. But universities walked so tall that they only had to shout loud enough that they were centres of excellence and everyone would bow. Universities walked so tall that they sometimes forgot about the ground".
>
> It is important to realise that what we are now doing people have been talking about on and off for years".[22]

However, assuming but not admitting that there was failure on the part of the universities, would that minimise the shortcomings in the performance of the DES particularly the avoidable frequent changes in policies and for creating a situation under which the universities were not able to plan ahead even of one year. The DES can also be criticised for raising hopes of the universities for continued growth in the backdrop the caution of Mrs. Williams on record and then shattering them finally in July, 1981.

The 1972 White Paper on Education followed by the announcement of the Conservative Secretary of State that the policy of expanding higher education would be continued could be argued to have had superseded the cautions of Mrs. Williams which were, in fact, not even the declared policy of the government. The White Paper envisaged about 30% growth in full-time student numbers in the universities over 72-77 and large capital investments in buildings and residences. It also envisaged that by 1981, 200,000 entrants annually would be registered in GB aged under 21 representing about 22% of the age group 18. The White Paper also envisaged a large capital programme for building and residences to achieve the growth in the universities. This provided the UGC with a "working hypothesis" for the 1977-82 quinquennium.[23] But throughout 1970s, demand stagnated, participation rate declined and consequently adequate physical capacity was available. However, the Paper had assumed a reduction in the post-graduate student number which was read as recovering from the Robbins euphoria.[24]

After a serious economic pressure on the government followed by the oil crisis in November, 1973 and the consequential escalation of the oil price in January 1974 making visible impact on all fronts of the economy which also affected the funding of the universities, there was a general indication that time had come to curb expansion of the activities of the universities. In 1975-76, the White Paper imposed cash limits as a new discipline on spending policy of departments.

However, an illusive stability and growth potential appeared through the publication of the demographic trends in February 1978, of the DES and Scottish Education Department's joint discussion document, Higher Education into the 1990s, which contained the possible implications of demographic trends for the pattern of higher education and how that might change between 1981-84. Three models provided in the documents aimed at growth to 21%, 18% and 15%, the lowest being 1% more than 14% growth that had been over the seven years.[25] However, it "... did not concentrate minds on the longer term implications of demographic trend."[26]

Earlier, it was 'indicated' that grants to 1980-81 were related to a provisional student objective for universities of 293,000 full-time students in 1981-82, The Government had adviced UGC in 1977 November that the objective should be 310,000 full-time students in 1981-82.

The Public Expenditure White Paper published in January 1979, contained a downward adjustment of the target of the student numbers and consequently, the planned numbers for the university sector were revised as stated in the Table-5.1.

The Government had informed the UGC that the reduction of 2000 target for 1981-82 in relation to earlier target for that year should be achieved by reducing the target for overseas students from 31,000 to 29,000.[28]

Table 5.1[27]

1979-80	:	292,000
1980-81	:	301,000
1981-82	:	308,000
1982-83	:	310,000

Although in July 1979, the DES invited the UGC to advise on the effect of various possibilities for modified grants upto 1982-83, it has been a mystery as to the advise given and with what consequences, for no record was available.

The new Goverment's House of Commons Select Committee on Education, Science and Arts started its work into the funding and organisation of the courses in Higher Education in December, 1979. In his communication to the Select Committee, the Secretary of State suggested *inter-alia* the following possible topics for consideration of the Committee in relation to the higher education.

"*(i)* subject balance in broad terms in relation to the future of highly qualified manpower. Precise manpower planning is no longer considered feasible because of the long lead time required by educational planning; but for the same reason broad guidelines on subject priorities within the higher education system would be valuable and need further study.

(ii) policies for preserving academic quality and new development in a period of static declining student numbers. With the prospect of constant or declining numbers on both sides of the binary line it is essential to develop management policies which allow room for new

developments by eliminating unnecessary duplication. This will require a response both at national and institutional level" (para. 1).[29]

The Select Committee, however, had its own approach about the various areas on which it would report including the full cost fees for overseas students the other forms of budgetary restraint for the universities and the decision to "cap the pool" by imposing cash limits.

Undeniably, the select committee in a democratic sturucture of the Government has high power and responsibility to the House of Commons. But what was strikingly lopsided was that in a structure in which the University Grants Committee existed as a Standing Committee of the Department of Education and Science charged with the responsibility *inter-alia* 'to advice the Government as to the application of any grants' and '... to collect, examine and make available information relating to university education throughout the United Kingdom', the Secretary of State in his own wisdom, decided to suggest to the Select Committee to consider policies that needed to be developed in relation to the subject balance keeping in view the future requirement of highly qualified manpower as also the broad guidelines on subject priorities within higher education system. It was also asked to consider policies for preserving academic quality and new development.

Even though the Select Committee was to cover the entire higher education area of which universities were one part, in a situation of the lawful existence of the UGC as a buffer body between the Government and Universities, the job assigned to the Select Committee should perhaps have, more appropriately, been assigned to the UGC. After all, the Select Committee had to interact with UGC. Moreover, the UGC consisted of more academics competent to examine and report on such questions as the academic quality and subject balance and could involve more academics as the necessity arose.

Late announcement of grants by the Government was another problem that the universities were facing. During 1979-80, the recurrent grant was increased three times to take care of the pay and price increases and in fact "... the universities did not know of their grants upto March, 1980 until January, 1980 and at that time still did not know of their grants upto July, 1980". This obviously proved to be "... inefficient method of funding which created short term financial uncertainties and discouraged rational planning by the UGC and by the Universities".[30] Gradually, the universities felt that due to the funding policies, they were not able to plan even ahead of one year as against the greater need to plan the activities in a situation of funds crunch.

The Jarratt Committee, appointed by the Committee of Vice-Chancellors and Principals (CVCP) in April 1984, with Sir Alex Jarratt as the Chairman with eleven members 'to promote and co-ordinate a series of efficiency studies of the management of universities had undertaken studies on a selective basis, and to report to the CVCP and to UGC on the results of the studies with such comments and recommendations as the Committee considered appropriate. While deliberating on the role of the Government, the Committee made the following recommendations:

> "It is all the more necessary for Government to make clear how it sees the role of universities because the funding horizon provided by the Public

> Expenditure Review processes are so short. Financial forward planning is made even harder by the considerable amount of additional chopping and changing which occurs at short notice. The cuts introduced by the Exchequer in the late summer of 1983 were an acute example of this as are the uncompensated extra costs imposed in recent budgets; but even the 'new blood' exercise, now in its final year, was inadequately signalled for the scheme to be used to maximum effect. If Government has to change the Rules, it should give either more notice or a longer period for implementation. Rapid changes in funding are not conducive to efficient use of resources".[31]

The above observation reflected the difficulties that the universities in general had to face and the treatment that the universities rightly deserved to meet the objectives of funding by the Government and the goals the universities stand for.

Five of the nine universities covered under the DES Research Project stressed that 'The major policy implication identified for DES is the need to restore a longer-term planning horizon".[32] According to the case writer of the University of Heriot-Watt, '... the DES should have recognised that in the university sector as a whole effective planning could not take place on a day-to-day basis in an atmosphere of increasing uncertainty over government intentions and should have taken steps to allow for the restoration of longer term planning'.[33] The case writer of the University of Hull, highlights, '.. the undesirability of abrupt major policy changes and that the replacement of a medium to long-term planning horizon is not conducive to good management or the most effective use of public funds ..."[34] The University of Sussex observed that "... the UGC's ability to engage in rational dialogue with the universities depends critically on broad guidance, a decent time horizon and reasonable consistency for DES".[35] These observations reflected what the case writers from the universities considered lacking on the part of DES during the period of 1979-81.

The DES, the case writer of the University of Salford stressed '... must give the UGC and therefore the universities, medium term and realistic financial prospects in a context in which UGC and the universities can work out their future strategies'.[36]

Throughout the period of late seventies till the final blow through the UGC letter dated the 1st July, 1981 uncertainty prevailed and that was due to either the absence of clear cut policy at the DES level or some kind of communication gap which had its toll on the university system over the years. This also reflects in the observation of the case writer of the University of Sheffield who felt that "... uncertainty in a situation of worsening provision weakens morale; the loss of a sensible planning horizon, the lateness of grant announcements, the need to effect change with extreme speed tend to convert rational planning into disjointed ad-hoc reactions".[37]

On the question of a clear-cut higher education policy and mechanism for integrated planning across higher education as a whole, the case writer of the University of Salford considered that '.. institutions require a clear view of the long term balance between the university and public sectors of higher education'.[38] The case writer also felt that 'the lack of any publicly stated policy for higher education from 1978 until late 1980/early 1981 meant that neither the UGC nor universities could make sensible planning decisions'.[39]

In the Final Report of the DES Research Project, the following[40] Policy Implications have been drawn for the DES from the comparative Analysis of the Case Studies:

(i) The need to develop and expound an effective higher education policy, and mechanisms which will allow for integrated planning across higher education as a whole.

(ii) The need to restore a longer term planning horizon and to understand the implications for the management of universities of not doing so.

(iii) The need to recognise that if the effective and efficient management of reduced funding is desired, it is essential that adequate lead times are provided and that D.E.S. planning is dynamic and flexible not static.

(iv) The need to recognise and endeavour to rectify, in formulating a policy for higher education, the distortions and imbalances created by the 1981-84 restructuring period, particularly those arising from the unsatisfactory age distribution and 'static' academic staff group.

(v) The need to accept that prior announcement of the provision of redundancy and restructuring funds is an essential, but crude, prerequisite to the orderly adaptation to reduced funding.

(vi) The need to review the relationship between the UGC and DES.

(vii) The need to recognise that the UGC should be supported appropriately at officer level.

(viii) The need to understand the impact on the management of universities of the overseas student fee policy.

Precisely, what have been mentioned above are those points which if they were taken care of earlier, the unprecedented difficulties that the universities in general had to face in varying degrees on a number of points of the system, could have been avoided and in any case minimised.

ROLE OF UGC - ACCOUNTABILITY VS. OBLIGATIONS

The role of the University Grants Committee both as a body created by the Government to advise it in the matter of grants to the universities and on the other hand, as the buffer body to ensure that the assessed needs of the universities to meet the national aspirations was, for obvious reasons, both crucial and delicate. On one hand, the terms of reference of the creation of UGC was to advise the government in respect of the activities of the universities which precisely meant that it was accountable to the government and on the other hand, there were expectations of the universities from the UGC that the latter would safeguard the interests of the former.

Any agency charged with the broad responsibilities of the kind mentioned above would find the job delicate, ardous and to an extent hazardous too, for the political pressures from the Government to implement the government policies become mandatory howsoever harsh or demanding they may be. Universities are organisations of the teachers and students which look forward to generous support of the Government in view of the role that they play in the national life. It is in this kind of game that UGC has more often than not, faced criticism. The Jarratt Report observed that the universities '... see the UGC as a tool of the DES, view that is readily reinforced when Government fails to provide the overall planning frame-work within which the university system is set. Moreover, the UGC is itself a committee advising the Secretary of State, the Chairman is formally a Second Permanent Secretary in the DES and the Committee is primarily supported by career Civil Servants on the DES pay roll.[41] However, before any conclusion is drawn in this regard, it will be in the fitness of things to look back and discuss the role of UGC.

The Government through its White Paper of 1972, promoted growth and provided grants therefor. The UGC Memorandum of General Guidance which though generally discussed an 'improvement factor' had also indicated an 'economy factor' for it envisaged an economy in expenditure per student from 100 in 1971-72 to 98 in 1976-77.

Even a general study and analysis of the statements that the UGC made from time to time, would make it clear that it was conscious of its responsibilities as well as limitations. For example, in its Annual Survey for the Academic Year 1974-75, approach of UGC in relation to universities was expressed in these words "... the principle that the universities with whom we deal are autonomous and responsible for their own decisions and their own management".[42] This clarified the approach of UGC in relation to the management of the universities in general. However, the Committee when it felt the responsibility to caution the universities, it did not lag behind to do so. In its 1975-76 Annual Survey, the UGC commented on the inter-institutional co-operation for it felt that it was necessary to point out the same to the universities. It had observed 'uneconomic proliferation of departments and courses resulting in wasteful use of resources, both within the university system and between institutions on both sides of the 'binary line'.[43] It therefore suggested 'sharing of facilities and resources and local coordination'.[44] Following its approach to autonomy, it again felt that such an '... attempt to impose co-operation or co-ordination from outside impigned upon academic freedom and autonomy. The DES Research Project considered that "Perhaps the committee should have taken a stronger line, given the concerns about the risks of uneconomic proliferation of departments. The time would come when it would have to evaluate more realistically the trade off between preserving autonomy and increasing the effectiveness and efficiency of university sector or higher education".[45] In retrospect, this opinion was natural, but at the relevant time, it must have been a delicate question to UGC for on one hand, it considered it necessary to caution the universities and on the other hand, it decided not to force any decision on the universities.

In the following year Annual Survey (1976-77), the UGC expressed concern about the deterioration in the 'average unit of resource' that the universities were getting since 1971-72 from public funds.[46] The DES Research Project felt that the UGC should have made some more relevant comments in this regard including '... the encouragement given to universities in the 1972-77 Memorandum of General Guidance to recruit tenured staff and enter into other commitments in advance of admissions of additional students'.[47] The UGC had also commented on the substantial increase on the tuition fees both for domestic and overseas students and "... the Committee envisaged this setting very serious and intricate problems for financing the universities, particularly with regard to overseas students".[48]

The UGC, the DES Research study observed was making '... a plea for full restoration of the quinguennial system, which was likely to fall on deaf ears given the economic problems facing the Government'.[49]

Commenting in the Annual Survey on the number driven philosophy, the UGC said "To sacrifice ... standards to over ambitious numerical expansion would be a disservice to both the universities and those who aspire to study in them".[50]

The Committee of Universities Association (CUA) held that "With the benefit of hindsight, the UGC and the universities should have paid more attention to the events and public statements of the 1974-75 crisis'.[51] According to Shattock and Berdahl, by 1977, the effectiveness of UGC was diminishing by the economic constraint and that 'it had abdicated its role as a positive strategic planning body'. The UGC, they considered, 'remained largely a reactive body preferring the system to be tidy rather than innovative'.

A dispassionate analysis of the performance of UGC would make two things clear. One: UGC implemented the policy decisions of DES as a body created by the latter which many a time were national policies and two: it (UGC) as a buffer body coutioned the universities whenever the Committee felt it was necessary to do so. However, it decided to 'suggest' rather than 'force', for it believed it was for the autonomous bodies and their managements to deliberate on the suggestions and act according to their wisdom.

It might be felt that if UGC had become more assertive, universities would have taken the suggestions and hints more seriously and that situation of preparations for the 1st July, 1981 blow would have had relatively less intensity. But on the other hand, any directive action of UGC would have been commented upon as an act of interference in the working of the autonomous universities and could blame for erosion of autonomy. The committee generally always expressed its concern but chose not to force the universities to act in any particular manner.

In processing the three hypotheses the UGC on being invited by DES to offer views, expressed that '... if universities were to consider more rapid expansion, they should be assured of adequate capital and recurrent resources."[52] This showed that the UGC as a buffer body was representing the case of the universities to the DES. On the other hand, despite the following[53] advice of the Chairman, UGC, in his letter (1/78) to stick to the overall target of 310,000, many universities did not heed the request":

> "The Committee would expect the university to give priority to meeting this objective which involves a change in the proportion of home undergraduate students in the student body as a whole from about 75.5% currently to 78.5% by 1981-82 ... we have to expect that every university will allow in its planning for a shift of at least 3% in favour of home undergraduate students ....".

At a time when the general election was just to be held after which the new conservative Government came to power, the communication conveyed by the Chairman, UGC about the 'greater degree of certainty' implied by the indication of grants beyond 1979-80 had created illusion and wrong impression.

> "The Committee has asked me to stress that the greater degree of certainty implied by the indication of grants beyond 1979-80 should enable universities to plan the provision and replacement of equipment with reasonable confidence and to eliminate uncommitted balance of grant".[54]

In retrospect, the role played by the UGC appeared to be what the Government approach was from time to time in regard to the higher education policy. Apparently, the UGC as the buffer body, expected also to look after the interests of the universities, did not raise any warning bell because as the body created by the Government, it could not perhaps have done so without hints from the Government, even if it wanted to. However, there could always be difference in opinion. Commenting on the performance of the UGC as the buffer body, Shattock and Berdhal said that by 1979, it was 'in serious disrepair'. Although, Shattock and Berdahl commented that the UGC had reached a stage of 'serious disrepair', they nevertheless agreed that it had made efforts to keep the universities informed of the developments that were taking place at the governmental level. It's position was really delicate. For example, when following the Public Expenditure White Paper of January 1978, the Government declared its policy to reduce the number of overseas students, the UGC had to ensure that the universities in turn actually follow that, but at the same time, it did not want to show any disrespect to the autonomous character of the universities.

With the new Conservative Government in power in May 1979 and its commitment to reduce public expenditure, came the inevitable reduction in grants in June, 1979 by 9 million pounds for 1979-80. In fact, the increase of about 20% in fees for overseas students from 9% meant a further reduction of 5.5 million pounds. The same UGC which had only about a month back assured in writing about the greater degree of certainty implied by the indication of grants beyond 1979-80, had to with the change of the Government, inform the universities in June, 1979 as follows:

"5. A number of further salary and wage settlements relevant to universities are expected to be determined during the coming months. It would be prudent to assume that the extra sums necessary for payment of these settlements will not in every case be compensated in full by additional grant".

The Committee, in view of the above, advised the universities by the same letter that "Having regard to these factors, I would urge you to examine very carefully all recurrent expenditure to which you are not irretrievably committed".[55]

Although the recurrent grant was later increased three times during 1979-80 to cover the pay and price increases the basic point was, as evident by its communication in May 1979, during the Labour Government, and in June, 1979 when the Conservative Government assumed power that the reasons containing different communications of changed tone, in both the times, were due to the fact that the UGC acted as the agent of the Government. It is for this reason that Sir Peter Swinnerton Dyer clarified that the UGC "... had conscientiously obeyed the shifts in Government policy and implemented them.[56] He also said that "The UGC had served the country and the universities well over seventy years"[57] adding further that during the 1980s, the UGC "had pressed universities for greater economy and greater selectivity while avoiding any major disaster".[58]

The UGC having already assessed the likely policy of the new Government, indicated[59] to the universities that there would be change and therefore it would "... review... allocations and students numbers to 1983-84 in the light of Government decisions on public expenditure". The UGC had advised the universities to restrict the number of home students of undergraduate courses in Oct. 1980 level, if necessary to 94% of the number of October, 1979.

Ostensibly, taking hints from the likely policies of the Government, the UGC had informed the universities in October 1979, about the possibility of full cost recovery of education from overseas students which would have impact on the UGC grants.

One of the allegations against the UGC was that in a likely situation of reduction of grants for funding of home students indicated in the circular letter, why the universities were asked to respond to the three hypotheses of grants situation which, as subsequently clarified by the UGC also included a 2% increase, besides the 'level funding' and 5% reduction in grants for the growth hypothesis, raised expectation and it was more so in view of the past twenty years of growth history and therefore did not help the universities to deliberate on the need of preparation for the difficult time that lay ahead.

On the 23rd July 1981, in the course of the question-answers between the Select Committee and Dr. Parkes, the latter was asked by the Committee as to how wide the scenarios were that he had discussed with the Government on the question of funding the universities, he had informed the Select Committee that "they stretched from a small improvement in the level of funding to a scenario which is slightly worse than the one that we at present have".[60] This partially explained why a growth hypothesis was communicated to the universities.

The much talked about UGC advice to the DES "... to describe what would happen to the university system under a variety of financial scenarios ranging from 'level funding' to a rate of withdrawal of grant greater than that which we have actually experienced",[61] and the actual advice given by the UGC in the autumn of 1979, remained a mystery for neither the UGC knew about its impact on the DES's policy, nor could the Select Committee lay its hand on it.[62] The following explanation of Dr. Parkes about the decision to issue the letter and its relationship to Government Policy is worth noting:

> "... it was our belief - and still is - that the universities are moving from a period of continuous growth, and therefore increased funding, which has been going on for 20 years or more, to a period where our funding will probably remain level in real terms for a number of years. That being so, the plans and expectations for growth which the universiteis had, and which in some cases have implied the appointment of staff ahead of time and this, that and the other, necessarily means that the change to level funding produces very considerable difficulties, particularly for a university which has been growing fairly rapidly. That being so, we wanted to probe this and therefore we set the level funding scenario, which we believe is the one which will probably apply to the system as a whole, but which is not necessarily - in fact, almost certainly not - one which we shall apply to individual institutions. By setting upper and lower targets, we tried to find out what were the important things in their thinking".[63]

Perhaps the UGC was unable to assess correctly the emerging situation of funding policy of the Government which disabled it to communicate the right message to the Universities. Does that mean that the UGC was not taken into full confidence by the DES while taking the unprecedented decision of reduction of grants pusing at least some of the universities to the wall.

Yet another allegation against the UGC was the favourable impression that it created in the minds of the universities during the two-hour dialogue meetings with each of the university between January and June, 1980 and the unfavourable decisions it conveyed by its letter dated the 1st July, 1981. On one hand, UGC held the discussion as 'unique in the history of UGC' in assessing the needs and justifications of the universities for fixation of grants, and on the other hand, the universities particularly those which were invited in the early months of 1980, had hardly had any reasonable time to prepare themselves to discuss with UGC in response to the three hypotheses. The claim of UGC was however rejected by many a critics.

What the UGC had considered to be 'unique', CVCP did not make any mention to the Select Committee on the 1st February, 1980 about the 'dialogue meetings'.

The grants for 1980-81 were announced when the second-half of dialogue meetings were still continuing. This implied that in fixing the grants for 1980-81, assessments of the dialogue meetings were not taken into account. It was perhaps due to that reason that the 1980-81 grants did not reflect any negative indication for the compensation for inflation in the form of a supplementary grant for 79-80.[64] According to the DES Research Project, "Not only did this practice reduce the enthusiasm of academics for cost cutting exercises, it did not assist the Vice-Chancellors in forcing their constituencies to face upto the new financial climate".[65]

In a situation where reduction in grants was inevitable, how the UGC, even when paying for the compensation of a previous year, did not clearly caution the universities that they should not mistake the compensation payment as a favourable sign is beyond comprehension. According to the CUA's Resource Allocation Group, "... it persuaded the university community that severe cuts would not be made in higher education and that Vice-Chancellors and other senior university figures who had 'cried wolf' every year since 1975 could safely be disregarded".[66]

Instead of giving clear warning to the universities, the UGC letter for 1980-81 grants dated the 28th May, 1980 (letter 9/80), only informed that "The Committee considers that, for 1980-81, universities would be wise to exercise caution on proposals for academic developments to which they are not committed and for which countervailing savings have not been found".[67] The Committee had also informed the universities that since the grant distribution had taken place prior to the conclusion of the dialogue meetings and before the impact on admission of the policy of the government on overseas students fees was known, there was no relationship of the 'level funding' policy. The universities were also informed that there was no relationship to the three hypothesis. However, these did not absolve the UGC from its responsibility to convey the appropriate and definite message of what was waiting in the store. On the question of the student numbers it was rather surprising that the UGC having earlier advised the universities in April 1979 (letter 13/79), to restrict, if necessary, admission in October 1980, to 94 per cent of the number admitted in 1979 had issued the letter dated the 28th May, 1980 (letter 9/80) that "The Committee considers that in 1980 most universities should be able to admit about the same number of home undergraduates as in 1979.[68] Again in a subsequent letter of UGC dated 15th October 1979 (16/79), it stated that "A reduction of entry in 1980-81 and subsequent years to a level below that expected in 1979-80 will be necessary..."[69]

It is significant that for the first time, while addressing the CVCP and talking *inter-alia* about the future level funding, Dr. Parkes stated that UGC intended to be more 'interventionist' than in the past and added that the Committee will urge the Secretary of State to sustain the level funding. He however, realized that "Even if we get level funding or something near to it, the question which then arises is for how long."[70]

It is true that many a time, one got the impression that UGC could do much to lessen the intensity of the crisis to the universities. But it is also evident from the analysis earlier here that the UGC had made efforts to keep the universities informed of the developments in regard to the funds, student targets and the general need of tightening the belts.

On the question that the UGC could have informed more definitely about the needs to tighten the belts, it is necessary to recall that the universities were not always adhering to all that the UGC was advising. For example, the advice of UGC relating to the student number was not adhered to. It may be that the universities had their own problems or assessments, because of which, they could not adhere to the advice of the UGC in this regard, but that is a different issue.

Selectivity Approach

For a variety of reasons, the UGC resorted to the selectivity approach. This had given rise to a good deal of apprehensions in the university system; but in an altogether new situation of resource crunch, the selectivity approach was perhaps inevitable.

For some time past, the possibility of the UGC adopting a selective approach in the matter of grant reduction was strongly believed to be on the cards. This was first officially indicated by the UGC in its letter dated 15th May, 1980 which *inter-alia* stated that "... it is not the Committee's intention to distribute the cut in resources equally between institutions and fields of study".[71]

Finally, the UGC's communication containing grant reduction and fixed student numbers for different universities including the subject mix was issued on the 1st July, 1981 from which the high selectivity of UGC became clear. The range of high selectivity is evident from the Appendix-2. While the UGC defended its action based on the inputs of the various subcommittees and main committee, many universities raised questions on the validity of the inputs. Those which were seriously affected faced enormous problems of adjustments on various fronts.

It is true that in a situation of resource crunch, which the UGC had to handle, 'selectivity' could not have been avoided, but what struck the university system was that the UGC should have given reasonable clear notice. Perhaps one and a half year's of clear notice to the universities so as to enable them to start preparation for the inevitable would have helped them. However, when that did not happen, the sudden decision of selectivity did certainly create a lot of problems in managing their affairs. But it is important that there is merit in the 'selectivity approach both from the point of view of quality control as also in a situation of limited resources'. On the question of research funding, the White Paper of 1991 clearly favoured selectivity. It announced that '... research funds should be distributed selectively, as now, on the basis of assessment of research quality. This will continue to reward quality, encourage innovation and make the best use of scarce resoures".[72]

The Jarratt Committee (1985) made the following recommendations for the UGC:

(a) The UGC should provide and make known its own views about the prospects and directions for higher education.

(b) There should be an increase in the frequency and scope of informal and confidential discussions between individual Vice-Chancellors and the UGC Chairman and Sub-Committee Chairmen.

(c) The UGC should encourage further inter-institutional collaboration.

(d) Within the next twelve months, the UGC should agree with each university a programme for implementing the recommendations in this Report and the relevant findings of the Special Studies, and should take progress into account when allocating grants.[73]

In the Final Report of the DES Research Project, the following[74] Policy implications for the UGC have been identified from the analyses of the case studies:

(i) The need to be more explicit, more open and to communicate more clearly and effectively with universities.

(ii) The need to recognise, when requesting universities to prepare contingency plans in anticipation of financial reductions, that a clear indication of the range of possible reductions should be given.

(iii) The need to have, and to be able to demonstrate, a better understanding of individual institutions and not simply a partial view of some of their subject areas.

(vi) The need to provide realistic planning horizons, hypotheses and timetables, and to be consistent in the advice it gives to universities.

(v) The need to recognise in its decision making processes that the nature of university courses and research programmes restricts the capacity of universities to respond rapidly to significant reductions in recurrent grant and student numbers, and that the most severely restricted institutions cannot be expected to respond to the same time-table as the more favourably treated.

(vi) The need to recognise in its decision-making processes the time scales involved in implementing changes particularly for the benefits to be reflected in the performance of the institution.

(vii) The need to examine the problems of, and develop policies for, small institutions, particularly within regions.

(viii) The need to recognise that cuts which are too large to be handled through belt tightening but not large enough to justify major surgery are difficult to handle, particularly within decentralised faculty structures.

(ix) The need to develop a better working relationship with the Scottish Education Department.

UGC Replaced by UFC

Following the recommendation of the Croham, Committee and the publication of the White Paper "Higher Education: Meeting the Challenge" (April, 1987), the Education Reform Act, 1988 passed by the Parliament, replaced the University Grants Committee on the 14th July, 1989 which had served the cause of university education for a long time and the new University Funding Council was established. The Secretary of State, while steering the Education Reform Bill through the Parliament had mentioned that the reason why UGC was replaced, was that it was only a standing committee "existed at the Secretary of State's pleasure", while the UFC, established by Statute, would have much more independence than UGC. The terms of reference for the UFC were that:

> "The Council shall be responsible subject to the provisions of this part of this Act, for administering funds made available to the Council by the Secretary of State for the purpose of providing financial support for activities eligible for funding under this section". The activities laid down are:

"*(a)* the provision of education and the undertaking of research by universities; and

(b) the provision of any facilities and the carrying on of any other activities by universities which their governing bodies consider it necessary or expedient to provide or carry on for the purpose of or in connection with education and research".

The Council is also empowered to make grants, subject to such terms and conditions as they think fit to the governing body of any university in respect of expenditure incurred or to be incurred by them for the purposes of any activities eligible for funding under this section. The Council became operative from 1st April, 1989.

However, how did the Chairman, UGC assessed the UGC's access to the Government and role and function of UGC would be clear from the following, mentioned in the strategy paper sent by UGC to the Secretary of State for Education and Science:[75]

> "11.16 - The Chairman of the UGC has always had ready access to Ministers. This has been of great value to the Committee and to the universities. We hope that it will also be possible for the whole Committee or for groups of members to meet Ministers more frequently than in the past".

We need to be constantly in touch with the universities, to help us both to advise Government on their needs and to judge how they are likely to respond to any initiatives which we are considering. We already have many contacts, formal and informal, with individual universities and we hope to develop them. We intend to consider the frequency and the organisation of visits by the Committee and the Sub-committees in order to ensure that they are as useful as possible. The recently introduced practice of seconding university administrators to our secretariat has already proved its value. We hope that this practice will continue and if possible grow.

The combined staff of the UGC and of NAB is less than the central staff of even the smallest Research Council. We accept that this is not comparing like with like, but it seems to imply that in the eyes of those who control our staffing the UGC and NAB combined are expected to know less, and do less, than even the smallest Research Council. What justifies the staffing levels of the Research Councils is that they have to operate an allocation system which is both open and discriminatory. Increasingly we shall have to do the same, and this will involve restoring part of the substantial cut which has been made in our staffing since 1979. That cut has already caused a deterioration in the level of service which we can provide to universities; and they have made it clear to us that they believe we are now understaffed".

The UGC had also brought to the notice of the Secretary of State to the need to modernise its office far better and effective management in the following words:

> "Finally we must remark on the low level of technology permitted in the UGC office. Given that we have to administer such large sums of public money, it is essential that the office is properly provided for. The fact that we have been designated as a cost centre has given us only very limited freedom to introduce modern equipment. We accept that the UGC may be no worse off than many Government offices. Nevertheless, we would severely criticise any university whose central offices were as ill-provided as ours".

Importantly, the UGC had also conveyed to the Secretary of State, its task as a buffer body between the Government and the Universities, as stated below:[76]

> "The UGC stands between Government and the universities as it has done for 65 years. Recent difficulties have led to its being criticised more than before; but they have also shown that an intermediary body is still essential. We are not the servants either of Government or of the universities. As one half of our task we shall continue to assert to Government the needs of the universities

for resources which will enable them to provide teaching and research of the highest quality as they must always aim to do. As the other half of our task we shall guide and encourage universities towards the changes which we are convinced they must make, and are willing to make, in order to serve the national interest into the 1990s and beyond."

A simple reading and a straight analysis will make it difficult for any one to accept the reasons mentioned by the Secretary of State that the replacement of UGC by UFC was aimed at better status and effectiveness despite the fact that UGC had several handicaps to effectively function in growing complex management period.

Commenting on this, Sir Peter Swinnerton-Dyer, former Chairman, UGC observed that "... the funding memorandum which regulates relation between the DES and the UFC manifests in every line that DES is not prepared to rely on the UFCs competance and good sense".[77] If the only reason to abolish UGC and to establish UFC is the statutory position, it is to be conceded that even the UGC could have been given the statutory position and powers with some modifications that the changed time demanded and that was also what the Robins Committee had recommended.

Commending the role played by UGC, Dr. Swinnerton-Dyer stated that "The UGC had always been non-political, and over the years, it had become a body of experts and addicted to planning".[78] The Government, he said "has become increasingly suspicious of non-political bodies, on the ground that any one who was not an overt supporter, is liable to be a secret enemy".[79] According to him, the University Funding Council

"... has suffered far more nitpicking interference from DES civil servants in the last two years than UGC did in the previous five years."[80] This refutes the claim of the Secretary of State that as a statutory body, UFC would be more effective than UGC.

UFC Replaced by HEFCS

The University Funding Council which was established in April 1989 replacing UGC, was broken into more than one Funding Council and at the same time enlarged by merging the Polytechnics and Colleges Funding Council (PCFC) abolishing the binary line and calling it "Higher Education Funding Council separately for England, Wales and Scotland. This was already hinted by Sir Swinnerton-Dyer when he said that '... whichever party wins the next General Election will have the merger of the UFC and the PCFC high on its Agenda".[81] The PCFC functioned only in England. In Scotland, the Scottish Central Institutes corresponded to the Polytechnics of England. This was authoritatively announced in the White Paper 'Higher Education — A New Frame-Work' which was presented to the Parliament in May, 1991 by the Secretary of State for Education and Science, the Secretary of State for Scotland, the Secretary of State for Northern Ireland and the Secretary of State for Wales. In his Foreword. to the White Paper, the Prime Minister of the United Kingdom *inter-alia* stated that:

> "In higher education, our key reform will be to end the increasingly artificial distinction between universities on the one hand and polytechnics and colleges on the other. This will build on our plans to transform education and training for 16-19 year olds by removing the barriers between the academic and vocational streams".

Importantly, the White Paper decided to abolish the binary line following which two very important consequences were to follow.

(i) to have a single funding structure for universities, polytechnics and colleges of higher education. Higher Education Funding Councils within England, Scotland and Wales to distribute public funds for both teaching and research; and new links to continue the present close relationship within Northern Ireland's existing unitary structure[82];

(ii) 'the extension of the title of university to those polytechnics which wish to use it and subject to the development of suitable criteria, to other major institutions' and abolishing the Council for National Awards.[83]

The White Paper also contained a number of policy decisions. In order to give effect to them, the Further and Higher Education Act 1992, was passed by the Parliament on the 6th March, 1992. Consequently, the University Funding Council (UFC) established in 1989, in place of UGC for England, Scotland and Wales, was replaced by the Higher Education Funding Councils each for England and Wales. The Scottish Higher Education Funding Council was established under the Further and Higher Education (Scotland) Act 1992.

The Further and Higher Education Act, 1992 provides that wherever necessary, any two or more Councils may exercise jointly to achieve more efficiency and effectiveness.[84] The Act also provides that on being directed by the Secretary of State, any two or more Councils shall '... jointly make provision for the assessment by a person appointed by them of matters relating to the arrangements made by each institution in Great

Britain which is within the higher education sector for maintaining academic standards in the institution.'[85] These provisions indicate that although separate Higher Education Funding Councils have been created to meet different political requirements for the country, being one, there would, for obvious reasons, be issues and areas where joint exercises would be essential in the ultimate interest of all without which, greater confusion and problems would arise.

ROLE PLAYED BY THE COMMITTEE OF VICE-CHANCELLORS AND PRINCIPALS (CVCP)

The Committee of Vice-Chancellors and Principals (CVCP) is a voluntary organisation founded in May 1918 for regular consultative meetings of Vice-Chancellors and Principals of the universities in England and Scotland. From the very beginning, the Committee has been represented by the Vice-Chancellors and Principals of those Universities in England and Scotland which are recipients of grants of the UGC and UFC. After the expansion of the university system, the membership increased to 60 from 22. This size would again increase following the large number of Polytechnics becoming university.

It is a consultative and advisory body which aims at "... to seek to reflect the collective view of universities and to keep all major university matters under regular review".[86] Although there is no formal framework, the CVCP has over the years grown into a stable and representative organization on behalf of the universities within its informal framework which are as follows:[87]

(i) to define and discuss matters of common interest to the universities;

(ii) to explore, formulate and adopt a common or central arrangement for the resolution of particular problems and where universities see advantage in so doing; and

(iii) to define and represent a university view on matters of policy to the UFC, to departments of government, to Parliament, to other educational bodies, industry and the public at large.

Broadly, for the furtherance of the above objectives, the CVCP discharges functions as follows:[88]

(i) to act as an invaluable forum for discussions between Vice-Chancellors, of common problems although the procedures are now more formalised;

(ii) to act as a centre for disseminating information relevant to universities e.g., collecting information from the media and parliamentary proceedings and disseminating them for the benefit of the universities. It also receives relevant information from the government which it studies and apprises the universities about the likely effects on the university system. This is considered as "invaluable to every university";

(iii) it has a service function and, therefore it has set up a number of specialist bodies which subserve a range of common university requirements, e.g. the University Statistical Record which maintains various statistical records relating to the university system, but is the responsible body for agreeing with the D.E.S. the nature and form in which such records should be kept for government and others; and

(iv) it has also a few other specialist bodies in different areas e.g. to consider changes in

school curricula in relation to entrance requirements and to promote staff training programmes and in the pay negotiations of all the staff. The Academic Audit Unit (AAU) established in 1990 to investigate, monitor and promote academic standards to ensure universities achieve and maintain their aims is an important unit.

With a view to making the decisions more effective, an Executive Committee has been established with elected members. It is well-organised to perform the functions in as wide an area as mentioned above and this "... it has acquired more by default than by intention".[89] Today, it "... is an informal and as devoid of power as ever it was. But its influence is very great indeed. It rarely makes pronouncements, but the pronouncement it does make carry great weight.[90]

With its long standing and a good track record, the CVCP is the only organization on behalf of the universities to project the views of the universities to the government and to the public and also guiding the universities in general with the collective wisdom of the body in various matters of importance much needed for the functioning of the universities in all areas. The CVCP has today, undoubtedly established an admirable credibility in the university system in UK.

For an organisation like CVCP, keeping the expectations of the university community, has never been an easy job. Clearly, the areas of functions of the CVCP are wide enough to cover all areas of functioning of the university system and it has, in fact, been performing its functions in all the areas as the necessity was felt by this representative body of elected members. How timely actions are taken and reactions of the CVCP are properly projected in any matter involving the interests of the university community and with what intensity and how much such matters really merit, are the real questions?

When the cash limits was imposed for the academic year 1975-76 which also marked the end of the growth in resources, the CVCP, in November 1975, had issued a statement entitled "Universities in a Period of Economic Crisis", reaffirmed its earlier views that the share of cuts in public expenditure should be borne by the universities and the university should play its role in facing and tackling the difficulties faced by them.

Simultaneously, it made three requests[91] to the government emphasising the importance of the university autonomy. One: to provide grants in such a way that the universities could plan its commitments and the funding done in real terms beyond one year, Two: to assure the universities for adequate funding after 1977 to help resume activities to meet their national and international standing, and needs, and Third: to assure the universities its commitment to restore effective long-term planning and financial arrangements. However, due to national trends and pressures on public expenditure, there was no positive result to the suggestions of CVCP.

During the same period, the CVCP, realising the resource crunch and the need for optimal utilization of various resources, gave a Report on 'Regional and subject co-operation between groups of universities and in some cases, groups of universities and polytechnics, on such matters as sharing services, sharing teaching and research facilities, etc. This was encouraged by UGC.[92]

Behind any voluntary organization's effective and

meaningful functioning, lies one of the two reasons either adequate recognition of the organization by the political and social structures or the organization is sufficiently strong and cannot be ignored by the social and political structures. Despite the fact that CVCP generally enjoyed the favourable position, it was not consulted either by the government or UGC on the question of recovery of full cost education of the overseas students as would be evident from the evidence to the Select Committee given by Sir Alec Merrison. It was only at the annual meeting of CVCP, he said, that the Chairman of UGC in the course of his talk, had only mentioned about what was "in the wind".[93]

Ideally, the role of CVCP *vis-a-vis* the universities should be that of a friend, philosopher and guide. While as a friend, it must fight and try to protect the universities from any possible injury as a philosopher and guide, it is expected to provide the right guidance to the universities. However, this did not happen when the UGC indicated to be more dirigiste for it did not comment critically. Neither in the memorandum that the CVCP had submitted to the Select Committee on the 1st February, 1980 nor during the examination of CVCP witnesses on the 13th February, 1980 was any reference made to dialogue meetings that the UGC had with the universities. At the same time, the said memorandum stated that the universities must work together to mitigate the worst effects of the financial stringency and also about the need to face boldly the prospect of inter-institutional arrangements. It concluded as follows:[94]

> "In difficult times, the necessary decisions may be very painful. Nevertheless, the university welcomes the opportunity to collaborate with UGC and with government agencies in carrying out this task,

while insisting that in the end, it should remain their own task and their own responsibility".

It appears that while the CVCP took a pragmatic approach on behalf of the universities to face the situation and share the crunch, it could have made the universities more alert and action-oriented and at the same time play its role to protect the universities' interest aggressively. However, perhaps there was an inherent problem of the CVCP which is "... an essentially heterogeneous body to be coherent and effective".[95]

Reacting to the 1981-82 Public Expenditure White Paper published in March 1981, which showed a fall in the planned expenditure, the CVCP in a Press Release dated the 12th March, 1981 had estimated that the total loss in income in 1983-84 would amount to between Pounds 130 million and 150 million or 11% to 12.5%, adding that:

> "But experience suggests that due to many other factors, such as incremental drift or incomplete compensation for inflation, the effective loss could easily be 15%.[96]

In the entire story of the circumstances leading upto the 1st July, 1981 letter of UGC, the advice of Mrs. Shirley Williams was of much significance. In retrospect, it was felt that had the universities paid due attention, the situation of the 'shock' following the aforesaid letter of UGC could have been averted or at least minimised the intensity. Why the universities did not take the advice seriously was not formally recorded. But, it was true that the government never declared its policy based on the advice of Mrs. Williams in the absence of which could the universities rightfully be expected to tighten their belts particularly in view of the structure and composition that they have had.

An important issue was raised as to whether the UGC had consulted the universities any time between the intervening period of the dialogue meetings and 1st July 1981. In his reply to the Select Committee, the Chairman, UGC stated that "... in addition to the 'dialogues' and much subsequent correspondence with individual universities, we have been in close touch with the Committee of Vice-Chancellors at all stages and have held meetings".[97] Although not quite clear he perhaps meant that the UGC relied on the interaction it had with CVCP about the need to communicate to the universities.

However, when the Chairman, CVCP, was examined by the Select Committee on the 23rd July 1981, he had replied that "... the universities had not had the long process of consultation and then advise, as in the past, but he thought the UGC had no option but to proceed at a totally unprecedented pace".[98] From this, one might conclude that although there was some discussion at some points and levels between the UGC and CVCP, either the CVCP did not consider the discussions so important as to communicate to the universities or the CVCP failed to act in that direction.

What role the CVCP as the representative body of the universities played after the UGC letter dated 1-7-1981 was important for the universities.

In the course of the evidence before the Select Committee, the CVCP advocated for additional funds for the universities and it made it clear that without that some of the universities would not be able to sustain injury which may lead to a formal bankruptcy.

The compensation proposal was prepared by the

CVCP and the same was submitted to the UGC which was taken up for consideration with the Government. The redundancy scheme was announced late in December 1981 along with the new blood scheme and information technology initiatives.

For obvious reasons, the CVCP as the representative body of the universities felt greatly concerned about the various factors that influenced the performance of the universities before and after the UGC letter dated 1st July, 1981. The Government also felt the absence of the right managerial effect. Finally, it was decided to undertake, on a selective basis, efficiency studies of the management of universities and make recommendations to CVCP and UGC. Keeping this in view, the CVCP appointed a Committee with Sir Alex Jarratt, Chairman, Reed International PLC and Chancellor of the Birmingham University and 11 other members which included the Prime Minister's Adviser on Efficiency and the Chairman, UGC. It also included a few other Vice-Chancellors and the Chancellor of the University of Aston. The composition of the Committee indicated the importance and level of the studies that the Committee was desired to undertake and to make recommendations.

However, while appointing the Committee, the CVCP made it clear in the terms of reference that "... the commissioned studies will not extend to issues of academic judgement nor be concerned with the academic and educational policies, practices or methods of the universities".[99]

The Committee submitted its Report in March 1985 making important and far-reaching recommendations including the role of universities, government, UGC and CVCP independently and separately the CVCP with the UGC.

The Committee made the following observations and recommendations about the role of the CVCP:

"4.23 - The CVCP is a voluntary association of the executive heads of universities and related institutions to which a limited number of roles - notably in connection with salary negotiations - are delegated. It is largely a forum for discussion and the dissemination of information but it is beginning to be a place where systematic views concerning the university system are developed. In recent years its role as an intermediary, interpreting the universities' collective views to the DES, to the UGC and to many other bodies, has grown in extent and importance.

4.24 - We feel that it must be for the CVCP to encourage and assist universities to adopt the improved practices outlined in this Report; and also to help channel the pressures that are arising from UGC and government with the same end in view. More generally it is for CVCP to encourage and foster best practice. An example of this is the recent initiative on auditing and accounting standards.[100]

In relation to UGC, the Committee made the following recommendations:[101]

(i) strengthen the relationship between the secretariats of the UGC and of the CVCP;

(ii) increase the dialogue between the UGC and the university system. Recently, the UGC has asked the CVCP to participate in a variety of joint planning exercises. Such developments can only be beneficial for all concerned; and

(iii) increase the number and scope of discussions,

in confidence, between individual Vice-Chancellors and the Chairman of the UGC and the Chairmen of the individual subject sub-committees. Close relationships between an individual university and the officer of the UGC particularly responsible for its affairs are also important".

The Final Report on the "Institutional Responses to Financial Reduction in the University Sector with specific reference to UGC's letter dated 1-7-1981", as a Research Project of DES made the following policy implications recommendations for the CVCP:

(i) the need to improve its effectiveness in representing the university system;

(ii) the need to become a more reliable channel of communication between the UGC and the universities; and

(iii) the need to collect and circulate details of particular cost-saving schemes and techniques.[102]

The CVCP is indeed a powerful organisation whose powers cannot be seen but felt through development of views of the community of intellectuals whose role in the national life is crucial. However, as it usually happens with such voluntary organisations, there is so much to be desired and lot to be done.

The role of the CVCP during the period leading upto the letter of the 1st July, 1981 was, as commented critically by some universities, "... too passive and ineffective, and was not a reliable source of communication between the UGC and the universities."[103] But much has been said in the following advice to UGC as confirmed in the Analysis of the Cases Studies of the DES Research Project of Sizer:

> "... it (UGC) should not rely upon the CVCP as a channel of communication with the universities until it is convinced it is reliable and effective one, nor should it be the primary channel of communication".[104]

PERFORMANCE OF THE UNIVERSITIES BEFORE AND AFTER THE UGC LETTER DATED 1ST JULY, 1981

The performance of the universities before and after the issue of the UGC letter dated the 1st July, 1981 was questioned and debated more often than not. But it must be admitted that the universities were primarily following the changing policies of the Government which at times were directions or the implied directions. However, at times unintented wrong implementation was done by some of the universities. For example, when the 'policy-led' expenditure was followed during 1960s, universities were bidding to UGC for higher student numbers for that was the basis for payment of grants by UGC. That had created a situation of unhealthy competition not only among universities, but within the same university amongst the departments for more resources and more staff. In the process, "In many instances, they were prepared to lower standards of entry in pursuit of expansion".[105] This was held by the UGC as 'disservice' to the universities as also to the students. It was true that the UGC never wanted that standards should be lowered in order to admit more students but due to the number driven formula, in some cases, the natural tendency was what actually happened. In fact, the UGC should have visualised that the formula might lead to such a situation. This also confirmed that wherever standard was compromised to admit more students that was due to a faulty policy.

In the discussion on the performance of the universities, a reference to the suggestions of the Mrs. Shirley Williams is unavoidable. Consequently, question would also be asked whether it was really a failure on the part of the universities to take the suggestions seriously? Although in retrospect, it was felt that the universities should have taken the suggestions with due care, the fact also remained that as a follow-up of the suggestions, neither the Government nor the UGC had issued any instruction to the universities in this regard, in the absence of which the universities which were so used to expansion that began in 1960s could not have decided of their own to curb their activities or, in other words, clip their own wings.

Although, it is widely said that the autonomy of a university lies in the freedom that it has in deciding what to teach, who to teach and whom to teach, but each of these is sometimes linked directly and sometimes indirectly, to the availability of funds. And that being so, which is in the hands of the Government or its agent - the UGC - the so called autonomy is more often than not, questioned.

Talking about the autonomy, the Jarratt Report stated that the universities in UK enjoy '... a large degree of constitutional autonomy'[106] which it explained "... is guaranteed by a Charter and Statutes ..."[107] This autonomy is really the frame-work within the system to function smoothly for achieving the objectives of the university. But when the purse is controlled by the Government, the 'constitutional autonomy' is hardly of any consequence. It is for that reason that the Jarratt Report subsequently said that "Despite the constitutional autonomy of universities, their freedom of action is significantly limited in practice".[108]

Undeniably, the universities had, from time to time, received signals of difficult times, but they were not taken seriously. However, the universities could not be blamed for that, for on one hand, at times, they had to face financial reductions and on the other hand, the Government did not announce that the expansion programme was over. For example, following the oil crisis, grants were reduced, but later to some extent, additional funds were provided which though were not adequate, nevertheless indicated the approach of the Government to keep up the support. In such a situation, the universities could not have been expected to tighten their belts right then.

At a time, in the first week of May 1979, when the general election was to take place and the change of the Labour Government by the Conservative Party was almost imminent which had the mandate to reduce the public expenditure, the Chairman, UGC, while informing the government's announcement of grants for the coming years and additions for the current year (1978-79), expressed by his letter, 'greater degree of certainty' beyond 1979-80. That had also created false hope in the university circle. Immediately after the Conservative Party came in power, by its Budget of June 1979, grant for 1979-80 was reduced by 9 million pounds.

For the first time after the arrival of the new Government, the UGC had indicated a major review to be undertaken by it and to plan admission in October 1980, restricting to 94% of the October 1979 level. However, since the letter of UGC (August 1979) was received in the middle of long vacation and before the universities could deliberate within their internal system on the possibilities to do so, another letter of UGC (October, 1979) was received which contained more important implications and that diverted the attention.

This letter related to the three hypotheses earlier discussed and the dialogue meetings held by UGC with each university separately, based on the responses to the hypotheses. Whether the universities should have prepared themselves in a better way to meet the situation created by the letter of the 1st July, 1981, could be debated, but the fact remained that going by the case writers' statements in the DES Research Project, what appeared in the UGC letter of July, 1981 were different from the impressions that most of the universities got during the dialogue meetings.

In the case of Heriot-Watt, the important message the Vice-Chancellor got was that the UGC was "looking for possible economy measures" which he assured. In fact, the university "felt sufficiently encouraged by the meeting to hope for more equitable funding in future years". The university did not, based on the meeting, take any specific action in this regard.[109]

The Vice-Chancellor of the University of Sussex had reported to the Senate that the dialogue meeting had produced no new information about the Governments intention, and the UGC had not taken the opportunity to comment on current issues such as redundancy, redeployment, rationalisation etc".[110]

The University of Salford was "content with the tone and conduct of the meeting, confident that the university's case had been well received" and therefore 'both Senate and Council received optimistic report of the dialogue meeting".[111]

No different was the case of the University of Stirling at the dialogue meeting when it got a 'positive impression'.

The University of Sheffield had the dialogue meeting at the end of May 1980 Before that, following the

UGC letter of three bypotheses, a well conceived document was prepared by the Academic Development Council on the request of the Senate. The University considered that "The dialogue meeting was cordial".[112] The UGC had only raised a point that the university 'had a lot of technical staff, and its departmental grants ran at a rather high level."[113]

As regards the Aberdeen, 'The Principal confirmed the meeting had been positive and encouraging'.[114] In fact, as case writers of the university stated "... those visiting the UGC were given no hint that Aberdeen would receive harsher treatment than the average for the system as a whole, or that any change of approach or even greater austerity was essential'.[115]

As regards Aston, in its case, 'UGC members did not ask very probing questions and no questions at all were asked on its financial position".[116]

For Hull also, the general impression was no different. The Case Writers stated that 'the dialogue meeting gave not the slightest inkling of the likely content of the grant letter of 1.7.1981; nothing that could have justified a sense of emergency, the preparation of contingency plans or further major cost reduction exercises'.[117]

From the reflections of the case writers on behalf of these universities, it is clear that the universities did not fail to act on any definite direction or even hint to prepare themselves for the situation created by the UGC letter of 1-7-1981 particularly keeping the dialogue meetings in view which the UGC itself had described as 'unique'.

However, for the universities, was it a question of defending themselves from the allegations that they failed to prepare - contingency plan against hints of difficult times that lay ahead and for not taking any initiative looking to the national environment; or was it a question of soul searching looking back into the domestic performance and taking lessons from the unprecedented happenings and thereafter preparing for any future disaster? Surely, for institutions like universities, it was a question of soul searching as bodies of intellectuals, repositories of knowledge and capable of interpretation of remote signals.

The unprecedented disturbances created in the universities following the UGC letter dated the 1st July 1981, raised several questions relating to both the preparation that could have been made to meet the situations without allowing any disturbances as also to face any inevitable disturbances, more boldly and ably.

It was well-known that the share of public expenditure in UK was constantly declining from the late seventies. It was 12.7% in 1976-77 which declined to 12.3 in 1978-79. Except the Housing Sector, Education was the only sector of all the other sectors, which suffered the most in terms of allocation. The first white Paper of the Conservative Government, presented in March 1980, actually reiterated its commitment of reducing the public expenditure. The White Paper declared the reduction of the total "progressively in volume terms over the next four years to a level in 1983-84 about 4 per cent lower than in 1979-80".[118] However, "the total rose substantially, by 6.3% on a slightly different yardstick of real inflation-adjusted terms".[119]

Although there were arguments to defend the universities against the allegations of failure to protect themselves from the difficult situation created by the UGC letter imposing cuts, there was a widespread feeling of absence of the right kind of managerial actions.

CONCLUSION

Undeniably, in view of the far reaching impact and influence of the university education and research on all sectors of the society which any Government is obliged to take care of greater attention and allocation of resources for the universities is inescapable. This position has to be maintained unless some day universities become fully commercial and entire cost is recovered from the benefifiaries - direct as well as indirect. In the existing system, if education sector is neglected, all other sectors are bound to suffer. Many a time, the immediate adverse impact of neglecting universities is not visible, but nevertheless the damage is caused. Greater attention and allocation of funds for strengthening the university system is a must for sustaining and improving the lots of the people of the society of any country. The Robbins Committee rightly said that 'a community that neglects education is an imprudent as a community that neglects material accumulation'. The Report also said that "To devote resources to the training of young people may be, au fond, as much entitled to be considered a process of investment as devoting resources to directly productive capital goods".

Rather more often than not, the Department of Education and Science, changed its policies about student number targets, quantum of grants and an overall approach for the universities. One way to look at the frequent changes could be that it was always alive to the needs of the changing time and, therefore, it was necessary for it to make changes from time to time. While one cannot reject this it is at least equally necessary to realise the problems that flow from frequent changes involving adjustments which more often than not, give rise to consequential difficulties in a system of the community of intellectuals.

On the operational side, late announcements and release of grants also created problems to the universities, much of which could have been avoided. Even for restructuring purposes, announcements for 'New Blood' and 'Information Technology' were made quite late and the universities were at a loss as to how to tackle the unexpected situation.

Talking about the role of the UGC, it has to be admitted that despite its inherent limitations which were not peculiar to it, but to any similar body, it did its best both to uphold the autonomy of the universities as also to keep them informed of the difficult time. However, on one point, it is difficult to defend the UGC and that is the 'dialogue meetings' which was called 'unique' by UGC and which created favourable impressions in the minds of the university representatives and yet negative treatment was given by its letter of the 1st July, 1981. The UGC could have played its role in a much better way than it actualy did.

As a voluntary organisation, the CVCP has limited role, but the success of that role play depends on how effectively it is done. The effectiveness of CVCP at a time when it was expected to play a crucial guiding and soothing role was minimal. The Jarratt Report has pointed out to the need of increased dialogues between UGC and universities for which the CVCP should play its due role. The DES Research project recommended that CVCP should become 'a more reliable channel of communication between the UGC and the universities'.

How far the universities are to be blamed for their failure to take seriously the various suggestions and hints to lighten belts, beginning from the suggestions of Mrs. Shirley Williams is a matter of dispassionate judgement. What one must not lose sight of is that characteristically universities are forward-looking organizations and, threfore, when necessary to tighten belts, the university community at large has to share the crunch. In that process, how seriously the various segments of the university society reacts is always a matter of chance for that would depend on a variety of factors, such as leadership at the given time, history and culture of the university, structure and composition of the decision-making bodies etc. Therefore, it was not unnatural that the universities did not take the hints seriously. It was more so in the backdrop of a history of growth approach for almost two decades.

Arguably, if business approach was adopted and better managerial methods and techniques had been employed, the injury could have been reduced, but not averted altogether. There is no doubt that there is a great change in the approach and attitude of the university system now, as compared to late seventies or even very early eighties.

Appendix-1

Summary of State of Financial Contingency Planning and Reviews of Academic Profiles as on 1st July, 1981

University	*Development of Financial Contingency Plan*	*Review of Academic Profile*	*Comments*
Aberdeen	No formal cost reduction programme and no financial contingency plan	No reviev had been undertaken	Savings targets had been increased

University	*Development of Financial Contingency Plan*	*Review of Academic Profile*	*Comments*
Aston	Financial contingency plan in place	Well advanced with review of academic profile	Arose largely from appointment of Prof. Crawford as Vice-Chancellor
Bath	No formal cost reduction programme or financial contingency plan	Academic profile regularly reviewed	Confident expectation of favourable treatment by U.G.C.
Heriot-Watt	No formal cost reduction programme or financial contingency plan despite difficult financial position	Academic review resulted in no proposals for change	Acting Principal from Sept. 1980 Illustrates limitations of faculty self-evaluation
Hull	Proposals made but no agreed plan to reduce expenditure and supplement income. No contingency plan	No review of academic profile Forward planning exercise resulted in unrealistic bids from faculties	Illustrates limitations of faculty self-evaluation
Salford	No financial continuing plans. Cost reduction actions taken	No review of academic profile but had revised quadrennial	Acting Vice-Chancellor from 1st Jan. 1981. Pressure for contingency

University	*Development of Financial Contingency Plan*	*Review of Academic Profile*	*Comments*
	which contributed to good financial position, but no formal cost reduction programme	plan adopted in Nov. 1978 on basis of hypothesis (b)	planning resisted because of uncertainty about likely future grant.
Sheffield	Financial contingency plan in place	Initiated a review of academic profile	Initiated through existing committee structure
Stirling	New Principal, commenced financial contingency planning Cost reduction actions taken	No indication academic profile under review	New Principal took up post in Feb. 1981 Proposals to be made direct to Court
Sussex	Had proposals for temporary cuts in expenditure but no financial contingency plan, Short term cost reduction actions taken	Progressing slowly in reviewing its academic profile	Slow progress of GRIPE contrasts with that of Aston and Sheffield

Appendix-II

Summary of Treatment of Participating Universities

Nature of University	*Nature of Treatment*		
	Relatively Well	*Middle Range*	*Relatively Harshly*
Ancient/ civic		Sheffield (Medical School) 6,860 students* 1979-1980 0% students (-8%)* –14% recurrent 11% overseas	Aberdeen (Medical School) 5,140 students 1979-80 -4% Students (-5%) -23% Recurrent 7% overseas
			Hull 5,070 students 1979-80 -17% students (-18%) –20% recurrent 7% overseas
Newer		Sussex 3,890 students 1979-80 - 5% students (-7%) -21% recurrent 12% overseas	Stirling 2,470 students 1979-80 -18% students (-26%) -27% recurrent 8% overseas
Technological	Bath 3,190 students (979-80 +2% students (+1%) - 7% recurrent 8% overseas	Heriot-watt 2,430 students 1979-80 -13% students (-17%) -13% recurrent, 12% overseas	Aston 4,670 students 1979-80 -22% students (-18%) -31% recurrent 17% overseas

Salford
3,940 students
1979-80
- 30%
students (-30%)
-44% recurrent
14% overseas

* Full-time Home and E.C. Students
# (1%) changes compared with 1980-81 actuals

Source: Tabte-l of the Case Studies of the DES Research Project, Institutional Responses to Financial Reduction in the University Sector" John Sizer, Loughborough (1987), (unpublished).

Appendix-III

Public Spending in the UK by Function

Item	*Percentage Shares* 1978-79	1985-86	1988-89
Employment and Training	1.6	2.4	2.7
Health and Personal social services	13.9	15.0	16.2
Law and Order	3.7	4.6	4.7
Defence	11.3	13.1	12.9
Other	10.5	8.5	8.5
Agriculture, Fisheries and Food	1.5	2.1	1.8
Transport	4.9	4.0	4.0
Industry, Trade and Energy	5.1	2.9	1.0
Housing	7.6	4.0	3.7
Education and Science	14.3	12.7	12.1
Social Security	25.6	30.7	32.2

Source: Table-5.4, Higher Education - Cost or Investment? Richard M. Mawditt, Bath (1990).

References

1. U.K., Department of Education and Science (DES), Institutional Responses to Financial Reductions in the University Sector, Final Report, John Sizer (1987), Table-6.
2. *Ibid.*, Table-4.
3. Higher Education Review, Spring (1980), Editorial.
4. *Ibid.*, p. 3.
5. *Op. Cit.*, p. 6.
6. Mawditt Richard M., Higher Education - Cost or Investment?, the author, Lectured at the University of Bath on 30th Oct. 1990, p. 4.
7. U.K., Committee on Higher Education, Report (Robbins Report), London, HMSO, 1963, p. 204.
8. *Ibid.*
9. *Op. Cit.*, p. 205.
10. *Op. cit.*
11. *Op. Cit.*,
12. *Op. Cit.*, p. 206.
13. *Op. Cit.*
14. Mawditt Richard, M., Higher Education - Cost or Investment?, the author, Lectured at the University of Bath on 30th Oct. 1990, p.16.
15. *Ibid.*, p. 17.
16. Wilkie, Tom, The Thatcher Effect in Science, *In The Thatcher Effect*, Ed. by Dennis Kavanagh and Anthony Seldon, Oxford, Clarendon Press, 1989, p. 316.
17. Scott Peter, Higher Education *In The Thatcher Effect*, Ed. by Dennis Kavanagh and Anthony Seldon, Oxford, Clarendon Press, 1989, p.198.
18. *Ibid.*, p. 199.

19. Swinnerton-Dyer Peter, Chairman, UGC letter dated 16.8.1984 to the Secretary of State of Education and Science, Section 1, para 1.1, p. 4.
20. U.K., CVCP, Report of the Steering Committee for Efficiency Studies in Universities, 1985 (Jarrat Report), p. 31.
21. *Ibid.*,
22. Higher Education, House of Commons Debate, Wednesday, 8-7-1981, Hansard, Vol. 8, No. 138, Col. 458-501, Extract from DES Research Project Report, John Sizer (1987), B.P. No. 1, p. 5.
23. U.K., Department of Education and Science, Institutional Response to Financial Reduction in the University Sector, John Sizer (1987), B.P. No.1, p.10.
24. *Ibid.*, pp. 10-11.
25. *Op. Cit.*, p. 27.
26. *Op. Cit.*, p. 45.
27. *Op. Cit.*, p. 34.
28. *Op. Cit.*
29. *Op. Cit.*, B.P. No. 2, p. 18.
30. *Op. Cit.*, p. 5.
31. U.K., CVCP, Report of the Steering Committee for Efficiency Studies in Universities, 1985 (Jarrat Report), para-4.8, pp. 31-32.
32. U.K., DES, Institutional Responses to Financial Reductions in the University Sectors, Comparative Analysis of Universities' Case Studies, John Sizer (1987), p. 40.
33. *Ibid.*
34. *Op. Cit.*, p. 40.
35. *Op. Cit.*
36. *Op. Cit.*
37. *Op. Cit.*
38. *Op. Cit.*, p. 41.

39. *Op. Cit.*
40. *Op. Cit.*, Final Report, p. 40.
41. U.K., CVCP, Report of the Steering Committee for Efficiency Studies in Universities, 1985 (Jarrat Report), para-4.8, p. 32.
42. Para-6 of the Annual Survey for the Academic Year 1974-75.
43. U.K., DES, Institutional Responses to the Financial Reductions in the University Sector, John Sizer (1987), B.P. No. 1, p. 22.
44. *Ibid.*
45. *Op. Cit.*, pp. 22-23.
46. *Op. Cit.*, p. 23.
47. *Op. Cit.*, p. 24.
48. *Op. Cit.*, pp. 24-25.
49. *Op. Cit.*, p. 25.
50. *Op. Cit.*, p. 26.
51. *Op. Cit.*, p. 26.
52. *Op. Cit.*, p. 30.
53. *Op. Cit.*, pp. 30-31.
54. *Op. Cit.*, p. 36.
55. *Op. Cit.*, B.P. No. 2, p. 5.
56. Swinnerton-Dyer, Peter, Rede Lecture, 1991, delivered on 10th May, 1991.
57. *Ibid.*
58. *Op. Cit.*
59. U.K., DES, Institutional Responses to the Financial Reductions in the University Sector, John Sizer (1987), B.P. No. 2, p. 6.
60. *Ibid.*, p. 10.
61. *Op. Cit.*

62. *Op. Cit.*, pp. 10-11.
63. *Op. Cit.*, p. ll.
64. *Op. Cit.*, p.10.
65. *Op. Cit.*, p.10.
66. *Op. Cit.*, p. 23.
67. *Op. Cit.*, p. 24.
68. *Op. Cit.*
69. *Op. Cit.*,
70. *Op. Cit.*, p. 27.
71. *Op. Cit.*, p. 34.
72. U.K., Higher Education - A New Frame Work, London, HMSO, May, 1991, p. 18.
73. U.K., CVCP, Report of the Steering Committee for Efficiency Studies in Universities, 1985 (Jarrat Report), p. 35.
74. U.K., Department of Education and Science (DES), Institutional Responses to Financial Reductions in the University Sector, Final Report, John Sizer (1987), Table-6, p. 41.
75. Swinnerton-Dyer, Peter, Development of A Strategy for Higher Education into the l990s - letter to Secretary of State for Education and Science dated 16.8.1984, p. 43.
76. *Ibid.*, p. 44.
77. Swinnerton-Dyer, Peter, Rede Lecture delivered on 10-5-1981.
78. *Ibid.*
79. *Op. Cit.*
80. *Op. Cit.*
81. *Op. Cit.*
82. U.K., Higher Education - A New Frame-Work, London, HMS0 1991, p. 4.
83. *Ibid.*

84. U.K., Further and Higher Education Act, 1992, Chapter-13, London, HMSO, 1992, Part-III, Section-82, p. 63.
85. *Ibid.*
86. U.K. INSIGHT, A Handbook of Information for University Administrators, CVCP, USDTU, University House, Sheffield, 1990.
87. *Ibid.*
88. Association of Commonwealth Universities, Commonwealth Universities Year Book, 1993, London, p. 2179.
89. *Ibid.*, p. 8.
90. U.K., Community of Universities, Ashby, Sir Eric, ACU London, 1988, p. 72.
91. U.K., Department of Education and Science (DES), Institutional Responses to Financial Reductions in the University Sector, John Sizer (1987), B.P. No. 1, p. 20.
92. *Ibid.*
93. *Op. Cit.*, B.P. No. 2, p. 7.
94. *Op. Cit.*, B.P. No. 2, p. 22.
95. *Op. Cit.*, B.P. No. 2, p. 22.
96. *Op. Cit.*, B.P. No. 2, p. 33.
97. *Op. Cit.*, B.P. No. 2, p. 41.
98. *Op. Cit.*
99. U.K., CVCP, Report of the Steering Committee for Efficiency Studies in Universities, 1985 (Jarrat Report), p. 6.
100. *Ibid,*, p. 34.
101. *Op. Cit.*, p. 33.
102. U.K., Department of Education and Science (DES), Institutional Responses to Financial Reductions in the University Sector, Final Report, John Sizer (1987), p. 41.
103. *Ibid,* Comparative Analyses of Universities, Case Studies, p. 46.

104. *Op. Cit.*, p. 47.

105. Christodoulou, A., *In The Proceedings of Discussion of "The Encroachment of Dirigisme on the Development of Arts and Science"*, Journal of the Royal Society of Arts, July 1981, p. 498, extract from the DES, Institutional Responses to Financial Reductions in the University Sector, John Sizer (1987), B.P. No.1, p. 3.

106. U.K., CVCP, Report of the Steering Committee for Efficiency Studies in Universities, 1985 (Jarrat Report), p. 8.

107. *Ibid.*

108. *Op. Cit.*, p. 8.

109. U.K., Department of Education and Science (DES), Institutional Responses to Financial Reductions in the University Sector, Comparative Analysis of Universities, Case Studies, John Sizer (1987), p. 20.

110. *Ibid.*, p. 20.

111. *Op. Cit.*, p. 21.

112. *Op. Cit.*, p. 22

113. *Op. Cit.*, p. 22.

114. *Op. Cit.*, p. 22.

115. *Op. Cit.*, p. 122.

116. *Op. Cit.*, p. 20.

117. *Op. Cit.*, p. 19.

118. Redell, Peter, The Thatcher Era - and its legacy, Oxford, 1991, p. 32.

119. *Ibid*, pp. 32-33.

6

Universities at the End of Restructuring Period

INCOME AND STUDENT NUMBERS

Baffled by the unexpected and unprecedented blow following the UGC letter, the universities represented their cases to the UGC and held discussions as a result of which, some adjustments were made and additional grants were provided for restructuring purposes particularly for 'New Blood' and 'Information Technology'. Some adjustments were also made in respect of the student number targets.

A comparative study of the position of the income from various sources in respect of the nine universities in 1979-80 and in 1983-84 and 1984-85 will reveal quite a few aspects of the nine universities in their efforts to generate non-government income.

The following table-6.1 shows the general income and the table-6.2 shows the specific income of these universities after which these two tables will be analysed.

An analysis of the figures of 1979-80 in relation to 1984-85 which was the last year of restructuring the system, the position reveals as follows:

Table 6.1[1] General Income

University		*1979-80*	A+B	*1983-84*	A+B	*1984-85*	A+B
Aberdeen	A	66.1	78.7	65.3	73.8	63.1	71.5
	B	12.6		8.5		8.4	
	C	1.7		2.0		3.2	
	D	1.1		1.4		1.3	
	E	-		-		-	
	F	1.2		3.6		4.4	
Total		82.7		80.8		80.4	
Aston	A	63.5	79.6	62.5	73.2	65.4	75.6
	B	16.1		10.7		10.2	
	C	5.2		7.0		4.5	
	D	0.1		0.2		0.2	
	E	-		-		-	
	F	2.9		6.2		6.4	
Total		87.8		86.6		86.7	
Bath	A	61.3	78.3	64.1	75.1	63.2	74.8
	B	17.0		11.0		11.6	
	C	3.1		5.5		5.6	
	D	-		-		-	
	E	-		-		-	
	F	3.2		2.9		2.9	
Total		84.6		83.5		83.3	
Stirling	A	69.4	86.6	67.5	77.9	65.5	76.0
	B	17.2		10.4		10.5	
	C	2.5		4.3		5.9	
	D	0.2		0.5		0.8	
	E	0.4		0.3		0.3	
	F	2.5		6.0		5.5	
Total		92.2		89.0		88.5	

University		*1979-80*		*1983-84*		*1984-85*	
Sussex	A	58.9	73.4	56.2	66.6	54.3	64.6
	B	14.5		10.4		10.3	
	C	3.7		6.5		6.9	
	D	-		0.1		-	
	E	-		-		-	
	F	3.0		5.1		5.5	
	Total	80.1		78.3		77.0	
Heriot-Watt	A	62.6	76.3	58.4	66.2	NA	
	B	13.7		7.8		NA	
	C	3.2		7.3		NA	
	D	0.1		0.2		NA	
	E	-		-		NA	
	F	1.1		3.3		NA	
	Total	80.7		77.0		NA	
Hull	A	63.7	84.8	70.1	82.1	71.3	82.8
	B	21.1		12.0		11.5	
	C	2.9		3.6		4.4	
	D	1.5		1.6		2.1	
	E	0.2		0.2		-	
	F	2.3		4.3		2.1	
	Total	91.7		91.8		91.4	
Salford	A	70.5	84.0	55.3	62.7	51.7	58.7
	B	13.5		7.4		7.0	
	C	3.9		6.9		7.9	
	D	-		0.2		1.3	
	E	-		-		-	
	F	1.9		2.2		2.8	
	Total	89.8		72.0		70.7	

University		1979-80		1983-84		1984-85	
Sheffield	A	66.1	81.0	69.7	78.8	68.5	77.7
	B	14.9		9.1		9.2	
	C	3.3		3.3		3.3	
	D	1.1		1.4		1.5	
	E	-		-		-	
	F	1.6		1.7		2.4	
Total		87.0		85.2		84.9	

A - UGC Recurrent Grant

B - Tuition Fees and support grants (Home students and EC students)

C - Overseas students

D - Endowments, donations and subscriptions

E - Local authority grants

F - Other general income

Table 6.2° Specific Income

University		1979-80	1983-84	1984-85
Aberdeen	A	1.5	0.7	0.8
	B	9.0	10.4	10.6
	C	6.8	8.1	8.2
Total		17.3	19.2	19.6
Aston	A	0.5	0.5	0.5
	B	9.4	10.9	10.6
	C	2.3	2.0	2.2
Total		12.2	13.4	13.3
Bath	A	0.5	0.4	0-4
	B	12.5	12.3	12.5
	C	2.4	3.8	3.8
Total		15.4	16.5	16.7

University		*1979-86*	*1983-84*	*1984-85*
Heriot-Watt	A	0.3	0.5	NA
	B	13.7	11.9	NA
	C	5.3	10.6	NA
	Total	*19.3*	*23.0*	*NA*
Hull	A	0.5	0.7	0.7
	B	7.6	7.3	7.8
	C	0.2	0.2	0.1
	Total	8.3	8.2	8.6
Salford	A	0.9	1.1	1.3
	B	9.0	14.8	18.4
	C	0.3	12.1	9.6
	Total	10.2	28.0	29.3
Sheffield	A	0.7	0.5	0.5
	B	11.6	13.0	13.3
	C	0.7	1.3	1.3
	Total	13.0	14.8	15.1
Stirling	A	0.8	0.4	0.4
	B	7.0	7.3	7.8
	C	-	3.3	3.3
	Total	7.8	11.0	11.5
Sussex	A	0.3	0.3	0.4
	B	19.1	20.3	21.4
	C	0.5	1.1	1.2
	Total	19.9	21.7	23.0

A - Computer Board Grant

B - Research Grants and Contracts

C - Other services rendered

(i) In the case of five universities, viz., Aberdeen, Stirling, Sussex, Heriot-Watt and Salford, the UGC recurrent grant stood reduced by 1983-84 and they were reduced further by 1984-85. In the case of Aston, although the grant stood reduced by the end of 1983-84 from 63.5% in 1979-80 to 62.5% but the same increased in 1984-85 to 65.4% i.e. higher than 1979-80.

(ii) Of the remaining three universities, viz., Sheffield, Bath and Hull, the UGC recurrent grant had increased by 1983-84 and again in 1984-85.

However, in terms of the UGC Recurrent grant and the tuition fees from the home and EC students together, the income position deteriorated in the case of all the nine universities. But despite the UGC recurrent grant being higher in the case of Bath, due to the decreased income from 17.0% in 1979-80 to 11% in 1983-84 and 11.6% in 1984-85 the total income from UGC and the grant on account of tuition fees together were 78.3% in 1979-80 while they were 75.1% in 1983-84 and 74.8 in 1984-85. Hull was no different where the two together was 84.8% in 1979-80 and 82.1% in 1983-84 and in 1984-85, it was 82.8%, the fee income having constantly decreased from 21.1% in 1979-80 to 12% in 1983-84 and 11.5% in 1984-85.

Identical position prevailed in Sheffield where the UGC Recurrent grant and fee income together was 81% in 1979-80 and they stood reduced at 78.8% in 1983-84 and further in 1984-85 to 77.7%. Unfortunately, income from fees of the overseas students in the case of these universities also did not increase. In Sheffield only, it increased marginally from 11.6% in 1979-80 to 13% in 1983-84 and 13.3% in 1984-85.

The question finally remained how did the

universities carry on their activities and fulfill commitments in a situation of deteriorated funding. The answer lied in generating non-government income - mainly through two channels - one was the Research and Contract and the other was 'general income'. This was true with all the universities except Bath. In Bath, the Research grants and contracts income was 12.5% in 1979-80 and in 1983-84, it fell to 12.3% and rose to 12.5% in 1984-85, the level of 1979-80. Much against this, the position in respect of all the remaining eight universities although the UGC Recurrent Grant and tuition fees including overseas students' fees deteriorated, the Research grants and contracts as also the general income together, came to their rescue as would be evident from the following Table-6.3.

Table 6.3[3]

University		*Recurrent Grants from UGC, Tuition fees including overseas*	*Research Grants and contracts and General Income and services rendered*
1		*2*	*3*
1. Aberdeen	1979-80	80.4	17.0
	1983-84	75.8	22.1
	1984-85	74.7	23.2
2. Aston	1979-80	84.8	14.6
	1983-84	80.2	19.1
	1984-85	80.1	19.2
3. Heriot-Watt	1979-80	79.5	20.1
	1983-84	73.5	25.8
	1984-85	NA	NA
4. Hull	1979-80	87.7	9.11
	1983-84	85.7	11.8
	1984-85	87.2	9.10

1		2	3
5. Salford	1979-80	87.9	11.2
	1983-84	69.6	29.1
	1984-85	66.6	30.8
6. Sheffield	1979-80	84.3	13.9
	1983-84	82.1	16.0
	1984-85	81.0	17.0
7. Sussex	1979-80	77.1	22.6
	1983-84	73.1	26.5
	1984-85	71.5	28.1
8. Stirling	1979-80	89.1	9.5*
	1983-84	82.2	16.6
	1984-85	81.9	16.6

* Figure of Services rendered for 1979-80 not available and hence not included.

Source: Based on Tables 7.1 and 7.2.

Table 6.4[4]

The Sources of Recurrent Income in UK Universities

Income source	*1974-75*	*1982-83*	*1983-84*	*1984-85*	*1985-86*	*1986-87*	*1987-88*
Exchequer grants	77.7	64.4	62.1	59.8	57.8	55.6	55.3
Fees							
- Home rates	2.9	8.1	7.7	7.6	7.3	7.1	6.8
- Part-time courses	0.2	0.5	0.5	0.6	0.6	0.6	0.7
Other support grants	0.3	0.3	0.3	0.4	0.3	0.4	0.3
Computer Board	0.8	0.8	0.8	0.8	0.8	0.8	0.7
Research grants	7.9	8.9	9.5	9.7	10.0	10.5	10.0
	89.8	83.0	80.9	78.9	76.8	75.0	73.8

Other government sources:							
Government departments	0.3	0.3	0.3	0.3	0.4	0.3	0.4
Hospital authorities	1.3	1.5	1.6	1.7	1.8	1.9	2.0
	1.6	1.8	1.9	2.0	2.2	2.2	2.4
Other							
Fees-other rates	1.1	4.3	4.6	4.8	5.3	5.6	5.6
Endowments	1.1	1.0	1.1	1.0	1.2	1.3	1.3
Other recurrent income	1.7	3.3	3.6	4.1	3.7	3.6	3.5
Research contracts	4.0	4.8	5.5	6.5	7.5	8.5	9.2
Other services rendered	0.7	1.9	2.4	2.8	3.2	3.8	4.2
	8.6	15.3	17.2	19.2	21.1	22.8	23.8
Total	100.0	100.0	100.0	100.0	100.0	100.0	100.0

Sources: Statistics of Education 1985; Universities, vol. 6, UGC, Table-34; Universities Statistics, vol. 3, Tables 1 and 3.

Notes: 1. The methods used to allocate income to each income source have changed over time: comparisons between years are likely to be less adversely affected by this problem for the 1980s due to greater consistency in the compilation of the income statistics in recent years; 2. Definition of various items (1982/83 to 1987/88): Research grants = grants from research councils and UK Government; Research contracts = grants from UK-based charitable bodies, UK industry, overseas and other sources; Other services rendered = special and short courses and other.

For all the universities in UK, the position of recurrent income beginning from 1970s till the later half of 1980s was as shown in Table-6.4.

In general, while the exchequer grants constantly reduced from 77.7% in 1974-75 to 59.8% in 1984-85 and further to 55.3 in 1987-88, income from fees, research grants and in particular income from research contracts increased considerably, 4% in 1974-75 to

6.5% in 1984-85 to a further upward movement to 9.2% in 1987-88.

The position of cash and short term deposits and investments of the nine universities at the end of 1979-80 and 1983-84 in relation to the general income was as shown in the Appendix-1. In, all the cases visible improvements took place. In terms of percentage of improvement of general income the highest was at Heriot-Watt (+) 40%, next highest being at Aston and Stirling - both (+) 30%. Lowest was at Hull (+) 6%.

On the students (Home and EC) number target position, while the UGC had specified, in July 1981, student number target of the individual universities, there was no target fixed for the intermediate years of the restructuring period, leaving, perhaps, some scope for minor adjustments. The UGC allowed a temporary addition to the student targets for science in a few universities which had admitted more students in Mathematical Sciences in October, 1982. The Annual Survey for 1983-84 observed that the home and EC student numbers were moving towards the overall target of 1984.[4]

Figure of full-time Home and EC student numbers in all the universities in U.K., by 1983-84 (or 1984-85) in relation to 1979-80 and 1980-81 are given in the Appendix-2 of Chapter-3.

Among all the universities, the maximum decrease by 1983-84 (or 1984-85) in relation to 1980-81 was at Salford (-) 30%. However, the overall decrease for all universities was 7%. The relative position in the nine universities covered by the project study was as shown in Table-6.5.

Table 6.5[5]

Changes in Full-time Home and EC Students Numbers by 1983-84 (or 1984-85)

University	Home & EC Students 1980-81	Increase (+)/Decrease (-) 1983-84 v. 1980-81 (Number)		(or 1984-85) - % change (%)	
Aston	4,438	(-)	798	(-)	18
Bath	3,234	+	26	+	1
Hull	5,120	(-)	920	(-)	18
Salford	3,928	(-)	1,178	(-)	30
Sheffield	7,441	(-)	581	(-)	8
Sussex	3,971	(-)	261	(-)	7
Heriot-Watt	2,540	(-)	420	(-)	17
Stirling	2,716	(-)	696	(-)	26
Aberdeen	5,195	(-)	255	(-)	5

IMPACT OF NEW BLOOD SCHEME

As part of the restructuring, the 'New Blood' scheme was an important aspect, for on one hand that aimed at the freshness of minds by inducting young teachers to provide vitality and rejuvenation to the teaching and research quality, on the other hand, through the replacements of old teachers by younger group, reduced the salary bill. Similar financial impact was also aimed at through other staff members - academic related, technical, secretarial and clerical as also manual and ancillary.

The table-6.6 shows the changes in the staff position of all categories between 1979-80 and the end of the restructuring period.

Table 6.6[6]

University	Percentage of changes in staff				
	Academic	Academic Related	Techni-cal	Secre-tarial & Clerical	Manual & Ancillary
Aberdeen	16.06	27.02	16.05	25.04	15.09
Aston	42.00	18.00	43.00	42.00	18.00
Stirling	6.07	26.03	9.06	12.01	12.09
Salford	28.06	24.07	37.00	29.04	28.06
Sheffield	12.09	21.00	12.00	4.08	18.08
Bath	+ 1.07	8.03	4.04	+ 1.02	+ 12.02
Heriot-Watt	1.05	3.05	9.00	11.09	16.03
Hull	13.03	14.04	20.05	29.04	16.03
Sussex	13.01	15.04	16.01	10.03	10.5

Note: Except in the case of +at Bath, in all cases it was (-)

Of the nine universities, Aston achieved the highest changes in respect of three of the five categories, namely, Academic, Technical and Secretarial and Clerical staff. For the Academic Related staff, the highest change was at Aberdeen followed closely by Sterling. As regards Manual and Ancillary, the highest was at Salford.

AGE PROFILE OF THE STAFF

The number and percentage of the staff members under various age groups in the nine universities in 1980 and 1984, showing the changes in the two periods is shown in the Appendix-2. If the age profile is broadly grouped under three, namely below 35, between 35 and 49 and 50 and above, the picture will be as shown in the table-6.7.

Table 6.7[7]

Staff Changes the Nine Universities

University		*Below 35*	*Between 35 & 49*	*50 and above*
1. Aberdeen	1980	183 (26.3%)	373 (53.6%)	140 (20.1%)
	1984	87 (15%)	367 (63.3%)	126 (21.7%)
2. Aston	1980	130 (24.3%)	230 (43.1%)	174 (32.6%)
	1984	35 (12.3%)	170 (59.4%)	81 (28.3%)
3. Bath	1980	97 (27.1%)	164 (46%)	96 (26.9%)
	1984	64 (17.7%)	184 (50.6%)	115 (31.6%)
4. Heriot Watt	1980	63 (23.5%)	155 (57.8%)	50 (18.7%)
	1984	47 (17.8%)	168 (63.6%)	49 (18.6%)
5. Hull	1980	107 (21.1%)	289 (57.2%)	110 (21.7%)
	1984	50 (11.2%)	291 (65.5%)	103 (23.3%)
6. Salford	1980	63 (33.3%)	280 (59.4%)	129 (27.3%)
	1984	41 (12.2%)	237 (70.3%)	59 (17.5%)
7. Sheffield	1980	215 (24.1%)	489 (54.7%)	189 (21.2%)
	1984	114 (14.9%)	495 (63.7%)	169 (21.7%)

University		*Below 35*	*Between 35 & 49*	*50 and above*
8. Sterling	1980	60 (23.1%)	171 (65.8%)	29 (11.1%)
	1984	31 (13%)	174 (72.9%)	34 (14.1%)
9. Sussex	1980	108 (23.6%)	266 (58.1%)	84 (18.3%)
	1984	70 (16.8%)	272 (65%)	76 (18.2%)

An analysis of the above table would reveal that in the age group of 50 and above between the 1980 and 1984, the percentage rose in the case of Aberdeen (by 1.6%), Bath (by 4.7%), Hull (by 1.6%), Stirling (by 3%). In the case of Sheffield, Heriot-Watt and Sussex, the increase was below one per cent. The picture was different at Aston where there was a reduction by 4.3% in the age group of 50 and above and at Salford by 9.8%.

In the age group between 35 and 49, the percentage of the staff members increased in the case of all the nine universities from 4.6% (Bath) to 16.3% (Aston).

The picture in the age group below 35 was negatively on the higher side in all the nine universities from 5.3% in the case of Heriot-Watt to as high as 21.1% at Salford.

On the position of the Academic staff, in its advice to the Government in 1984, the UGC, expressed its concern about the urgent need for '... a steady renewal of ... academic staff to sustain ... intellectual vitality and the effectiveness of ... teaching and research'.[8] It pointed out the 'imbalance' in the age structure as follows:

(i) Less than 30 per cent of all non-clinical academic staff are aged 50 or over and in a dozen institutions the figure is below 20 per cent. This is mainly the result of the contraction of the past three years; between August 1981 and March 1984 about 2000 staff over the age of 50 took voluntary retirement. The substantial further number of voluntary retirements which is expected this September can only make things worse.

(ii) Less than 15 per cent of staff are under 35 because recruitment in the early 1980s was well below the levels of the 1970s. This has been only partially offset by the new blood scheme.

(iii) About 60 per cent of staff are aged between 35 and 49. This is the result of high recruitment in the late 1960s and early 1970s. Most of the members of this large group will not reach retirement age until the first decade of the twenty-first century.

The UGC also pointed out to the imbalance in the staffing pattern of different subjects. The Committee recommended that "... there should be a minimum annual recruitment of 3.5 per cent of the total number of academic staff".[9] It also opined that for comparison, a university system with a balanced age structure would have about 40 per cent of staff over 50, about 20 per cent under 35 and about 40 per cent between 35 and 49'.[10] The voluntary early retirement scheme is to a large extent responsible for the imbalance.

As regards the non-Academic staff, the UGC conveyed to the Government that when it visited the universities, it was 'impressed' "... by the loyalty and dedication of their non-academic staff, who are frequently expected to show great flexibility in adopting to changes in working requirements and environments".[11] It also recognised that the "Technical, Secretarial and Clerical staff play a vital part in the universities, teaching and research activities".[12]

LEADERSHIP QUESTION AND QUALITY

When the universities faced the problems arising out of the cuts of grants, students number restrictions and subject mix, imposed by the UGC letter, "... the government formed the view that the universities were incapable of rapid and effective response, a condition supposedly due to their ineffective or poor management practice. It was in this context that the question of leadership in the system and the managerial experiences and practices came up under focus which were discussed at various levels particularly to identify the shortcomings and to take precautions for any future disaster so that there would be no question to 'breakdown' or a situation that might lead to 'bankruptcy'.

The institution of Vice-Chancellor is recognised universally, by whatever name called, as the Principal Academic and Executive Head of the University System. He is responsible for all that happens in the university from the most important policy decision to, at times, a mundane matter. A Vice-Chancellor has been defined as:

> "The person who is expected, above all, 'to embody the spirit of academic freedom and the principles of good management in the University, is the Vice-Chancellor. He stands for the commitment of the university to scholarship and pursuit of truth and can ensure that the executive wing of the University is used in its activities".[13]

The Robbins Committee observed that 'it is difficult to overstate' the importance of the position of the Vice-Chancellor, who '... is at once a member of the governing body and the Chairman of the main academic councils. He must, therefore, be at the centre of all discussions involving broad questions of internal policy or relation with the outside world. He must represent his institution in all formal or informal relation with the University Grants Committee; he must be present at meetings of the Committee of Vice-Chancellors and Principals; he must keep up in touch with potential benefactors, and he must be aware, in general, of developments in various branches of learning".[14] The expectations of these qualities from the Vice-Chancellor precisely tells the multifarious responsibilities of the Vice-Chancellor who, in effect, has necessarily to be a dynamic personality of progress and change and provide leadership to the entire system. Undoubtedly, the responsibilities are too many in characters and too heavy as burden. It is for this reason that the Robbins Committee again observed that "No other enterprise would impose on its Chairman the variety and burden of work that the modern university requires of its Vice-Chancellor".[15] The Universities are more complex than ever before. The Jarratt Committee recognised the universities as 'complex organisation with multiple objectives and functions'. It has mentioned the following as some examples, which make the managerial and administrative process complex:[16]

(a) *Range of academic activity:* There is an immense range and variety of activity undertaken within each university. This is reflected in the number of departments in some institutions - there are for example as many as 120 in Edinburgh. The diverse physical environment, equipment, library facilities and personnel needed for research and teaching over such a wide range of activity complicate judgements about objectives and resource allocation.

(b) *Professional loyalties:* Between a third and a half of the total staff which universities employ are 'professionals' in widely diverse fields. Moreover, such staff often regard their status as physicists, surgeons, lawyers or technicians as being at least as important as their membership of a university. This can give rise to divided loyalties and conflicts of interest. It adds to the task of uniting an institution to work to a common purpose and objectives, and provides a managerial challenge.

(c) *Participation:* The tradition of self-government, which lies at the heart of a university's constitution, has extended over the years to wider groupings in the institution who have, or wish to have, a voice in both academic and business affairs. Such participation can provide a strong unifying force within the institution; but it can also be used to delay or block difficult but necessary decisions. This can be particularly marked at a time of scarce and declining resources.

(d) *The tenure issue:* There has been much comment in recent years on the inflexibility imposed on universities by the terms and conditions of service of staff, and of academic staff in particularly. Essentially, tenure gives permanent employment in the employing university, with a contract that can only be broken in special circumstances. There are frequently restricted to various forms of misconduct, or inability or willingness to do the job; in general, tenure does not allow for dismissal on grounds of redundancy.

Before proceeding further, it would be proper to know whether the universities had suffered due to the absence of the right managerial experience in tackling and handling the problems that primarily arose due to the UGC letter dated 1st July, 1981 - both before and after - and whether any steps were considered to avoid such situations in future.

Although some case writers were not quite willing to address the question, only two case writers responded - they were from Sussex and Salford. According to the case writer of the Sussex,[17] in the unexpected difficult situation, there were "..internal obstacles to coherent planning of the university's future". He also added that "The Vice-Chancellor's influence was circumscribed by two of his three deputies being also the 'managers' and representatives of the Arts and Science areas with far greater effective authority over the deployment of resources, and by a large and representative Planning Committee, and by an even larger Senate". Absence of co-ordination between the academics and administrative officers was mentioned to be another problem for on one hand administrative officers were required "... under pressure to produce annual budgets and returns for the UGC, resorted to arbitrary mechanisms and to formulae; whilst the academics produced generalised statements, not conspicuously based on consultation and systematic analysis of evidence, which were ill-received by the academic community".

In the case of Salford, the case writer came out with a number of points[18] in this regard, namely,

- never believe your own propaganda;
- never act in the belief that independent assessors are totally independent;
- Departments failed to identify and support enough activities of high quality, and, in particular, failed to promote public and peer acceptance of the quality of their work;
- Numbers (i.e. department size) became too dominant a feature of the Judgements about resources; and
- The university was insufficiently sensitive to the public debate and to the signs of problems for the system as a whole.

The summarised views, lessons learnt and 'Good' Managerial Practice and Unsatisfactory Experience as revealed through the Case Studies are given in the Appendix-3.

Although other case writers did not address the question at all or in any reasonable detail, the fact remained that the structure, composition and above all the history of the particular university had had their impact on the question. While managerial experience is certainly a good tool to meet difficult situations, there will always be operational problem if on the other hand, the structure and composition of the management of the university are not in tune with the modern need. In particular, because universities are dominantly the management of the teachers where the administrative officers are, in true sense, to help the system to achieve the central objectives of teaching and research, and the teachers being what they are, it is difficult for any Vice-Chancellor to convince all, at least the majority, to go in for hard decisions. It is for this reason that Prof. John

Sizer based on his experience of self evaluation exercises of universities in other countries, observed that "... they tend to break down under conditions of financial stringency and contraction. There is a general reluctance to face reality and make hard choices, and a preference for equal treatment and maintenance of the existing range of subjects".[19]

Recognising that for managing the complex university system, high quality managers are necessary and particularly when they have to be managers of change so as "...to be successful in developing and implementing a plan for significant reduction in core funding, possibily accompanied by similar student number reductions, which recognises the need to protect the institution's strengths and weaknesses and requires selectivity in the allocation of resources",[20] through the analysis of the Case Studies, certain managerial guidelines emerged as given in the Appendix-4.

While there might not be any disagreement about the various guidelines, the fundamental question that remained was how the individual leadership at the given time performed and how flexible the structure was, for they would determine whether there was the right type of leadership and whether the leader had the minimum flexibility in the structure to steer the university through rough weather. Even for the leader of the highest quality to deliver the goods, it is necessary that he should have the right kind of structure and support.

Finally comes the question of the Leadership and Managerial Role of the Vice-Chancellors. Addressing this important question, the Jarratt Committee Report identified that "... the Vice-Chancellor's primary roles are as: giving academic leadership as Chairman of the Senate, acting as Chief Executive with responsibility to

Council, representing the University in relation with the local and regional communities and representing its interests to a whole variety of national and international bodies".[21]

For obvious reasons, different Vice-Chancellor in office perceive the role according to his own background and understanding of the system and more importantly how he conceives the office of the Vice-Chancellor. The style of functioning of the individual which comes with the individual, is another important factor. The Jarratt Report observed that "Vice-Chancellors will always have differences of style arising from their own personalities".[22] The Report observed that 'we have been especially struck both in the Reports and from our discussions, with wide range of management styles and modes of operating which characterise the Vice-Chancellors..."[23] It stated that 'In some cases, the Vice-Chancellor sees his role quite clearly as providing leadership and exercising executive authority; in others he sees his role primarily as that of a Chairman seeking consensus".[24]

The task of the Vice-Chancellors as leaders of the system becomes all the more difficult when on one hand, he has to achieve for the university all that the various decision-making bodies decide and on the other hand, he does not have the commensurate powers. The Report observed that "the Study Reports show one common factor - that Vice-Chancellors have virtually no formal constitutional powers other than those which may be delegated to them to act on behalf of Council, Senate or a Committee. They rely on the influence which stems from leadership and persuasion. It does, however, lie within the powers of Council to strengthen formally the executive role of the Vice-Chancellor".[25]

In order that the universities have the proper

leadership what is prerequisite is selection of the Vice-Chancellor. Addressing this crucially important issue, the Robbins Committee recommended that:

> 'Senate should give clear lead as to the qualities they look for in their new Vice-Chancellor; governing bodies or their appointed committees should then examine thoroughly the selected fields of search and consider the potential candidates within them".[26]

The Jarratt Committee considered the task of the process of selection of Vice-Chancellors as 'vital' and as he has to provide leadership to an academic organization, it conceived that "... it is probable that a large proportion of appointees to such posts will continue to be senior academics from within the university system".[27] In view of the fact that the Vice-Chancellors will be drawn from within the system, it suggested that "this being so, it is important in our view that senior academics across the university system, from whom the next generation of Vice-Chancellors will be chosen, should be given the opportunity to improve their managerial skills through appropriate training and to gain some experience outside the university system through periods of secondment and staff exchange".[28] The Jarratt Report also observed that "The tradition of Vice-Chancellors being scholars first and acting as a Chairman of the Senate carrying out its will, rather than leading it strongly, is changing. The shift to the style of chief executive, bearing the responsibility for leadership and effective management of the institution, is emerging and is likely to be all the more necessary for the future".[29]

As reflected in the Case Studies of the DES Research Project, "positive and decisive leadership" and "high quality manager of change of appropriate academic standing" have been preferred to "executive leader" used by the Jarratt Committee.

According to the Case Studies, it is clear that 'exceptional leadership and managerial skills' are the prerequisites for the Vice-Chancellor who have 'few executive powers, in a self-governing community of scholars. This is particularly necessary in the universities with long established, strongly decentralised faculty structures'.[30] Precisely, the Vice-Chancellor should provide that leadership which not only creates the environment conducive to creating 'excellence' in teaching and research but also brings reputation to the university as a centre of innovation, creation and preservation of knowledge for the present and future society and world of learning.

JARRATT'S RECOMMENDATIONS

In the direction of restructuring the university system, the recommendations of the Jarratt Committee which included *inter-alia*, the Chairman of UGC and the Prime Minister's Adviser on efficiency, are not only important but have had far reaching impact. Besides the observations and recommendations relating to the Office of the Vice-Chancellor or Principal, some other recommendations have also been made for the universities. Those recommendations are extremely relevant to any Vice-Chancellor to be effective in the discharge of his duties.

In order to find out the reaction of the universities to the recommendations of the Report, the UGC had invited responses from the universities on the various recommendations. They were analysed by Prof. John Sizer as shown in the Table-6.8.

Table 6.8[31]

Recommendations of Jarratt Committee and Responses from Various Universities

Recommendations of the Jarratt Committee	*Summary of Responses from Universities*			
	Accepted	*Qualified or partial acceptance*	*Rejected*	*No Response*
1	*2*	*3*	*4*	*5*
1. Role of Councils	78 (97%)	2 (2%)	0 (0%)	1 (1%)
Councils to assert their responsibilities in governing their institutions notably in respect of strategic plans to underpin academic decisions and structures which bring planning, resource allocation and accountability together in one corporate process linking academic, financial and physical aspects.				
2. Role of Senate	79 (98%)	1 (1%)	0 (0%)	1 (1%)
Senates to continue to play their essential role in coordinating and endorsing detailed academic work and as the main forum for generating an academic view and giving advice on broad issues to Council.				

1	*2*	*3*	*4*	*5*
3. Plans	79 (98%)	1 (1%)	0 (0%)	1 (1%)
Developing a rolling academic and institutional plan which will be reviewed regularly and against which resources will be allocated.				
4. Planning and Resources Committees	61 (75%)	15 (19%)	4 (5%)	1 (1%)
Establish a planning and resources committee of strictly limited size reporting to Council and Senate with the Vice-Chancellor as Chairman and both academic and lay members.				
5. Budget Delegation	56 (69%)	22 (27%)	2 (3%)	1 (1%)
Budget Delegation to appropriate centres which are held responsible to the planning and resources committee for what they have achieved against their budgets				
6. Vice-Chancellors and Principals	78 (97%)	1 (1%)	0 (0%)	2 (2%)
Recognise the Vice-Chancellor not only as academic leader but also as chief executive.				

1	2	3	4	5
7. Heads of Departments Appointing Heads of Depts. by Councils on the recommendation of the Vice-Chancellor after appropriate consultation with clear duties and responsibilities for the performance of their departments and the use of resources.	59 (73%)	17 (21%)	3 (4%)	2 (2%)
8. Performance Indicators and Cost Awareness Developing reliable and consistent performance indicators, greater awareness of costs and more full cost charging.	73 (90%)	7 (9%)	1 (1%)	0 (0%)
9. Staff Development Appraisal and Accountability Introducing arrangements for staff development, appraisal and accountability.	72 (89%)	8 (10%)	0 (0%)	1 (1%)
10. Committees Saving academic and other time by having fewer committee meetings, involving fewer				

1	2	3	4	5
people, and more delegated authority to officers of the university, especially for non-academic matters.	72 (89%)	88 (10%)	0 (0%)	1 (1%)

Role of Councils

A glance at the above table indicates the overwhelming acceptance (97%) of the recommendation in respect of the Role of Councils. In fact, as mentioned by Sizer, "Many have established Jarratt type Policy and Resources Committees, restructured the Council agendas to differentiate between strategic technical and statutory business".[32] They have also revised the Committee structures and delegated extensive powers to sub-committees.

Role of Senate

With regard to the role of Senate, more favourable response was received (98%). It is because in a large number of cases, the position was 'current practice', or 'already implemented'. Some had also informed the recommendation was a 'standard practice', since long.

Plans, Planning and Resources Committees

As regards the Rolling Plans, the response was again overwhelming (98%). However, for establishing a planning and resources committee, *inter-alia* with lay members, the percentage of acceptance was only 75% with another 19% partial or qualified. As analysed, "Many of the qualified or partial acceptance relate to the role of lay members and to the chairmanship of the committee, and others wish to retain existing structures which they believe meet the spirit of the recommendation".[33] On the whole, 'A large number of institutions have established Policy and Resources Committees in the form recommended. Some have amended the responsibilities and membership of existing committees to meet the recommendation, and others already had such Committees'.[34]

Budget Delegation

On the question of Budget delegation, as will be seen from the above table 6.8 the lowest response (56%) was received in favour of the recommendation. However, qualified or partial acceptance was 27%. Many of this group 'argued against full delegation in small single faculty institutions'. Sizer comments that "Many appear to lose sight of the accountability and performance assessment aspects of budgetary planning and control systems".[35] Identifying the reasons for this tendency, Sizer felt that "They tend to view budgetary control purely in terms of the exercise of tight financial control".[36] It also appears from the analysis of the responses that many did not fully understand the underlying spirit of the recommendation.

Vice-Chancellors and Principals

The most important recommendation that the Jarratt Committee made in the context of the leadership need and executive approach was about the Vice-Chancellor. Responses in favour of the recommendation was very high (97%). The reason for this high response was due to the fact that a large number responded to this recommendation as 'current position', 'already operating'. However, a small number informed that they would take appropriate action. In the case of the University of Wales and the Cambridge University, the role of the Vice-Chancellor is different, for there "...he chairs a number of key committees but has otherwise limited powers".

Some felt that "...the use of the 'chief executive' analogy in relation to the office of the Vice-Chancellor in that it might be thought to imply the direct imposition of central control which would not be appropriate, and would in fact be damaging to the governance of a large academic community".[37] However, it is important to note that the Jarratt Report did not conceive the dominant chief executive. The analysis has pointed out to the '... concern expressed that a Chief Executive of the Jarratt type would require management machinery and management powers foreign to many British Universities, and for this to be acceptable these powers would have to be defined carefully".[38]

Heads of Departments

In the academic and the developed administrative structure of the universities, Heads of Departments occupy very important position, for they have necessarily to perform both academic as well as administrative functions. It is for this reason that the Jarratt Committee has suggested that they should be given some training in managerial techniques.

But the responses received to the recommendation of the Jarratt Report was, according to Sizer, 'not altogether satisfactory and in terms of percentage, it was 73%. After analysing the responses, Sizer commented that "They confirm that many universities may not have understood fully the recommendations in the Jarratt Report, and that some institutions have looked at each recommendation in isolation rather than seeing them as an integrated whole".[39]

Performance Indicators

Of the various recommendations of the Jarratt Committee, its recommendation to develop reliable and consistent performance indicators, greater awareness of costs and more full cost charging was of great significance. Although the need and desirability of measuring the performance of the institutions of higher education was felt long ago, no concrete step was taken across the system, for it was considered to be 'horror in academic circles'.

In the 1985 Green Paper, concern was expressed ... that higher education does not always respond sufficiently to changing economic needs'. Jarratt also suggested that 'A range of performance indicators should be developed, covering both inputs and outputs and designed for use both within individual institution and for making comparisons between institutions'.[40] The Jarratt Committee was bold enough not only to make the recommendation for the performance indicators but also to suggest the indicators. It suggested indicators in three groups as shown in Table-6.7.

Table 6.7[41]

Performance Indicators Proposed in the Jarratt Report

Internal performance indicators include

- market share of undergraduate applications (by subject)
- graduation rates and classes of degrees
- attraction of masters and doctoral students
- success rate of higher degrees (and time taken)
- attraction of research funds
- teaching quality

External performance indicators include

- acceptability of graduates (post-graduates) in employment
- first destination of graduates (post-graduates)
- reputation judged by external reviews
- publications by staff and citations
- patents, inventions, consultancies
- membership, prizes, medals of learned societies
- papers at conferences

Operational performance indicators include

- unit costs
- staff/student ratios
- class sizes
- course options available
- staff workloads
- library stock availability
- computing availability

The main recommendation on performance indicators has two aspects, namely, *(i)* performance indicators and *(ii)* cost awareness and full cost charging. Therefore, responses to the recommendations were also required accordingly. The 'accepted' responses was 90%. The qualified or partial acceptance was 9% which represented the cost awareness aspect of the recommendation.

Responding warmly to the recommendation of the Jarratt Committee on performance indicators, the UGC and CVCP had set up a Working Group which had proposed a more detailed set of indicators than those suggested in the Jarratt Report. The Group had mentioned that majority of the institutions were using 'some indicators over a long period, primarily input and process indicators'. They reviewed the use of indicators in the light of the Jarratt Report and the CVCP/UGC statements. However, a few had expressed difficulties to develop indicators of teaching quality.

The universities, in general, recognised the need to create their information system so as to link the departments to the central data-processing system. Management Information System was recognised at all levels in a number of universities.

Based on the guidelines prepared by the Working Group of the UGC/CVCP, performance indicators were developed, but they were still subject to further examination. It was for this reason that Sizer observed that 'Because of the need to evaluate carefully the extent and basis of full cost charging and to develop the appropriate cost and management information systems, the implementation of this recommendation will be an ongoing process for a number of years'.[42]

The Working Group of the UGC/CVCP developed three broad indicators and five characteristics as shown in the Table-6.8.

In a situation where a widely acceptable evaluation methodology is yet to be developed, the existing basis can best be used for limited purposes of inter-departmental and interuniversity comparisons between the variables produced by the Group. The following[44] variables could be used to compare the performance of universities:

- unit costs;
- percentage of students not completing their degree course;
- percentage of graduates with a first upper second class honours degree;

Table 6.8[43]

Broad Indicators and Characteristics developed by the Working Committee of UGC/CVCP

Broad Indicators	*Characteristics*
1. Input indicators: these are concerned with the resources and factors employed in order to produce each institution outputs.	1. They should relate to the objectives of the universities, especially those concerned with teaching and research.
	2. They should be specific, quantifiable and standardize so that comparisons can be made within and between institutions.
2. Process indicators: these relate to the way in which resources and factors combined and used in order to produce each institution's outputs.	3. They should be as simple as possible in order to aid understanding of the activities of universities about which they provide information
	4. They should be acceptable, credible and free from bias.
3. Output indicators: these describe the outputs produced by universities.	5. They should provide useful information about the operations and activities of institution and they should be expected to provoke question about these operations and activities.

- percentage of graduates unemployed or in a short-term job (six months after graduation)
- research grants per full-time academic; and
- research rating (calculated from the UFC's research rating exercises.

Based on the above variables, Appendix-5 and

Appendix-6 provide information in respect of all the UK universities. However, the authors have cautioned that the information 'should not be taken seriously even though the individual indicators may look plausible at first sight'.[45] Locating the possible reasons for this, the authors explain that 'the main problem is that the individual indicators do not compare like with like. For example, although it may be interesting to know that university A awards a higher proportion of first class degrees than university B, this information is of little use per se for evaluation purposes since we do not know whether the difference between A and B is a result of better teaching in A or a result of A attracting students with more innate ability.[46]

Really speaking, it does not seem practical to overcome this kind of situation between universities. Pragmatically, either one has to compromise with the inherent limitations of the methodology or make effort to categorise universities based on the similarities of tolerable differences. But even that would change from year to year. However, how far that would serve the purposes of the Government in question need to be answered.

Keeping all the possible difficulties in the methodology, "perhaps the only way to measure performance is to take an extremely broad view of what universities do and the processes they use to achieve their ultimate objectives".[47] But everybody in the game should remember the following warning given by the authors:

> "Our final word is one of warning. No one has yet devised a single indicator of performance which commands wide support amongst the academic community. Performance measurement is still very much in its infancy stage and those using

performance indicators, whether they refer to teaching and research activities, should use them with great caution and considerable humility".[48]

Staff Development Appraisal and Accountability

Basic to achieving objectives of any type and magnitude, is the human beings of the right attitude and skill. For achieving the various goals that the Jarratt Committee recommended, it stated that "The attitude of mind of the staff and the will of the institution to achieve the necessary change are crucial. Without these, little will be achieved of value".[49] It was found that there was no systematic annual appraisal of staff excepting in most cases reviews undertaken at the time of confirmation, crossing of efficiency bar or for promotion.

While the responses to 'Accepted' category was 89%, another 10% was partial or qualified which were from small institutions. Many institutions informed having established Staff Development and Appraisal Committees. However, the 'accountability' aspect attracted limited attention.

The CVCP established the first Universities' Staff Development and Training Unit (USDTU) in 1989 with pump-priming funding directly from the then UGC. Later, CVCP took over partial funding of the Unit by subscriptions from all-member universities. The USDTU also planned to generate income for its activities. The USDTU's statement is as follows:

> "To advise on and support the development of strategically planned and comprehensive programmes of staff development and training in individual institutions, in regional networks and at national level across the university system, in order to

enhance the potential of universities and departments and individuals within them, to achieve their objectives and to respond effectively and efficiently to changing external and internal circumstances".[50]

In so far as the activities in the universities are concerned, the position is as follows:[51]

- there is increasing staff development activity in universities at institutional, regional and national levels;
- more staff development co-ordinators are gradually being appointed to full-time position;
- staff development needs are being met in a number of ways not limited just to the provisions of courses; and
- universities are using a wide range of internal and external providers to meet their staff development needs.

Committees

Although 89% responses conveyed full acceptance of the recommendation, there was another 10% which was partially accepted or qualified in nature. Looking to the significance of the recommendation, which aimed at saving the precious time of the academics so that they could devote more time to better productive activities, the recommendation has been implemented 'positively by virtually all institutions'. Many had already restructured the committee system and others were in the process of so doing.

CONCLUSION

Despite all out efforts on the part of the nine universities in question the income position deteriorated despite increased fees from home and EC students by 1984-85. It was the non-government income - mainly through two channels - 'research and contract' and 'general income' that helped the universities to tide over the problems. However, in Bath, while income from research contract did not improve in 1984-85 in relation to 1979-80, the income from 'other services rendered' increased from 2.4% in 1979-80 to 3.8% in 1984-85.

While as acknowledged by the Annual Survey for 1983-84, the home and EC student numbers was moving towards the overall target of 1984, the position of per cent of changes in staff was a mixed one. Even on the age profile, late announcement of the 'New Blood Scheme' and 'Information Technology', although helped the universities a good deal, finally did not enable them to achieve the desired level.

Coming to the question of leadership and its quality, firstly that will depend on the selection of the individual who occupies the position and secondly situation in which he has to function including the structure and organisation of the university. A professional manager may relatively find it easy to bail out a business house from a difficult position, but in the case of an institution of higher education, chances are generally fifty-fifty because of the composition of the system. Teachers and students are the main components who are emotional and the occasional aggressive behaviour of students make things difficult particularly when hard decisions are to be taken.

The mandate to generate non-government income and more importantly not only to keep up the name and fame of the university, but try to improve further, needs full support and understanding of the teachers and students. These make the job of the Vice-Chancellors difficult and delicate. It is for this reason that the Robbins Committee said that "No other enterprise would impose on its chairman the variety and burden of work that the modern university requires of its Vice-Chancellor". This was what Robbins observed thirty years before. Today, the variety of burden could easily be multiplied by a factor of four.

The Jarratt Committee recommendations particularly the Performance Indicators and devolution of powers, when fully implemented, would surely show significant changes. But by that time, it would be time to look for new changes in the fast changing world.

Appendix-I

CASH AND SHORT TERM DEPOSITS AND INVESTMENTS

(amount in thousand pounds)

University	*End of 1979-80*		*End of 1983-84*		*Change*	
	amount	*% of Gen. Income*	*amount*	*% of Gen. Income*	*amount*	*%*
Aberdeen	86	0.4	4283	14.3	+4197	+14
Aston	1724	10	7939	40	+6215	+30
Bath	2222	21	4819	29	+2597	+ 8
Heriot-Watt	1055	12	3934	28	+4989	+40
Hull	1162	9	2921	15	+1859	+ 6
Salford	3264	23	8759	49	+5495	+26
Sheffield	185	1	6045	15	+5860	+14
Stirling	400	5	4175	35	+3775	+30
Sussex	2414	18	6606	34	+4192	+16

N.B : The Data in this table may not have been prepared on the same basis by all institutions.

Source: Table-12 of Final Report of the DES Research Project "Institutional Responses to Financial Reductions in the University Sector", John Sizer, Loughborough, 1987 unpublished).

Appendix-II

AGE ANALYSIS OF STAFF, 1980 Vs. 1984

Age Group Years	*1980*		*1984*		*Change + or (-)*	
	No.	*%*	*No.*	*%*	*No.*	*%*
ABERDEEN						
Under 30	57	8.2	34	5.9	(-) 23	(-) 2.3
30 - 34	126	18.1	53	9.1	(-) 73	(-) 9.0
35 - 39	154	22.1	111	19.1	(-) 43	(-) 3.0
40 - 44	135	19.4	132	22.8	(-) 3	+ 3.4
45 - 49	84	12.1	124	21.4	+ 40	+ 9.3
50 - 54	59	8.5	70	12.1	+ 11	+ 3.6
55 - 59	57	8.2	35	6.0	(-) 22	(-) 2.2
60 and over	24	3.4	21	3.6	(-) 3	+ 0.2
Total	696	100	580	100	(-)116	–
Under 35	183	26.3	87	15.0	(-) 96	(-) 11.3
50 and over	140	20.1	126	21.7	(-) 14	+ 1.6
ASTON						
Under 30	29	5.4	13	4.6	(-) 16	(-) 0.8
30 - 34	101	18.9	22	7.7	(-) 79	(-)11.2
35 - 39	73	13.7	72	25.2	(-) 1	+11.5

Age Group Years	1980 No.	1980 %	1984 No.	1984 %	Change + or (-) No.	Change + or (-) %
40 - 44	75	14.0	47	16.4	(-) 28	+ 2.4
45 - 49	82	15.4	51	17.8	(-) 31	+ 2.4
50 - 54	89	16.7	46	16.1	(-) 43	(-)0.6
55 - 59	53	9.9	27	9.4	(-) 26	(-)0.5
60 and above	32	6.0	8	2.8	(-) 24	(-)3.2
Total	534	100	286	100	(-)248	–
Under 35	130	24.3	35	12.3	(-) 95	(-)12.0
50 and over	174	32.6	81	28.3	(-) 93	(-) 4.3
BATH						
Under 30	19	5.3	18	5.0	(-) 1	(-) 0.3
30 - 34	78	21.8	46	12.7	(-)32	(-) 9.1
35 - 39	53	14.9	77	21.1	+ 24	+ 6.2
40 - 44	54	15.1	47	13.0	(-) 7	(-) 2.1
45 - 49	57	16.0	60	16.5	+ 3	+ 0.5
50 - 54	49	13.7	56	15.4	+ 7	+ 1.7
55 - 59	32	9.0	40	11.0	+ 8	+ 2.0
60 - 64	15	4.2	19	5.2	+ 4	+ 1.0
Total	357	100	363	100	+ 6	–
Under 35	97	27.1	64	17.7	(-)33	(-) 9.4
HERIOT-WATT						
Under 30	13	4.8	14	5.3	+ 1	+ 0.5
30 - 34	50	18.7	33	12.5	(-)17	(-) 6.2
35 - 39	62	23.1	67	25.4	+ 5	+ 2.3
40 - 44	56	20.9	55	20.8	(-) 1	(-) 0.1

Age Group Years	1980 No.	1980 %	1984 No.	1984 %	Change + or (-) No.	Change + or (-) %
45 - 49	37	13.8	46	17.4	+ 9	+ 3.6
50 - 54	26	9.7	27	10.2	+ 1	+ 0.5
55 - 59	20	7.5	16	6.1	(-) 4	(-) 1.4
60 and over	4	1.5	6	2.3	+ 2	+ 0.8
Total	268	100	264	100	(-) 4	–
Under 35	63	23.5	47	17.8	(-)16	(-) 5.7
50 and over	50	18.7	49	18.6	(-) 1	(-) 0.1
			HULL			
Under 30	33	6.5	13	2.9	(-) 20	(-) 3.6
30 - 34	74	14.6	37	8.3	(-) 27	(-) 6.3
35 - 39	110	21.7	81	18.2	(-) 29	(-) 3.5
40 - 44	109	21.6	111	25.0	+ 2	+ 3.4
45 - 49	70	13.9	99	22.3	+ 29	+ 8.4
50 - 54	45	8.9	62	14.0	+ 17	+ 5.1
55 - 59	37	7.3	29	6.6	(-) 8	(-) 0.7
60 and over	28	5.5	12	2.7	(-) 16	(-) 2.8
Total	506	100	444	100	(-) 62	–
Under 35	107	21.1	50	11.2	(-) 57	(-) 9.9
50 and over	110	21.7	103	23.3	(-) 7	+ 1.6
			SALFORD			
Under 30	11	2.3	11	3.3	(-) 1	+ 1.0
30 -34	52	11.0	30	8.9	(-) 22	(-) 2.1
35 - 39	73	15.5	57	16.9	(-) 16	+ 1.4
40 - 44	110	23.3	73	21.7	(-) 37	(-) 1.6
45 - 49	97	20.6	107	31.7	+ 10	+11.1
50 - 54	67	14.2	44	13.0	(-) 23	(-) 1.2

Age Group Years	1980 No.	1980 %	1984 No.	1984 %	Change + or (-) No.	Change + or (-) %
55 - 59	46	9.7	13	3.9	(-) 33	(-) 5.8
60 and over	16	3.4	2	0.6	(-) 14	(-) 2.8
Total	472	100	337	100	(-)135	–
Under 35	63	13.3	41	12.2	(-) 22	(-) 1.1
50 and over	129	27.3	59	17.5	(-) 70	(-) 9.8
SHEFFIELD						
Under 30	47	5.3	33	4.2	(-) 14	(-) 1.1
30 - 34	168	18.8	81	10.4	(-) 87	(-) 8.4
35 - 39	193	21.5	167	21.5	(-) 26	–
40 - 44	172	19.3	177	22.8	+ 5	+ 3.5
44 - 49	124	13.9	151	19.4	+ 27	+ 5.5
50 - 54	89	10.0	91	11.7	+ 2	+ 1.7
55 - 59	60	6.7	57	7.3	(-) 3	+ 0.6
60 and over	40	4.5	21	2.7	(-) 19	(-) 1.8
Total	893	100	778	100	(-)115	–
Under 35	215	24.1	114	14.6	(-)101	(-) 9.5
50 and over	189	21.2	169	21.7	(-) 20	+ 0.5
STIRLING						
Under 30	15	5.8	5	2.1	(-) 10	(-) 3.7
30 - 34	45	17.3	26	10.9	(-) 19	(-) 6.4
35 - 39	88	33.9	68	28.5	(-) 20	(-) 5.4
40 - 44	50	19.2	65	77.2	+ 15	+ 8.0
45 - 49	33	12.7	41	17.2	+ 8	+ 4.5
50 - 54	18	6.9	21	8.8	+ 3	+ 1.9
55 - 59	6	2.3	8	3.2	+ 2	+ 0.9
60 and over	5	1.9	5	2.1	(-) 1	+ 0.2
Total	260	100	239	100	(-) 21	–

Age Group Years	1980 No.	1980 %	1984 No.	1984 %	Change + or (-) No.	Change + or (-) %
Under 35	60	23.1	31	13.0	(-) 29	(-)10.1
50 and over	29	11.1	34	14.1	+ 5	+ 3.0
			SUSSEX			
Under 30	34	7.4	15	3.6	(-) 19	(-) 3.8
30 - 34	74	16.2	55	13.2	(-) 19	(-) 3.0
35 - 39	92	20.1	72	17.2	(-) 20	(-) 2.9
40 - 44	124	27.1	93	22.2	(-) 31	(-) 4.9
45 - 49	50	10.9	107	25.6	+ 57	+14.7
50 - 54	43	9.4	43	10.3	-	+ 0.9
54 - 59	34	7.4	26	6.2	(-) 8	(-) 1.2
60 and over	7	1.5	7	1.7	-	+ 0.2
Total	458	100	418	100	(-) 40	–
Under 35	108	23.6	70	16.8	(-) 38	(-) 6.8
50 and over	84	18.3	76	18.2	(-) 8	(-) 0.1

Source: U.K., Department of Education and Science, Institutional Responses to Financial Reduction of the University Sector, Comparative Analyses of the Universities Case Studies, John Sizer (1987), Table-9.

Appendix-III

Good Managerial Practice, Lessons Learnt and Unsatisfactory Experience as revealed through Case Studies of the DES Research Project

1. Salford

Six further lessons are identified in Salford's case study:

(i) The establishment and maintenance of steady planning targets for individual parts of the university (i.e. the 1984-85 plan).

(ii) The encouragement of initiatives with some appropriate reward mechanism (e.g. SCEL Ltd., and CAMPUS senior lectureships).

(iii) The establishment of a planned and co-ordinated public relations programme directed at emphasising in appropriate contexts the university's strengths and particular appeal.

(iv) The development of management structures where policy decisions are the subject of broad agreement after being tried and tested in appropriate fora, with implementation being the clear responsibility of individuals.

(v) Encouragement to departments to find particular strengths and to exploit them, in the context of agreed university aims and objectives.

(vi) The development of effective support mechanisms for declared policies (e.g. integrated chairs).

Two lessons learnt and unsatisfactory experiences are given:

(i) A failure to make sufficient allowance in the very early planning stages for the continued erosion of the value of the U.G.C. grants.

(ii) The slowness with which the reward mechanisms for unconventional but significant educational activities and successes can be built into the traditional academic career structure.

Satisfaction came from:

(i) The encouragement of the belief that all groups cannot only critically examine and discuss university policy but have the obligation to offer constructive suggestions as a reciprocal action was a significant factor in the coordination and management of the university's response to the cuts and the maintenance of a significant volume of activity and initiatives.

(ii) the insistence on the priority of an approved

academic plan based on available resources and which required appropriate action for its implementation helped to maintain the belief in the values and purposes of university teaching and research.

2. Stirling

Stirling's case writer observes that morale is not high, in spite of having come successfully through a severe reorganisation, and there is concern regarding future uncertainty. He considers the importance of the role of departmental and sectional heads in keeping motivation at a high level cannot be overemphasised.

3. Hull

For university management, a general, if obvious, conclusion from Hull's experience is the importance of identifying the correct policy quickly and then pursuing it consistently. It was clear that on two issues, delay in so doing worked to its disadvantage:

(i) It took four years from the winter of 1979 to arrive at a fully integrated policy in respect of the recruitment of overseas students and this represented a lost opportunity.

(ii) Acceptance of the U.G.C.'s 1984-85 student number targets in the Spring of 1982 rather than of 1983 would have entailed less diversion of effort from the real problems of academic planning and management. A policy of opposition to UGC., coupled with a campaign for additional student numbers, was not only unrealistic, it was contradictory.

It was not until the end of the restructuring period that Hull moved towards a more proactive and fundamental policy of restructuring. It had been argued earlier in the case study that the university could not have accepted this degree of change during the first two years of restructuring or at least not without serious damage to morale; and that the preservation of academic morale was of utmost importance. The consequence was, however, that the rate of change towards the end of the period and in the following year became frantic when it was realised that 1984-85 represented the base for the next stage of restructuring and time of still greater selectivity and competition between universities. In this context, an explicit corporate plan was crucial in expressing commitment to agreed policies and in stating priorities for development and for protection in an overall frame-work of contraction. The case writers conclude that their case study may be seen by some as portraying a typical pre-Jarratt milieu. One of the intentions had been to show the difficulties and complexity of management of the university as an autonomous body for which Jarrat attempts to provide an answer. Since the end of the restructuring period, there had been considerable structural and managerial change. Universities are concerned with the longer term, and changes should not be judged within the context of a three year time scale.

Commentary

The case writers' conclusion that it is important to identify the correct policy quickly and pursue it consistently is consistent with the contrasts drawn in the comparative analysis between Hull's approach to developing a plan and that of Salford, Aston and Stirling, which did not have strongly decentralised faculty structures; and also with the comment that time is not a luxury available to a university facing a financial crisis.

Sussex

The Sussex case writers draw a number of important implications from their study:

(i) From the experience of Sussex, it can be clearly seen that it is not possible to have 'equal misery'. Inequalities are inevitable as units start in unequal positions, and therefore it is preferable to plan where they will fall, rather than allow them to fall where they do through force of circumstance. Accross the board cuts sustain weaker areas at the expense of the strong and it would be the better policy to 'bite the bullet' and make selective decisions. The high

proportion of interviewees recognised in retrospect that Sussex had collectively ducked decisions and that more selectivity might have been possible.

(ii) Top-down planning can cause resentment and staff are more likely to accept decisions if they feel they have a hand, however small, in their making. Forward planning can provide opportunities for communnicating and collecting feedback from staff. Pushing problems downwards to be dealt with at lower levels by imposing targets can weaken staff's loyalty to the overall institution and poor corporate communication can exacerbate this effort. Comments that the threat of cuts was worse than the cuts themselves give evidence to the importance of communication; it is necessary to avoid rumours and to ensure people know where they stand. Likewise there must be channels to ensure that communication is two-way.

(iii) The dilemma of a dual managerial/representative role not only places undue pressure on individuals but also is not conducive to productive and innovative planning. In a period of retrenchment the top down managerial roles and bottom up representative roles need to be clearly differentiated.

(iv) The experience of the Library showed the benefits to be gained from flexible working arrangements in alleviating the problems of staffing imbalances. However, flexibility can be over-exploited as could be seen in the experiences of groups which had taken large amounts of unpaid leave. High levels of unpaid leave cannot be sustained as a long term policy.

(v) Where differential treatment is involved, clear and comprehensive reasons for decisions must be available, and readily supplied if requested to avoid breeding frustration and mistrust.

Commentary

The case writers' conclusions are consistent with the commentaries in the comparative analysis, and also with the guidelines developed in Sections 4 and 5.

Heriot-Wait

The Heriot-Watt project team identified the pressing need to obtain additional funding for research from non-government sources and to recover overheads.

Sheffield

Sheffield produced a single list of implications which were included in Parts II and III.

Bath

This comparative study was not as applicable to Bath as it was to the other universities in the study. Bath was relatively well treated in 1981, but the case writers emphasise it had been through a similar traumatic exercise in the early 1970's. It was not surprising therefore that it did not have to re-examine its policy structures and that very many aspects of its good management practices are embedded in methods, techniques and administration which had been applied over ten years. The pressures that were faced in the early 1970's were reflected in the way in which the management structure, particularly the executive authority vested in the Vice-Chancellor, and a small group of senior university officers, had brought about the management process, which was streamlined as compared with elsewhere. Bath had introduced at a very early stage an early retirement benefit scheme; it was one aspect of good management practice that had assisted it throughout the last decade. Furthermore the unit cost comparisons over the 1981-84 period clearly show the university to be no better treated than most of those universities severely cut in 1981-84. Recovery of contract overheads and the methods of recovering finance for the use of university facilities had been a major feature of good managerial practice before the 1981-84 exercise. Business enterprise and taking a share in the equity of companies which had been established from within the university is another major area which Bath is taking advantage of.

Commentary

Although less detailed than the other case studies, because Bath was favourably treated in 1981, the good management practices identified in the case study are consistent with the guidelines developed in Sections 4, 5 and 6.

Source: U.K., Department of Education and Science, Institutional Responses to Financial Reduction in the University Sector, Comparative Analysis of the Universities', Case Studies, John Sizer (1987), pp. 190 -192.

Appendix-IV

Managerial Guidelines for Vice-Chancellors and Principals as emerged through DES Research Project

1. Build, and ensure supported by, a strong and cohesive managerial team with clearly defined responsibilities, capable of the sort of extra dedication, involvement and utilisation of imagination which characterises a first class team. Assess the needs for, and acquire, appropriate management and leadership training and development for all members of the team. Avoid members of the managerial team having both top-down managerial roles and bottom-up representative roles.

2. Recognise the importance of understanding the external environment, in particular,

(a) being aware of external factors and influences at work and being able to interpret these authoritatively within the institution;

(b) being able to relate to and work effectively with external bodies; and

(c) keeping a finger on the pulse of the local business and wider community.

3. Employ computer based models for financial forecast-

ing, student number and staffing projections, and support management at all levels with computer based financial planning and control systems, management information systems, and performance appraisal procedures.

4. Develop detailed departmental profiles.

5. Recognise, when faced with the prospect of financial reductions, the need to build up financial reserves so as to provide the maximum flexibility to adapt to reduced financial circumstances. If advance warning is received of a possible range of financial reductions, prepare financial contingency plans to see the institution through any short term financial crisis, and consider carefully whether the contingency plans should be made available in the university.

6. Whilst recognising a vigorous political campaign of protest and appeals to a central funding body following the announcement of significant reductions of grant, may assist in maintaining internal cohesion and morale, separate the political campaign from the development of academic and financial plans. Do not delay the planning process whilst awaiting the results of appeals.

7. Ensure the chairman and lay members of Council/Court understand fully Council's/Court's responsibilities, and the role they have to play in support of the Vice-Chancellor/Principal in ensuring the institution faces upto the need to set priorities, make hard choices, and develop an integrated financial and academic plan; in monitoring its implementation, and if necessary, ensuring appropriate corrective action is taken.

8. Involve an influential, respected and informed group of senior academics in obtaining agreement to the planning process, in the preparation of a plan and its subsequent implementation.

9. Communicate and consult extensively with departments, staff and student unions in order to obtain agreement to the planning process, its time table and the criteria to be employed in evaluation, and to identify them with the philosophy of the plan.

10. Within a tight, step-by-step time table, employ a top-down, bottom-up, top-down approach to the preparation of the plan, with an extensive information gathering exercise preceding the top-down proposals, extensive consultation about the proposals and a willingness to give serious consideration to bottom-up responses, leading to top-down plans for approval by Senate and Council. Do not rely on faculty or school self-evaluation; recognise there may be a reluctance to make hard choices and a preference for equal treatment and maintenance of the existing range of subjects.

11. Whilst recognising the need for widespread communication, consultation and participation in the preparation of plans, accept may have to tolerate extensive argument, debate and controversy as part of the process of gaining acceptance of hard and difficult choices.

12. When preparing top-down proposals:

(a) Recognise the impact of financial reductions on the university's capacity to undertake research and concentrate in a limited number of fields. Identify those departments and units whose past research performance and future potential warrant their being selectively supported.

(b) Employ small, specialist and adhoc groups when it is necessary to identify, and evaluate quickly, policy options and to propose plans for the implementation of strategies for complex and/or specialised areas.

(c) Recognise, if actions have not been taken previously, opportunities exist to reduce costs and generate additional income in non-academic areas.

(d) Establish a central development/innovation fund to provide for flexibility in implementing the plan.

(e) Avoid raising expectations and making unrealistic promises, which may create debts to be paid that subsequently may prove to be embarrassments and lead to discontent and dissension.

13. Make positive efforts, and involve all staff, to continually promote the external image of the university and to

secure additional income. Develop and implement a planned and coordinated public relations policy programme directed at communicating to appropriate audiences the institution's distinctive characteristics, strengths and appeal.

14. Develop positive personnel policies and procedures. Involve unions in the development and implementation of these policies. Recognise that at an appropriate stage in relations with unions careful consideration should be given to whether it would be helpful to commission an independent review of the university's financial position. As far as possible employ concept of a single pool of staff and regard early retirement as one element of a policy which encompasses unpaid leaves of absence, vacancy review procedures and staff training and redeployment. Avoid equating voluntary redundancy with academic incompetence. Respect the dignity of individuals, adopt personal approaches to agreeing early retirement arrangements, and encourage continuing association and identification with the university. Recognise the negative aspects of intimation of possibility of compulsory redundancies and only contemplate in last resort.

15. Ensure that planning, resource allocation, accountability and monitoring of performance are effectively integrated. As far as possible develop plans for responsibility centres. Allocate resources, devolve plans for responsibility centres. Allocate resources, devolve financial responsibility and accountability and provide incentives to generate additional income, directly to responsible heads of department, and subsequently monitor their performance. Avoid intermediate planning and resource allocating bodies, such as faculties, which may be unwilling to make hard choices and implement selectivity, and cannot subsequently be held accountable for their actions.

16. Ensure that plans and decision-making processes are sufficiently dynamic and flexible to allow for externally generated developments, and for initiatives to be taken quickly in response to external opportunities.

17. Recognise the changing, more demanding, and at times conflicting managerial and representative roles of heads of departments, and the need for periodic replacement. Plan

for succession and provide appropriate managerial and leadership training and development for current and future heads of department. Ensure heads of department do not neglect staff appraisal and development by implementing formalised departmental and university systems. Ensure as far as possible that heads have appropriate administrative support.

18. Advise academic departments, schools and faculties to examine relationships between the component parts of their student-staff ratios, i.e. average student contact hours, average class size, and average lectured hours, and the structure and context of their courses, and to consider the impacts on these ratios of modularisation, increased flexibility and joint courses.

19. Recognise that further reductions in the UGC's recurrent grant and other unexpected financial setbacks may occur and, after testing the sensitivity of the financial plan to variations in the key assumptions, develop a contingency plan. If revisions to the plan are necessary, employ the top down, bottom up, top down approach to secure agreement and commitment to the changes.

20. Communicate extensively with all departments, staff and student unions regarding progress in implementing the plan to maintain a shared commitment to its successful implementation.

Source: U.K., Department of Education and Science, Institutional Responses to Financial Reduction in the University Sector, Comparative Analysis of the Universities', Case Studies, John Sizer (1987), pp.196-198.

Appendix-V

Some Popular Performance Indicators, 1986/87

University	*Unit costs* thousand pounds*	*% of students not completing their degree course*	*% of graduates with a first or upper second*	*% of graduates unemployed or in a short-term job***	*Research grants per full-time academic (thousand pounds)*	*UFC research rating (1984-88)#*
1	2	3	4	5	6	7
Aston	2617	16.8	48.1	9.7	8.4	2.53
Bath	3002	14.1	57.7	8.6	8.3	2.86
Birmingham	3335	10.5	43.3	8.2	8.5	3.29
Bradford	2789	16.0	41.9	8.9	5.8	2.56
Bristol	3797	7.3	52.1	11.9	9.4	3.80
Brunel	2926	21.8	45.9	6.3	12.2	2.27
Cambridge	3201	3.4	66.2	9.3	11.2	4.77
City	3466	19.3	45.3	4.7	6.6	2.11
Durham	2641	5.2	47.8	6.5	6.4	3.20
East Anglia	2853	9.6	42.9	17.2	5.9	3.27
Essex	2372	14.6	43.5	13.5	6.5	3.69
Exeter	2661	8.8	45.1	10.2	3.8	3.07
Hull	2598	12.3	41.9	9.5	5.7	2.72
Keele	2580	16.3	42.5	13.9	6.0	2.14
Kent	2310	13.3	43.6	14.9	6.2	2.85
Lancaster	2927	8.7	43.5	9.3	5.2	3.28
Leeds	3613	10.9	37.8	14.7	7.0	3.12
Leicester	3132	9.7	42.4	10.6	8.4	2.87
Liverpool	3596	14.3	35.0	16.6	8.4	3.22
London	4293	16.5	43.2	11.8	14.9	3.44
Loughborough	3139	10.3	47.2	11.0	10.9	2.74
Manchester	3519	12.8	40.7	12.0	7.7	3.59

1	*2*	*3*	*4*	*5*	*6*	*7*
UMIST	3963	14.8	43.3	7.9	15.0	3.71
Newcastle	3430	16.9	35.2	7.5	8.3	3.50
Nottingham	3183	9.2	47.3	9.6	9.0	3.38
Oxford	3083	7.0	56.8	9.6	13.8	4.79
Reading	3172	12.0	51.1	9.3	7.6	2.89
Salford	2972	19.5	43.9	10.2	6.0	2.24
Sheffield	3162	9.9	41.4	12.9	7.2	3.31
Southampton	3436	19.1	43.4	9.6	12.3	3.72
Surrey	3454	14.7	43.6	9.2	11.7	3.28
Sussex	2827	12.2	44.1	16.1	9.2	3.42
Warwick	2749	11.5	47.7	10.3	9.8	4.24
York	2566	8.7	54.0	13.5	9.9	3.79
Aberdeen	3236	23.6	33.3	10.2	6.0	2.78
Dundee	3585	22.4	31.8	8.0	11.5	2.70
Edinburgh	3695	14.0	37.7	12.4	10.7	3.31
Glasgow	3512	20.8	29.8	10.6	10.2	3.32
Herriot-Watt	3154	21.5	28.2	11.4	11.5	2.27
St. Andrews	2590	11.8	47.8	8.9	6.2	3.14
Stirling	2420	14.9	32.5	16.9	5.7	2.43
Strathclyde	2795	21.6	39.1	9.6	9.7	2.85
Queen's	3044	11.5	33.4	11.7	4.8	2.56
Ulster	2176	15.9	33.3	19.9	2.6	2.19
Wales	2904	15.7	39.1	12.6	9.1	2.74

Notes: * Unit costs = general expenditure on academic departments per FTE students.

** Six months after graduation.

All data for 1986/87 except for UFC research rating, which was based on the period 1984-88.

Sources: University Statistics, vols. 1 and 2; Universities' Statistical Record, Cheltenham, for data on first destination of new graduates; 'Research Selectivity Exercise 1989: The Outcome', Universities Funding Council, Circular letter 27/89 for research rating data.

Ref: 'Performance Indicators in Higher Education', Jill Johnes and Jim Taylor, The Society for Research into Higher Education and Open University Press, Buckingham, UK.

Appendix-VI

Rank of Each University on Several Indicators

University	Rank of each university (1 = 'best')						
	Unit costs	% of students not completing their degree course	% of graduates with a first or upper second	% of graduates unemployed or in a short-term job	Research grants per full-time academic	UFC research rating (1984-88)#	Overall (rank of average rank)
1	2	3	4	5	6	7	8
Aston	9	36	7	20	22	38	21
Bath	21	25	2	8	25	28	10
Birmingham	32	14	23	7	20	17	12
Bradford	13	33	30	10	39	37	31
Bristol	43	4	5	31	16	4	9
Brunel	18	43	13	2	5	41	18
Cambridge	30	1	1	13	9	2	2
City	36	38	14	1	30	45	33
Durham	10	2	9	3	32	22	4
East Anglia	16	10	26	44	38	20	29
Essex	3	27	21	37	31	8	20
Exeter	11	7	15	22	44	25	19
Hull	8	21	30	15	41	34	26
Keele	6	34	27	38	36	44	39
Kent	2	23	19	40	34	30	24
Lancaster	19	6	21	13	42	19	14
Leeds	41	15	35	39	29	24	38
Leicester	24	11	28	26	22	27	22
Liverpool	40	26	38	42	22	21	42
London	45	35	25	30	2	11	26
Loughborough	25	13	12	27	10	33	16
Manchester	38	22	32	32	26	9	30

1	2	3	4	5	6	7	8
UMIST	44	29	23	5	1	7	11
Newcastle	33	37	37	4	25	10	23
Nottingham	29	9	11	18	19	13	7
Oxford	23	3	3	18	3	1	1
Reading	28	19	6	13	27	26	15
Salford	20	39	17	22	36	42	37
Sheffield	27	12	31	35	28	16	27
Southampton	34	8	22	18	4	6	6
Surrey	35	28	19	11	6	19	13
Sussex	15	20	16	41	17	12	17
Warwick	12	17	10	24	14	3	5
York	5	6	4	37	13	5	3
Aberdeen	31	45	41	22	36	31	44
Dundee	39	44	43	6	8	35	36
Edinburgh	42	24	36	33	11	16	32
Glasgow	37	40	44	26	12	14	35
Heriot-Watt	26	41	45	28	8	41	41
St. Andrews	7	18	9	10	34	23	8
Stirling	4	30	42	43	41	39	43
Strathclyde	14	42	34	18	15	30	28
Queen's	22	17	39	29	43	37	40
Ulster	1	32	41	45	45	43	45
Wales	17	31	34	34	18	33	34

Sources: University Statistics, vols. 1 and 2; Universities' Statistical Record, Cheltenham, for data on first destination of new graduates; 'Research Selectivity Exercise 1989: The Outcome', Universities Funding Council, Circular letter 27/89 for research rating data.

Ref: 'Performance Indicators in Higher Education', Jill Johnes and Jim Taylor, The Society for Research into Higher Education and Open University Press, Buckingham, UK.

References

1. U.K., Department of Education and Science, Institutional Responses to Financial Reductions in the University Sector, John Sizer (1987), Final Report, Table-10 (unpublished).
2. *Ibid.*
3. U.K., Performance Indicators in Higher Education, SRHE and Open University Press, Buckingham (1990), Basic Source: Statistics of Education, 1975! Universities, Vol. 6, UGC, Table-34, Universities Statistics, Vol. 3, Table 1 and 3, p. 38.
4. U.K., Department of Education and Science, Institutional Responses to Financial Reductions in the University Sector, John Sizer (1987), B.P. No. 3, p. 16.
5. *Ibid.*, Final Report, Table-3.
6. *Op. Cit.*, Table-8.
7. *Op. Cit.*, Table-9.
8. Swinnerton-Dyer, Peter, Chairman, UGC to the Secretary of State for Education and Science, letter dt. 16.8.1984, p. 22.
9. *Ibid.*, p. 22.
10. *Op. Cit.*, p. 22.
11. Op. Cit., p. 25.
12. *Ibid.*
13. India, The Education Commission Report (1964-66), New Delhi, p. 334.
14. U.K., Higher Education Report (Robbins Report), HMSO, London 1963, p. 221.
15. *Ibid.*
16. U.K., CVCP, Report of the Steering Committee for Efficiency Studies in Universities (1985), (Jarrat Report), pp. 9-10.

17. U.K., Department of Education and Science, Institutional Responses to Financial Reductions in the University Sector, John Sizer (1987), Comparative Analysis of Universities, Case Studies, p. 48.
18. *Ibid.*, pp. 48-49.
19. *Op. Cit.*, p. 50.
20. *Op. Cit.*, p. 195.
21. U.K., CVCP, Report of the Steering Committee for Efficiency Studies in Universities (1985), (Jarratt Report), p. 26.
22. *Ibid.*, p. 26.
23. *Op. Cit.*, p. 26.
24. *Op. Cit.*, p. 26.
25. *Op. Cit.*, p. 26.
26. U.K., Committee on Higher Education, Report (Robbins Report), London, HMSO, 1963, p. 222.
27. U.K., CVCP, Report of the Steering Committee for Efficiency Studies in Universities (1985), (Jarratt Report), p. 26.
28. *Ibid.*
29. *Op. Cit.*, p. 26.
30. U.K., Department of Education and Science, Institutional Responses to Financial Reductions in the University Sector, John Sizer (1987), Comparative Analysis of Universities, Case Studies, p. 199.
31. UGC, An Analysis of Institutions' Responses to Constitutional Recommendations in the Jarrat Report, John Sizer (1987), pp. 9-42.
32. *Ibid.*, p. 10.
33. *Op. Cit.*, p. 21.
34. *Ibid.*
35. *Op. Cit.*, p. 27.
36. *Op. Cit.*, p. 27.

37. *Ibid.*
38. *Op. Cit.*, p. 5.
39. *Op. Cit.*, p. 35.
40. U.K., CVCP, Report of the Steering Committee for Efficiency Studies in Universities (1985), (Jarratt Report), p. 36.
41. *Ibid.*, p. 53.
42. U.K., Performance Indicators in Higher Education, SRHE and Open University Press, Buckingham 1990, Basic Source: Statistics of Education, 1975! Universities, Vol. 6, UGC, Universities Statistics, Vol. 3, Tables 1 and 3, p. 34.
43. Performance Indicators in Higher Education, Jill, Johnes and Jim, Tayler, SRHE and Open University Press, Buckingham 1990, p. 7.
44. *Ibid.*, p. 9.
45. *Op. Cit.*, p. 9.
46. *Ibid.*
47. *Op. Cit.*, p. 185.
48. *Ibid.*
49. U.K., CVCP, Report of the Steering Committee for Efficiency Studies in Universities (1985), (Jarratt Report), p. 34.
50. CVCP USDTU Update, - A Progress Report on Achievements and Targets, London (1990), p. 6.
51. *Ibid.*, p. 37.

7

UNIVERSITIES BEYOND 1990s

RECALLING THE PAST

The rich and glorious history of the university system of the United Kingdom particularly of England and Scotland, have contributed significantly to the national development in all sectors of activities of the Society. The traditions of about eight hundred years of the university system of England and of over five hundred years of Sctotland have provided inspirations to many individuals and institutions beyond the boundaries of U.K. and Europe.

After the Second World War, the universities faced a number of challenges - beginning from reconstruction, re-equipping and re-building of houses, to the basic need of funds. But the most challenging problem, which was basically national, was the unprecedented demand that was estimated for places in higher education in the sixties. Besides, there was the pressing need to train a

---

Original members of the OECD countries include Austria, Belgium, Canada, Denmark, France, the Federal Republic of Germany, Greece, Iceland, Ireland, Italy, Luxembourg, the Netherlands, Norway, Portugal, Spain, Sweden, Switzerland, Turkey, the United Kingdom and the United States. The following countries became Members subsequently through accession at the dates indicated hereafter: Japan (28-4-1963), Finland (28.1.1969), Australia (7.6.1971), New Zealand (29-5-1973).

scientific and technological workforce for economic prosperity of the country which was also necessary for an appropriate place in the international scenario. In 1960s as well as in early 1970s, in most of the OECD countries including UK, there was massive expansion of higher education which however slowed down in the late seventies.

The growth, after having dropped, picked up in the late eighties. The reasons for this were mainly two. "The first was primarily egalitarian: higher education institution provided opportunities for the rapidly growing number of young people who were completing their secondary education. The second was economic: they trained the highly qualified workforce that was needed by the economics of the industrial world".[1]

In UK, the society was characterised by mass affluence. But the 1960s witnessed 'the rediscovery of poverty' a condition which once socially refound, could not be forgotten completely.[2] The Labour Government of Harold Wilson was re-elected in 1964 and again in 1966 on a programme of welfare and modernisation. Resultantly, 1960s witnessed unprecedented expansion of higher education.

Primarily, due to the pressures on the Public Expenditure, the Conservative Government which came in power in May 1979, lost no time to reduce the grants to the universities. The reduction of grants by 6% to 44% averaging 17% for all the universities in UK pushed the universities to the wall which was nothing less than 'traumatic'. The universities had to steer through a really rough weather which the system had not known earlier. Pushed to such a situation, they faced the forced challenges and ultimately got over the problems experiencing a good deal in various aspects of management. The problems were not of the same degree in all the universities; nor was the modus-operandi of tackling the problems the same. That made the picture of problems difficult in different universities. But finally, after having had a tough time for the first time on the whole, what was the morale of the universities which faced serious problems of adjustments. For some, it was almost a situation of 'bankruptcy'.

Analyses of the Case Studies reveal that Salford's asset was its own internal consensus and it believed itself to be 'innovative, enterprising and resourceful'. Aston which initially faced demoralisation gained 'a sense of purpose and cohesion'. At Heriot-Watt, mainly due to the leadership quality, the University moved towards 'cohesiveness, vitality and sense of purpose, reinforced by the prospect of a united community at Ricarton and the success in achieving certain goals by self-help'.

Sheffield was also in good spirit and remained 'Cohesive' and 'Morale rose throughout the restructuring period'. In Stirling, however, staff morale was not high due to "the acute awareness of the university's size and its incompatibility with its commitments to breadth of academic coverage". Turning to Bath, which did not suffer by the UGC letter of the 1st July 1981, was 'in good heart'.

At Hull, the major problem was to maintain the morale of the staff due to "salary settlements and the limitation of senior/junior staff ratios as with problems of restructuring". In Sussex, actions for retrenchment affected 'cohesion', and the staff 'suffered a lowering of status which was a severe blow to their self-esteem'. In the Arts and Social Studies Area, there was a detectable malaise of spirit akin to disillusionment".[3]

Interestingly, the Case Studies concluded that "the implementation of the cuts of 1981 did not have universally negative impacts on cohesiveness, vitality, sense of purpose and mission, nor on morale, nor were the impacts wholly positive".[4]

Undeniably, in the decison-making of any government in a democratic set up, there are political compulsions which may sometime be popular and at other times be difficult and unpopular. It has to be admitted that of the various sectors of the management of the government, it is education and more particularly higher education which has its impact on all other sectors. It is the higher education which is capable of supplying trained personnel for all other sectors, e.g. agriculture, health, power generation and supply, transport, aviation and communication system and service sector, without which, it would virtually be impossible to keep up the other sectors efficient.

The role of higher education being what it actually is, the pertinent question that need be answered is what kind of priority the higher education sector should be given for the purpose of public funding? Should it be given the same priority as would other sectors get or be given higher priority and if so, in relation to which sectors. If it is to be given the highest priority, there is no question of debate. Depending on how the government percieves the role of higher education that it would take policy decision on the funding pattern.

However, there is no reason why in a not so comfortable financial position, grants should have been released late to the universities. For obvious reasons, the role of a 'buffer' body like UGC or UFC could not be independent of the Government's control and therefore, the former's performance had high degree of -

built-in connection with the plans and policies of the Government. For example, as observed by the Jarratt Report, the UGC could not announce the grants to the universities earlier than February for the Government indicated the levels of grants to UGC only in January. Consequently, the UGC allocated the grants in February and March for the next financial year and that too, not a firm commitment. The link is apparant. That is how the flow of funds affected the universities.

The Report has further observed that at times despite UGC's efforts to provide guidance to the universities in advance, that did not really help as the-Committee's financial projections could not be more reliable than the figures in the Public Expenditure Paper.

In a dynamic society, models and patterns are always changing ones. Beginning from the late seventies and particularly from the beginning of 1981-82, changes in policies have taken place more often than not, and if one takes a dispassionate view of comparing the characters and attitudes of the universities of 1970s and those of 1990s, glaring difference would be noticed.

Universities are no longer the seats of learning only, but centres of providing knowledge and skills against rising payments. But what could be dangerous is the tendency, though under pressures, to earn more and more. While earning is a mandate, there must be some unwritten understanding so that the universities do not go beyond a point to generate income. Should universities do all that the commercial organisations do? The simple answer is no, for nobody conceives that universities should function the way commercial organisation do.

It is true that in some positive respects, the

universities have adopted commercial approaches eg. creation of companies in the campus, efforts to be cost effective, generation of income, raising the level of efficiency by various means of modern management techniques and on the whole, an overall awareness of maximizing the returns from investments.

In a system of public funding, where there are pressures on the public expenditure, it is necessary to explore all the possibilities to be cost effective and generate income to reduce public funding, for "It is now a fact of life that providers of education and training in public and private sectors need to find more ways of generating income".[5] This has become a *sine-qua-non* for survival. According to a study that was undertaken by OECD, "whatever the pros and cons, the fact remains that institutions of higher education, and particlarly universities, all have the potential capacity to operate as service enterprises and under some conditions to cover a big part of their expenditure from the sale of their services.[6] This means more contract research and consultancy.

But, there has to be a widely known difference and demarcating line between the universities and commercial organisations. Precisely, the universities should accept all the means, methods and techniques of the commercial organisations to be efficient but not go for a profit making as the sole objective like the commercial organisations.

In the process of efforts to earn more money through contract research and consultancy, it is necessary to ensure that such efforts are not counterproductive. It need be ensured that time of the management, the valuable hours of research in the area of basic research for more applied research in order to secure and accomplish the contract research, ultimately does not cost more, and leave any long-term adverse impact on the university. If the basic research level is not kept up to the right level, the danger will be that a time may come when the industry may think that the universities do not have sufficient to offer for "... senior industrialists in Britain are now speaking with alarm of the weakening of basic research of the universities due to continuing government insistance that we concentrate more effort on application".[7]

Based on a stock taking account,[8] at the end of 1980s, the Universities of UK have, despite unprecedented problems, achieved a good deal. Despite the sharp fall in the number of 18 year old in the population, demand for higher education has constantly risen, rather sharply. Attraction of overseas students for places in UK universities have continued to rise despite the high fees based on full cost of their courses. Industry and other employers retrain and up-date their more than 600,000 employees in the universities.

University-Industry interaction has increased by 15% during 1980s benefitting each other for applied research activities. Research earnings per full-time academic increased by 35% in real term since 1984-85. The overall dependence on public exchequer has come down from 63% to 47%.

However, there are certain areas which caused concern - for example, a sizable fund was needed to replace the old equipment for quality teaching and research. Concern was also expressed for the increasingly decreased time devoted to research and scholarship. There was also a strong need to provide additional resources to provide places for the growing home student numbers. Raising the level of efficiency only cannot bridge the gap.

REVIEWING THE PRESENT

Really speaking, universities are now facing, if not threats, challenges, unlike July, 1981 which was designed by the Government.

With the abolition of the binary line and a large number of Polytechnics becoming university, this will now make the situation more competitive in all areas from attracting students both home and overseas, to bidding for contract research. The changes that now seem imminent for the universities will be more than the changes they have undergone in the last fifty years.

The number of universities in UK was 42 till 1959, which rose to 46 by the end of 1960s, the decade of unprecedented expansion. With the addition of 40 Polytechnics which have been given the status of 'university', the number of universities in UK is now 86. This number may rise further as some more Polytechnics become 'university'.

The challenges are many and for that purpose, universities need to plan based on various inputs of vision and mission so that they are able not only to survive in the keen competition but make headway to achieve greater heights. The identified challenges are:

- Managerial and Academic restructuring.
- Raising of the level of the Research activities to exploit the private sectors and achieve excellence.
- Opportunity of students for personal contact and tuition by quality and devoted teachers.
- Need to have a long term plan so that when not only the growth may slow down, halt, but gradually move downward that does not affect the system. This is necessary for although the

number of qualified entrants to full-time higher education system has been increasing faster than anticipated, based on the demographic trends, sooner or later, the levelling of the growth is imminent. Rising cost of education will force a large number of students to go in for the non-formal channel of education.

Basic to meeting the challenges and achieving the goals is a smooth structuring of the university. By design, the universities function through active participation of academics where decision-making processes are all through the committee structures having academics of different mind, approach, attitude, values and interest. Hard decisions suggested or endorsed by the Vice-Chancellor or by a committee are mostly subject to the approval of some other committee or committees, where again, different values, approach and interests clash. But the positive aspect of high participation of academics when supported, weilds great strength to the system.

Not being the professional managers, the academics do not always appreciate the limitations of running the show purely on academic considerations ignoring the economic aspects which has important and inescapable impact on the overall management of university. In such a structure, it is an up-hill task for any Vice-Chancellor to initiate hard choices or to implement them even when they are imposed by a central authority.

The Jarratt Report deliberating on the position of participation, observed that - "The tradition of self-government which lies at the heart of a university's constitution, has extended over the years to wider groupings in the institution who have, or wish to have, a voice in both academic and business affairs. Such participation can provide a strong unifying force within the institution; but it can also be used to delay or block difficult but necessary decision. This can be particularly marked' at a time of scarce and declining resources".[9]

In the changed situation, where hard decisions are required to be taken more often than not, conflicting situations are bound to come to fore.

SIGNALS FOR FUTURE

For meeting the challenges that now lay ahead of the universities and to achieve the goals, the pre-requisite is to be decisive and be ready to take hard decisions. For all these, does it mean that the universities need a shake-up in their structure so that the limited commercial approach match reasonably commercial structures?

It is futile to talk of a 'return' of investment of every penny in a structure in which the Chief has to work-out plan and spend anxious moments of great uncertainty of whether or not the implications of investments *vis-a-vis* return howsoever good they are, will go through the highly independent committee system. In an organisation of commercial structure and commitments, the Chief has all the powers vested in him or in the Board.

Paradoxically, in the university system, besides the committee system, how satisfied the academics are with the functioning of the Vice-Chancellor have impact on the smooth sailing of the tenure of the Vice-Chancellor. This, however, does not undermine the need and impact of the right managerial capacity of the Vice-Chancellor for without that in todays complex management of the university system, he cannot handle the affairs for besides the internal problems, the Vice-Chancellor has to interact with the external authorities, bodies and organisations and political forces.

A careful assessment and analyses of the functioning of the universities in the last two decades provide reasonable signals that the socio-economic pressures have changed the characters of the universities from a position of 'Ivory Towers' to one of the 'masses', moving from the campus to everywhere possible *inter-alia* through continuing and distance education both to reach the benefits of the academic world to the people as also to ensure a reasonable return of investments from the beneficiaries.

As part of the Educational Technology, increasing use of computers and other electronic means for teaching, learning and research activities indicate adequately that in not too distant a future, education system will be forced to survive through 'packages' by using extensively these aids. Such packages might be both computer based and mainly document based with some visual aids. Inescapably, these have to be done because firstly class room teaching will be very costly and secondly, there would be continuous efforts to reduce the cost of education.

In the current management system, "cost" has already become a matter of first consideration for anything that one thinks today. The question that invariably always comes up is, what is the cost involved and what is the return? Today, it is not possible that one would think only of the 'academic' value without relating the same to 'economic' value -be it teaching or research. These provide signals for the future. Inescapably, the universities would be forced to function more or less along the lines of the commercial organizations in a limited way aimed of course at very different products and results. Now that the 21st century is knocking at the door what would be the scenario of higher education is a big question. It is therefore necessary to dwell upon the likely scenario in the 21st century.

DEFINING 21st CENTURY

When we say 21st century, that really does not mean 2000 AD or 2001. Nor does that mean 2090 or 2099. That really should mean the scenario that could be visualised more on realistic basis - rather than as prophesies, keeping of course in view the assets of good practices along with those which are archaic, outdated and outmoded having lost relevance in the context of the changed and fast changing scenario as also the traditions which are more obstacles than paving ways to effective functioning of the system.

NEED OF CHANGE

Fundamentally, universities are instrumental to changes in the society, but such changes come through the products of the universities and not through the universities themselves. Paradoxically, they themselves change slowly and that is their characteristic: "Universities have often had the effect of prolonging and stereotyping ideas and modes of thought for a century or more after the rest of the world has given them up".[10] In fact, it "...is surprising how slowly an intellectual revolution affects the course of ordinary education".[11] Talking about the tradition, "... universities, even the newest, poorest and smallest in the modern world, still preserve missions, ideas, values, conventions, and customs, that in the life of their professors and students, still recall those of their predecessors in Paris, Oxford and Bologna during the 13th century.[12]

Such characteristic may be debated as to how far that meets the fast changing needs of the society. But whatever be the merit or demerit of such characteristic, the universities have continued to flourish and over the years, deeply rooted in the society and that is because "... the university as an institution has survived wars, political and religious persecution, poverty and negligence."[13]

Although slowly, but steadily, '... changes have taken place in the university system and they include the scientific and epistemological break in the concept of knowledge current in the 16th century (Kahn 1992), the changes caused by the industrial revolution toward the end of the 18th century, and the development of modern nation states in the 19th century."[14] Changes of the twentieth century particularly after the Second World War and in 1980s and 1990s were phenomenal which will be discussed later.

Clearly, universities do change, but they change slowly and when the need of change is apparent in the society. They have the inherent strength to survive through difficult times. If the universities had not responded to the needs of the society, they could not have survived for centuries together. Whether universities need to change faster than before to keep pace with the society is debatable. It has to be admitted that since the late seventies, changes in the society have become fast and in the 1990s they are faster. This means when there was a pressure, the universities changed faster than ever before. The question is how fast the universities changed and should respond to change themselves.

CONTRIBUTORY FACTORS TO CHANGES

Never before the oil crisis of 1970s, and the consequential economic problems, did people raise any question about the high or otherwise, the aspect of expenditure on higher education for it was always considered different from other sectors for it contributed to the preservation of culture, tradition and knowledge, and innovation and discovery of new knowledge. But with the economic pressure and the pressure to reduce public expenditure, attitude and approach changed and higher education came under scrutiny. An oft repeated question is to what extent investment in higher education has paid dividend to the society. Unfortunately, the general impression is that it has not paid the expected dividend. There was one more reason for the pressure and that was growing demands on various other social sectors of the same society which patronized and respected higher education. At times, defence budget made inroads in some countries into the education budget.

Changes that began from the early 1980s both in terms of clientele, demand and a new, rather unprecedented, economic pressure forced the universities all over the world for change in their outlook to the concept of education as against what was so far reared with respect, in the minds of the people.

Firstly, due to pressure to reduce public expenditure and secondly the general impression that the system has failed to pay dividend of the investments, attitude towards higher education has changed rather fast in the last about a decade and a half; the reason is thus socio-economic. And that has happened world over. This change in attitude has brought about changes in every aspect of the university system - be it a general attitude of the people, government and students, financing courses, methodology of teaching and the overall environment of the system. For example, except in USA, teachers were involved in a very limited way to earn for the universities, be it contract research, consultancy or in any other way. Hiring out university space to outsiders was not known, at least not common at all. Selling or leasing out university buildings and land for financial reasons was not known earlier. These changes have come in the university system fast, and the reason was and still is the resource crunch and change in the attitude of the society. This mainly, I will now not say alone, is responsible for all consequential changes.

That was how the turning point came and that was the beginning of change of the concept of education leading to the changing scenario. A simple comparison of the concept of education, function of the universities then, till 1970s, and now in 1990s, would indicate the fast changing track.

SUCCESSES AND FAILURES OF THE SYSTEM

Undeniably, despite the fact that the universities have not paid the society the due dividend, it is irrefutable that the contributions of the higher education is enormous. For example, what would have happened to the bulging population of the world if higher education had not made its contribution for higher production of food with modern technology? What messy it would have been if the technology had not contributed to innovate and increase the production of the daily necessities of today's complex life and how chaotic it would have been without new and improved technology of transport, communications, energy and even housing? How painful it would have been if advanced techniques of medical sciences had not come to our rescue through the gift of higher education and research. All these are the contributions of the higher education sector.

Undoubtedly, the system has contributed great scholars, statesmen, scientists, teachers, physicians, social reformers, managers and thinkers. It is perhaps because of the very high expectation from the system that the society is not satisfied with the performance of the system. It is also perhaps because the society thinks that the higher education system alone is the hope to survive and improve the lot of the people, that so much is talked about and criticisms are, at times, extreme.

Accepting that the university system is the saviour of the world of today and tomorrow, a dispassionate assessment would tell us that the system has its successes and failures. Successes such as those mentioned above are shrouded in silence, but failures spotlighted in notoriety.

Successes have really helped the society to survive today. As regards failures, many think that the problems of clashes, crimes/terrorism, disharmony, disparity and destructions are the results of failures of education. While this is debatable, the fact is that today peace is indanger and economic disparity is all over in different degrees. For all these it is the education system that is responsible fully or is it political designs and ambitions that are also responsible in no small measure, leading to distress and destruction of people and property.

Changed political scenario of the world, liberalised economy of a large number of countries coming into being of new trade agreements and norms, all these together, have thrown numerous challenges to the knowledge based society for which university system is the only saviour to train and educate people and also to implement the various plans and programmes of economic order and welfare schemes.

It is important to bear in mind that the basic concept of the role of the university has not changed, and that will never change. The basic concept is to provide trained personnel in different areas of needs of the society so that people are able to fulfill their needs and aspirations. Besides, conceptually, university is the repository of knowledge and an instrument of change through the people for the good of the society which is dynamic in character.

In the plethora of literature on higher education, a good deal has been written that the university education should be related more to the needs of the real life rather than it performing only the knowledge transmission function. However, how far this has been achieved in a normal course and under pressure is debatable albeit many think the university system has failed to fulfill this.

Inescapably, whatever be the strengths and weaknesses of the system, it must be rejuvenated to meet the challenges of the 21st century so that it becomes alive and alert to the needs of present and future and is able to deliver quality products in a changing scenario, involving changes in design and a built in capacity to constantly improve in a new world looking for continuous improvement in quality.

Before we discuss how to rejuvenate the system and ensure built-in dynamism in it, it is necessary to discuss what would be the possible scenario of higher education in the 21st century.

VISUALISING THE SCENARIO IN THE 21ST CENTURY

Realistically, the scenario that could be visualised in the twenty-first century would have to have some basic relationship and some resemblance of the past, particularly immediate past, in relation to the possible scenario at least of the first two decades of the 21st century.

Arguably, the university in the twenty-first century would continue to:

- function as a centre for transmission of knowledge and generation of new knowledge, which means teaching and research - both basic and applied.
- perform the function of hiring of teachers, framing of courses and selection of students.
- extend to the society at large the benefits of knowledge, facilities and expertise, through Extension Services.

While the functions of the University will broadly continue to be the above, drastic changes in the concept and structure would be the prerequisites to meet the needs of the market force of the 21st century which will be elaborated later. It is only the university which alone can keep the knowledge based society going and flourishing to make breakthroughs. Breaking new ground through research and innovation and providing more and more specialised but flexible trained people would be one of the basic demands of the 21st century.

Basically, because of the pressure of the number, more and more institutions will come into play their role. But survival will depend on the competitive capacity based on their performance. The changing social and economic scenario all over the world indicate that flexibility, adaptability, capacity to dramatic changes, with fine tuning, would be the need of the 21st century.

Universities and colleges would have to build credibility themselves, make the whole operations simple, efficient, cost-effective and meaningful like a good national business house, if not multinational. Briefly, the scenario could be visualised as follows:

(i) in place of the present control of the government or any of its agency, on the creation of new institutions, there should be a shift from 'restrictions' to 'growth' and at the same time, 'monitoring' the quality and grading them by an efficient Agency of the Government, for information of the students and society. For this, declared policies have to be made so that people are aware of that. The situation should be more like a business which although one can start if he has the money, but have to conform to the prescribed norms of the Government,

(ii) privatisation of higher education has to be allowed, with built-in check and balance provision. For this, the control should be nebulous. It should be more to allow freedom than to intervene. But the government should be able to do so if matters go beyond control and against national policy,

(iii) higher education will effectively be a market of 'seller' and 'buyer'. Institutions will be forced to market its transparent facilities and capabilities so that students as clients could choose based on their tastes, needs and buying capacity and institutions as 'sellers' would make best

efforts to satisfy their clients with quality and environment. A strong built-in market research mechanism is necessary to obtain feed back about the performance of students,

(iv) in order to maintain quality, the university, however, has to have its own selection procedure,

(v) module-based fees structure would have to be prescribed; differential fees based on the market value of the courses would be the need.

(vi) structure and organisation of the university have to be business house like and professionalism has to be the thrust of all functions of the university; cost-effectiveness would be the dominating demand of the time for survival. Professional managers have to be given freedom in their areas. This would also relieve the teachers of many avoidable non-academic work. Commensurate pay and perks packages have to be given to the teachers and professionals in relation to the quality of services demanded.

(vii) educational technology would be applied more and more to reduce cost without compromising the requirement of contact classes to maintain quality.

(viii) more and more modular courses and transfer of credits would have to be designed with less and less rigidity in rules to provide maximum flexibility.

(ix) in order to relate education more and more to the world of work, structure and content of courses should be such that on one hand, reasonable specialised knowledge and skill is given, on the other, students should be capable of doing work in another area also for which related interdisciplinary courses should be provided. Precisely, some specialisation and a built in flexibility to get adjusted with any related area of work would be a special demand in the 21st century.

(x) big residential campus has gradually to be reduced in area, to minimise the upkeep cost and consequential problems of township which involves lots of managerial time and also money; that also diverts attention from the main function of the University. However, alternative facility either through higher housing allowance or a separate package of contract arrangement for housing by an appointed agency, has to be found out.

(xi) government and civic bodies should extend incentives by way of concessions through tax laws and municipal charges for even if the institutions start functioning like business houses, savings on these accounts would be used only for public purposes which is so vital for national health and mind, and without which no nation can survive.

(xii) university-industry working together has to be a way of life for mutual benefits and also national interest.

(xiii) non-formal stream of education has to develop faster to cope with the increasing demand of higher education.

(xiv) Extensive use of information media both in management and education through worldwide information network, TV E-Mail, Internet

and Video conferencing would be necessary both to reduce cost and importantly, to get the benefit of sought-after expertise from any part of the world.

(xv) Achieving full autonomy by the institutions is a *sine-qua-non* for efficient functioning in the 21st century. Government should decide that if the institutions do not ask for more than 30% grant of the operative budget, it will not ask them to conform to any given rule, except any national policy.

(xvi) Basic Research funding policy and programmes should be transparent and clear.

(xvii) Applied Research should be maximised with industry which will also help generate income and productivity.

A CASE FOR RE-ENGINEERING IN THE HIGHER EDUCATION SYSTEM

Admittedly, despite the inherent potential of the system, a dispassionate and objective assessment of the strengths and weaknesses of the institution of higher education of today and the likely needs of the 21st century would tell us that they are not equipped to meet the new challenges.

If the institutions have to do all that are visualised in the foregoing paragraphs, they need some major changes in the concept, structure and organisation and radical and dramatic changes in the processes. Most of the institutions are trapped in rigidity of traditions or archaic rules. In order to change, to meet the needs of the changing time, radical changes would be essential.

The universities as institutions being what they

are, having deep rooted traditions and tenacities with a continuous history of about 800 years, can they really change to meet the challenges of changes and if so, how much through designed reforms. These institutions are not just places of some activities for material gains, but centres where the main players of the game are teachers and students to whom emotions, traditions and values are important in their pursuit of teaching and learning rather than material gains.

Yet over the last about one and a half decade, some changes and reforms have taken place in the universities for they realized that the changes were necessary to survive. American universities have the culture to 'change', to suit the changing needs. Many European countries have also made some changes particularly the universities in UK following the cuts in government grants in 1981 and reforms following the Jarratt Report. However, whether these universities think that the changes that have taken place adequately equip themselves to meet new challenges of the world of tomorrow, or a reengineering is unavoidable, is again debatable.

RESULTS OF RE-ENGINEERING IN BUSINESS HOUSES

Many business houses succeeded in bailing out themselves from red or a situation leading to that, through the application of re-engineering. Even those business houses doing well, but looking for doing much better, applied re-engineering and gained enormously. From experiences, there are three types of companies that took to, and can take to reengineering. They are:

Type One: Companies which found themselves in deep trouble on all fronts of activities and services, applied re-engineering. Not only they came out of red, they are doing well.

Type Two: Companies which assessed themselves and realized that they were approaching trouble zone and decided with vision, to apply re-engineering and thus avoided trouble and gained sufficiently.

Type Three: Companies which were in comfortable position, doing very well, but had ambition and aggresive plans to leave behind their competitors, actually achieved their goal through dramatic changes of re-engineering method.

In simple and clear words, the three categories could be explained as: "Companies in the first category are desparate; they have hit the wall and are lying injured on the ground. Companies in the second category are cruising along, at high speed, but see something rushing toward them in their head lamps. Could it be a wall? Companies in the third category are out for a drive on a clear afternoon, with no obstacles in sight. What a splendid time, they decide to stop and build a wall for the other guys"[15]

APPLICATION OF RE-ENGINEERING TO UNIVERSITIES

In today's global resource constraint and crunch, there is hardly any university belonging to the third type which comfortably goes 'out for a drive on a clear afternoon, with no obstacles in sight'. Most of the universities belong to the first type where they are struggling to survive. There could be a lucky few belonging to the second type.

With an inherited system of a built-in resistence to change, particularly to change 'fast', and specifically to change 'dramatically', how far re-engineering can be applied to the system is certainly a question which does not have any ready answer. However, there is little chance that without 'dramatic' changes in the system particularly in the 'processes', demands of the 21st century can in any reasonable measure be met. The only silver lining is that the universities have responded favourably to the pressures of changes in the last about 15 years. This provides hopes for the future.

Believing that the university system is basically capable of changes as evidenced by the changes of 1980s and now in 1990s, we must think of applying re-engineering and examine the areas that need dramatic changes to ensure an efficient, effective and viable system for the society.

Re-engineering, to define, is "the fundamental re-thinking and radical design of business processes to achieve dramatic improvements in critical, contemporary measures of performance, such as cost, quality, service and speed".[16]

Conceptually, re-engineering is through the application of '... the real power of technology' not 'to make old processes better but enabling the organisation to break old rules and create new ways of working".[17] The four key words are-

Fundamental, Radical, Dramatic and Processes

The word 'Fundamental' essentially poses the following questions: "Why do we do what we do? And why do we do it the way we do?" In relation to the universities answer to the first question is not unclear for objectives of the universities have already been discussed and they have remained and will basically remain the same. What is important is why do we do it the way we do? It is here that the universities have to bring about dramatic changes and that would come through the 'processes' which will be discussed later here.

KEY WORD - RADICAL

This means 'root' and 'Radical design means getting to the root of things: not making superficial changes or fiddling with what is already in place, but throwing away the old.[18]

There are many areas in the structure and organisation of the system which need changes in the 'root', not improvement on the existing ones. Structures of the universities are rather complicated and that does not help the system to work efficiently. Functioning through such structures involves a good deal of time and energy leaving little time to devote to make the system more efficient, smooth and cost effective. It is necessary to re-write the constitution of the universities which should involve the constituents in broad decision-makings, but executive powers should be left to the professionals to involve least procedures, to achieve the end result.

Key Word - Dramatic

In the concept and meaning of re-engineering 'dramatic' is the directional signal as opposed to marginal improvements in any particular area of function of the system. Generally, marginal improvement keeps happening in all organisations. But 'dramatic' change means whole - hog change. This aims at achieving the same basic objective, but with greater efficiency in terms of time, money, people and speed. There are many areas where dramatic changes are necessary.

Key Word - Processes

All the definitions of re-engineering ultimately converge to the processes of function of any organisation to achieve dramatic changes with the help of information technology. It can also be explained as rejecting the old processes of 'assembly line' and achieving the purposes of many, through one or very few ones in an altogether new approach.

Our system of - higher education has many archaic, out-dated procedures which must be replaced by the new ones. Some of the areas are the following:

(i) Basic structure of the university. In fact, "One of the characteristics of the current debate on the future of higher education is the wide-spread call for changes in the structure".[19]

(ii) Decision-making processes. They need be quick, free from rigidity and implementable.

(iii) All matters relating to the students. They need to be more simple and comfortable to remove all 'irritants' of procedures.

(iv) Availability of equipment, teaching and research facilities. New procedures need be adopted for procurement and maximum return should be ensured before investments.

(v) Appointments and all service matters like, leave, housing and travelling should be flexible removing all rigidity.

(vi) Budgetting allocation and monitoring should be done on scientific norms and transparency is desirable.

The above is by way of illustrations only. Individual institutions would be the best sudge to find out the areas needing re-engineering. Once the institution decides to take up each area and examines the various aspects from the angles of - clients, cost, time, overall impact (and at times aesthetics), the need will be apparent and the ways to go about would also be clear.

If the institution sees the fundamental need, to go deep to the root, then new approaches and processes can be found out for dramatic changes. That will make the life of the clients and constituents comfortable and reduce the operational cost to meet the pressures of the new needs of the 21st century.

Re-engineering, *per-se*, is not, even by any remote definition of the concept thereof, an approach or attempt to bring about some improvements on the existing ones, but 'throwing away the existing areas', identified for re-engineering, and introducing an altogether new one which will ensure cost-effectiveness, speed, efficiency, convenience, and above all, making a positive impact on the organisation.

The idea of application of re-engineering in the higher education system may not easily be conceived for the traditions are likely to come in the way. Moreover, the character and aims of the higher education are very different from those of the business houses. Yet, as the 1980s and again 1990s indicate, it would be the market force that would ultimately push the system to go in for reengineering as there may not be any alternative to this. However, what has to be seen is whether the system does it when crisis is at the door step or it does so with due vision assessing the needs of the future. That would be interesting.

References

1. France, Financing Higher Education - Current Patterns OECD (1990), pp. 7-8.
2. U.K., Social Welfare, Paul Corrigan, IM, UK Society - Work, Urbanism and Inequality, Ed. Philipo Abrams

and Richard Brown, The Pitman Press, Bath, GB (1984), pp. 315-16.

3. U.K., Department of Education and Science, 'Institutional Responses to the Financial Reduction', Comparative Analysis of Universities Case Studies, John Sizer, (1985), p. 14.
4. *Ibid.*
5. U.K., Generating Income for Educational Institutions, John Wheale, Kogan Page Ltd., London (1991), p. 7.
6. France, "Educational Costs, Expenditure and Financing: An Analysis of Trends: OECD, Paris, 1986, internal document Extract from Financing Higher Education - Current Pattern, OECD, Paris, 1990.
7. U.K., What can we do for Our Countries, the Contribution of Universities to National Development, Proceedings of Commonwealth Universities, Western Australia, Perth, Feb. 1988, ACU, London, p. 50.
8. U.K., CVCP, The State of the Universities, London (1991), pp. 3-5.
9. U.K., CVCP, Report of the Steering Committee for Efficiency Studies in Universities, London, 1985, p. 10.
10. P.16, The University as an Institution Today, Attonso Borrero Cabal, UNESCO, Paris (1985).
11. *Ibid.*
12. *Ibid.*, p. 17.
13. *Ibid.*, p. 18.
14. *Ibid.*, pp. 15-16.
15. P. 35 Re-engineering the Corporation Manifesto for Business Revolution, Michael Hammer and James Champy, Nicholas Brealey Publishing Ltd. (1993), London.
16. *Ibid.*, pp. 35-36.
17. *Ibid.*, p. 33.
18. *Ibid.*
19. P. 16., Key Address by Professor Harold T. Shapiro, President, Princeton University, at the first Richard A. Harvill Conference on Higher Education, The University of Arizona, November 23, 1992.

and Richard Brown, the [illegible] Press, [illegible] 1976, pp. 313-[illegible]

3. U.K. Department of Education and [illegible], [illegible] Approaches to [illegible] Education: [illegible] Analysis and [illegible] [illegible] [illegible] [illegible]

4. Ibid.

5. [illegible] [illegible] [illegible] [illegible] [illegible] Institutions, [illegible] [illegible] [illegible] Ltd., London, 1971, p. [illegible]

6. [illegible] Educational [illegible] Expenditure [illegible] [illegible] An Analysis of [illegible] OECD [illegible] 1986 [illegible] [illegible] [illegible] [illegible] [illegible] [illegible] Pattern, OECD, Paris, 1984.

7. U.K., [illegible] [illegible] [illegible] Committee [illegible] [illegible] [illegible] [illegible] [illegible] [illegible] [illegible] Commonwealth Universities, Western Australia, Perth, 1988, A.C.U., London, p. [illegible]

8. [illegible] The State of the Universities [illegible] (1991), pp. [illegible]

9. [illegible] [illegible] [illegible] Steering Committee on [illegible] [illegible] in Universities, London, [illegible]

10. [illegible] The University as an Institution Today, [illegible] [illegible] [illegible] [illegible] Paris [illegible]

11. Ibid.

12. Ibid. p. 114.

13. [illegible] p. 14.

14. [illegible] p. [illegible]

15. [illegible] [illegible] The [illegible] Management [illegible] Science, Revolution and [illegible] [illegible] [illegible] [illegible] [illegible] Ltd. [illegible] London.

16. Ibid. pp. [illegible]

17. Ibid. p. 98.

18. Ibid.

19. [illegible] [illegible] address by [illegible] [illegible] [illegible] [illegible] [illegible] [illegible] [illegible] [illegible] [illegible] University of Arizona, November [illegible] 1982.

Index

Financing Education

Resource Generation in Education

Financing Education

Resource Generation in Education

Vol. II

D.K. GHOSH
Registrar, Indian Institute of Technology, Bombay

Foreword by

R.A. MASHELKAR
Director-General, Council of Scientific and Industrial Research (CSIR)
Government of India

COSMO PUBLICATIONS
1997 **INDIA**

First Published 1997

FINANCING EDUCATION (2 Volumes)

ISBN 81-7020-769-x (Vol. II)

ISBN 81-7020-736-3 (Set)

Published by:

MRS. RANI KAPOOR
COSMO PUBLICATIONS
for GENESIS PUBLISHING PVT. LTD.
24-B, Ansari Road,
Darya Ganj,
New Delhi-110002, INDIA

Typeset by:
Manav Computer House

Printed at :
Mehra Offset Press

Foreword

India has witnessed a phenomenal growth in the University system since independence. The number of Universities has grown from 19 to nearly 200 while the student strength has increased from just over one lakh to over 4,5 million. On an average, nearly 5 lakh graduates and about 4500 doctorates are produced annually. Higher education is thus no longer the prerogative of just the affordable few, but it is equally accessible to the vast majority of youth determined to acquire higher knowledge and skills. This will certainly lead to a reduction in social inequalities, a prime factor for social development. Further, the opening up of our economy has brought in tremendous employment opportunities. It is therefore necessary to enthuse motivation in students to acquire competitive skill.

The increasing dependence of the educational sector on government funds, and the financial crunch associated with the continuous expansion of the higher educational infrastructure, has brought in inherent ills like influenced selectivity in admissions, decrease in standards of teaching and evaluation, etc. All these have an adverse bearing on the quality of our output. *Qualitative growth* is an imminent imperative, which cannot be sacrificed on any account. The National Policy on Education formulated in 1986, had pre-empted the absolute need for quality enhancement in its observation, "*In the context of unprecedented explosion of knowledge, higher education has to become dynamic like never before, constantly entering unchartered areas*", and thereby clearly signaled the importance of the academic effecting changes necessary to produce talent capable of meeting the challenges of globalization. Basically, this change should involve enhancing quality of education and creating motivation for competitiveness among the teachers and the taught. The underlying emphasis naturally points to a system with sound financial base. It is now essential for the universities and other higher educational institutes to devise and adopt sustainable mechanisms for generating income. This is inescapable too because, the prime beneficiaries of any increase in Government's allocations to the educational sector, are bound to be the agencies responsible for promoting programmes for total literacy.

When viewed in this background, the present book is a very timely contribution from the author. Dr. Ghosh's experience of over three decades in the Higher Education systems provides requisite insights into the type and efficacy of the various mechanisms for external earnings by the Universities. The individual chapters have been well thought out, are comprehensive and indicate a deep understanding of the issues involved. The lucid background given in chapter 1 enables a clear comprehension of the effects of resource crunch on the university system the world over; and explains the Punnayya Committee recommendations setting targets of income to be generated by the universities over a period. Chapter 2 dealing with routes for resource generation explains the various logistic factors necessary for achieving a sustainable mechanism and aptly focuses on the crucial leadership factor. Chapter 3 emphasis on the need to motivate sponsored work, both in fundamental and applied research, in a systematic and structured manner. Emphasis on relevant examples and models for practical applications is justifiably explained. Means for income generation through Continuing Education Programme (CEP), Alumni Associations and investments of funds are again highlighted and it is good to see that the necessary precautions to be taken to create a balancing mechanism are also pointed out. Chapters IV and V deal with University - Industry interaction as an important means of mutual growth and resource generation. The necessary interface factors essential for these interactions have been properly highlighted again.

This book is a good referral text to universities/ institutes, particularly in the new context of depleting funds and desirability of generating extra budgetary resources. It should become an integral aspect of curriculum planning in the higher education system. I congratulate the author for this timely and valuable work.

R.A. Mashelkar
Director-General
COUNCIL OF SCIENTIFIC &
INDUSTRIAL RESEARCH (CSIR)
GOVERNMENT OF INDIA
NEW DELHI

Contents

Preface

To-day, the idea of a book on how to go about to generate resource in the higher education system sounds sense. But in 1980s, there could be a few articles written to establish how absurd the idea was. Over the last one decade, it has been accepted all over the world that, firstly, public money must be spent with a sense of accountability and secondly, the system must generate additional income within its frame-work. While in USA, this generally has been accepted for quite some-time, from 1980s, the approach became stronger, and in Europe and other countries also, the approach was accepted and their universities have been earning and doing well in this direction.

In India, despite the fact that save a few universities and institutions like IITs, resource constraint has always been there, the approach to generate income never found favour primarily because many a people of the system thought that it was the responsibility, of the government to fund education as a social responsibility and others thought how could those involved in a sacred activity of generating and transmitting knowledge get involved in resource generation.

Slowly, but steadily, the pressure has since been built up in India, as it did in Europe notably, UK. With the liberalisation of economy and the escalating cost of higher education bringing pressure on the public exchequer, the inevitable has happened. Universities and institutions have now to generate additional income to meet the rising costs of higher education. Most of the universities have already been under serious financial constraints, many facing crisis with mounting deficits. In such a situation, the first requirement is to reduce and arrest the growing expenditure and at the same time, to generate income.

It is true that every university-institution wants to generate additional income and some efforts must have been made at some point of time or other, but with little achievement. This is likely to happen unless the efforts are planned, structured and the constituents are involved in the efforts.

Primarily, for three reasons, I decided to write a small but reasonably as comprehensive as possible, a book on how to go about for resource generation. One: I have been in the system for over 30 years and I think that when the universities-institutions look for some literature to check what can be done and how to move in this direction, there is hardly anything that could one find. Keeping this in view, I thought an effort in this direction may perhaps be of some use. Second: study on resource crunch and resource generation have of late been rather my areas of greater interest and also part of my profession. After spending some reasonable time to study these aspects in respect of different countries, and occasionally writing in these areas and speaking in some universities, many seniors and colleagues had suggested from time to time that I should try to write a small book so that universities and colleges may have some material in this regard in a structured manner. And the third and the most important reason to make this humble effort is that in 1991-92, when I undertook a study of the Resource Management in the Universities in UK and finally wrote a book on that, I had realized that it would be worthwhile to have some literature to try to providing a structure as to how to go about for resource generation.

Although, in my mind in 1991, I had no doubt that what the universities of UK had faced in 1980s, we, in India, would be facing the crunch in not too distant a future. Rather sooner thereafter, than later, came the crunch in our system also, in a formal way.

In the book, I have used the words 'university' 'institute' and 'college'. Basically, I meant all. Therefore, if I have used the word 'university' in a particular place that does not mean that 'Institute' or 'College' is not covered and *vice-versa*. One has to see how relevant the context is. Most of the suggestions are, however, common to all.

The first Chapter of the book is devoted to explain why there is a resource crunch. The idea is that we should know that the resource crunch which has now come to us in a formal way, came to the developed countries in 1980s and they too had problems. This Chapter also tells about the crunch in other developing countries and the steps taken by them to tide over the crisis.

With a background of the crunch starts the real area of the book covering Chapters 2 to 5.

Chapter 2 introduces the Routes for Resource Generation and there is really no short cut to generate income. The leadership factor is crucial to all efforts to achieve success. Of course, the leader has to have a good team to translate the vision to performance. This Chapter discusses the need of Vision Statement, Missions therefor, and the Strategies to fulfil the Missions. It has also discussed the need to project the image of the university/institution to achieve the objectives and spelt out how this depends on a variety of relationship - internal and external.

Chapter 3 discusses in detail, the Sponsored Research Projects, Continuing Education Programme (CEP),

Alumni Association, Fees and Income from Investments etc. How each of these, particularly the Sponsored Research Projects and CEP contribute to resource generation has been spelt out clearly and how they should be explored. Information about the national R & D support, the funding agencies, areas of research have also been provided which indicate that the university sector has hardly taken the advantage of the funding facilities for Research activities. International position for R & D and the funding by the Government of Japan have been provided for the readers.

Chapter 4 may perhaps be considered as the most important one for it discusses why industry interaction is necessary and how to go about for that. Mostly, it is mistaken that industry interaction is necessary only to generate income. While this is certainly an important part of the interaction, the real benefit is that for national development, extensive, effective and meaningful interaction between academics and industry is a *sine-qua-non.* Discussing the national R & D expenditure in various sectors, e.g. central government, state governments, public sector and the private sector and also giving details of the growth of R & D units in each of the plan periods since 1950, the chapter discusses with reasonable details about the international scenario of R & D expenditure with special reference to UK and Japan.

Taking advantage of the liberalised economic policy and the new possibilities that stem from that, it is necessary to boost the university-industry interaction. Finally, the chapter spells out through recipes how to go to market to generate income and what are the essentials to build up credibility and to sustain the same for meaningful interaction. It also discusses some of the common problems of interaction and also the new trends in the university-industry interaction.

Chapter 5 is devoted to describe that for the purpose of interaction with industry how interface factor is important for it is with the effectiveness of the interface authority that all that is intended to happen can be achieved. It has been suggested in the chapter that besides a senior faculty who should continue to be incharge of Research and Development, keeping in view the needs of the changing time, the concept of University Company which has successfully worked in the university system in UK is worth trying in the Indian context also. For the colleges also, the concept can be applied in the form of Consortium.

Chapter 6 is really the concluding chapter discussing the collections of the proceeding five chapters of the book.

I must put on record that this book has been written with the financial support of the Curriculum Development Programme (CDP), Government of India, at IIT Bombay.

I am grateful to Dr. R.A. Mashelkar, Director-General, Council for Scientific and Industrial Research (CSIR), Government of India, New Delhi, for writing the Foreword for this book.

Besides my usual official responsibilities, completing a book could not have been possible without the whole-hearted co-operation of my colleague Anil Kumar who has worked with me beyond the hours known for office work. Rajan, another colleague too worked hard for the same purpose. I am not only thankful but grateful for their active support in my effort to accomplish the work.

I am grateful to Professor, S.C. Sahasrabudhe, our Deputy Director and Professor, S.L. Narayanamurthy, Dean (R&D) for their valuable suggestions on certain chapters. For the same reason, I must express my thanks and gratitude to Professor Arvind P. Kudchadker, our former Deputy Director.

At home, I owe a lot to my wife Lily who provided an ideal condition to work for the book and despite visible inconveniences, she readily and smilingly provided me the ideal condition to accomplish the work. So did my daughter Rinki My son Rahul was a real help in my work. I must thank him for many good suggestions from time to time. He also provided me a lot of material connected with management.

Finally, being conscious of my limitation and also of the fact that this is an effort first of its kind, it may suffer from many shortcomings. All views are my own views, I shall greatly value the suggestions of the worthy readers on this humble effort for improvement.

Mumbai,
15th January, 1997

D.K. Ghosh

1

Resource Crunch – A Global Phenomenon

INTRODUCTION

Admittedly, resource crunch in higher education is a global phenomenon. Resultantly, need to generate income by the system itself has become important and crucial and that is why the Government of India and the various Governments as also the University Grants Commission have been emphasising on this need. To answer the question why there is a global resource crunch, we have to go back and analyse the consequences of the Second World War which have changed the social, economic and cultural scenario of all the countries all over the world—in varying degrees, and at staggering pace. But today, the impact is complete, the problems are broadly common, and hence, efforts are not very different in different countries.

DEVELOPED COUNTRIES

Consequences of the Second World War made all round impact in various spheres of life throughout the world. Perhaps the most striking impact was the realization of the role of higher education, particularly the role of science and technology to achieve economic prosperity and superiority of powers. Settlements of a large number of personnel on their return to home, after the Second World War led to population growth and demanded expansion of higher education. Decolonization by the United States and European countries in the years after the Second World War, also led to the return of a large number of personnel to their respective countries.

It was no coincidence that practically all over the USA and Europe, 1960s were in general the period of expansion of education, particularly higher education. The 18 year olds i.e., those who were born after 1940s demanded the facility of higher education. On its part, the government was also keen to create a trained manpower force through higher education system particularly technical education. Resultantly, there was massive expansion of higher education during 1960s.

Conspicuously, the later-half of 1970s marked all over the world, a slowing down trend in the pace of expansion, particularly due to the strikingly high public expenditure that higher education demanded. From the beginning of 1980s, changing climate was visible in the universities in USA and Europe to curtail expenditure, at least to arrest the escalating investments in higher education. The message to generate income became clear and changing attitude and culture were clearly seen making impact, of course in different degrees, in different countries.

One reason for the pressure to reduce investments in higher education was the pressing demand of various other social sectors. In Japan, public funding in higher education declined maximum, from 83.10% in 1970 to 63.10% in 1987[1] Next to Japan, it was UK, where public

1. P. 94, Financing of HE - Current Practices, OECD, Paris, 1990.

funding declined from 71.20% in 1970-71 to 55% in 1986-87 as shown in table 1.1. That was also the trend, of course in varying degrees, in some other developed countries. Table 1.1 also shows the sources of income of higher education in some selected countries from which it is evident that public funding in higher education declined.

Table 1.1[2]

Sources of Income of Higher Education in Selected Developed Countries

Country		*General Public Funds*	*Fees*	*Other Incomes*
UK	1970-71	71.20	6.30	22.40
	1986-87	55.00	13.70	31.30
France (all Institutions)	1975	93.00	2.90	4.20
	1984	89.50	4.70	5.80
Japan Public	1970	83.10	2.00	14.90
	1987	63.10	8.80	28.00
USA Public	1969-70	61.10	15.10	23.70
	1984-85	59.30	14.50	26.30

For historical reasons, there was a good deal of commonality in the higher education system between UK and India. However, since 1980s there have been many changes in UK, following a general policy of reducing the public expenditure by the newly elected Conservative Government (1979), led by Margaret Thatcher. Within a few months of its installation, allocation for universities was reduced by the

2. *Ibid.*

government and from July 1984, through the University Grants Committee (now bifurcated into three Funding Councils called Higher Education Funding Council—one each for England, Scotland and Wales), grants of the universities were reduced on a selective basis by 6% to as high as 44% which posed serious problems to the universities. For some universities, it was a threat of survival and for some it was a question of 'bankruptcy'. While announcing cuts of grants in July 1981, a three-year period of restructuring was given and the cuts were effective from 1984-85.

From that time, the UK higher education system has undergone a sea change in almost all respects although universities had initially reacted to the government's action and were not quite willing to accept and participate in various restructuring activities including special efforts to generate income, but as time passed by, they gradually realized the reality and slowly restructuring took place. Criticising the indifference and inaction of the universities to the suggestions of the Minister of State for Education and Science of the previous Labour Government as early as in 1969, that they should increase student-teacher ratio, encourage students to study within the reach of home, make more efficient use of buildings and equipments, avoid duplication of facilities etc., in a debate in 1981, in the House of Commons, a Member of Parliament said that the Universities did nothing since then (since 1969 warning) to the suggestions of the Minister. He observed that ".... universities walked so tall that they only had to shout loud enough that they were centres of excellence and everyone would bow. Universities walked so tall that they sometime forgot about the ground"[3] Universities had to face

3. PP. 458-501, House of Commons Debate (HE), 8.7.1981, Hansard, Vol. 8, No. 138.

enormous problems of restructuring, but when pushed to the wall, finally all of then rose to the occasion and they are now doing well. They have become transparent, efficient and cost-effective. Universities have moved out of UK to market their expertise and services 'aggressively' and generated income through international consultancies. They have also been successful in attracting more foreign students despite the fact that from 1979, very high fees are charged. It is interesting that students from Europe are charged the same fees as are applicable for home students. Fees prescribed for the foreign students are aimed at recovering the full cost of their education. Within the country, University- Industry interaction was given a boost which helped both the universities and industry.

Precisely, there is a global trend to be 'cost effective' in a situation of steep competition and scarce resources. Universities in UK and elsewhere have achieved this in varying degrees, through.

- Reduction of Expenditure,
- Enhancing Efficiency at all levels including use of Educational Technology, and
- Generation of Non-Government income by boosting the existing sources and tapping new ones.

DEVELOPING COUNTRIES

India was no exception in respect of the expansion of higher education in 1960's. As against 25 universities including 'deemed university' (actual number of universities was 19), 700 colleges and 2,65,917 students enrollment in higher education at the time of independence (1947-48), by 1970-71, the numbers rose to 93 universities, 3604 colleges and 19,53,640 students respectively.

During 1970s, slowing down of expansion was noticed in the developing countries also. In India, however the number continued to increase primarily due to population bulge. In the case of the developing countries, besides the demand of various social sectors, the need of investments in sector that could help develop the economy was an additional important pressure, e.g. agriculture, power generation, rural development, etc. Precisely, resource crunch in higher education was felt all over the world in 1980s.

In India, while the universities have always faced the resource constraints, particularly the state universities in general, the real crunch has been felt only now. However, it is really more a realization of the 'crunch', than the 'crunch' itself for the funding agencies have now been pressing the universities to generate non-government income and be on their own, which earlier the government agencies did not clearly say so, as a matter of declared policy. Even the universities thought why they should raise non-government income, for they were doing a service to the nation and a commercial approach was not desirable.

In the developing countries of Asia, in relation to 1960s, the public expenditure in general declined except China and South Korea. The following table 1.2 will show the position in this regard.

Resultantly, the universities faced resource crunch. Table1.3[5] will show how the crunch is felt by the higher education sectors in some selected developing countries.

In order to face the crunch, universities in these countries have drawn up plans and programmes for there is no getting away from the reality and, therefore,

5. *Ibid.*

Table 1.2[4]

Public Expenditure on Education as a percentage of total Government Expenditure in Selected Developing Countries of Asia

Country	*1965*	*1975*	*1985*	*1989*
China	NA	4.2	8.1	12.4
India	8.7	9.4	9.4	8.5*
Indonesia	NA	13.1	9.3	4.3#
South Korea	15.4	13.9	28.2	23.3
Malaysia	18.5	19.3	16.3	18.2
Phillipines	25.0	11.4	7.0	NA
Thailand	20.1	21.0	18.5	16.6

* 1987 figure

\# 1988 figure

Table1.3

Resource Crunch in some Selected Developing Countries

Country	*Crunch Felt*
Indonesia	* Sharp reduction in development budget from Government. * Reduced level of operation and maintenance expenditure. * Increased fees to fill up the gap of reduced Government support.
Thailand	* Declining Government Support. * Drastically reduced level of Expenses.

4. Compiled from Funding for Higher Education in Asia and the Pacific, UNESCO, Paris (1990).

Republic of Korea	*	Reduced Government Grants for Higher Education.
	*	Reduction in Expenditure.
Phillipines	*	High Inflation Rate in late '80s (24%)
	*	Financial constraints.
	*	Looking for generation of Income.
China	*	Gradual Reduction of free boarding.
	*	Gradual imposition of Tuition Fees.
	*	Reduction in Expenditure.

sooner the steps are taken, better it is before it is too late. Even China has effected a few unprecedented changes in this regard. The following table 1.4[6] will provide the picture.

Admittedly, no government can sustain the fast escalating expenditure on higher education, particularly when there are pressures on other social sectors, and sectors demanding heavy investments for developing the economy. At the same time, it is true that the universities find the funding by the government at a level which does not help them raise and keep up the level for running the system in all the areas e.g. the fast rising expenditure on salary component, general inflation factor, upkeep of the campus, removal of obsolescence, equipping the library and the liberal assistance to the students. Even for research activities, there is hardly any funding worth the name except through projects and that too only a few universities are able to win them; many do not even make serious efforts.

6. *Ibid.* (complied)

Table 1.4

Broad Plans and Programmes to reduce Expenditure and generate Income in Higher Education in Selected Developing Countries

Country	Plans and Programmes
Indonesia	* Develop Private Sectors. * Improve Planning and Management, Quality, Reliance, Efficiency and Equity. * Emphasize on Cost Recovery–Bank–Government negotiation. * Flexibility and adaptability to changing circumstances, emphasize on developing administration capabilities through Management Information System (MIS).
Thailand	* Creation of Endowment Fund. * Technical Services for generating income. * Boosting Existing Sources. * Follow AIT Pattern (Separate Vice-President for funds development).
Republic of Korea	* Funding from Private Sectors by incentives to Donors. * New approach that part of profit of Industry for Higher Education. * Higher Education-Industry Interaction. * Generation of income by lending Assets to outside agencies on lease basis.
Phillipines	* Fees – but limited normally to 15%. * Residue subsidy on income basis. A – Below 30,000 B – Upto 40,000

	C – Upto 80,000
	D – Upto 1,00,000
	E – Beyond 1,00,000
	* Maximizing Income from auxiliary facilities and land holdings.
	* Tapping Alumni, Business and Industry for funds.
China	* Charge tuition fees.
	* Charge boarding expenses.
	* Move to International Market.
	* Developing profitable services for wider society commercial enterprise.
	* Special tax policies for commercial activities.

INDIAN SCENARIO–ESCALATING EXPENDITURE

Over a period of four years from 1984-85 to 1988-89, of the eighty universities who responded to a study of the Association of Indian Universities, in a number of universities, the expenditure had increased by more than 100%. In the case of the other Universities also, the increase posed problems. Table 1.5 will provide the picture in this regard in a representative manner.

It is true that while the increase of expenditure is alarming, the fact remains that it is a global phenomenon. It is so primarily because of the inevitable growth of expenditure due mainly to the inflation factor and again that is a global reason, although the inflation rate differs from sub-continent to sub-continent and country to country. During the aforesaid period, impact of the Fourth Pay Commission was also another reason for the increase in non-plan expenditure.

Table 1.5[7]

Sr. No.	*University*	*Budget Expenditure during (1984-85)*	*(1988-89) (Rs. in lakhs)*	*Percentage Increase*
(1)	*(2)*	*(3)*	*(4)*	*(5)*
	A. Universities with more than 100% increase			
1.	Karnataka	558.4	1332.7	138.66
2.	Poona	436.5	1036.9	137.55
3.	JNU	537.2	1200.1	123.40
4.	Manipur	110.7	231.9	109.49
5.	Bangalore	456.6	920.4	101.58
	B. Universities between 75% and 100% increase			
6.	Roorkee	643.3	1283.5	99.52
7.	Kurukshetra	431.2	858.2	99.03
8.	Anna	531.6	1032.3	94.19
9.	Visva Bharati	408.1	775.2	89.95
10.	Delhi	1086.8	2028.9	86.69
11.	Guru Nanak Dev	407.9	750.2	83.92
12.	H.S. Gaur	313.3	559.9	78.71
13.	Sambalpur	141.7	252.1	77.91
14.	Himachal Pradesh	313.2	552.1	76.28
15.	Punjab	685.9	1203.8	75.51
	C. Universities between 51% and 75%			
16.	Venkateswara	491.3	799.9	62.81
17.	Gujarat	406.5	626.7	54.17
18.	M.S.	728.9	1189.6	63.20

7. Compiled from Financial Deficits in Universities, AIU, New Delhi (1991).

(1)	(2)	(3)	(4)	(5)
19.	Calicut	427.0	722.9	69.30
20.	Shivaji	332.3	552.2	66.18
21.	BHU	2368.1	4105.7	73.38
22.	Calcutta	814.7	1304.7	60.14

RISING COSTS AND SINKING RESOURCES

Such a situation as has been described in the previous paragraphs, of constantly rising costs ultimately led the universities to the deficit trap irrespective of the fact that the universities were central or state, albeit the former were always funded much better than the latter. During the period 1984-85 and 1988-89, the position of surpluses or deficits of eighty universities of a study undertaken were as shown in Table1.6[8].

For a better understanding of the deficits of Table1.6, names of the universities have been identified as given in Table1.7[9].

From Tables 1.6 and 1.7, it is clear that out of 80 universities, only two did not have deficits. Of the remaining 78 universities, as many as 20 suffered deficits for all the five years of the study together. The largest number of universities (36) had deficits for 1 to 2 years. Today, the condition is worse than before for the crunch has ultimately appeared publicly in a declared manner.

It is interesting that the reasons of deficits were not due to the good or bad financial position of the governments which were responsible for funding for ".. all the

8. P. 6, Financial Deficits in Universities, AIU, New Delhi.
9. *Ibid.*, p. 8.

Table 1.6

Sl. No.	*Universities*	*No. Deficit in any year*	*Deficit for 1 to 2 yrs.*	*Deficit for 3 to 4 yrs.*	*Deficit for all 5 yrs.*	*Total no. of Universities*
1.	Central Universities	Nil	4 (5.0)	3 (3.7)	Nil	7 (8.7)
2.	State Universities	2 (2.5)	20 (25.0)	19 (23.8)	8 (10.0)	49 (61.3)
3.	Agricultural Universities	Nil	10 (12.5)	6 (7.5)	Nil	16 (20.0)
4.	Deemed Universities	Nil	2 (2.5)	4 (5.0)	2 (2.5)	8 (10.0)
5.	Total (All Universities)	2 (2.5)	36 (45.0)	32 (40.0)	10 (12.5)	80 (100.0)

Note: Figures in parentheses indicate the percentage to total responding universities i.e. (80).

responding universities in the States of Bihar, Himachal Pradesh, Madhya Pradesh and Manipur suffered from deficits even though the States had surplus during the period of analysis."[10] On the other hand, "the universities of Andhra Pradesh, Uttar Pradesh, Tamil Nadu, Jammu and Kashmir, Maharashtra, Punjab and West Bengal emerged out with surpluses while the States experienced deficits."[11] The third picture that emerged from the study was that both the universities in Gujarat, Assam, Karnataka, Orissa and Kerala as well as these States had deficits.

The causes of deficits as analysed were:

(i) inadequate grants;

10. *Ibid*, p.13

11. *Ibid.*

Table 1.7

Identification of the Universities having Deficits for Varying Duration during 1984-85 to 1988-89

Sl. No.	Type of Universities	No Deficit in any year	Duration of Deficit: 1 to 2 yrs.	Duration of Deficit: 3 to 4 yrs.	Duration of Deficit: All the 5 yrs.
(1)	(2)	(3)	(4)	(5)	(6)
1.	Central Universities	Nil	Hyderabad BHU, Visva Bharati, JNU	NEHU, Jamia Milia, Delhi	Nil
2.	State Univer-sities	Padmavati Mahila, Tamil	Bombay, Poona, Kurukshetra, Maharshi Dayanand, Himachal Pradesh, Jammu, Gulbarga, Karnataka, Mangalore, Jiwaji, Ravi Shankar, Manipur, Sambalpur, Punjabi, Anna, Bharthiar,	Nagarjuna, Venkateshwara, Dibrugarh, Guj. Ayurveda, South Gujarat, Bangalore, Mysore, Calicut, Cochin, HS Gaur, Devi Ahilya, Guru Ghasidas, SNDT, Marathwada,	Kakatiya, Patna, M.S. Univ. S. Patel, Kerala, Shivaji, Tilak, Maharashtra, Annamalai

(1)	(2)	(3)	(4)	(5)	(6)
			Mother Teressa, Rohilkhand, Calcutta, Vidyasagar,	GND Amritsar Avadh, North Bengal, Roorkee	
3.	Agricul-tural Universities	Nil	A.P. Agri., Marathwada, Krishi, Konkan Krishi, M.Phule Krishi, Y.S. Horti., Univ. of Agri. and Sc., Kerala Agri., Punjab Agri., TN Agri., GBP Agri., ND Agri.	Birsa Agri., Rajindra Agri., Orissa Univ. of Agri. and Tech., C.S. Azad Agri.	Nil
4.	Deemed Universities	Nil	Guj. Vidyapith Gurukul Kangri	IISc., Thapar Inst. of Engg., BITS, Gandhi-gram Rural Institute	Indian School of Mines, Banasthali Vidyapith

(ii) inefficiency in the distribution of funds;

(iii) rigidity in the method of funding;

(iv) adhocism in budgetary allocation by the State Governments; and

(v) financial mismanagement by universities.

Clearly, it is the government which was responsible for the causes *(i)* to *(iv)* while the universities were responsible for the cause *(v)*. Going by this, it has to be admitted that primarily, it is the funding pattern and distribution system that are responsible for the deficits of the period in question. It is also true that to an extent, mismanagement contributed to the already inadequate grants and for that the universities were responsible. In the context of today, mismanagement must be converted into good management, else already indifferent to bad health of the universities will lead to more serious problem.

WHAT IS THE MANDATE NOW?

Clearly, the facts and figures as discussed earlier make it amply clear what the global scenario is, and also what is the position in the Indian Universities. Precisely, there really is a no getting away situation from the reality that we must learn to handle our affairs with due vision, dedicated mission and perfect strategy to achieve the various objectives that lie ahead in the situation that we are already in. In the current context, broadly, the following objectives could be set for the universities and institutions of higher learning in the area of resource management:

(i) to rejuvenate the management and make it efficient and promising;

(ii) to reduce expenditure as far as possible;

(*iii*) to arrest the growing expenditure on as many counts as possible; and

(iv) to Generate Income by:

(*a*) boosting the existing sources, and

(*b*) tapping new sources.

Although the broad objectives are two, in reality, quite a few associated issues would be required to be tackled to achieve the objectives. For example, to reduce the level of expenditure or to arrest the growth in respect of certain areas, the prerequisites are to study the possibilities and act accordingly for which a suitable mechanism should be developed.

For generation of income both to boost the existing sources as also to tap new ones, there must be a planned study and concerted efforts across the system. Stray or half-hearted efforts cannot result into anything. Now that most of the governments have pegged the grants at a particular level giving the mandate that the universities should generate income to meet additional requirements of funds, they are now forced to find ways and means to balance their budgets.

There are two ways to look at the situation. One is that it should be accepted as a challenge to move to the direction of reduced dependence on the government support and achieve greater autonomy. The other is to try to restore the old pattern. This, however, is neither beneficial nor possible. It is not beneficial for even when government was paying grants on routine basis either as block grants or incremental grant, the universities were in no better position. They lived in depressed deficits as is clear from the facts and figures already discussed. In the context of the liberalised economy, every organisation has to learn to earn and live within its capacity. Really speaking, it is 'fait-accompli'. The mandate is thus quite clear and therefore, it is not possible to restore the old pattern.

JUSTICE PUNNAYYA COMMITTEE ON RESOURCE POSITION

In the context of the New Economic Policy of the Government of India from 1991, and the alarming burden of the fast increasing expenditure in higher education, the University Grants Commission was already seized of the problem of providing funds. For the first time, the commission (UGC) had appointed in 1992, a High Powered Committee consisting of nine members, under the Chairmanship of Justice Dr. K. Punnayya. The terms of reference for the Committee are shown in the appendix-I of which, the following two are relevant for the purpose of this book:

* To study the extent to which the institutions are raising their own resources, and to suggest specific measures for augmenting the proportion of resource raising by the institution.
* To recommend incentives to institutions to raise a higher proportion of internal resources and to develop norms for utilisation of internally generated resources.
* To explore and recommend ways of improving overall efficiency of institutions.

The Report which was submitted in 1993 covered various aspects of resource position, generation of income and management thereof. The summary of recommendations of the committee are given in the Appendix-II. Relevant to this book are only those aspects which are related to resource generation and management thereof. The Committee deliberated on the following broad issues:

* Role of the Government in Financing Higher Education;
* The present pattern of Funding Universities;
* The Patterns of Funding the Universities with special reference to Central Universities;
* Proposals for Funding Central Universities in the future;
* Norms for fixing Non-plan Grants of the Universities (Central);
* Efficiency to achieve accountability, quality assurance and cost-effectiveness;
* Income Generation by Universities and its utilisation;
* Review of the existing schemes of financial assistance for needy students and measures for a scheme of freeships and scholarships;
* Institutions deemed to be Universities;
* Delhi Colleges; and
* Colleges affiliated to the Banaras Hindu University.

CURRENT SOURCES OF INCOME OF THE UNIVERSITIES

Over the years, dependence on the government funds has increased considerably. Another striking absence in the matter of funding education now is that in 1950-51, local bodies contributed to education, to as much as 10.9% of the educational expenditure, as against 05.6% in 1982-84. Income from fees aggregated to a high of 20.4%. in 1950-51 compared to 07.5% in 1982-84. This however does not mean that fees have been reduced. What has happened is while expenditure increased manifold, income from fees remained unrevised creating thereby an increasing gap.

It is relevant to know how much income the central universities generate internally *vis-a-vis* the government grants through UGC. Table1.8 is perhaps a classic example where the income from fees varies from as low as 0.56% in the case of Visva Bharati to a reasonable percentage (at 1991-92 level) of 9.88% in the case of the University of Delhi. The other two universities whose income from fees is less than one per cent are BHU and JNU.

Table 1.8[12]

Source of Income of Central Universities (1991-92)

University	*Government*		*UGC*	*Fees*	*Endowments*	*Others*	*Total*
	Central	*State*					
Aligarh	–	0.05	93.30	5.91	–	0.74	100.0
BHU	0.49	0.03	91.60	0.62	0.08	7.18	100.0
Delhi	–	–	88.68	9.88	0.62	0.82	100.0
JNU	–	–	95.75	0.59	–	3.66	100.0
Jamia	–	–	94.90	4.24	–	0.86	100.0
Hyderabad	–	–	94.82	2.03	–	5.15	100.0
Pondicherry	–	–	95.05	9.66	–	0.29	100.0
Visva Bharati	–	0.04	97.60	0.56	–	1.80	100.0

While the Non-plan expenditure has been increasing at rates higher than the inflation rates, there has not been any revision of fees or even when revision took place, that was not in relation to the growth of expenditure of the university in any way.

12. Punnayya Committee Report, Chapter-IX, Table-IV.

Tracing the possible reasons for this situation, the report observed that 'The universities are regarded in India largely as noble and charitable ventures, as an essential part of the welfare programme, with little concern for cost effectiveness and income generation.'[13] However, it is not altogther true that no efforts were made to revise the fees. The fact is whenever efforts were made to revise the fees that did not materialise, due to stiff opposition from the students. Attempts in this regard were always regarded both by the universities as also government sometime as 'delicate' and sometime 'risky' Consequently, the better option of not revising or even not attempting to do that, was adopted. The other source of income is miscellaneous under 'others' which also varies among the central universities from as low as 0.29% in the case of the Pondicherry University to 7.18% in the case of BHU.

Even when income from fees is negligible, as a single source of income, even today fees are considered significant, although in the overall budget, it is insignificant. Income from examinations has not been shown separately. However it is not always a source of income although there is enough scope to reduce expenditure on the conduct of examinations through some reforms and better management to make it profitable.

On one hand, dependence on the government funds has increased and on the other hand during the above period, the number of universities (including deemed universities) grew fast from 30 in 1950-51 to over 130 by 1984. This makes it clear how fast and heavy have been the order of additional burden on the government for funding higher education. The number of colleges

---

13. *Ibid.*, Chapter IX, Para-9.3.

grew at a faster pace from 750 in 1950-51 to over 5000 by 1984.

Clearly, it is primarily the government funding that keeps the universities going. Table 1.8 shows that the government grants through UGC was as high as 97.60% in the case of Visva Bharati. Even the lowest was as high as 88.68% in the case of the University of Delhi. All others received grants amounting to more than 90%. The government grants are paid on negotiated basis every year.

For obvious reasons, unit costs once arrived at cannot remain the same. The Punnayya Committee has, therefore, recommended that "Ultimately maintenance grants to a university based on unit costs of all its activities would require revision from time to time". What is important, in this connection, is the basis of arriving at the unit cost (or per student cost). Unit costs are also bound to be different for different subject-mix. For example, it cannot be the same for an Engineering course and a Science course and between the latter and Humanities. Punnayya Committee has suggested that an expert committee should find out the reasons of difference of unit costs of different subjects e.g. between Social Sciences and Humanities and Sciences.

The Committee had taken seven parameters to arrive at the 'academic expenditure':

(a) Costs involved in the teaching departments (salaries of teaching and non-teaching staff in the teaching departments plus other expenses);

(b) Costs on examinations;

(c) Library expenses;

(d) Student facilities;

(e) Expenses on hostels;

(*f*) Scholarships and fellowships; and

(*g*) Publications.

SUGGESTIONS FOR GENERATION OF INCOME

For the purpose of generation of income, the Punnayya Committee has suggested that steps be taken by the Universities to generate additional income as shown in Table 1.9, most of which are conventional and some are non-conventional.

Table 1.9[14]

Suggestions of Justice Punnayya Committee of UGC for Resource Generation

Source	*Recommendations*
1. Fees	
(*a*) Tuition Fees	To revise with immediate effect and be periodically adjusted keeping in view the rate of inflation. There should be differential rates keeping in view the employment opportunities. They should also be related to the recurring cost of the course.
(*b*) Other fees (Admission, examination, Library, laboratory, sports and other facilities	To review and revise the entire fee structure and recover a significant part of recurring cost.
(*c*) Hostel and Mess Fees	To recover actual recurring cost and gradually, capital cost.

14. *Ibid.* Chapter IX.

(Water, Elect-
ricity, seat rent)

2. *Other Sources of Income*

   (a) Renting out facilities, e.g. auditoria, class rooms, computer services, play-ground, guest-house, hostels, lawns, messes, etc.

   (b) To recover municipal service charges from campus residents as also for facilities like telephone, computing, etc.

3. *Consultancy Mechanism*

   Universities to constitute appropriate consultative mechanism for mobilising resources. UGC to extend support.

It is true that for the first time, UGC had appointed a committee such as the Justice Punnayya Committee to examine and recommend on matters very important for the health of the higher education system. The committee had to look into many aspects of financing of higher education and make its recommendations. While many of its recommendations are being examined, two of its recommendations have been acted upon which have a far reaching impact in favour of the universities. One is, not to adjust the additional income generated by the Institute while determining the annual maintenance grant, and to provide an appropriate incentive grant to the universities on the additionally generated income. The other is the hundred per cent income tax concession on all donations to the universities and an additional tax concession to donors for sponsoring selected research projects. The Finance Ministry has already amended the Income-tax Act to provide 100% and 125% tax exemption respectively.

NEED FOR DATA SERVICES

In many areas of its deliberations, the Committee felt handicapped due to the absence or non-availability of relevant statistics. Although UGC publishes some statistics, but they are inadequate to do any useful research or meaningful comparison and analysis. It is necessary to publish dependable statistics in relation to the various activities of the universities in properly devised formats for computer feeding and analysis.

Undeniably, it is a gigantic task involving vigour and funds. It may be worthwhile to handover the responsibility to a professional organisation which may be authorised to collect statistics from the universities and colleges and publish them at reasonable cost. If all universities, colleges, relevant government departments and others purchase them, that will serve purposes of all. Even if UGC may have to provide some funds to the professional organisation to collect and publish statistics, that would be cost-effective in real terms. The UGC should, in that case prescribe such conditions as may be necessary to serve the purpose. In any case, it is high time that more statistical data and importantly dependable statistics of our higher education is available for a number of purposes—from policy decision to performance indicators. Alternatively, a University Statistical Board may be established. But, that may not be cost-effective. The question of professionalism would also arise.

In UK, to meet such needs, Universities' Statistical Record was established in 1968 under the joint auspices of UGC and CVCP (Committee for Vice-Chancellors and Principals) for more comprehensive statistics on staff and students in higher education. Computer based information is collected and provided covering:

(a) undergraduate and post-graduate students,
(b) the first destination of graduates,
(c) academic and academic related staff, and
(d) continuing education courses.

Justice Punnayya Committee has recommended that some studies be undertaken and norms be prescribed for various purposes. While some of them have correctly been left to be finalised by UGC or other bodies, one feels that the Committee could have made, with the authority and mandate that it had, specific recommendations for in that case, they would have been acted upon fast, as have been on its recommendations that the universities should be allowed to keep the resources generated by them with an incentive matching grant for UGC as also the tax exemptions on donations.

CONCLUSION

Admittedly, there is a resource crunch all over the world and there is no getting away from the reality to generate income by the universities themselves boosting the existing sources and in particular tapping the new ones. It is perhaps more important and necessary to learn to be cost-effective. That there is a positive need to be efficient, needs and argument for it is well admitted that mismanagement is in no less measure, responsible for the precarious financial position of the universities.

Justice Punnayya Committee has recommended that the universities should generate at least 15% of the total recurring expenditure at the end of the first five years and at least 25% at the end of ten years for which universities must draw up specific plans.

If the universities are to generate at least 15%

income at the end of five years, say by 2001, and 25% at the and of 2006, it is imperative that they must draw up plans and programmes; in the right direction without loss of time.

How should the universities go about, what should be the mechanism of rejuvenating the financial and what routes they should follow to achieve the desired goals, are the real questions which would be discussed in the following chapters.

Appendix-I

TERMS OF REFERENCE OF JUSTICE PUNNAYYA COMMITTEE*

Terms of Reference

1.1. The UGC in its order no. F.1-78/92 (CPPII), dated 11 November, 1992, set up a High Powered Committee under the Chairmanship of Justice Dr. K. Punnayya to examine the present financial situation in regard to central universities, institutions deemed to be universities, colleges affiliated to Delhi University and Banaras Hindu University, and technical institutions funded by the Government of India. It also asked the Committee to make necessary recommendations and suggest methods to determine their financial needs, and to suggest changes, if any, which could be introduced in the system of grants to these bodies in future.

1.2. In the operative part of the order mentioned above, the Commission observed that the system of covering the deficit for determining non-plan assistance was proving difficult to continue because it discourages raising of internal resources and its implications, for larger assistance every

---

* Report of Justice Punnayya Committee – Introduction, para-1.1 and 1.2.

year. The Commission also regarded the scheme of plan assistance as ad hoc. The Commission therefore, desired that the Committee should examine the manner in which plan and non-plan grants should be determined, the rational norms that should be adopted, and look into the pattern and system of expenditure of institutions fully funded by the UGC. The terms of reference for the Committee are reproduced below with the number(s) of the chapter(s) dealing with each term of reference given in parenthesis.

i. To examine the present policy, norms and the pattern of providing development and maintenance grants to central universities, deemed universities, Delhi colleges and technical institutions, from the University Grants Commission/Ministry of Human Resource Development, and to suggest policies and norms for determining grants in the future, (Chapters IV, V, XII).

ii. To examine the inter-university variations in development and maintenance grants (per student, per department, and any other relevant criterion) with a view to develop objective parameters governing such grant. (Chapter VII)

iii. To examine the pattern of utilization of the grants, (Chapter IV).

iv. To examine the pattern of allocation of grants between teaching, research and non-teaching functions and to suggest norms relating to expenditure on the above functions, (Chapter VII).

v. To examine the feasibility of developing norms for individual items of expenditure under the development and maintenance grants and, to suggest such norms; and specifically, to examine whether students/research students strength should be related to faculty strength and the strength of the non-teaching staff, any other criteria in this regard. (Chapters VI, VII).

vi. To consider the extent to which flexibility should be available to the institutions for increasing or decreasing expenditure on the individual items under the maintenance grants, (Chapter IV).

vii. To explore and recommend ways of improving overall cost efficiency of the institutions, (Chapter VIII).

viii. To study the extent to which the institutions are raising their own resources, and to suggest specific measures for augmenting the proportion of resource raising by the institutions, (Chapter IX).

ix. To recommend incentives to institutions to raise a higher proportion of internal resources and to develop norms for utilization of internally generated resources, (Chapter IX).

x. To review existing scheme of financial assistance for needy students such as free studentship, scholarships, students loans and to recommend measures for initiating such a scheme with a view to assisting students from disadvantaged sections of the community, and promoting equity in higher education, (Chapter X).

xi. To consider any other item ancillary to the above which the committee may consider relevant, (Chapter VIII).

Appendix II

SUMMARY OF RECOMMENDATIONS*

1. Any additional resources generated by a university institution may be kept in a separate fund to be utilised for furtherance of the objectives of the university/institution. (1.12).
2. The UGC may provide a matching grant as an incentive to universities generating additional resources. (1.12).

---

* Summary of Recommendations of Justic Punnayya Committee, Appendix-I,

3. There should be a 100% income tax concession on all endowments and contributions made to the universities, and additional concessions to donors sponsoring selected research projects in the universities. (1.12.).

4. While universities should be encouraged to angment their resources for covering a larger proportion of the costs of education than at present, the incrcased burden must be borne mainly by those who can afford it. (1.13).

5. State or Government funding must continue to be an essential and mandatory requirement for support to higher education. The Government/State must continue to accept the major responsibility for funding the essential maintenance and developmental requirements of the universities. (1.14).

6. The basis of funding of a central university may be linked to its specific objectives and to its pursuit of excellence, innovativeness, all-India character, and ability to provide access to the weaker sections of society. (5.6.).

7. Research funds may be provided in the development grant as special inputs for strengthening the university's research infrastructure. (5.6).

8. Central universities may switch to an appropriate mix of input funding and student funding systems, which may be standardised for comparable courses of study, by the UGC, over a period of time. (5.7).

9. In regard to student funding, consideration of merit as well as of social and economic backwardness should be taken into account. (5.8).

10. Quality, efficiency and innovativeness must be consciously rewarded and institutions failing to improve financial and academic discipline should face disincentives. (5.9).

11. The unit cost system of calculation of eligibility for grants should replace the existing incremental

system which may be retained till the end of the current Five Year Plan period. (5.10).

12. From the Ninth Plan onwards, grants should be related to the unit cost of activities as a rule, except for new programmes for which unit costs are not determined, or would be difficult to determine. (5.10.II).

13. The Government must ensure that the maintenance grant covers the wage bill of the universities, including periodical increases in increments, DA. and other service charges. (5.10).

14. Heavy subsidies in many of the activities covered under the maintenance grants, such as supply of electricity, transport, water supply etc. and in many other items have to be reviewed and reduced to a substantial extent so that the maintenance grant can be stabilized at a certain acceptable level. (5.11).

15. Maintenance grants to a university based on unit costs of its activities would require periodical revision. (6.1).

16. Expenditure due to increase in the number of staff has to be reviewed and curbed firmly wherever necessary. (6.2).

17. An optimum division between academic and non-academic costs should be arrived at to help in stabilising the maintenance expenditure. (6.2).

18. The universities should be competent to operate their maintenance grant flexibly except for the creation of any new post of any category. (6.3).

19. 20% of the annual maintenance grant may be released to the universities in April-May, 60% in September-October and the remaining 20% in December. (6.4).

20. Part of the development grant may be provided for organisation of new academic programmes and development of existing programmes.

21. Development grants should be linked to an academic audit system, and to performance indicators, to be developed by each university. (6.5).
22. Central universities must avoid offering conventional courses, except when they are specially needed. (6.5).
23. In viewing academic infrastructural facilities, no distinction should be made in regard to the plan and non-plan grants and the entire system must be viewed as a whole. (6.5).
24. Each university must have a perspective plan which must be linked to its objectives, environment and potential. (6.9).
25. The UGC must have a well-developed system for defining objectives and the profile of each central university and for monitoring their development. (6.9.).
26. The UGC should constitute a Standing Advisory Committee of experts, who would continue on a reasonably long-term basis, for evaluating the perspective plans drawn up by Central Universities and for monitoring them. (6.9).
27. The UGC should have special provision of funds in the plan for which all universities may compete to organise new courses of study and undertake research in identified areas. The UGC may identify areas for such courses of study and research. Selection of institutions for funding must be on clearly identified parameters. (6.9).
28. The Vice-Chancellors may be provided with a specified discretionary fund to be used for promoting excellence in teaching and research without incurring any recurring liability. (6.9).
29. Once the Five Year Plan of a university is finalised, the university should be competent to implement these schemes within the broad guidelines of the UGC. (6.10).

30. Each university should have a Statutory Building Committee and it should not be required to seek the approval of he UGC for construction of a building, once the plan and the estimates bave been approved by the Building Committee. (6.11).

31. The University must have an efficient system for dissemination of information regarding the deployment of resources and the implementation of academic and non-academic plan programmes. (6.12).

32. The development plans of the universities should be linked to the perspective plans of the universities and there should be a statutory Planning and Monitoring Committee for each central/deemed university. (6.13-6.14).

33. The universities and the UGC must improve the organisation of an efficient reliable and prompt information system capable of storage, retrieval and analysis of the same. (7.1-7.3).

34. The UGC must develop a system of presenting annually a set of selected information on academic, administrative and financial parameters, of the institutions, particularly, those which are fully funded by it. This information should be utilised in decision-making processes. (7.12-7.13).

35. Two parallel quantitative norms for determining the non-Plan grants, viz *(a)* the optimum proportion of total maintenance grant for a particular activity, and *(b)* the optimum per student recurring cost p.a., have been suggested. (7.19).

36. The academic cost i.e., the expenditure directly related to teaching and research should be 60-65%, academic administration should be 10-12% and on other departments, auxiliary services etc. within 20-25% of the total maintenance grant. Till further refinement in calculation, the basis of maintenance grants is calculated as under: (7.47).

37. ADA, Pension, Arrears pay etc. to be provided on actual basis. (7.41).

Activity	Social Sc./Humanities Cost per student	Science
i) Academic/Teaching Cost	Rs. 11,680/-	Rs. 21,640/-
ii) Academic/Admn. Cost	Rs. 4,500/-	Rs. 4,500/-
iii) Other Department/ auxiliary Services and miscellaneous expenses	Rs. 6,070/-	Rs. 6,070/-
Total	Rs. 22,250 or 22,300	Rs. 32,210 or 32.200

38. The maintained institutions in the A.M.U., the B.H.U. and Visva Bharati be paid maintenance expenditure on incremental basis till meeting the same from other agencies is finalised. (7.50).

39. The student-teacher ratio should be 1:12. (7.52).

40. The teaching to non-teaching staff ratio should be brought to 1:3 and employees like gardeners, safaiwalas, watch and ward etc. be engaged on contract basis to the extent possible. (7.55).

41. The minimum work-load for Professors, Readers and Lecturers should be 40 hours per week and the work distribution for actual teaching and tutorial, examination, research, own reading, administrative work, and on assistance to students have been spelt out in detail. (7.57).

42. On the pattern of the U.K. the Indian Universities should adopt the Academic Audit system and the UGC may give the highest priority to it as this will not only promote academic efficiency, but also cost effectiveness. (8.19).

43. Priority should be given to the introduction a monitoring system for Performance Indicators. (8.20).

44. While the Government/UGC may continue to be the major funding agency, the universities must generate internal resources which should become sizeable in course of time. (9.2).

45. The tuition fees may be revised upwards with immediate effect and may be periodically adjusted,

keeping in view the rate of inflation. The tuition fee may have to be different within a university, for different courses of study. The revised fee should be made applicable to the new entrants. (9.8).

46. The fees for library, laboratory, and sports should be revised upwards to recover a significant part of the recurring cost. (9.9).

47. Hostel fees should be revised with immediate effect to meet all the actual recurring cost and, in due course of time, a part of the capital cost as well. The student community should be involved in the discussions to raise resources where their interests are affected. (9.10).

48. There is a need to review the municipal, civil and other services which are extended to individual members of the university, in their personal capacity and they should be charged appropriately to recover the cost. (9.11).

49. The income derived from enhancement of fees should be utilised to augment fellowship and scholarship programmes for ensuring access to the weaker sections. (9.12).

50. For generating income, the universities should let out their infrastructural facilities like playgrounds auditoria etc. and also organise short-term courses for which there is demand. They should also solicit endowments contributions and actively participate in consultancy without affecting the academic activity of the institutions. (9.13).

51. The resources generated by the universities should constitute at least 15% of the total recurring expenditure at the end of the first five years and at least 25% at the end of 10 years. (9.19).

52. With a view to mobilising resources from within the country and abroad the Alumni Association may be set up in each university with the assistance of an Advisory Body consisting of the well wishers of the University. (9.20).

53. A significant proportion of the internally generated resources and incentive grant from the UGC for the purpose be put in a corpus fund. The UGC may also provide corpus fund grant to institutions, in addition to, maintenance and development grants. (9.24).

54. The income from the corpus fund be utilised for infrastructural development of the university. (9.24).

55. Income generated by the university be used to build up the basic academic infrastructure without having any recurring liability (particularly staff appointment) besides providing support to needy students. (9.25).

56. UGC may comprehensively look into expanding and/or appropriately targeting the existing schemes for providing fellowships, scholarships, freeships and student concessions. (10.1).

57. The existing scheme of the Department of Welfare to provide tuition and living expenses to SC/ST students needs streamlining. (10.2).

58. There is a need to strengthen the 'Book Bank' scheme institutions. (10.4).

59. UGC may introduce broad-based student scholarship schemes for post-graduate students studying in central universities; this may be extended to 20% of the total student enrollment at post-graduate level. (10.9).

60. Central universities should award freeships or admit students at concessional rate of fee to meritorious students belonging to socially and economically weaker sections of the society. (10.12).

61. UGC may explore the possibilities of introducing soft loan scheme in collaboration with the nationalised banks. (10.14).

62. Government in course of time may shift the funding of universities to a system of students funding for ensuring access of higher education to socially and weaker section of the society. (10.17).

63. In respect of institutions deemed to be universities the present mode of determining the maintenance grant may be replaced by grants based on input cost, the modalities for which could he determined by a group to be set up by UGC. (11.16.i).

64. The pattern of provision of development grant suggested for Central Universities should apply by and large to the institutions deemed to be universities. (11.16.ii).

65. A statutory body for extending financial assistance to Delhi colleges be constituted and UGC may not directly fund Delhi colleges. (12.10).

66. The Governing Bodies of Delhi colleges should be reorganized and conferred adequate powers and authority. (12.11).

67. The UGC in consultation with Government of India should set up a Committee regarding the future set up for the Delhi colleges in light of the foreseeable demand for new colleges in the National Capital Territory of Delhi. This may inter-alia require multi-campus structure or alternatively starting new universities. (12.12 and 12.13).

68. Recommendation made for resource generation in respect of Central Universities should be applicable to Delhi Colleges. (12.12).

69. The Academic Audit System and Performance indicators should be finalised in consultation with the colleges and made applicable to them. (12.15).

70. The 4 colleges affiliated to BHU may continue their affiliation to BHU until they voluntarily relinquish it. (13.2).

71. A Banaras Hindu University College Funding Council be constituted under the Chairmanship of Pro-Vice-Chancellor, BHU, which will receive funds both from UGC and U.P. State Government for disbursement to these colleges. (13.3).

2

Routes for Resource Generation

THE LEADERSHIP FACTOR

The leadership factor has always been crucial to any organisation for the directions and motivations have basically to flow from the leader. The leadership quality is directly related to conceiving vision, developing missions, and motivating people for successful organisation of efforts to ensure that the objectives are achieved and that too, with speed, efficiency and cost-effectiveness.

Primarily, leadership has to provide vision, opportunities to work and motivate competent people to work with dedication and commitment and guide them, as necessity arises, both invisibly and whenever needed visibly, so that objectives are achieved. For the leader, to visualize difficulties and see that there are preparations to face them, is another important requirement. For an institution, where the clients are many and much of peace, progress and programmes depends on its relationship particularly of the leader with a number of external groups of people and organisations, the job of the leader is undoubtedly difficult.

In an institution like a university, the Vice-Chancellor is the leader as the academic and executive head of the system. Leading a public institution of intellectuals such as a university, where democratic structures are predominant is both difficult and delicate. How onerous and arduous are the duties of a Vice-Chancellor have been acknowledged by the Robbins Committee of UK in these words, "...no other enterprise would impose on its chairman, the variety and burden of work as the modern University requires of its Vice-Chancellor."[1] Even when one does his duties with best of his ability and intention, it hardly guarantees satisfaction to the constituents of the system or others. Dr. D.S. Kothari, former Chairman, University Grants Commission, had so wisely advised the Vice-Chancellor in these words "... Vice-Chancellor must reconcile himself to the harsh reality that successes are shrouded in silence while failures are spotlighted in notoriety."[2]

As the leader of the system, and by virtue of his position as academic and executive head of the university, the Vice-Chancellor has to play the most significant role. He functions as a 'bridge' between the executive and academic wing of the university and as he is the head of both the wings, he is a 'teacher' and an 'administrator'. Existence of a cordial relation between these two wings is a prerequisite for fostering fellow feeling in the university campus and thereby help develop a corporate life[3]. Such an environment is very necessary to making missions success.

Finally, whatever mechanism of resource generation is developed and tools available to go ahead in this

1. UK, Committee on Higher Education Report (Robbins Report), London, HMSO, 1963, p.106.
2. Address by Dr. D.S. Kothari at the Vice-Chancellors' Conference (1969).
3. University System in India, Ghosh, D.K., Rahul Publishers (1983), p. 247.

direction, much will depend on the leader how he steers through rough weather for the routes and procedures are not smooth. However, there is no doubt that planned efforts with commitment bring success.

THE VISION STATEMENT

In a world of resource crunch, who would not like to go for extra generation of income. But what should be the starting point for a planned and sustained programme of resource generation? Success of any effort in this direction depends on how well the institution has structured the programme. Again, the question is how to go about? "The best starting point for generating extra income or resource is a clear overall view of your institution's identity and direction. Making a vision statement is one way of achieving this."[4]

What is Vision Statement? It is really speaking a dream of the future as the institution expects to reach. It is the most important starter to reach all that the institution thinks that it should be, for its good health, contributions to and reputation in the society. The vision statement may also include key features of the institution as also the major changes or dream that it wants to translate into reality. Since vision is essentially what an institution wants it to be in future, the vision statement could be anything that the top management conceives for the institution. It could be that although the institution is financially sound, in the changing scenario, it wants:

* To be ahead of time than others in the field, through re-engineering;

---

4. Generating income for educational Institution—A business planning approach, John Whealer, Kogan Page Educational Management Series, London (1991), p.11.

* Improvements in some other areas to increase efficiency;
* Closing down some of its activities, which are no longer too relevant and likely to lose relevance in the near future; and
* New areas to be introduced which have greater relevance in the changing scenario.

The institution can then decide the time frame for each of the above within which missions are desired to be fulfilled.

It is important that the Vision Statements also include all the associated aspects, for unless that is done, success cannot be achieved; not even reasonably. For example, in a situation of resource crunch, the institution being already in a deficit trap, would certainly not only like to bail itself out from that, but would also like to reach a situation comfortable enough for the institution which means generation of adequate income which is stable, and to do that, quite a few associated steps would be needed.

What kind of Vision Statements should be made when the institution is in a debt trap and wants to reach a comfortable position in terms of money and also wants to build good reputation as an academic institution? The following (Table 2.1) could, in such a case, be Vision Statements of the institution including the associated aspects which are complimentary to the main vision statement.

Realistically, the main vision statements are two, namely, to move from the position of deficit to surplus, and to improve teaching and research and thereby serve the basic purpose of academic institution. But there are two other vision statements which though independent,

Table 2.1
Vision Statement

Vision		*Time Frame*
Finance		
Deficit to Surplus	:	3 years
Teaching and Research		
Making Teaching more relevant and Research current	:	2 years
Administration		
A Responsive and Efficient Management	:	1 year
Reputation		
A Better Image Projection	:	1 year

are complimentary to the main vision statements. For example, unless the institution is geard well to handle various problems and issues connected with the main vision statements, it would be difficult to achieve the objectives. For this, it is necessary to ensure that it has the right kind of management. Similarly, when the institution moves out to public, industry and government agencies for funds, it should also make sure that its image is good for that makes the entry easy to discuss proposals for funds.

THE CRUCIAL FACTORS

Admittedly, the crucial factor to achieve success for the institution so as to reach the vision statements is to involve the entire system for which the prerequisite

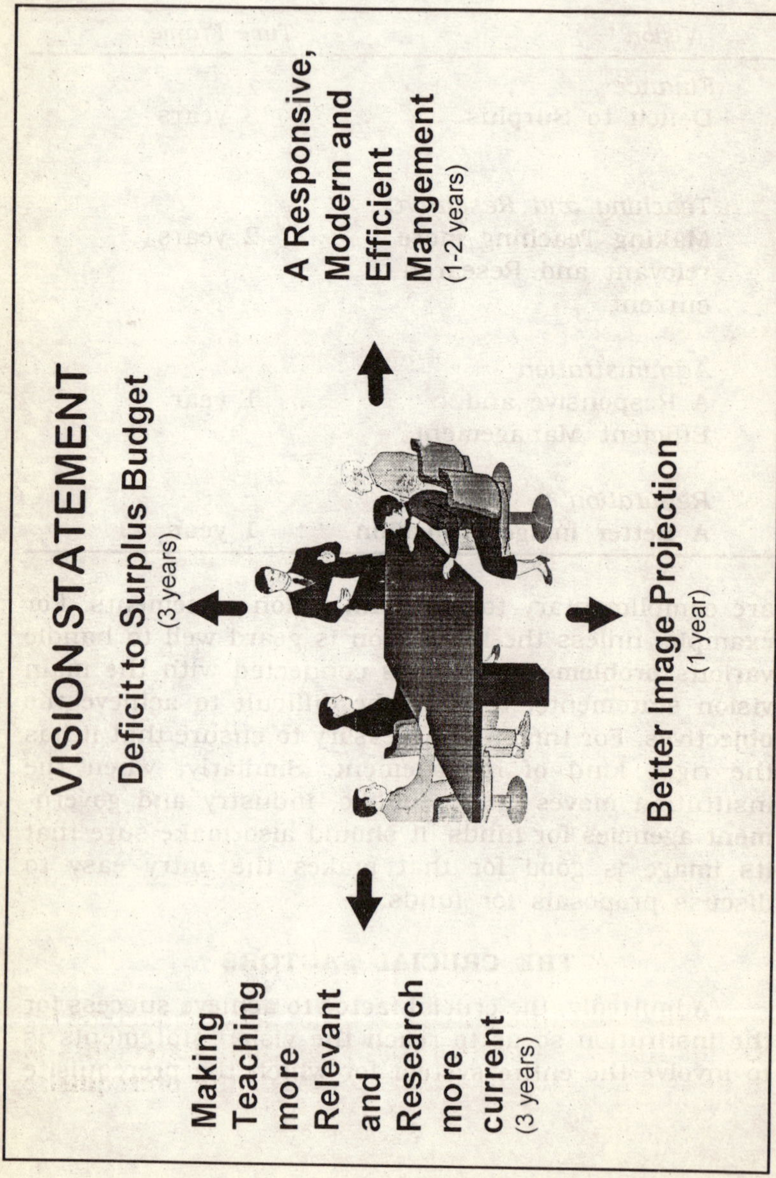

Fig. 2.1. Vision Statement

is to set up a 'communication process that allows a voice to everyone'. It is likely that in the process of involving all the groups, it will take more time and, at times money. It is also natural that in the process of consultation, not all will understand the right way, and therefore not agree with the vision statements. In fact, some may be passive and some may even oppose. Even then, consultation is a must for it always pays, rather than paying heavily later for not consulting the various segments of the institutional community. Of course, the institution has to deliberate and decide how best the various groups should be consulted. Each institution has its own culture, and local needs and therefore, there cannot be any prescribed structure.

However, while there cannot be any structured route in this regard a few hints could be useful. In the process of communication, it may first begin with the heads of various departments both academic and administrative. A visual presentation is considered more effective. In turn, the heads of departments may repeat at their departmental level with the structured document.

Students are a very important component in any educational institution. Their participation has far reaching impact on any of the efforts to achieve the objectives. The first communication with the selected group of students should be with the head of the institution doing the main talking, and thereafter the discussion should be taken over by faculty members who are known for their good image and influence on the students. Later, the Professor-in-charge of the students affairs may arrange more discussions at different level of the students. That would depend on the size of the institution and the student number.

As against the top-down approach discussed above, a bottom-up approach on the lines of Total Quality

Management (TQM) could be the other alternative. But that may not be workable in the current situation for it is loaded with more uncertainties and risks.

There is another crucial factor to achieve success and that is team work. This can successfully be done once the communication down-the-line is satisfactorily established. However, as an institution, it would already have some team work with which it should work its process of communication to involve people for the vision statement. Clearly, for achieving the Visions through Missions, good team work is a *sine-qua-none.*

THE MISSION STATEMENT

From 'Mission to Performance' is the process that ultimately would decide how far the vision statement has been achieved. Unless a mission statement is operational, 'it is just good intention'. Peter Drucker holds that 'A mission statement has to focus on what the institution really tries to do and then do it that everybody in the organization can say. This may contribute to the goal.'[5] It is important to note that whatever an institution wishes to do must not violate the values that it stands for. In case of violation, Peter Drucker holds 'you are likely to do a poor job'.

There are three 'Musts' of a successful mission, says Peter Drucker. They are: Opportunities; Competence; and Commitment. Each one is important both individually and together to fulfill the missions that the institution undertakes. Without opportunities, it is not possible to start the job, and the job must not be undertaken if the competence is not assured. Therefore,

---

5. Managing the Non-profit organisation–principles and practices, Peter Drucker (An Indo-American Co-operative Publishing Report, Macmillan India Ltd. (1993), p. 4.

competence is an integral part of the efforts. Finally, it is the commitment which is very crucial for without that there cannot be success, and partial success cannot be the objective.

'Mission' in this context means the broad routes to achieve the vision statement. One of the vision statement of Table 2.1 is to move from deficit to surplus position. While, it is a one sentence statement or desire or dream, how that can be achieved and what should be the routes for that. It has numerous implications. For example, in the first instance, if deficit has to be wiped out, the institution must take actions on two fronts. One: to examine where and how it can reduce expenditure and which are the items of expenditure that need be arrested from further growth. Second: Efforts to generate extra income by exploring various possibilities. This is really the more positive aspect of the two actions for there are limitations to reduce expenditure and curb the growth of expenditure particularly when inflation is high. All actions have to be taken simultaneously. In the process of achieving the vision of moving from deficit to surplus, the institution must decide the Missions relating to the vision. The Missions in relation to the above vision would be as shown in the figure 2.2.

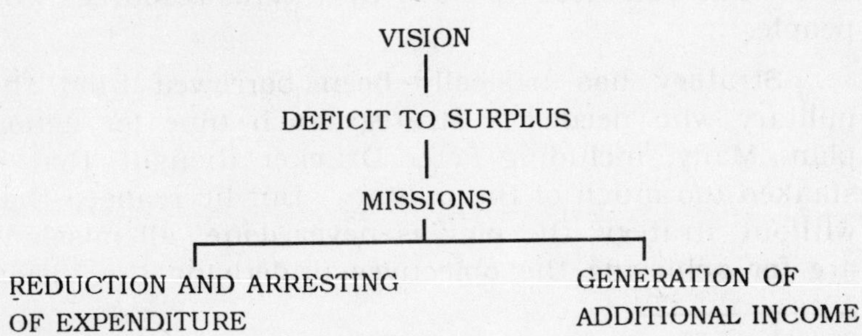

Fig. 2.2.

As the thrust of the book is generation of income, separate chapters have been devoted covering the processes that could lead to generation of income particularly through Sponsored Research Projects and interaction with Industry as also Alumni Associations. Matters covered in this chapter relate to the various aspects relating to the reduction and arresting of expenditure which are crucial to any exercise or attempt to eliminate deficit and then to move to surplus. For a surplus budget, generation of additional income is a must for which detailed discussions have been made in the Chapters 3 and 4.

STRATEGIES FOR IMPLEMENTATION OF MISSIONS

No mission can be successful without developing the correct strategies. As mission emerges out of the vision statement, strategies are developed keeping in view the Missions. Peter Drucker holds that mission and plans 'are the good intentions'. But to see the missions or the plans actually happening, what is must is the right 'strategy' which Drucker calls 'Bulldozers'. The importance of the strategy is that 'They convert what you want to do into accomplishments. Thy are particularly important in non-profit organisation.'[6] It also '... tells what you need to have by way of resources and people.'[7]

Strategy has basically been borrowed from the military who needed a strategy each time for action plan. Many, including Peter Drucker thought 'that it smaked too much of the military'. But he realised that without strategy, the plan is never done. All missions are for achieving the objectives underlying the Vision

6. *Ibid.*, p. 59.

7. *Ibid.*,

and they can happen only by developing the right strategies.

STRATEGIES OF MISSIONS

Reduction of Expenditure and Generation of Income

For fulfilling the Missions, strategies have to be developed so that in an organised and systematic manner, actions could be taken. Strategies to fulfill the two Missions (fig 2.2) mentioned could be as shown in the Table 2.2.

Table 2.2.

Strategies to Fulfill the Missions

Time Frame: 3 Years

Reduction of Expenditure	*Arresting Growth of Expenditure in selected areas*	*Generation of Income*
(1)	*(2)*	*(3)*
* Identify items to reduce expenditure, over 1-3 years	*Electricity *Stationery	* Sponsored Research * Consultancy
* Eliminate, after review, redundant areas or avoidable functions and save manpower and associatedexpenditure	* Telephones * Rents	* Alumni Association * Continuing Education Programme
* Manpower need *vis-a vis* Modernization and saving recurr. ing expenditure * Retirement	* Fuel * Selected Areas of Maintenance * Advertisement	* Donations, Grants, etc. * Library facilities to External Members

(1)	*(2)*	*(3)*
* Contract appointments		* Fees Mechanism to be developed * Renting out space and facilities (Equipment, etc.)
* Reduce expenditure on examinations through better management and some reforms	* Salary component fix limit	* Gymkhana Physical facilities and expertise * Sale/Lease out unusable land and create Endowment Fund.
* Reduction/ Abolition of subsidies	* Overtime * Reduce campus size if possible to reduce maintenance expenditure	* Flexible Investment Policy Short-Term–Long-Term through professionals

Reduction and Arresting of Expenditure – Money Saved is Money Generated

Strategies or routes are to be decided to fulfill the Missions of the one sentence vision to move from deficit to surplus, over a period of three years. The institutes should undertake detailed exercise to reduce expenditure for which it should appoint different teams with at least one professional from outside. A team of insiders with an outsider is necessary to achieve the objective in the best possible manner and speed. Separate team or even the same team as for reduction of expenditure, may undertake exercises to identify areas to arrest growth of expenditure as, by and large, both have the same character.

Reduction of manpower is a must to achieve reduction in expenditure. Even efficiency is affected because of an unwanted and unwilling extra staff. In some organisations, manpower need has been reduced by as much as 15% over a period of five years. As it is, most of the institutions are over-staffed particularly non-teaching. It is not only through automation, but by changing age-old rules, many unwanted pockets of an activity can be avoided to reduce the manpower need, besides bringing efficiency. Depending on the size of the institution, the scope can be found out.

Manpower need of any educational institution has hardly ever been assessed in relation to the size of the institution and its activities. Historically, without proper assessment, additions of manpower have been made in stray manner from time to time. That is the story of almost all institutions. The staff members are neither trained nor motivated; they have remained almost neglected and their development left to chance. If somebody has made mark in commitment, devotion, intelligence and innovation, that was because the individual happened to be basically a good material and therefore availed of opportunities to prove his worth and grew in career. After all, in every institution, there are always some committed persons who keep up the show. But we are talking about the majority and not for a few exceptions who are any way good by themselves.

Almost without exception, administrative staff, not being considered important, always took a back seat in the system for they were not considered fundamental or even an integral part of the system as it was thought that the process of teaching and learning could be complete without the help of this component. However, over the time, due to the expansion of the system and the need to comply with many requirements of the government particularly those relating to money, and a whole lot of other information needed from time to time in a democratic setup, staff, particularly well trained and motivated ones, has become essential. Even within the system itself, because of the council and committee structures, services of a large number of staff are sun-avoidable. A well trained and motivated staff can prove to be complimentary to all the efforts of the institution.

It is quite possible that through simplification of procedures of meetings of councils and committees, on one hand, man-power need can be reduced and on the other hand, additional savings can be achieved due to less consumption of papers and use of machine and in that chain, a lot of other invisible cost factors. That would also achieve efficiency and speed. However, how this should happen in a particular institution has to be decided by a conscious approach and by involving the people of the system. To achieve the objective, re-engineering may be the answer.

Turning to the role of the administrative staff, it has to be borne in mind that if it is not positive, it causes negative impact on the system. Therefore, it is realized that a minimum number is a must, but the staff members should be trained, motivated and committed ones.

As has been discussed and analysed in the Chapter one, it is the salary component of the budgets of almost all the institutions that eats away most of the recurring resources. However, this includes the salaries of both teaching staff as also the non-teaching staff for teaching purposes.

Justice Punnayya Committee, reviewing the present pattern of funding universities and commenting on how the universities have more staff than they need, observed that 'The nature of the system of appointment of staff in the universities regarding job security in regard to the academic and non-academic staff in various departments, make it difficult for universities to dispense with their services when not required or shift them to a new set of activities.'[8] The Committee further commented that 'The net result has been that the staff is retained causing heavy burden on the maintenance expenditure. In many cases, staff on research projects retained on humanitarian grounds or on court orders becomes an additional load on the university budget.'[9]

Identifying the reason why demands for more maintenance grants are made, the Committee strongly recommended curbing increase in staff strength. It observed that — 'One of the causes for increase in the maintenance grants has been the increase in the staff costs due to additional employment. While incremental changes in salary and remuneration structure and periodical increases in allowances and costs are inevitable, expenditure due to increase in the number of staff has to be reviewed and curbed firmly wherever necessary. Developing detailed internal information system and working out the per unit cost in regard to non-academic activities and the enforcement of an optimum division between academic and non-academic costs should help in stabilizing the maintenance expenditure.'[10]

It is necessary to prescribe a limit of non-teaching

---

8. Justice Punnayya Committee Report, Para 4.13 of Chapter-IV.
9. *Ibid.*,
10. Para 6.2 of Chapter-VI.

staff in relation to the teaching staff. Generally, at present the ratio of teaching-non-teaching staff is about 1:5. It should be brought down to 1:3. This is also what the Punnayya Committee has recommended.

As regards the teacher student ratio, except in the case of the new universities, the committee has suggested a 1:12 ratio. In one of its recent analysis of UNESCO on the data on public expenditure on education, "in ninety countries shows the overall share of teachers emoluments in total public expenditure on education to be around two-thirds."[11]

Yet one more source of major saving is from the income of examinations with some reforms in the examination system and better management thereof. Although some universities manage to save from examinations, there are other universities which still sustain loss on that account. This, in today's situation is unthinkable, illogical and against all norms of management. Despite strong and specific recommendations by both the Radhakrishnan Commission (1948-49) and the Kothari Commission (1964-66), for examination reforms, hardly any visible reforms have taken place although UGC had made its efforts. However, prerequisites to any meaningful reforms are appropriate changes in the courses of studies.

Briefly, there is reasonable scope both to reduce expenditure as also to arrest some of the growing items of expenditure. What is not happening is a determined planned effort to achieve the objectives. How far this is true, will be clear the moment the institution looks back to find out whether any serious efforts were made in this direction and how much. Failing once in achieving the target does not mean forgetting the need.

---

11. World Education Report, UNESCO, Paris (1991).

Similarly, it should be examined how growth of expenditure can be arrested. For example, expenditure on electricity, if it cannot be reduced, at least ways and means can be found out to ensure that expenditure does not increase. This can be done by avoiding wastages and by installing some modern devices which makes it efficient.

MAKING TEACHING MORE RELEVANT AND RESEARCH CURRENT

For an institution, there cannot be a more important vision than making teaching more relevant, and research current for it is the quality of education and research that an institution is known for. The Missions in relation to this Vision could be as given in the figure 2.3 and strategies as given in figure 2.4.

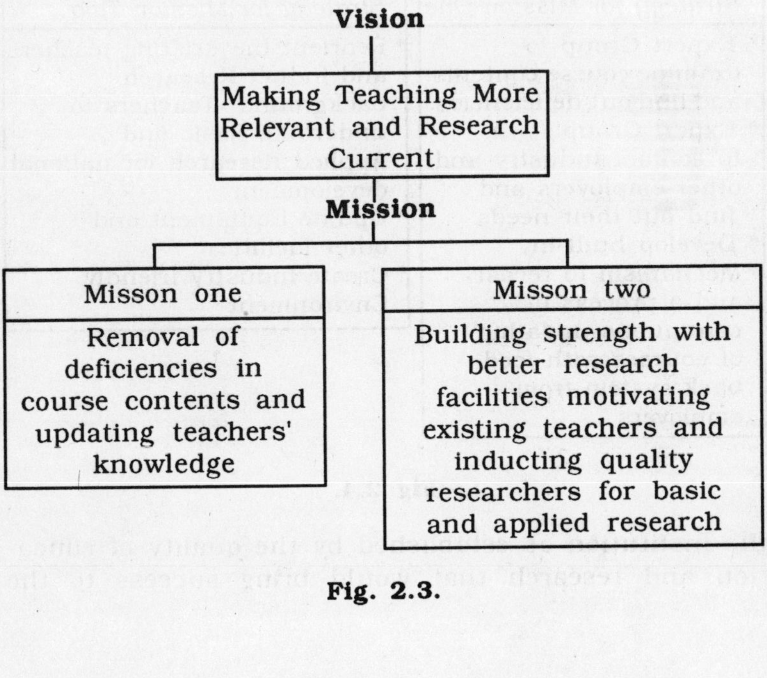

Fig. 2.3.

Having decided the above two Missions, the next step is to develop strategies which will pave the way to achieve the objectives of the missions. Strategies for this could be as shown in the figure: 2.4.

MISSION AND STRATEGIES

Removal of Deficiencies in Course Contents and Updating Teachers Knowledge

Basic to all questions and efforts to achieve the Vision statement is how relevant are the courses provided, and how effectively teaching is done, and what is the level of research work carried out by the teachers and students in the institution. It is the reputation of

Strategies for Missions

Strategy for Mission One	*Strategy for Mission Two*
* Expert Group to examine course contents and find out deficiencies. * Expert Group to contact Industry and other employers and find out their needs. * Develop built-in Mechanism to recast and a process of continuous updating of courses with feed-back system from employers	* Reorient the existing teachers and induct Research background Teachers to undertake Basic and Applied Research for national development. * Update Equipment and other facilities * Create Industry friendly Environment

Fig. 2.4.

the institution as established by the quality of education and research that would bring success to the efforts of income generation whether from its alumni, industry or public.

The need for relevant good courses of studies, effective teaching and high level of research activity cannot be over emphasised. The quality of students who pass out from the institution and their demand in the industry and government, is a good indicator as to how relevant the courses are, and how effectively teaching is done. This requires constant updating of the syllabi and for that, the prerequisite is to establish a linkage with the industry and other employers about their needs. This has to be a way of life in the system and not once in a while. Such a need has always been there, but in the changing scenario, the need is pressing. In UK, internal performance indicators include:

— market share of undergraduate application (by subject),
— graduation rates and classes of degrees,
— attraction of research funds,
— teaching quality,
— acceptability of graduates (post-graduates) in employment,
— first destination of graduates (post-graduates), and
— reputation judged by external reviews.

It is not only the course contents, but the programme itself should be evaluated from time to time in relation to the market needs. A programme which has lost its relevance should be scrapped and a new programme should be developed and introduced. This would help the students to get jobs which, in turn, would promote improvement, efficiency and productivity with the skilled manpower.

Now that the economy is open, market is international rather than domestic and competition is the basis of business, well trained students with education of the fundamentals of the subject and a reasonable application capacity thereof coupled with the capability to comprehend the scenario around are generally what would be welcomed by the employers. This leads to good personality development. Students education "... should not consist of projects tailored simply to fit the size of the job, dispensing with his or her spiritual, intellectual, and moral development. The university can fulfill the needs of society in general and business in particular if it produces students with a high level of personality development."[12] There is no dearth of jobs for those who meet the needs of the employers. This was true always, but it is much more so today in the liberalised economy of the country. An alert skilled man is the need of the employer.

In the industry, employment is no longer on the basis of just a paper certificate. While a certificate is surely the gate pass, it no longer can guarantee security of job, not to talk of growth in career. Inability of the students to apply, in their world of work, the fundamentals of their subjects which they are supposed to have acquired in the college coupled with the lack of flexibility and adaptability, disappoint the employers first, and ultimately themselves. This aspect has to be taken care of, with the best of ability and commitment of the institution.

Promoting Basic and Applied Research for Generating Income

Conceptually and functionally too, universities are both Teaching and Research for really speaking, they

12. The University as an Institution Today, Alfonso Borrero Cabal International Development Research Centre, Ottawa, UNESCO Publishing, Paris (1993), p. 103.

are integral part of each other. No university is known anywhere in the world which is designed to carry out only research. And there is no university in any part of the world which does not teach undergraduates and/ or post-graduates. All universities have the basic function of teaching with invariably at least some research activities which may vary from very significant to even rather—insignificant—both in terms of actual output and extent but some reasonable research activities would surely be carried out in all the universities.

The Robbins Committee of UK held that:

> "We are in total disagreement with the extreme view that would remove research altogether from the universities and concentrate it in research institutes, leaving the universities to devote themselves wholly to teaching, and we are confident that the experience of the world is against such a separation. We would not dispute that at times a university teacher is confronted with conflicting claims on his time and attention; but the need to reconcile differing professional obligations is not peculiar to the university teacher. We would not dispute either that some students could be better taught. But the remedy for this is to be sought in improved arrangements for teaching and these need not be made at the expense of research."[13]

The importance of research needs no justification. In fact, it is the level of the research activity that a university is known for. It is true that teaching is the basic function of any university which, in a way, is a 'taken for granted' activity. Therefore, even when quality teaching is done, it does not arouse that much

13. UK Committee on Higher Education Report (Robbins Report), London, HMSO, 1962, p. 208.

excitement in the academic world as would a new research result do. The dynamism of the university system is bound to come out with better norms to promote research for there is a real concern to excel in research at the national and international level.

In order to create and keep up the demand in the industry and various funding agencies for consultancy work and for sponsored research work, it is necessary that the institution builds good basic research base. At the same time, unless there is application of research activities, there is no social and economic benefits to the nation. Therefore, for undertaking application oriented research activities keeping in view the current needs, basic research is a must.

Without strong basic research activity, over the years, capacity for applied research is likely to diminish. It is also important that the institution carefully selects the areas for research which should be current. It is that which would help the institution to project its research capabilities to the outside agencies to attract them for gainful interaction and generation of income. For this, the prerequisites are, to allocate funds as an investment for generation of income, and to identify a group of researchers to undertake identified areas of basic research to form the foundation for applied research.

Funding and Research Ranking Relationship

It is true that all the institutions do not have separate allocations for research, and even among those which have allocations, they are inadequate. While there is no denying of the essentiality of reasonable funds without which research work cannot be undertaken, it is also a fact that larger allocation of funds does not necessarily mean better results. Reliable and systematic statistics are not available to find out how much various universities and institutions spend on research. No parameters have also been developed for research rating or to compare the universities and other institutions on their research attainments. Resultantly, it is not possible to discuss the relationship of funds with the quality of research, except that it needs no argument that without funds, no research work can be undertaken.

In UK, where there is a system of research ranking of the universities, mixed examples are available. For example, of the various Cost-centres in U.K., viz. (*i*) Biological Sciences (*ii*) Chemistry, (*iii*) Computer Science, (*iv*) Engineering (*v*) other social studies, (*vi*) Business Management Studies; and (*vii*) Humanities, for the years 1986-87, 1987-88 and 1988-89, an analysis of data given in appendix I reveals mixed results. Within the same Cost-centre, it is found that there are examples of all types.

In Biological Sciences, Oxford spent £K-2422 in 1986-87 securing a research rank of 8; next year (1987-88), it spent £K2912 and secured a better rank of 6 and in 1988-89, it spent the highest in these three years £K3522 and also secured a still higheer rank of 3. But Surrey, with lesser investment of £K 1916 in 1986-87, it secured the 'first' rank in research in the same Cost-centre area. In the next two years also, it kept up its level of first rank when again it's spending were less than that of Oxford. In Biological Sciences, the same way, the performances of the Warwick, Dundee and Stirling were better than Oxford with lower investments.

In Chemistry, UMIST spent £K1283 in 1986-87 and secured the research rank '1' while London University with more than double spending £K2738 secured a much lower rank of '19'. Similar trend continued between these two institutions in the next years too (1987-88 and 1988-89).

An example of lowest spending and lowest ranking is the Sheffield University for the Chemistry Cost-centre. Sheffield spent the lowest £K254, £K296 and £K440 during 1986-87, 1987-88 and 1988-89 with research ratings of 38, 43 and 35 respectively which are lowest out of the seventeen universities included in the analysis except Birmingham for 1988-89 which ranked only two points lower than Sheffield in that year.

In the Computer Science Cost-centre, Heriot-Watt spent only £K820, £K644 and £K356 in 1986-87, 1987-88 and 1988-89 and secured the rank '1', '1' and '15' respectively. As against this, the London University spent £K9962, £K3560 and £K4286 in 1986-87, 1987-88 and 1988-89 respectively, but secured the rank of '11', '7' and '7' respectively. The Edinburgh University, however, secured better ranks with lesser investments. It spent £K2201, £K1629 and £K2223 during the aforesaid years, and earned the ranks of '1', '2' and '1' respectively.

In the Engineering Cost-centre, the cases of the London University and the University of Warwick are noticeable. Of the eighteen universities of the study, London University spent highest in all the three years under reference — £K15610, £K15280 and £K16989, but the research ranks earned by it were '4', '3' and '3' respectively while the University of Warwick with lesser spendings in all these years £K3634, £K3986 and £K4782, it earned the rank '1'. Southampton also secured ranks better or close to Oxford while it spent about one-third of the spending of Oxford. Even the University of Edinburgh spent only £K1536, £K2840 and £K2308 and earned better ranks than others, particularly during 1987-88 and 1988-89. This again is the repetition of the trend mentioned earlier.

From these analyses, it is clear that it is not just funds but other factors too that are responsible to show quality research and they are: area of research, expertise, infrastructure, some previous work already done, research environment, scope of interdisciplinary interaction etc.

RESPONSIVE MODERN AND EFFICIENT MANAGEMENT

In relation to the Vision statement for a Responsive, Modern and Efficient Management, the MISSIONS could be as shown in the figure 2.5. Strategies in relation to this could be those given in the figure 2.6.

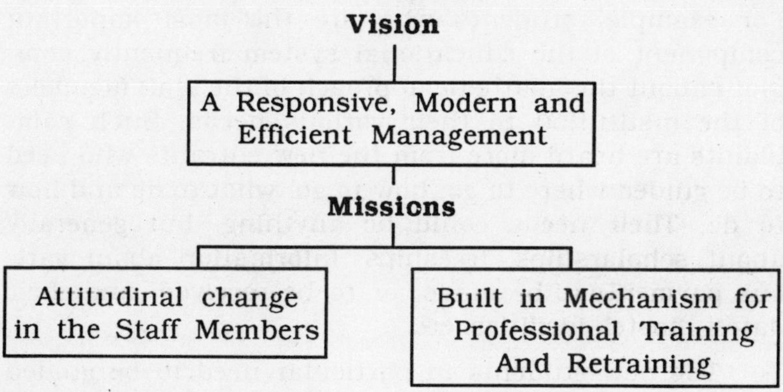

Fig. 2.5.

In relation to the above two Missions, strategies for

them could be developed as given in the figure 2.6.

Strategies

* Identify strengths (rather than weakness) of staff members and utilise services	* Involve the staff in policy planning and implementation * Delegate Responsibilities to achieve missions * Monitor the performance	* Priority training on Responsiveness * Professional training to promote creativity

Fig. 2.6.

MISSIONS AND STRATEGIES

Need to Change Attitudes

Attitudinal change is the prerequisite to any attempt to make the management responsive and efficient. Staff members must be sensitive to other clients and act to satisfy them which is almost absent today. For example, students who are the most important component of the educational system frequently complain about the apathetic approach of the staff members of the institution to their various needs. Such complaints are heard more from the new entrants who need to be guided where to go, how to go, what to do and how to do. Their needs could be anything, but generally about scholarships, freeships, information about various payments to be made, or to be received, and their dates, hostel facilities etc.

The new students in particular need to be guided as to how to avail of the various other facilities and where would they get the forms they are looking for, and the like. When they face apathetic treatment, they feel lost, they feel agitated. As the students start knowing people and places over some time after admission, they find out their ways to get work done.

Responsiveness of staff members to the students is the most important requirement. In fact, it may not be wrong to say that responsiveness or demonstration of willingness and interest to help is more than actually doing the work for anybody, and more so to the students. A gentle and sweet way to say 'no' has, in fact, more impact than a harsh and bitter way of doing the work. A ready willingness to help and co-operate the students is very important to the new students who are in particular vulnerable ones.

The staff members should appreciate the difficulties of students and at times, demonstrate their assistance and co-operation that they feel concerned for the needs and well being of students. It should be remembered that help is not only to be given but also be seen. Today's students are tomorrow's teachers, managers, bureaucrats, captains of industry and even leaders of the country. Impressions that the students carry at various stages of their learning life in the institution are always remembered and that could be sweet, bitter or even irritating to remember.

What should be the approach and attitude of a responsive, modern and efficient management to that group of client for whom basically not only the administration, but even the teachers are drawn to the system, perhaps needs no elaboration. If the modern management considers the students as 'client' of the system, the approach and attitude should be what we find in a multinational bank where as one enters, the official sitting inside immediately welcomes with a smile, shows interest to know what he can do to the visitor and he does quickly what he can do, with the best of his ability. Even when he is not the right person to do the work, or if there is some problem requiring a discussion with a senior colleague, he either himself moves and sorts out, or takes the visitor to the senior colleague to help out the situation. This means that the motto is service to client. No different should be the motto of staff members to clients in the higher education system.

Similar should be the approach and attitude not only to other visitors, but also to the faculty and other category of staff members.

In the new situation every staff member should perform his duties with competitive speed and efficiency. It is also necessary to remember that as more and more fees would now be recovered from the students, they would in turn demand good and better services from the institution. Therefore, we should make preparations to meet the new situation if we want to avoid a fire-fighting situation and unhappy consequences.

Time has changed, and that survival is now on the basis of the return of the investments that the institution makes in terms of salary, space and other facilities to the staff members, must be made clear to everybody to find out the cost-effectiveness. It is high time that every institution develops a modern, efficient and responsive management, shedding the archaic, outdated and outmoded 'administration', based on the century-old approach which believed more in the culture of 'how not to do', rather than 'how to do'. If the institution wants that it's efforts to generate money should succeed and its programmes are organised with efficiency as also cost-effectiveness, the management should be such that it is able to respond promptly and positively, to provide all the necessary assistance to the system.

Every staff member has some strengths along with some weaknesses. In order to utilize the precious time, it would be advantageous to make use of the strengths rather than spending time to correct the weaknesses. However, whenever, that becomes very necessary, that may have to be done. Involving the staff members in policy planning and delegating their responsibilities and powers would always prove productive. However, monitoring and guiding occasionally is a must.

Professional Training

A small well trained staff is far better than a large number of unwilling and inefficient staff members. However, it is easier said than done for changing the attitude is a hard job. Since the book aims at the various mechanisms for generating income, it is not possible to discuss much in this area. But, it must be remembered that basic to all efforts in different directions, is the need of an efficient and committed management.

In the new situation when high fees would be recovered from students, they would also expect improved services from the staff members who basically belong to a service sector. There should be definite programmes to provide improved level of efficiency of the staff members and to upgrade their abilities through the right kind of training and retraining and exposure. In fact, what is needed is a built-in mechanism for professional training of the staff. They should conceive and develop professionalism. Once that happens, rest is not difficult, rather may follow.

BETTER IMAGE PROJECTION

For the purpose of projecting better image, multi-dimensional implications are involved requiring careful handling of the affairs. In relation to the Vision of projecting better image of the institution, the Missions will be as shown in figure 2.7.

Vision

Better Image Projection

Missions

Internal Image Factors for students and parents

External Image Factors for various Agencies

Fig. 2.7

The strategies for a better image projection could be those shown in figure 2.8 involving a large number of agencies.

Missions and Strategies

Image building, image correction and image projection—be it of an educational institution, commercial organisation or an individual — is as essential an aspect of career as the existence itself for after all, it is the reputation that matters and makes matters smooth and it is also that which contributes to image building. But this cannot be done overnight, nor is it possible to do that without visible good work. When it is a question of image of an educational institution, image building is more difficult than a commercial organisation or an individual for its reputation and image depends on a number of functions and performance thereof, and each area has its own clientele to be satisfied. It is the cumulative impact of reputation in all the relevant areas of functions that helps build the right image.

For a commercial organisation, the target groups

STRATEGIES FOR BETTER IMAGE PROJECTION

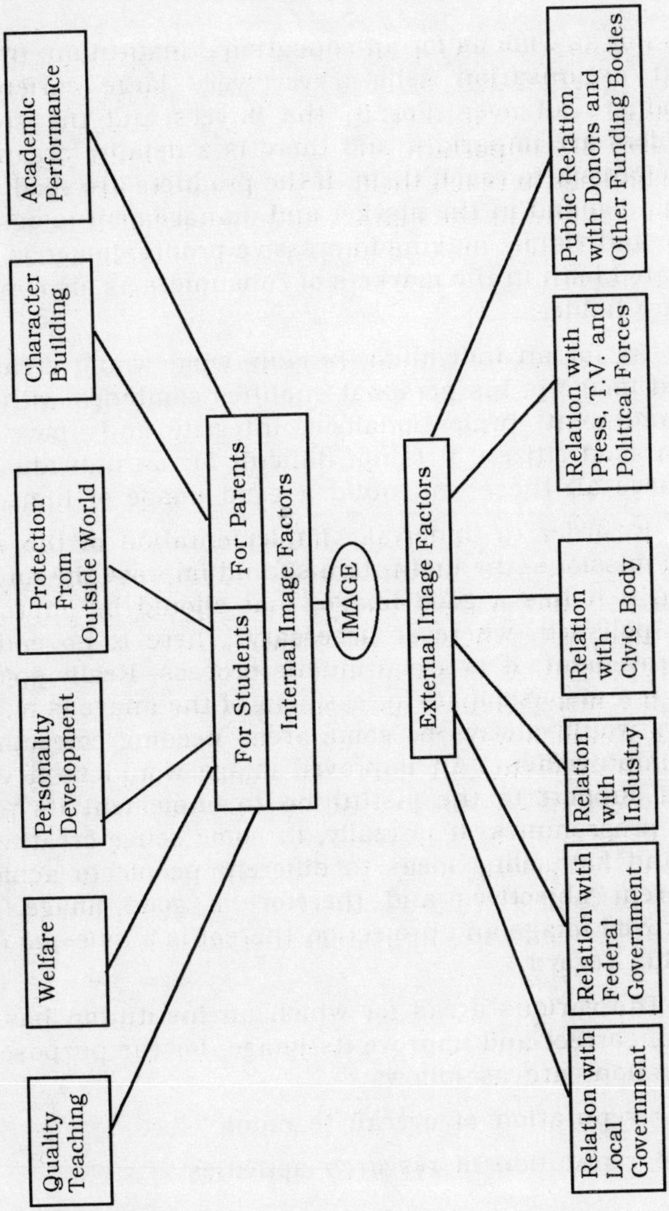

Fig. 2.8. Strategies for Better Image Projection

are not as wide as for an educational institution, unless that organisation sells a very-very large variety of products all over. For it, the buyers and the share-holders are important and there is a definite organized mechanism to reach them. If the products are good with good demand in the market and management is aggressive and viable, making impressive profits, image is just created both in the markets of consumers as also on the share-holders.

As for an individual, broadly what would create a good image is his personal qualities combined with his commitment, professionalism, integrity and above all, as a good citizen. It is not difficult for an individual to achieve all these and build a good image of himself.

In order to undertake implementation of the specific missions, the institution should improve the image. Even if it has a good image, that should be improved and polished, wherever necessary. There is no end to improvement; it is a continuous process. Really speaking, if a dispassionate assessment of the image is made, there would always be some areas needing corrections for improvement. An improved image would be a very good support to the institution to implement its plan and programmes. It is really, in some sense creating a ground for selling ideas to different people to achieve different objectives and therefore a good image, an improved image and projection thereof is a *sine-qua-non* in this regard.

The various areas for which an institution has to build, correct and improve its image, for the purpose of projection, are as follows:

* reputation of overall teaching;
* reputation of research activities;

* reputation of discipline;
* reputation of teachers;
* reputation of students; and
* reputation of management.
* reputation of participation in social activities.

Primarily, an institution has to satisfy the student with all facilities including quality teaching, welfare, personality development, protection from any outside interference etc. At the same time, for the same students, parents have to be satisfied that their sons and daughters are making good progress in studies and character building. And not infrequently, some parents for whatever right or wrong reasons, would express unhappiness in different degrees and manners if they feel in any way that the overall progress of studies is not good or that his son or daughter has influence of undesirable elements or factors leading to uncertainty in career.

With the public at large, the institution has to have good relation for without the co-operation and support of the society around, the institution would find many things difficult. Even for fund raising purposes, such relation is a must.

A cordial relation with the civic body, local government officials and the governments both state and federal, is again a prerequisite for a large number of operational purposes, including of course grants for various purposes. It is important for the institution that its relations with the funding agencies is not only good, but impressive.

Briefly, since an educational institution is funded by a number of groups, e.g. students, governments, industry and donors, it has obligations to a larger number of people than what a commercial organisation or an individual would have to care for.

In a democratic structure, some relationship with the political force is desirable, if not necessary. As representatives of the people, they have say in any matter they think right. In any case, institutions should take care to see that there is no negative relationship with any political force. They should not have any grouse against the institution. At times, although their praise may not help, their negative attitude and remarks may cause harm or create difficulty for the institution. Even a neutral relationship may not be against the interest of the institution, rather than negative one which is surely against its interest.

Again, in a democratic setup, Press and TV are important. Their help as media to reach the people is really an advantage. Whether it is a first time image building or correction or improvement thereof, the media is the best help. A good relationship with the Press and TV is necessary as they would always prove to be helpful. However, lot of care is necessary to interact with them.

CONCLUSION

Basic to all efforts to generate income for which a number of efforts are required, is the right kind of leadrship. Leadership is equally important whatever field it is, to bring about improvement; even to keep up the state of affairs at a level considered good. Unless the right leadership is there, even if a bright Vision is conceived by the institution just because it happens to have a few members on its governing body who are able and visionary, it will be difficult for the institution to develop perfect Missions. Different still it will be to involve the various segments of the institution to implement the Missions for that is the crucial factor in the process. Unless there is an involvement of the various components of the system, the chances of success is little.

Efforts to reduce expenditure and arrest the growth of expenditure have to be made with definite targets and determination and not half heartedly. Seriousness or otherwise of the efforts is watched by all concerned of the system. If there is a visible demonstration of the genuineness of efforts and some of which are seen through the actions of the leader and the important functionaries, the impact is more on the system and possibilities of success would be more. However, reduction and arresting of expenditure should be such that none of the action is counter-productive. Here lies the real sense of proportion. In any case, even if the institution is able to arrest the growth of the overall expenditure for a few years, that itself would be an achievement.

For generation of income through various means, Chapters 3 and 4 have been devoted.

In the context of the fast changing needs, any institution which aims at making improvements must necessarily ensure that the course-contents that it teaches to its students are relevant both in terms of knowledge per-se, as also to meet the needs of the employers. And if this has to be achieved, developing a mechanism to find out the needs of the employers on regular basis is a *sine-qua-non*.

Importance of undertaking basic research in a few areas hardly needs any justification. For generation of income, applied research is a must. But unless basic is strong, applied cannot stand strongly, and ably.

Today, there is an element of management everywhere from library — laboratory, to space utilisation, procurement and supply of equipment and consumables, service to the teaching and students, and finally the fund raising and management thereof. Inefficient management always makes the teaching and research activities slow, and at times difficult due to many irritants that grow out of inefficiency. In view of this, what is more important is a change in attitude from the culture of "how not to do", to "how to do." However, the need of professional training is always there to update the technique of modern management.

Really speaking, building, correcting and projecting image of the institution is extremely important for ultimately it is image that matters. And image is built only when it has established reputation in a number of areas. However, an educational institution has a number of clients to depend on, and to satisfy with, which is no easy job in a democratic structure. Nevertheless, sincere efforts and proper planning can bring success in the efforts in this direction.

Appendix-I

Research Expenditure and Rankings

University	*Expenditure and Ranking*					
	1986-87		*1987-88*		*1988-89*	
	K Exp.	*Ranking*	*K Exp.*	*Ranking*	*K Exp,*	*Ranking*
I. Cost Centre (Bioloqical Scs.)						
1. Birmingham	1030	15	1020	20	1013	25.5
2. Cambridge	1986	11	2341	11	3410	11
3. Kent	263	4	598	2	410	6

University	*Expenditure and Ranking*					
	1986-87		*1987-88*		*1988-89*	
	K Exp.	*Ranking*	*K Exp.*	*Ranking*	*K Exp,*	*Ranking*
4. Leicester	1289	3	1429	4	1879	2
5. London	5151	14	5639	15	7470	14
6. Oxford	2422	8	2912	6	3522	3
7. Surrey	1916	1	2299	1	2799	1
8. Warwick	1750	2	2026	3	1776	4
9. Dundee	619	9	818	8	857	8
10. Edinburgh	2604	6	2851	7	3214	7
11. Stirling	1136	5	1513	5	1788	5
II. Cost Centre (Chemistry)						
1. Birmingham	324	37	571	3.6	541	37
2. Bristol	1014	14	1092	11	1285	15
3. Cambridge	960	13	1041	14	2019	6
4. Leeds	768	26	1094	13	1289	17
5. Liverpool	505	21	652	15.5	801	12
6. London	2738	19	3025	19	3827	14
7. UMIST	1283	1	1401	2	1632	3
8. Oxford	1632	7	1607	10	3399	1
9. Salford	587	22	484	32	205	44
10. Sheffield	254	38	296	43	440	35
11. Sussex	559	18	528	26	756	16
12. Southampton	1207	2	1238	5	1391	5
13. Warwick	402	17	777	4	505	21
14. York	706	4	823	3	966	7
15. Aberystwyth	102	34	147	35	_	_
16. Aberdeen	344	32	370	33	500	26.5

University	Expenditure and Ranking					
	1986-87		1987-88		1988-89	
	K Exp.	Ranking	K Exp.	Ranking	K Exp,	Ranking
17. Ediburgh	792	11	682	24	1385	9
18. St. Andrews	443	5	307	25	670	10
III. Cost Centre (Computer Science)						
1. Aston	75	36	154	32.5	62	44
2. Bristol	20	10	67	35	238	18
3. Cambridge	494	10	474	13	348	16
4. Leicester	487	9	229	21	217	26
5. Leeds	76	34	129	39	177	39
6. London	2962	11	3560	7	4286	7
7. UMIST	587	14	365	22.5	740	12
8. Oxford	631	6	541	8	574	10
9. Sussex	469	8	478	5	422	14
10. Warwick	196	23	233	19	319	17
11. York	805	4	368	15	240	32
12. Aberystwyth	209	19	358	4	353	5
13. Swansea	25	40	79	40	159	33
14. Edinburgh	2201	1	1629	2	2223	1
15. Glasgow	189	28	295	22.5	378	22
16. Heriot-Watt	820	1	644	2	356	15
17. Reading	399	3	607	1	453	2
IV. Cost Centre (Engineering)						
1. Birmingham	2232	31	4144	10	4423	12
2. Bradford	1386	38	1391	37	1657	37
3. Bristol	1337	20	1578	15	2365	8
4. Brunel	2078	14	1969	14	2314	13

University	Expenditure and Ranking					
	1986-87		1987-88		1988-89	
	K Exp.	Ranking	K Exp.	Ranking	K Exp,	Ranking
5. Cambridge	3316	15	3690	12	3148	25
6. Essex	947	4	1009	46	868	11
7. Leeds	3117	19	3433	30	3439	23
8. London	15610	4	15280	3	16989	3
9. Manchester	2095	17	1818	26	1555	36
10. UMIST	4817	8	3570	17	4203	18
11. Oxford	2600	5	2942	4	3150	5
12. Salford	1757	31	1392	38	1995	34.5
13. Sheffield	2525	19	3336	9	3670	9
14. Warwick	3634	1	3986	1	4782	1
15. Edinburgh	1536	13	2840	3	2308	7
16. Glasgow	1527	22	1834	21	2889	45
17. Heriot-Watt	2581	12	3054	8	4179	4
18. Southampton	4715	2	5009	5	5173	6
V. Cost Centre (other Social Studies)						
1. Bath	775	5	844	5	686	11
2. Birmingham	3963	1	4329	1	4867	1
3. Brunel	1533	2	1513	2	1540	2
4. Cambridge	939	12	824	16	852	24
5. Essex	251	31	289	32.5	434	31
6. Exeter	185	34	277	32.5	511	28.5
7. Lancaster	340	29	348	29	294	36
8. Leeds	499	22	539	22	639	33
9. Oxford	1551	14	2083	10	1977	13
10. Sussex	1533	3	1836	3	1899	4
11. Warwick	997	8	1059	11	1289	12

University	Expenditure and Ranking					
	1986-87		1987-88		1988-89	
	K Exp.	Ranking	K Exp.	Ranking	K Exp,	Ranking
12. York	1442	4	1421	4	2247	3
13. Aberystwyth	23	40	17	46	54	44
14. Bangor	396	7	492	7	525	9
15. Edinburgh	636	20	750	17	992	16
16. Glasgow	748	17	734	19	1130	14
17. Heriot-Watt	275	6	296	6	282	6
VI. Cost Centre (Business Management Studies)						
1. Bradford	1373	9	1529	8	2239	9
2. City	2037	6	2642	5	2844	8
3. Durham	787	1	1653	9	1792	1
4. Oxford	207	2	184	1	217	2
5. Warwick	2100	5	3397	3	4971	3
6. Edinburgh	233	14	291	16	405	13
7. Glasgow	531	8	778	6	512	10
8. Heriot-Watt	173	13	191	9.6	167	22
9. Stirling	838	7	1047	–	1418	7
VII. Cost Centre (Humanities)						
1. Birmingham	348	2	366	2	417	1
2. Bristol	20	22	16	34	69	24
3. Cambridge	317	7	438	9	557	4
4. Leicester	104	8	80	15	118	12
5. London	1040	4	1357	3	1763	3
6. New Castle	190	1	183	1	127	6
7. Warwick	50	19	81	23	55	28.5
8. York	27	20	152	7	138	9
9. Cardiff	138	4	133	4	62	18.5

University	*Expenditure and Ranking*					
	1986-87		*1987-88*		*1988-89*	
	K Exp.	*Ranking*	*K Exp.*	*Ranking*	*K Exp,*	*Ranking*
10. Edinburgh	69	21	49	30.5	57	31
11. Glasgow	104	14	96	22	180	15
12. St. Andrews	131	10	170	12	150	18.5

3

Generation of Income through Sponsored Research Projects, Continuing Education Programme, Alumni Association, Fees and Investments, etc.

BENEFITS OF RESEARCH PROJECTS

While presenting the Union Budget 1994-95, the Finance Minister in his speech recognized that "The role of science and technology is critical for modernizing our economy and making it globally competitive". In order to provide more funds for government sponsored research, the Finance Minister raised the outlay for the Department of Science and Technology by 19% from Rs.189 crores in Budget Estimates 1993-94 to Rs. 225 crores in 1994-95.

For a variety of reasons, sponsored research projects are important to an institution particularly from the point of view of research potential to contribute to the socio-economic development of the nation through science and technology. In addition to the basic objective which also brings reputation to the institution, sponsored research projects also help generate resources in three ways.

First, through the creation and acquisition of a number of facilities which after the project is closed, remain to be the assets of the institution. Depending on the kind of assets, some are useful for regular teaching or research, or both. In an institution where a number of research projects are carried out, there is a consequential saving on equipment and at times, consumable. Money saved is money generated. Hence, this contributes, of course in varying degrees, to resource generation through various savings.

Second, the overhead charges on the projects. It is true that 15% overhead is generally allowed by many funding agencies, but that is utterly inadequate. Even this 15% is not uniformly given for in the case of Project costing more than Rs. 40 lakhs, the funding agency decides the total overhead to be allowed. However, if an institution is able to bag a number of research projects every year, they together, contribute to some generation of income although part of this is required to keep up the facilities for research activities. Some agencies do not provide the overhead. In fact, in the long run without adequate overhead, the institutions will find it difficult to keep up the quality of infrastructural facilities for carrying out research project activities for on one hand due to resource crunch, they may not be able to spend for that even at the current inadequate level and on the other hand, without such facilities, the funding agencies may some day find that for carrying out sponsored research projects at the institution, the latter is not equipped. It is a long felt need that the overhead charge should be increased to at least 30%. In the developed countries, it is higher: in some, it is about 50%. This would enormously help the institutions to keep their facilities updated.

Third, the interest earnings through proper investment policy and planning of investments for shorter duration with the specified financial institutions as per the Investment Rules of the government. Such earnings, if not significant for all institutions, is also not negligible. Ordinarily, steps to implement the approved projects by the Principal Investigators start only on receipt of the first instalment of grants from the funding agency. Except a small amount that may be needed immediately, remaining amount would be needed normally after about two months to six months by which time, some purchases through procedural formalities may materialise and staff wherever involved, would join. Instead of allowing the funds to remain idle, short-term investments at least for 46 to 60 days can always be made to earn interest. For bigger projects, involving purchase of costly equipment from abroad, investments can be for longer period as these purchases are always time consuming. What is most important is an alert group of people to co-ordinate with the Principal Investigators and to keep latest information about investment and wherefrom, within the Rules, maximum interest can accrue. For effective co-ordination, an interface body is required and that will be discussed in the chapter five.

FUNDS AND FUNDING AGENCIES

With a view to providing opportunities to the academics and scientists to enable them to undertake research work in their areas of specialisation, Research Projects are funded by the various central government Ministries, Departments and Agencies, including Public Sector Industry. Similarly, various State Governments also provide some fundings within their means and interest.

FUNDING OF PROJECTS DURING SEVENTH PLAN

During the seventh plan period (1985-86 to 1989-90), 16 Science and Technology Departments/Agencies provided a total of Rs. 297.75 crores for 5314 new projects involving 856 institutions belonging to different sectors, the percentage of funding to various sectors were as shown in the figure 3.1.[1]

It is interesting that out of the 22.04% of the university sector, 12% was bagged by two universities alone viz. Banaras Hindu University and the University of Roorkee, amounting to Rs. 805.75 lakhs. However, the average support per university stood at Rs. 49.72 lakhs for five years. In the case of the five IITs and IISc., the average support per institute was Rs.1073.89 lakhs. And for the colleges, the average support per college was only Rs. 9.59 lakhs.

Total Rs. 297.75 Crores

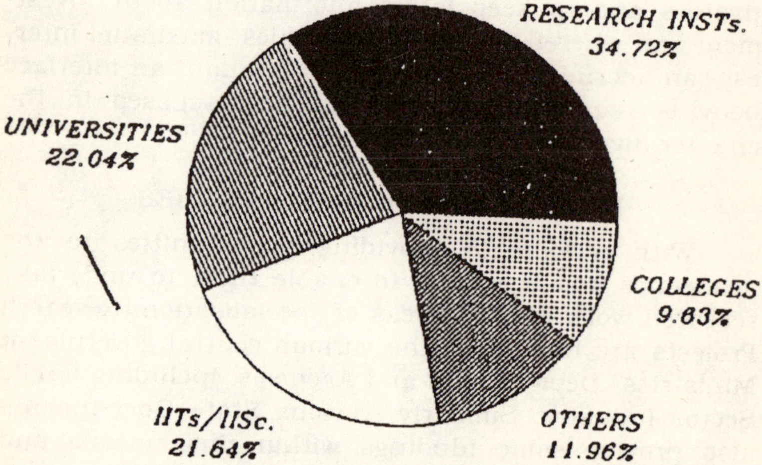

Fig. 3.1.[1] R&D Support to various Institutions During the 7th Five year plan

1. Funding Pattern of Sponsored Research by Scientific Agencies (1985-86 to 1989-90), Govt. of India DST, New Delhi Sept. 1990, p. 11.

As regards distribution of the number of institutions which received support from the various funding agencies, they were as shown in the Figure 3.2.[2]

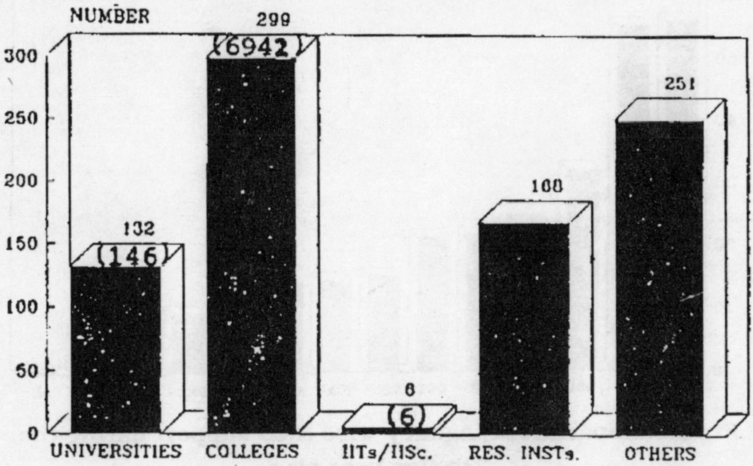

Fig. 3.2.[2] Number of Institutions Supported during the 7th five year plan

Total Number of Institutions: 856

(Figure in the parenthesis indicate the number of total universities, colleges and IITs + IISc. in 1989-90).

Funds that each of the sixteen Science and Technology Departments/Agencies provided during the Seventh Plan period to 856 institutions mentioned above were, as given in the Figure 3.3.[3]

The fundings of Rs. 297.75 crores were for 5314 projects, the number that each of the above

2. Funding pattern of sponsored research by scientific agencies (1985-86 to 1989-90), DST, Sept. 1990, Chart-8 p.11

3. *Ibid.* p. 8.

funding agencies had sanctioned was as shown in the Figure 3.4.[4]

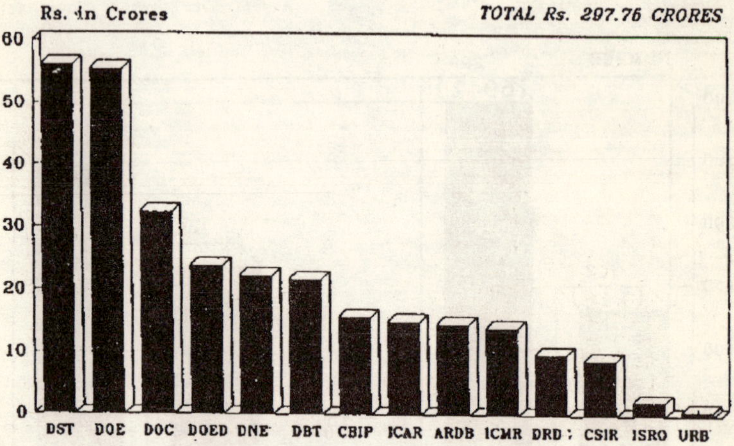

Fig 3.3[3] Department/Agency-wise R&D support during the 7th five year plan

Information from UGC and Doen is Incomplete

Based on the total funding of Rs. 297.75 crores for five years, the annual average funding by the central government sector including public sector industry was 59.5 lakhs. In subsequent years, the position improved considerably in terms of the number of projects and money.

During the Seventh Plan period, the University Grants Commission provided assistance to the universities and colleges amounting to Rs.10174.82 lakhs for Science and Rs. 4966.71 lakhs for Engineering and Technology as shown in the Table-3.1.

4. Funding pattern of sponsored research by scientific agencies (1995-96 to 1989-90), Govt. of India, DST, 1990, p.a.

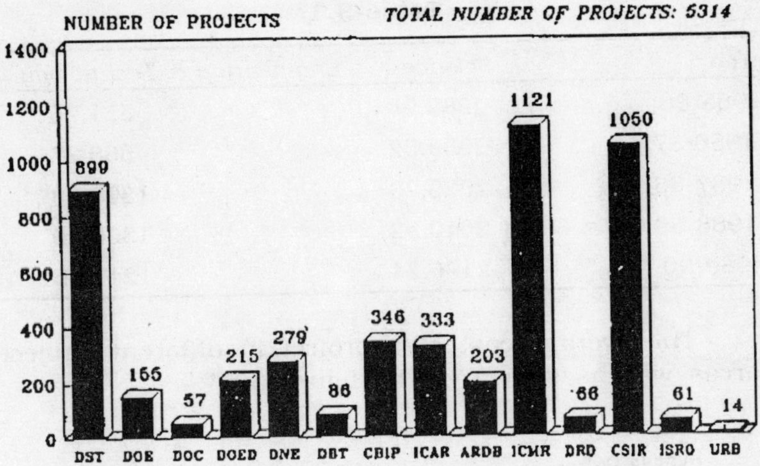

Fig. 3.4[4] Number of R&D projects supported during the 7th five year plan

Information from UGC and Doen is Incomplete

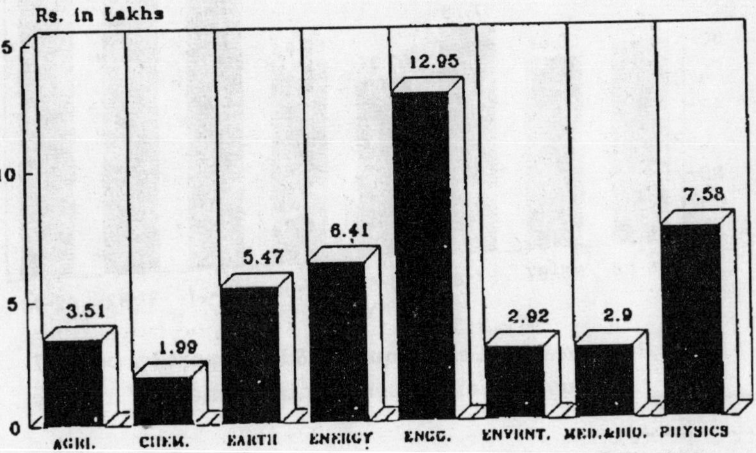

Fig. 3.5[6] Average cost of a project in different subject areas during the 7th plan

Table-3.1[5]

Year	*Science*	*Engineering & Technology*
1985-86	1982.91	551.95
1986-87	1959.52	568.27
1987-88	2025.23	1328.63
1988-89	2010.92	1300.00
1989-90	2196.24	1217.86

The average cost of a project in different subject areas was as shown in the figure 3.5.[6]

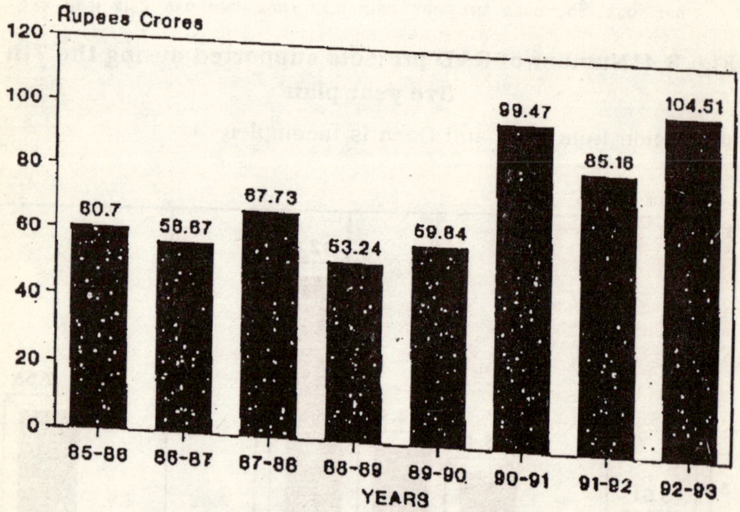

Fig. 3.6 Growth of extramural R&D support by central government departments/agencies

5. R&D Statistics 1992-93, GOI, DST, New Delhi, p. 39, Table 6.7.
6. Funding pattern of sponsored research by scientific agencies (1985-86 to 1989-90), Govt. of India, DST, 1990, p. 9.

FUNDING AFTER SEVENTH PLAN

After the Seventh Plan, ended in 1989-90, in a normal course, the Eighth Plan should have started from 1990-91. However, 1990-91 and 1991-92 were the Annual Plan periods. The Eighth Plan period actually started from 1992-93. Compared to the position of the seventh plan period, during these years, there was increase in the number of projects, approved costs (during the year) as also in the number of funding agencies as would be evident from the Table 3.2.

Table 3.2[7]

Types of Institute	*1990-91*		*1991-92*		*1992-93*	
	No. of Projects	*Approved Cost*	*No. of Projects*	*Approved Cost*	*No. of Projects*	*Approved Cost*
(1)	*(2)*	*(3)*	*(4)*	*(5)*	*(6)*	*(7)*
DAE	N.A.	N.A.	83	333.82	88	443.56
DBT	48	1607.33	108	2171.75	93	3289.90
DOC	5	234.94	7	467.91	4	325.42
DOED	27	190.20	44	341.00	41	241.00
DOE	14	931.68	23	309.96	29	373.75
DOD	28	1489.28	12	195.18	6	532.69
DOM	N.A.	N.A.	3	24.50	N.A.	N.A.
DST	286	2196.76	355	2678.90	262	1982.36
DOEN	30	152.30	24	91.69	68	411.15
DNES	38	322.85	21	335.11	6	238.01
MOW	16	63.66	Nil	Nil	2	149.65

7. Research and Development Statistics – 1992-93, Govt. of India DST, New Delhi, Table-10.1, p. 55.

(1)	(2)	(3)	(4)	(5)	(6)	(7)
CBIP	180	948.31	Nil	Nil	23	215.25
CSIR	202	592.28	109	351.87	147	567.06
DRDO	59	454.90	84	577.85	31	289.26
ICAR	115	488.51	50	296.40	107	728.22
ICMR	157	168.70	123	154.61	99	210.35
IMD	2	16.84	2	12.15	Nil	Nil
ISRO	11	54.27	13	53.67	8	40.51
SAIL	N.A.	N.A.	8	71.89	Nil	Nil
UGC	N.A.	N.A.	80	48.19	406	413.01
URBD	7	34.48	N.A.	N.A.	N.A.	N.A.
Total	1225	9947.29	1149	8516.45	1420	10451.15

Source: Data collected and compiled by DST.
Note: N.A. = Not Available.
Glossary of Abbreviations is given in Appendix I

In 1990-91 alone, 1225 projects were approved as against 534 in the Seventh Plan of Five Year period. Beginning from the Seventh Five Year Plan period (1985-86) to the beginning of the Eighth Five Year Plan including the annual plan years 1990-91 and 1991-92, the year-wise growth of support by the Central sector was as shown in the figure 3.6.[8]

During the year 1990-91 to 1992-93, the distribution of funds among the five classified types of institutions and the subject area-wise distribution of the projects were as shown in the tables-3.3 and 3.4 respectively.

8. Research and development Statistics, 1992-93, Govt. of India, DST New Delhi, p.56.

Table 3.3[9]

Distribution of Extramural R&D Projects by Types of Institutes

(In lakhs)

Types of Institute	*1990-91*		*1991-92*		*1992-93*	
	No. of Projects	*Approved Cost*	*No. of Projects*	*Approved Cost*	*No. of Projects*	*Approved Cost*
Universities/Colleges	567	2533.77	572	2858.17	896	3414.89
Deemed Universities	64	798.34	92	886.97	76	1468.74
Institutes of National Importance	187	1314.64	201	1457.33	147	953.28
National Laboratories	202	3949.44	194	2638.37	212	4075.88
Others	205	1351.10	90	675.61	89	538.36
Total	*1225*	*9947.29*	*1149*	*8516.45*	*1420*	*10451.15*

Source: Data collected and compiled by DST.

Table 3.4[10]

Subject Area-wise Distribution of Extramural R&D Projects

(Rs. Lakhs)

Types of Institute	*1990-91*		*1991-92*		*1992-93*	
	No. of Projects	*Approved Cost*	*No. of* Projects	*Approved Cost*	*No. of* Projects	*Approved Cost*

9. Research and Development Statistics, 1992-93, Govt. of India, DST, New Delhi, Table-10.3, p.58.

10. *Ibid.*, Table-10.2.

(Rs. Lakhs)

Types of Institute	*1990-91*		*1991-92*		*1992-93*	
	No. of Projects	*Approved Cost*	*No. of* Projects	*Approved Cost*	*No. of* Projects	*Approved Cost*
Agriculture	124	422.05	89	562.74	155	1429.73
Engineering	353	3376.07	264	2799.29	223	2941.00
Medical Sciences	173	528.01	137	649.30	170	930.45
Natural Sciences						
Biological Sciences	233	2587.23	327	2438.49	400	3256.70
Chemical Sciences	106	415.90	132	582.12	213	695.88
Earth Sciences	149	1949.72	72	399.24	69	409.55
Mathematics	11	26.73	4	9.22	46	54.24
Physical Sciences	76	641.57	124	1076.05	144	733.60
Total	1225	9947.29	1149	8516.45	1420	10451.15

Source: Data collected and compiled by DST.

The figures of the last seven years indicate the trend of an increase; the average annual growth rate being 18.17 per cent.[11]

INTERNATIONAL SCENARIO - JAPAN

It may be interesting to present a picture of Japan, and with that of some other developed countries, by an international comparison of research expenditures in

11. *Ibid.*, p. 59.

the universities as shown in Table 3.5.

Table 3.5[12]

International Comparison of Research Expenditure in Universities (1989)

Countries	*Research* exp. (billion yen)	*Govt.* sources (%)	*Exp. per* researcher (million yen)	*Ratio of* total exp to GNP (%)	*Ratio of* government sources to GNP (%)
Japan	1,140	57.4	15.5	0.28	0.16
USA	4,540	85.7	33.6	0.42	0.36
UK	590	74.1	22.5	0.35	0.26
Germany	780	93.0	20.2	0.41	0.38
France	580	93.6	14.7	0.35	0.33

Note: 1. Definition of research expenditure may differ by country.
2. Conversion into Japanese Yen is based on purchasing power parity of OECD.
3. USA and UK figures are for 1988.

An analysis of the Table 3.5 will reveal that Japan spent next only to USA on research. While USA spent 4540 billion yen, Japan spent 1,140 billion yen which is double of France - 580 billion yen. However, in terms of government spending for research in the universities, France spent highest (93.6%) while it was 57.4.% and 85.7% in Japan and USA respectively. Next to France, it was Germany - 93%. The reason why of the five developed countries, research expenditures in the universities through government sources was highest in France and Germany, was that higher education is free there and it is the government's responsibility of funding the entire higher education.

Expenditure per researcher (million yen) was highest in USA - 33.6 million yen, with UK the second.

12. The University Research System in Japan, MONBUSHO - Ministry of Education, Science & Culture (1993), p. 11, *Source:* OECD.

position in this regard - 22.5 million yen, higher than Japan - 15.5 million yen.

In Japan, of the total research expenditures in all fields, industry spent 71%. Of the remaining 29%, universities spent 17%. The remaining 12% was spent by the government in the government's research institutions. Of the 17%. expenditure on research in the universities, government met 57.4% of that, from its funds.

In 1993, the MONBUSHO (Ministry of Education, Science and Culture. Government of Japan) spent 73.6 billion yen as grants directly to the researchers or groups of researchers working in the universities and research institutes on the basis of merit, as adjudged by the Science Council Research Grant Committee. The grants are made so that the researchers are able "...to make significant contributions to the advancement of science". This total grant of 73.6 billion was allocated for awards for the purposes mentioned in the Table-3.6.

Excepting the General Scientific Research for which 24 billion yen was spent, the highest was 17.6 billion yen for Priority Areas Research and Special Project Research in the areas of 'strong scientific and social needs'. It is interesting that 3.9 billion yen was spent for overseas scientific research. This was for 'survey or research conducted abroad', and is indicative of exploring possibilities of investments for expansion programmes abroad. The third highest allocation is of 6.6 billion yen for 'Applied research whose outcome is likely to be put into practical use.

Over a period of 11 years, research grants that Monbuso alone paid to the individual researchers and groups of researchers increased from 39.5 billion yen in 1983 to 73.6 billion yen, in 1993, as given in the Table 3.7.

Table 3.6[13]

Research Grant Category

Grant Figures-1993

Special Promoted Research 2.4 billion yen	Internationally renowned research which is likely to produce outstanding results.
Special Long-term Research 2.1 billion yen	Long-term research in the field of specially strong scientific and social needs such as cancer research and fusion research.
Priority Areas Research, Special Project Research 17.6 billion yen	Fixed term targeted research in the field of strong scientific and social needs such as materials science (solid state physics, chemical materials, new materials), information electronics (information science, electronics), life science (bio-science, cancer, neuro science), earth, space science (environmental science, geophysics, space) energy science (new energy, energy saving) humanities and social sciences (for one area 50 - 600 million yen, period 3-6 years).
Cooperative Research 2.7 billion yen	Research carried out by researchers belonging to different institutions.
General Scientific Research	Research carried out by a researcher or a group of researchers belonging to the same institution. The most popular category of the programme are sub-divided into three categories according to the amount of funds required:

13. The University Research System in Japan, MONBUSHO, 1993, p.12.

24 billion yen	Category A 10-50 million yen Category B 3-10 million yen Category C less than 3 million yen
Encouragement of Young Scientists 5.3 billion yen	*Research by a young researcher (37 yrs. or less) of an institute (category A), research by a school teacher or a researcher of the town (category B)*
Developmental Scientific Research 6.6 billian yen	Applied research whose outcome is likely to be put into practical use.
Overseas Scientific Research 3.9 billion yen	Survey or research conducted abroad
Scientific Research Promotion 2.4 billion yen	Support urgent and important research
Publication of Scientific Research Results 2.3 billion yen	Support to diffuse the research results and information materials of high scientific value.
Creative Basic Research 2.3 billion yen	Promotion of new programs for the development of science.
Research grants for JSPS Postdoctoral Fellows 1.9 billion yen	Research carried out by JSPS post-doctoral fellows including those from overseas)
(JSPS: Japan Society for the Promotion of Science). It is a quasi-government organisation that conducts various programmes in line with national policies to promote science.	

Table 3.7.[14]

Trends in the Amount of total Research Grants by MONBUSHO

Year	*Yen (in billion)*	*increase over* previous year
1983	39.5	3.9
1984	40.5	2.5
1985	42.0	3.7
1986	43.5	3.6
1987	45.08	3.6
1988	48.88	8.4
1989	52.6	7.6
1990	55.8	6.1
1991	58.9	5.6
1992	64.6	9.7
1993	73.6	13.9

Although on the face of the above trend, in an inflation-striken world, the amount of increase from 39.5 billion yen in 1983 to 73.6 billion yen in 1993 in the eleventh year, is not any big increase. But, in a country like Japan where inflation has been minimum, the increase is impressive. The percentage of increase in 1992 over the previous year was 9.7 and it was 13.9% in 1993, as against very little increases during 1984 and 1987, fluctuating between 2.5 and 3.6.

Turning to the total government budget related to science and technology (including personnel and administrative expenditures) in 1993, it was 2,266.8 billion yen, the share of the various agencies of the government was as shown in the Table 3.8.

14. *Ibid.*, p. 13.

Table 3.8[15]

Japan Government Budget for Science and Technology

	Agency	Amount in billion yen	(%)
1.	Ministry of Science, Education and Culture (MONBUSHO)	1,046.3	46.2
2.	Ministry of Agriculture	80.4	3.5
3.	Ministry of Industrial Trade and Industry (MITI)	282.2	12.4
4.	Science and Technology Agency (STA)	581.6	25.7
5.	Others	276.5	12.2
	TOTAL	2,267.0	100.00

In the research support programmes of the Department of Education, Science and Culture of Japan, categorisation of research grants indicates that MONBUSHO takes into account all round needs within its 5 areas of responsibilities.

CONTINUING EDUCATION PROGRAMME (CEP)

Basically intended to extend the facilities of expertise and infrastructure of the institution, to the various outside organisations to update knowledge and skill of their personnel, CEP programmes are organised. Such programmes besides extending knowledge and skill to others, also help generate income for the institution. For every programme, a suitable fee is charged which leaves some margin after meeting all expenditure to conduct the programme. A number of such programmes

15. *Ibid.*, p. 11.

can generate significant income. The programmes also bring income to faculty for lecturing and for other instructional work. A few others also can earn for helping in organising such programmes.

Every department of the institution should draw up its plan to organise CEP, six months, if not one year, in advance. Even Departments like Economics, Psychology and of course Management, Physics and Chemistry can organise CEP for the industry- big or small. Engineering Departments are of course in a better position to offer CEP for industry managers who are willing to pay higher fees for such training depending of course on the quality of the programme. Precisely, Continuing Education Programme (CEP) provide benefits:

* To the professionals through updating of their knowledge and skill by the academics and experts and the facilities that the institute has;
* To the employers of professionals for when their personnel are trained, they get better services – both in terms of quality and efficiency;
* To the organising institution in two ways, One: a satisfaction of extending the infrastructure facilities and expertise to the society. Two: generation of income;
* To the individual faculty who participate in the programme by way of knowledge transmission and in that process, updating themselves in better ways and of course some monetory benefits as honorarium. Additional perspective for teaching and research activities.
* To other staff members of the Institution who help in the organization of the programme gaining experience and earning some money.

Initially, for the purpose of organising CEP, faculty members of each department have to think both individually and collectively and do the following:

* Conceive programmes which in the cóntext of the current liberalization, would be of interest to the industry. and other organisations to get their staff trained;
* Fix target groups and sell the idea particularly benefits of training: prepare simple but attractive Brochure and mail them to the target groups. Additionally, personal contact over telephone will help
* Prepare an estimate for a minimum number of trainees to ensure cost-effectiveness and about thirty per cent saving for the institution after meeting all expenses. Greater care should be taken fixing the fees that the trainees should pay, keeping in view all expenses, e.g. space, facilities, printing, postage, stationery, telephones, transport, honorarium to experts (internal and external) and some remuneration to staff members, and a saving of about 30% for the institutions;
* Finalise list of experts and facilities and their availability and fix dates;
* In case the training programme is of a longer duration, say more than 3 to 5 days, provide opportunities and facilities to avoid boredom by arranging visits, entertainment programmes, etc;
* Depending on the type of programme, visits to relevant places and discussion with different groups would be beneficial.

It will always be advantageous to create a database of experts and facilities for organising more and more programmes. Reading and reference material should be provided for that would always be useful to the trainees both to read during the training period as also to carry them home for future use. Precisely, for organising the programmes, the following are important points to be kept in view:

* Identification of target groups and conceiving the right kind of programmes - by all departments;
* Minimum number of trainees so as to be cost-effective;
* Maximum number that should be limited to for effective training programme;
* Which period(s) of the year would suit the organisation to spare their staff members for training; and
* Organisations which should first be approached and the target groups.

FORMING ALUMNI ASSOCIATION

Alumni of any institution are great sources for a number of benefits, the foremost of them being that they are the most sincere and effective Ambassadors of the Institution to talk about their *alma-mater* which indirectly contributes to building its reputation. Besides, if properly designed to involve the alumni through the formation of an Association, they could contribute according to each one's capacity and desire, to the funds of the institution.

Contributions of the Alumni could be either in cash for the general purpose or leaving to the institute to decide for any specific purpose such as hostel improvement, class room modernisation, creation of a corpus for scholarships, modernisation of laboratory, construction of a building or a wing of the building. The donor may also specify the purpose for which the money is to be utilized.

However, there are certain prerequisites to form and organise Alumni Association to ensure that the efforts are sustained well to bring-forth the desired benefits both to the Alumni and the Institution. They are as follows:

* to create a data base of the alumni with correct address with telephone numbers, fax, E-mail, information about family, organization where working, etc.,
* to involve the alumni first, briefing them about the activities of the institution - achievements, plans and programmes, and
* to offer some programmes which might interest them such as coming and meeting together on a particular day of the year and spend the time with family members and enjoy. Discussion on any specific subject can also take place together, such as, how they would like to see their *Alma-mater* in the next 5-7-10 years and what they can offer. This should be for all the alumni both in India and abroad.

What is important in this effort is to create an interest among the alumni for their *alma-mater* without giving the slightest hint in the beginning that they are being contacted for purposes of help only. Any alumnus would feel happy when his/her *alma-mater* remembers him. Once involvement is complete that they could be approached to contribute.

In USA, alumni contribute a lot to their *alma-mater*. For that, universities maintain contact with them. For example, in the University of Georgia (USA), the President of the University sends a birth day greeting to every alumnus. In fact, one of the important functions of the President of any American university is to raise funds and his office would do all that is necessary to keep contact with the alumni wherever they are in any part of the world.

The President of the Massachusetts Institute of Technology (MIT), which is internationally known for excellence, writes to every alumnus a very personal letter by addressing as "Dear MIT Graduate", giving general information about the development and innovations that the Institute has had in the recent time and asking them to help it to keep up its global name. As incentives to the alumni as donors, firstly the name is published in the Alumni/AE Activities Annual Report and depending on the amount of donation, the donor becomes member of different organisations within the MIT. For example, the annual donors of US $5000 or more become members of the 'Killian Society'. Those who donate US $2000 to 4999 annually becomes members of the 'President's Fund'. Annual donors of US $500 to 1999 become members of 'Great Dome Associates'. For those who donate US $100 to 499 on an annual basis from the five most recently graduated classes become members of the 'Century Fund'.

For small contribution of US $35 or more to the MIT Alumni/AE Fund, 8 issues of Technology Review are sent to them at a lesser value of US $25. This is however available only for those who may have graduated in the last two years.

As mentioned earlier, raising of funds is one of the

crucial functions of the President; many of them spend as much as 50% of their time for fund raising. The current President of MIT along with one of his senior colleagues travelled to Europe and Asia several times to mobilise resource generation and to establish formal relationship with many institutions and companies for collaborative activities. Through the efforts of the successive Presidents for raising funds particularly through the alumni, the universities have been able to create sizable endowments. For example, Harward University has an endowment of about $ 2000 million. Stanford and Princeton each having an endowment of $ 800 million. Even a public university, namely Texas at Austin has an endowment of about $ 1600 million. Annual interests that these endowments earn meet a good part of their budgets.

While there are some universities and other institutions in India whose alumni, of their own, formed Association in different cities, meet at least once a year which is more or less social meetings over dinner and small talking, most of the universities do not have alumni associations. It is a matter of initiative for even some of the old colleges have their alumni associations. But they meet for they like to meet. No initiative of the institution is seen in any way.

Our higher education system is huge with more than 200 universities and institutions of higher learning and over 8000 colleges. Besides all universities, even if 25% of the colleges form their associations, they can gain a lot. It is important that the alumni should be kept in touch with the activities of the institution and they should be offered something in return. Occasional calls, greetings, remembering for convocation and other important functions and ceremonies would help.

Now that 100% income tax exemption is available on donations to universities, IITs and national laboratories, and 50% to other institutions, it should be used as an incentive for donation from the Alumni of the Institutions.

In the process of contacting the alumni, the institution must ensure that it is cost-effective. A Market oriented approach is a must in all such efforts. For example, Stanford University has development office which has managers for different alumni groups. To ensure cost-effectiveness, graduates who donate '....$25 to $75 receive three to four more letters and those who pay a little more than $75 get a telephone call, and so on. Basically, the whole development effort is based on segmenting the market and working up the most cost-effective marketing mix of the tools for raising money.'[16]

For obvious reasons, all graduates do not respond, but nevertheless, all have to be remembered. This happens since there cannot be a universal appeal. Therefore, in Stanford '..... they have approached their fund-raising experimentally. They do not feel there is a universal appeal that you can make to all Stanford graduates. Different strokes for different folks was a lot better.[17]

Punnayya Committee has recommended that:

> "Each University should take initiative to organise and set up an effective Alumni Association with a view to mobilizing resources from all over the country and abroad. An Advisory Body consisting of the well wishers of the university may be set up

---

16. Kotler Philip, in his interview with peter F. Drucker, Managing the Non-Profit Organisation - Principles & Practice. p. 75, Indo-American Cooperative Publishing Reprint, 1993.

17. *Ibid.*, p. 76.

to pursue action in this regard".[18]

Precisely, it is high time that all universities and other institutions should establish Alumni Association. The following action plan may be taken in that direction:

* An Institutional level advisory committee preferably with the head as chairman;
* Invite through news paper insertions, all former students to join association. Simultaneously, mail letters to all the graduates of the past years. Also contact through personal sources;
* Create data of the Alumni - update the list of graduates with personal information like: address, date of birth, telephone, fax, E-mail, family size and names, professional status: service/business, current interest, etc;
* Allow first year to involve the alumni;
* From second year onwards – alumni may be invited to contribute according to their wish and capacity;
* Design incentives, on the basis of contributions in modified way of MIT approach; and
* Pragmatically, Stanford approach of 'Different strokes for different folks' is better workable.

The Committee may meet at least once in two/three months and review the activities, conceive new plans and programmes to achieve the objectives.

Income Through Fees

The Table 2.2 (chapter two) indicate some conventional as well as suggested non-conventional sources of income. Of the conventional sources for generating

18. Chapter IX, Para 9.20 of Punnayya Committee Report.

ADVISORY COMMITTEE FOR ALUMNI ASSOCIATION

(A suggested model)

Number of members	*Description*
	CHAIRMAN
One	Vice-Chancellor/Director/Principal.
Three	Three Alumni who have evinced interest preferably from different fields.
Three	Three Alumni who are in Industry and business.
One	A serving faculty who is an Alumni to act as Member-Secretary.

income, it is the fees which is commonly the item that the institution thinks first to augment income. In the background of resource crunch and the mandate to generate income by the institutions, one finds almost a wave-like move to raise various fees which some time is rather abrupt, not with proper preparation and notice, the whole of which becomes the burden of the parents. However, this is also the phenomenon in most of the countries for besides the question of raising fees, perhaps the more important question is since higher education is capable of giving greater direct economic benefit to the student, why should he not pay the cost of education. Why should tax payers money be spent on him.

Historically, higher education in India has been cheap—be it non-professional or professional courses. But there are reasons why it has been so. First, after the independence, there were rising aspirations of the people that higher education would bestow a status in the society and of course, give direct greater economic benefit to the individual. Second, the government had adopted the open-door policy of admission to provide opportunities for higher education system. Third, as a welfare state in the background of the socio-economic condition of people, there was a general policy of keeping the fees low.

Generally, no revision of fees was made over 20-30 years. Even for the professional education for which the cost of education and the direct economic benefit was so high, the fees were low to establish any relationship. Even among the central universities for whom the funding and a number of guiding rules are from the University Grants Commission, the scales of fees were different as is clear from the chapter one.

There cannot be any two opinion that fees should be revised. But, *three* guiding principles should be followed. One, there should a gradual, rather than abrupt rise. Second, the fees should be related to the market value of the programmes. Even there should be a differential between urban and rural areas. Third, reasonable and smooth facilities of loans and freeship for poor and meritorious must be provided.

Justice Punnayya Committee while recommending for upward revision of fees, was also conscious of the need to provide freeships and loans and to make these facilities smooth. With regard to the free or concessional studentships, the Committee said that, "We recommend that, along with the implementation of revision of the fee structure, the central universities should award freeship to meritorious students belonging to the socially and economically weaker sections of the society, and admit students at concessional rates of fee".[19] Talking about the extent to which these facilities should be

19. Para 10.12 of Chapter-X of the Punnayya Committee Report.

extended, it recommended that '... in the first instance, be limited to 10% of the entire student strength of the institution. However, the university can operate this with flexibility.[20]

As regards the facilities of loans for studies, the committee deliberated on the feasibility of providing soft loan by the nationalised banks and recommended that:

> "The UGC may also explore the possibilities of introducing a soft loan scheme in collaboration with the nationalised banks. The success of such a scheme in central universities on an experimental basis will enable the UGC to decide the scope of extending it to all the universities. The sole criterion for selection of a student in this case must be merit and economic backwardness. The extent and manner of assistance may be determined by the universities. In other words, the extent of tuitions and living costs to be supported by the loan programme will be determined in each individual case by the university, based on economic need and local circumstances"[21]

Pointing out to the need of complying with the formalities of satisfying the Banks who may give loans, and the credit worthiness of the applicants, the Committee recommended that:

> "........ this should not be rigorous and that interest charges should be the low, period of return should be long, and appropriately phased. Government may also consider bearing the interest charges and allowing a generously phased return of the loan. It should be made amply clear that the university

20. *Ibid.*

21. *Ibid.*, para-10-14.

should not be made responsible for the recovery of the loan or pursuing of action for this purpose. However, we would expect the universities and the banks to act in close collaboration".[22]

The Punnayya Committee was conscious of the complicated procedural formalities of administering such programmes. It therefore observed that "it must however be recognised that loan schemes are difficult to administer. While these are intended to promote equity, the rigidity of conditions governing sanction and of elusive employment opportunities, are factors which may act as deterrents, unless the scheme is designed carefully and pursued earnestly. The programme must be flexible enough to suit the requirements of the weaker sections".[23]

In USA, while the fees are high, the facilities of freeships and loans are abundant. In UK, for all undergraduate home students fees are reimbursed whether by the government or by the Local Education Authority (LEA). Such facilities ensure equity and justice so that no deserving student is denied the opportunity of higher education due to his inability to afford the cost of education.

In most of the countries while fees for the home students were raised, fees for the overseas (foreign) students were raised much more. In UK, a differential fees structure was introduced for the first time in 1979 for overseas students towards a policy of recovering the cost of education. However, in 1966, a beginning was made to charge a lumpsum amount from the overseas students separately for post-graduate and under-graduate students. Interestingly, students from European

22. *Ibid.*

23. *Ibid.*, para-10-16.

countries are not considered 'foreign' but 'home' and they pay fees at the level that the UK students pay.

From 1981-82, when the government imposed cuts on grants, fees from the foreign students became one of the major source of income. Every year, the universities fix target numbers and develop strategies to attract foreign students. For the last over two years, many universities of UK and Australia have been sending teams to India to attract foreign students. In UK, over 10% students are from foreign countries, while in India, it is less than one per cent. In Australia, the percentage of foreign students is over 9% while in Canada, it was over 6%.

By providing a little better infrastructure facilities for the foreign students and making the admission procedure smooth, it is quite possible to attract more and more foreign students particularly from other Asian and African countries. For this, what is needed is a well thought out policy and plan to attract foreign students.

Besides the fees from the foreign students another source of generation of income from the foreign students could be to ask for a refundable deposit, say, one year's fees and earn interest on such deposits. This will also help the students to go back to their home after completing their studies for many a time, some of them face financial difficulties to clear many dues and the money needed for return journey.

Income Through Renting out of Facilities

More or less like the other conventional sources of income, are the renting out space and facilities of the institutions.

In varying degrees, institutions have had some income through renting out the facilities of space, but generally they have not been exploited fully. In most cases, the institutions have not made efforts to obtain the return from the high investments in the costly and sometime rare equipment that they have. If the outside agencies are invited to use the various facilities of equipment, on one hand the institution will gain in terms of money and on the other hand, the industry or may be another institution not having the same equipment would gain by its use by one time or occasional payment which would be cheap and help avoid investments. Similarly, facilities of space and equipment in the Gymkhana may be exploited for resource generation.

What is needed in this regard is to prepare a document of facilities of space and equipment that the institute possesses indicating the time of the year and hours of the day (wherever necessary to keep this in view) when they can be used. The document may then be circulated to the potential users. In order to sustain the work that would stem from such an offer, the institution must structure this, e.g.. interface contact person for quick decisions, and the person or persons who would be responsible to maintain and actually making available the facilities. Unless the procedure is smooth and the given facilities are in shape as offered through the document, the users would be discouraged to approach.

Income through Library facilities by External Members

Not so conventional source of income is the external use of facilities of books and in particular the Journals. Most of the institutions spend sizably on library books and journals. In the knowledge-based society, there would be a large number of external people who would like to avail of the facilities of books and journals if only they know how and at what cost. In particular, selling xerox copies of selected topics or articles at a given price could fetch reasonable income. However, again that has to be structured and publicised. More importantly, quick supply of xerox copies is the vital question to sustain any such scheme.

On a selective basis, throwing the library facilities open to the outsiders may also fetch additional income. Precisely, efforts should be made, to begin with, to raise the income to meet the upkeep expenditure of the library and later, to make the library independent at least the running cost of the library including salary.

However, for the obvious reason, the scope would vary from university to university and place to place. And again a library having more books and journals in science and engineering would be able to earn more than others.

Income through Interest of Investments

Earning of interest through proper long-term and short term investment is a potential source of resource generation. In most of the institutions, this aspect of resource generation is not professionally exploited. It is true that the institutions do not generally have surplus funds- to invest. But what is important is whether the funds be it of non-plan or plan budget or for specific purposes, are invested wisely on short- term or long-term basis to earn maximum interest.

For short-term investment, every day, the cash-flow of the institution is required to be watched and investment be made to earn interest. It is here that an alert mind is necessary to ensure what amount can be invested, where and for what rate of interest. This requires the following:

(i) which are the days of the week when the institution would receive known income, e.g. fees, rents, repayments, other deposits,

(ii) which are likely dates of receipt of grants from the government or any other agency, e.g. Municipalities, Trusts, Foundations and how much can be invested and for what period,

(iii) how much of the receipts would be needed to meet routine expenditure, and capital expenditure, if any. Salary requirements are well-known,

(iv) which are the dates or the periods when funds for specific research or consultancy or for any other purpose would be required so that investment ranging from 46 days to 90 days may be made, and

(v) updated information about investments in various financial institutions - short-term and long-term.

Creation of Income through Sale/Lease of Unusable Land

The most non-conventional suggestion for generation of income to create an Endowment Fund for the institution, is to deliberate and decide whether some part of land of the institution is not likely to be used in the foreseeable future and can be sold/leased out. In many cases, maintaining the land, particularly the security of that, is a problem by itself. In case the institution has, for long, land that has not been used and there is no possibility of using the land in the foreseeable future, it will be in the interest of the institution to dispose of the land to fetch capital money for creating an Endowment Fund, sizable interest on which will provide support to the institution after a period of say 10 years. However, the institution must keep adequate land that may be needed over the next 20-30 years. There should be a limit of expansion to prevent consequential problems.

Ordinarily, most of the institutions have sizable land which are generally gifted either by the government, Municipality or a Trust or Foundation for its establishment. The crucial question is whether the institution has the authority to dispose of the land. Generally, the institution would not have the authority, but if the donor permits legally, there should not be any difficulty to dispose of the land. It is not a simple proposition. But it is worth examining. In UK, during 1980s, some universities have sold their land and buildings to tide over the financial crisis.

Leasing out of land would mean denying any right of the Institution for at least 30 years and at the same time not getting any good return. In view of this, selling is a better proposition if that is possible, rather than leasing out. However, as selling may appear to be difficult, it may be easy to lease out, but at what return, should be ensured.

The next chapter has been exclusively devoted to resource generation through consultancy.

Income from Donations

Historically, donations by trusts, foundations and individuals were more conventional than perhaps even the fees. In the pre-independence period, universities and other institutions received sizable donations for their establishment, development, creation of chairs and for other facilities. Unfortunately, in the post-independence period, with the more and more government support, the earlier attitude of helping the cause of education has waned.

Realizing the need of public support for education, particularly when the products of institutions are used by the industry and other organisations, the government has since provided for 100% income tax exemption for donations to the educational institutions to be approved by the Income Tax Authority. A weighted 25% i.e. a total of 125% income tax exempting can be obtained for funding research projects in the universities, IITs, deemed universities and scientific laboratories under the aegis of the Defence Research and Development Organisation (DRDO), the Department of Electronics (DoE), the Department of Bio-Technology (DBT) and the Department of Atomic Energy. These concessions were long felt and awaited. Now that the desired concessions are available, it is for the institutions to plan and approach the industry and others, to donate for various purposes, e.g. for creation of Endowment Funds, construction or maintenance of hostels, teaching, laboratory buildings, for equipping, modernising laboratories and for library books and journals, specific resence etc.

CONCLUSION

As compared to the funds, number of projects and participation of the institutions in the Seventh Plan period and in the subsequent years (till 1992-93), visible improvements are noticed. Although funds are always limited, it is generally believed that there is no lack of funds for a good proposal. Keeping in view the huge higher education sector of the country consisting of about 250 universities and institutions of university level, besides over 8000 colleges having over three lakhs teachers, there is much to be desired.

It is true that a large number of the institutions do not have the necessary strength of experts and facilities to ably compete at all India level to win the projects, but there is no denying the fact that the strengths which are already available in the institutions are not utilised optimally. Whether that is due to the absence of motivation or an inherent passive approach of the teachers, or absence of the right kind of environment for that, is another issue. In the changing situation, what is needed is a sustained effort on the part of the institutions to participate in the research activities both basic and applied to explore the various possibilities of breaking new frontiers of knowledge and to apply them to real life to improve the economy of the nation. Every department of every institution should discuss and plan out how best it can take the advantage of funding by the various government agencies.

For a variety of reasons, Continuing Education Programmes (CEP) need be encouraged in the institutions. *First*, it generates income both for the institution as well as for the faculty which is a positive incentive. *Second*, by organizing CEP, the institution extends its expertise and facilities to the society to update knowledge of those who need them for enhancing their professional competence for productivity which help the economy. *Third*, involvement of a number of participants of other organisations in the activities of the institutions help create well-wishers of the institution which it should always look forward as a long-term investment.

It is necessary to tap the vast resources that lie in the alumni and make use of their strengths. The alumni can be helpful to the institution in a number of ways. In fact, they could prove to be the best ambassadors of the institution both to contribute financially as also to carry the message of goodwill and reputation to all over the country and outside the country. The prerequisite to tap the vast resources of alumni is to create a data of the alumni at least of the last 30 years. This by itself is an uphill task, if it is for the first time that the data is to be created. However, once created, it is then a matter of adding the new names to the existing data.

While creation of data and updating the same from time to time is the basic job to organize activities for the alumni, the other important job is to develop a mechanism to maintain contact with them in a number of ways. Of the various ways, one could be sending them from time to time some designed information about the institution to keep them informed of the important activities and plans of the institution. This will keep up their interest in their *alma-mater*. Creating an Alumni Association and involving some of them in some activities of the institution is another way to sustain their interest. However, sending information to those alumni who are abroad particularly if that number is big, is expensive. But, such expenses should be viewed as a long-term investment.

How much financial contributions can come from the alumni is a matter of relative situations for that will depend on a few factors such as how well data is created, how best interest is created among the alumni and kept that up, and what percentage of them are in a position to contribute financially. This is bound to vary from institution to institution, but there is no doubt that every institution can substantially gain through its alumni if properly planned and tapped.

Income through fees is the most conventional one. Of the various reasons why fees should be raised is that since higher education gives direct benefit to the individual, why others should pay for his education. However, by educating the people, nation is also benefitted and therefore it is neither justified nor practically possible to recover the full cost of education. But the level of fees that are charged in India is perhaps one of the lowest in the world for in a period of 20-30 years, there has not been any revision. However, in order to be realistic to the situation, revision should be gradual and simultaneously adequate opportunities of freeships and loans should be provided to make sure that due to the higher fees, no deserving poor and meritorious student is deprived of the higher education. It will be a loss to the nation even if a single meritorious student is denied higher education just because he does not have money to pay for that.

Another source of generating income is to make optimal utilisation of the space and facilities such as equipment etc. by making them available on payment to a selective few. To sustain this, necessary planning and interface body should be created. It is also necessary to ensure that the facilities that are intended to be used to earn, are in good shape.

Use of the library facilities by external people can be a good source of income besides a satisfaction that the facilities are extended to a larger community of our own society. For this also, what is needed is to identify which are the facilities that can be offered and whether the desired service structure is there so that it is possible to sustain the additional workload. Once money is accepted to provide facilities, there should not be any failure to provide them. A reputation of promise of good service and keeping that up, is a pre-requisite to undertake any each venture.

It is time that the managers of the institutions particularly those involved in the financial management get themselves equipped and updated about the rules and regulations of investments. An alert mind is a *sine-qua-non* for generating income through investments.

The suggestion to sell/lease land although non-conventional, needs serious thinking for a long-term resource planning of the institution. If workable, it can prove very helpful.

Although the culture of donations to the institutions has waned over the years, but in view of the incentives now available in the income-tax, efforts to get donations are likely to succeed now than before.

Efforts are important for it is only through efforts, may be sometimes repeated ones, that success comes.

Appendix-I

GLOSSARY OF ABBREVIATIONS

DAE	:	Department of Atomic Energy
DBT	:	Department of Bio-Technology
DOC	:	Department of Coal
DUED	:	Department of Education
DOE	:	Department of Electronics
DOD	:	Department of Ocean Development
DOM	:	Department of Mines
DST	:	Department of Science and Technology
DOEM	:	Department of Environment
DNES	:	Department of Non-Conventional Energy Sources.
MOW	:	Ministry of Welfare

CBIP	:	Central Board of Irrigation and Power
CSIR	:	Council for Scientific and Industrial Research
DRDO	:	Defence Research & Development Organisation
ICAR	:	Indian Council of Agricultural Research
ICMR	:	Indian Council of Medical Research
IMD	:	India Meteorological Department
ISRO	:	Indian Space Research Organisation
SAIL	:	Steel Authority of India
UGC	:	University Grants Commission
URBD	:	Ministry of Urban Development.

4

Industry Interaction — Why, and How to go About?

WHY INTERACTION WITH INDUSTRY

Primarily for the national development and not merely for generating income, extensive, effective and meaningful interaction between academics and industry is a *sine-qua-non*. Although on the face of it, it may appear that an interaction with industry is necessary to generate income but that is only one aspect of the many benefits of such interaction.

Universities and other institutions generally conduct basic research. However, results of basic research unless applied for the benefits of the society have limited and little value. Ordinarily, it is through the industry that application of basic research results reach the society at large, and then to the national and international benefits. In USA, it is estimated (1990) that about 19% of university research is now carried out in programmes that involve linkage with industry in a fundamental way.[1] However, even when university research is 'basic research', that does "... not mean that such research is not guided by practical

1. American Universities and Technical Advance in Industry, Nathen Rosenberg and Richard R. Nelsons, Research Policy 23 (1994), 323-348, North Holland, P. 323.

concerns"[2] and '... it is a gross misconception to think that if research is basic this means the work is not motivated by or funded because of its promise to deal with a class of practical problems. Nor does it mean that university scientists and engineers are not building and working with prototypes of applicable technology.'[3] The percentage of academic research in USA funded by industry was estimated to be 6.9% in 1990 from 3.9% a decade earlier.

Through a survey of industrial R & D managers, undertaken in mid 1980s - at the Yale University, it was clear "... how university research contributes to the advance of industrial technology, and into industrial fields where this role is most important."[4] The respondents to the questionnaire were asked to rate the importance of research done at universities to technical advance in their line of business. The managers 'had rated the contributions of university research as very important or important Theoretically, what is true in USA, is true elsewhere, in so far as the value of contributions of the academics to the industry is concerned.

This tends to establish that the industry is the greater beneficiary of the interaction. But the universities too gain for besides the achievement of contributions to the industrial development, there is monetary benefit that the university as an institution gets, and in the process the individuals involved in the research activities and application thereof. A linkage of the academics with the industry is therefore not only desirable but essential for technology development and

2. *Ibid.*, p. 340.
3. *Ibid.*, p. 340.
4. *Ibid.*

industrial application and for bettering the quality of life of the people. And that is beneficial to all—industry, institutions and the society at large.

In view of this, in the developed countries, investments of industry in Research and Development is sizable. In the changing scenario, such investments are now being made more and more, through collaborative R & D activities. In the developed countries, companies spend about 10% of their revenues on R & D. A company like Toyota spends about US$ .5 billion which is about three times of our national budget on technology.

In India, for their own reasons, industry has hardly any worth the name R & D. Nor do they spend in any significant order on R & D through universities. While industry may have their own reasons on practical reasons, the fact remains that such a state did not promote product development or even upgradation. Resultantly, involvement of the academics of the institutions has been minimal. If there was a demand from the industry, interaction would have taken place in a natural way of demand and supply.

RESEARCH AND DEVELOPMENT EXPENDITURES: INDIAN SCENARIO

National R&D Expenditure

In 1992-93, of the total Rs. 5141.64 crores of national expenditure on R & D, government spending accounted for 73.6% (Centre and State together) with 11.4% by the public sector. Private Sector spent only 15% as shown in figure 4.1.[5]

5. R&D Statistics, 1992-93, Govt. of India, DST, New Delhi, p. 2.

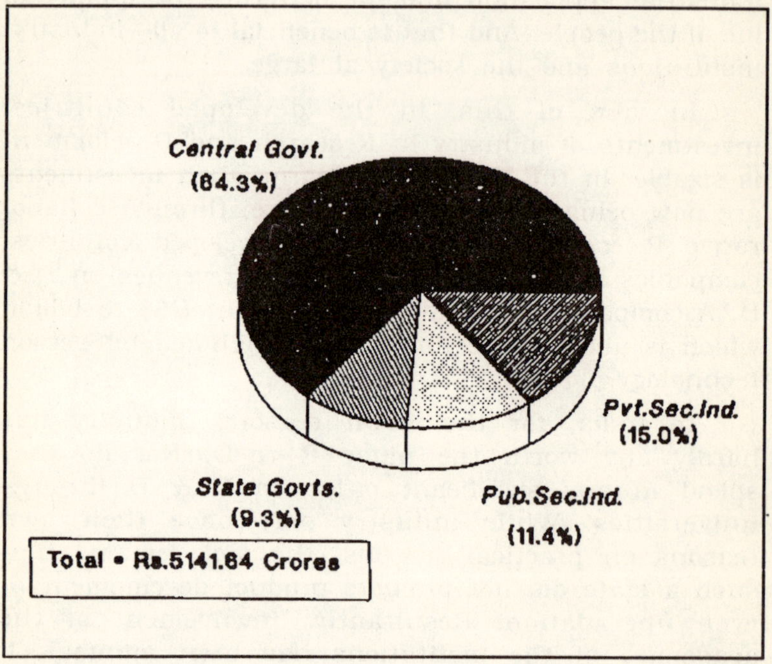

Fig. 4.1. National R&D Expenditure by Sector 1992-93

By objectives, the amount of Rs. 5141.64 crores was spent as given in Table 4.1, the percentage share being mentioned against each.

Central Government R&D Expenditure

During 1992-93, of the total national R & D expenditure of Rs.5141.64, the Central Government share of expenditure was 64.3%. With the Public Sector share of expenditure of 11.4%, it was 75.7%. Of this, 71.6% expenditure was by the major scientific agencies. These agencies accounted for 54.2% of the

Table 4.1[6]

Percentage Share of National Research and Development Expenditure by Objectives, 1992-93

Objective	*Percentage*
Defence	19.2
Development of Agriculture, Forestry and Fishing	17.6
Promotion of Industrial Development	16.4
Space	9.6
Production, Conservation and Distribution of Energy	7.9
Development of Transport and Communication	6.7
General Advancement of Knowledge	5.4
Development of Health Services	5.5
Protection of Environment	4.6
Others	7.1
Total	100.00

national R & D expenditure as given in Table 4.2.

Five agencies namely, DRDO, DOS, ICAR, DAE and CSIR together accounted for 80.1% of the 54.2% of the national expenditure on R&D. DRDO alone consumed 28.4%.

A comparative position of the expenditures by the Central, State and Private Sectors for a period of five years (1989-90 to 1993-94) is shown in Table 4.3.

6. Table 1.1, Research & Development Statistics, Govt. of India, Dept. of Science & Technology, New Delhi, p. 3.

Table 4.2[7]

Percentage share of R & D Expenditure by Major Scientific Agencies during 1992-93

Sr. No.	Scientific Agency	Percentage share of R&D Expenditure
1.	Defence Research and Development Organisation (DRDO)	28.4
2.	Department of Space (DOS)	17.6
3.	Indian Council of Agricultural Research (ICAR)	12.1
4.	Department of Atomic Energy (DAE)	11.4
5.	Council of Scientific and Industrial Research (CSIR)	10.6
6.	Department of Environment	7.8
7.	Department of Science and Technology (DST)	5.8
8.	Department of Bio-technology (DBT)	2.1
9.	Indian Council of Medical Research (ICMR)	1.5
10.	Department of Ocean Development (DOD)	1.5
11.	Department of Electronics (DOE)	0.7
12.	Department of Non-Conventional Energy Sources (DNES)	0.5
	Total	100.00

There is a clear trend from Table 4.3 that albeit at slow pace, private sector expenditure is increasing from 13% in 1989-90 to 15% in 1992-93 and to 15.69% in 1993-94. Even State government expenditure also shows increasing trend. Resultantly, central government spending reduced from 78.74% in 1989-90 to 75.67% in 1992-93 and a further estimated decrease to 74.51% in 1993-94.

7. Table 1.3, Research & Development Statistics, 401, DST, New Delhi, p. 6.

Table 4.3[8]

Research and Development Expenditure for Five Years in Various Sectors

(Rs. in Crores)

Sector	*1989-90*	*1990-91*	*1991-92*	*1992-93*	*1993-94 (Estimated)*
Central including public sector	2933.92 (78.74)	3058.27 (76.95)	3467.29 (76.83)	3891.09 (75.67)	4272.42 (74.51)
State	301.23 (8.85)	365.92 (9.20)	408.58 (9.00)	478.78 (9.31)	561.13 (9.78)
Private	490.59 (13)	549.98 (13.83)	636.94 (14)	771.77 (15)	899.88 (15.69)
Total	3725.74	3974.17	4512.81	5141.64	5733.43

Source: Data Collected and compiled by DST.

Note: Figure in the parenthesis is the percentage share of private sector in National R&D expenditure.

The only reason why private sector's investment on R&D is growing could be the economic liberalisation, a realization on the part of the private sector that both to survive and to grow in the competitive situation, investment in R&D was essential.

Public Sector R&D Expenditure

In the Public Sector, in 1992-93, the total R&D expenditure was Rs.586.71 crores at current prices which was highest so far, registering an increase of 21.1% over 1991-92 when it was Rs.484.39 crores. Compared to 1980-81, when the R&D expenditure of the Public Sector was only 86.37 crores, the figure of Rs.586.71 crores was surely impressive. However, 86.8%

8. Table 1, R&D Statistics (1992-93), 401, DST, p. 63.

of this expenditure was incurred under a few Ministries/Departments as given in Table 4.4.

Table 4.4[9]

Public Sector Investment on R&D by Major Industry Groups, 1992-93 covering 86.8% of the total Public Sector R&D Expenditure

Sr. No.	Ministry/ Department	R&D Expenditure in 1992-93 (Rs. Lakhs) 1992-93
1.	Defence Production and Supplies	19753.45
2.	Heavy Industry	8878.59
3.	Petroleum and Natural Gas	6824.61
4.	Steel	5460.63
5.	Telecommunications	3412.71
6.	Chemicals and Petrochemicals	2866.32
7.	Atomic Energy	1981.32
8.	Electronics	1729.85

However, although in 1992-93, R&D expenditure by the Public Sector was an impressive 586.71 crore as compared to Rs. 86.37 in 1980-81, the percentage share in national R&D expenditure remained to be the same, namely 11.4%. Even in other years between 1981-82 to 1991-92, the relevant percentage did not increase or decrease substantially. It remained between 10% to 11% with the highest in 1983-84 i.e. 11.7% as would be evident from Table 4.5

9. Compiled from Table 3.4, R&D in Industry, 1992-93, Govt. of India, DST, New Delhi, p. 43.

Table 4.5[10]

Trend of R&D Expenditure by Public Sector and the Percentage Share in National R&D Expenditure

Sr. No	*Year*	*R&D Expenditure (Rs Crores)*	*Percentage growth in expenditure over the previous year*	*Percentage share in national R&D expenditure*
1.	1980-81	86.37	-	11.4
2.	1981-82	107.55	24.5	10.7
3.	1982-83	122.46	13.9	10.2
4.	1983-84	161.66	32.0	11.7
5.	1984-85	171.22	5.9	9.6
6.	1985-86	198.62	16.0	9.6
7.	1986-87	235.70	18.7	9.4
8.	1987-88	288.47	22.4	10.1
9.	1988-89	342.12	18.6	10.2
10.	1989-90	412.90	20.7	11.1
11.	1990-91	414.53	0.4	10.4
12.	1991-92	484.39	16.9	10.7
13.	1992-93	586.71	21.1	11.4

State Sector R&D Expenditure

In the State Sector, the R&D expenditure during 1992-93 was Rs.734.63 crores, the State-wise position of the number of R&D units and the R&D expenditure was as shown in Table 4.6.

10. Table 3.2, R&D in Industry, 1992-93, Govt. of India, DST, New Delhi, p. 41.

Table 4.6[11]
State-wise Private Sector Industrial R&D Units and R&D Expenditure, 1992-93

Sr. No.	*State*	*No. of R&D Units*	*R&D Expenditure (Rs. Lakhs)*
1.	Maharashtra	384	34703.43
2.	Tamil Nadu	134	8098.81
3.	Karnataka	112	5829.77
4.	Gujarat	102	4885.36
5.	West Bengal	68	3978.16
6.	Andhra Pradesh	64	3767.53
7.	Delhi	41	3029.81
8.	Haryana	44	2379.83
9.	Uttar Pradesh	71	2070.47
10.	Bihar	10	1105.09
11.	Others	98	3614.54
	Total	1128	73462.80

Of the 1128 R&D Units, 76.6% were located in six States - Maharashtra, Tamil Nadu, Karnataka, Gujarat, West Bengal and Andhra Pradesh, which accounted for 83.4% of the total R&D expenditure of the state sector in 1992-93. From the table, it is also clear that the biggest State, viz. Madhya Pradesh, does not figure independently but, under 'others' because of the small number of units and R&D expenditure.

Private Sector R&D Expenditure

According to the figure of 1992-93, there were 1124

11. Table 2.6, R&D in Industry, Govt. of India, DST, New Delhi, p. 26.

R&D Units in the Private Sector. However, until the Third Five Year Plan (1961-66), it had only 5.9% units, the highest was during the Sixth Plan (1980-85) 25.2% as shown in Table 4.7.

Table 4.7[12]

Growth of R&D Units in Private Sector during different Plan Periods

Sr. No.	*Period*	*Number of R&D Units*
1.	Before 1950	30
2.	First Five Year Plan (1951-56)	15
3.	Second Five Year Plan (1956-61)	21
4.	Third Five Year Plan (1961-66)	45
5.	Annual Plans (1966-67 to 1968-69)	45
6.	Fourth Five Year Plan (1969-74)	148
7.	Fifth Five Year Plan (1974-79)	212
8.	Annual Plan (1979-80)	41
9.	Sixth Five Year Plan (1980-85)	283
10.	Seventh Five Year Plan (1985-90)	232
11.	Annual Plan (1990-91 and 1991-92)	49
12.	During 1992-93	3
	Total	1124

The R&D expenditure of the Private-Sector *vis-a-vis* the Government sources, in relation to the national expenditure for the period 1980-81 to 1992-93 was, as given in Table 4.8.

12. Table 2.1, R&D in Industry, Govt. of India, DST, p-20

Table 4.8[13]

Trend of R&D Expenditure by Source

(Rs. Crores)

Year	*R&D Expenditure*		
	Private Source	*Government Source*	*Total National*
1980-81	120.69 (15.9)	639.83	760.52
1981-82	147.00 (15.6)	793.73	940.73
1982-83	196.98 (16.3)	1009.05	1206.03
1983-84	207.83 (15.1)	1173.27	1381.10
1984-85	233.19 (13.1)	1548.36	1781.55
1985-86	251.94 (12.2)	1816.84	2068.78
1986-87	291.63 (12.0)	2143.77	2853.07
1987-88	310.27 (10.9)	2542.80	2853.07
1988-89	417.62 (12.5)	2929.64	3347.26
1989-90	490.59 (13.2)	3235.15	3725.74
1990-91	549.98 (13.8)	3424.19	3974.17
1991-92	636.94 (14.1)	3875.87	4512.81
1992-93	771.77 (15.0)	4369.87	5141.64

Note: Figures in brackets are the percentage share of private source in National R&D expenditure.

From a meagre Rs.120.69 crore, in 1980-81, in terms of money, a quantum jump is seen compared to 1992-93 when it reached Rs.771.77. But when compared in terms of the percentage share to the national expenditure on R&D, it was higher (15.9%) in 1980-81, than it was in 1992-93 (15%). From this angle, its share of expenditure to national R&D expenditure has declined.

13. Table 2.2, R&D in Industry, Govt. of India, DST, p. 22.

INTERNATIONAL SCENARIO OF R&D EXPENDITURE

World R&D Expenditure

For the purpose of international comparison, the commonly used indicator is the percentage of GNP devoted for research and development activities. In ralation to the GNP for the entire world (1990), the percentage of expenditure on R&D was 2.55. In that year, the developed countries spent 2.92 rising from 2.22 in 1980 and 2.62 in 1985. In the case of the developing countries, the figures were 0.52% in 1980, 0.54% in 1985 and 0.64% in 1990. The figures of expenditures and the comparison could be seen from Table 4.9.

Table 4.9[14]

Estimated World R&D Expenditure and the Relationship to GNP

	R&D Expenditure (US $ billion)			*R&D Expenditure as % of GNP*		
Region	*1980*	*1985*	*1990*	*1980*	*1985*	*1990*
World	*208.4* (100%)	*271.9* (100%)	*452.6* (100%)	*1.85*	*2.22*	*2.55*
Developed	195.8 (94%)	258.9 (95%)	434.3 (96%)	2.22	2.62	2.92
Developing	12.6 (6%)	13.0 (5%)	18.3 (4%)	0.52	0.54	0.64

For 1990, the World R&D expenditure was 452.6 billion US $ of which 43.4% was in USA with 23.2% in the whole of Europe. Share of the entire Asia was only 20.2% while the former USSR spent 12.3%. The

14. Table 8.1, R&D Statistics, (92-93) GOI, DST, New Delhi, p. 46.

remaining was in Africa - 0.2% and 0.7% in Oceania. R&D expenditures in these continents in 1980, 1985 as well as 1990 are as shown in Table 4.10 and Figure 4.2.[16]

Table 4.10[15]

R&D Expenditure and its Share in World total by Continents

Continents	*Expenditure on R&D in billion US dollars and % share in brackets*		
	1980	*1985*	*1990*
Africa	1.1 (0.5)	0.9 (0.3)	1.1 (0.2)
America	70.4 (33.8)	118.9 (43.7)	196.6 (43.4)
Asia	31.7 (15.2)	47.2 (17.4)	91.2 (20.2)
Europe	70.7 (33.9)	65.6 (24.1)	105.0 (23.2)
Oceania	2.2 (1.1)	2.1 (0.8)	3.0 (0.7)
USSR	32.3 (15.5)	37.2 (13.7)	55.7 (12.3)
World (Total)	208.4 (100)	271.9 (100)	452.6 (100)

As a matter of new trend, huge investments are now made by American, European and Japanese companies on R&D. For example, IBM and Hewlett-Packard have an estimated 30 per cent of their R&D outside US. On the other side, about. 250 R&D facilities in USA have been created by more than 100 companies from Japan, Germany, UK, France and South Korea.[17] Dr. R.A. Mashelkar referred to the new concept of techno-globalisation that is being promoted in Japan implying

15. Table 8.2 R&D Statistics, (92-93) GOI, DST, New Delhi, p. 46.
16. *Ibid.* p. 47.
17. World can be our Technical Oyster, Dr. R.A. Mashelkar, The Telegraph, Calcutta, 22.8, 1995, p. 13.

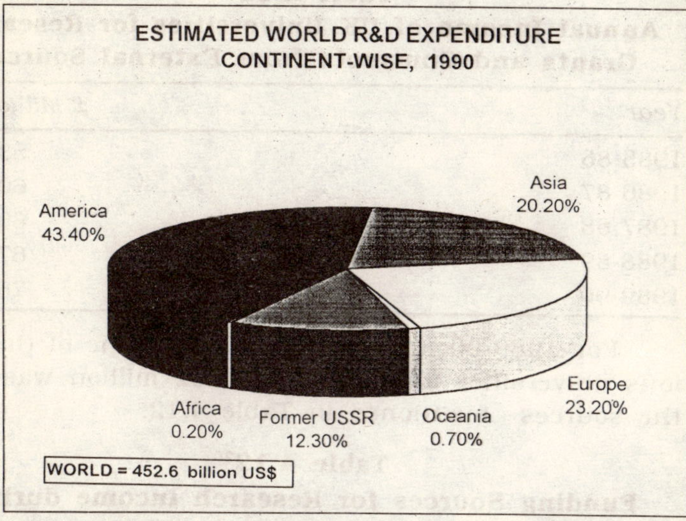

Figure - 4.2 [16]

"widening cross border interdependence between individual technology based firms as well as economic sectors, especially through the restructuring of high and medium technology industry".[18]

University-Industry Interaction in UK

In UK, consequent to the 1981 cuts of university grants by the Thatcher government on an average 17% the universities were forced to generate, through a good deal of restructurisation, non-government income. Besides other areas to generate income, universities had to work aggressively in many areas including industry interaction. In 1982-83, the income from research grants and contracts from external sources for all the universities was only £230 million, which increased fast in the subsequent years as shown in the Table 4.11.

---

18. *Ibid.*

Table 4.11[19]

Annual Income of UK Universities for Research Grants and Contracts from External Sources

Year	*£ Million*
1985-86	535
1986-87	607
1987-88	604
1988-89	673
1989-90	762

For 1989-90, external research income of the various universities amounting to £762 million was from the sources mentioned in Table 4.12.

Table 4.12[20]

Funding Sources for Research income during 1989-90 for UK Universities

	Funding Agency	*Million Pounds*
1.	Research Councils	265
2.	UK based Charitable Trusts	156
3.	UK Govt. Departments	106
4.	UK Local Authorities	4
5.	UK Public Corporations	9
6.	UK Industry and Commerce	96
7.	UK Health and Hospital Authorities	14
8.	European Community Grants	38
9.	Other Overseas Organizations	43
10.	Other sources	31
	Total	762

19. University Funding Council: Present and Future Policies, Prof. Graeme Davies, Chief Executive, Universities Funding Council, UK, (1991) — not published.

20. *Ibid.*

It is interesting that the top eighteen universities of fifty one (at that time) gained 75% of external research income. Perhaps such a situation is bound to be there in every country for the obvious reason that building a strong research group depends on a number of factors and that cannot happen in every university. Nevertheless, on the whole, participation of the university community in contract research and consultancy is important both from the points of view of income and utilisation of capabilities of universities on one hand, and the industry utilising the capabilities of academics and harnessing them for the society at large on the other.

University-Industry Co-operation in Japan

In Japan, recognizing "the growing importance ascribed to science and technology has created new demands and expectations on university research to contribute to the solution of social problems" and therefore, the Ministry of Education, Science and Culture (MONBUSHO) conducts various programmes "to encourage increased co-operation between the universities and industry", as shown in Table 4.13.

Table 4.13[21]
Programme of the Govt. of Japan to Encourage Increased Co-operation between Universities and Industry

Measures		*Contents*
Measures extended by the university side	Joint research with industry	A system of joint research was created in 1983 by the MONBUSHO to encourage researchers from private companies on topics of common in-

21. P. 17, University Research System in Japan, MONBUSHO, 1993.

Measures	*Contents*
	terest. Research funds are also received from the participating companies. This system has been expanded in scale year by year. (FY 1993 budget: Yen 5.0 billion)
Contract research	This system enables instructors and researchers by national universities to conduct on a contract basis, research commissioned by private companies, government institutes and other external bodies. The cost of such research is borne by the external body. The consignor or his designee) receives patent licensing priority for upto seven years. (FY 1993 budget: Yen 9.6 billion)
Measure extended by the University	National universities accept about 200 projects (excluding commissioned examinations, etc.) a year under this system.
Contract researchers	This system provides researchers and engineers employed by private companies the opportunity to conduct graduate-level research in national universities. This system, which had been formerly limited to scientific and engineering fields, was opened up to all academic fields including humanities and social sciences in 1989. More than 1200 contracted researchers are now conducting research projects at national universities under this system. (FY 1993 budget: Yen 0.5 billion)
Centres for cooperative research	To promote full-scale cooperation with the private sector through joint and commissioned research, the MONBUSHO

Measures		*Contents*
		has been establishing centres for co-operative research within the national universities since 1987. At present, there are 33 such centres established in the national universities. (In 1993, centres were established in Iwate University, Shinshu University, Tottori University, and Oita University.)
Measures extended by industry side	Donations	National universities are authorized to receive donations from private companies and other outside organizations for promoting scientific research and educational activities. In 1987, a system of endowed chairs and funded research departments was introduced through private donations. At present, there are 52 endowed chairs and 12 funded research departments in a total of 22 universities, and two funded research departments in one national inter-university research institute. The donations are utilized flexibly in line with the donors objectives, and play an important role in vitalizing scientific research in various fields. (FY 1993 budget: Yen 50.2 billion)
Other measures	Joint research by Monbusho Grants	Under the category of "Developmental Scientific Research" of the Grants-in-Aid program for scientific research (developmental and applied research with a high potential for practical use), joint research is encouraged between universities and industry. (FY 1993 budget: Yen 6.6 billion)
	JSPS Programme	JSPS has established an "Advisory Committee on University-Industry

Measures	*Contents*
	Research activities" consisting of eminent members of academic and industry to study the fields of research which have a high potential for advancement through university-industry cooperation. As a result at present, two specialized research and development committees have been established: the Committee on Atomic Cluster Research, the Committee on JSPS also creates industry-university cooperative research committees on specific themes, through which researchers from the two sectors have an opportunity to discuss basic and technological problems. (Forty-one such committees are operational at present).

National Research expenditure in Japan in 1993 was 13,772 billion Yen of which 71%, i.e. 9,743 billion Yen was shared by the industry, 17% i.e. 2,408 billion Yen research expenditure was in the universities and the remaining 12%, i.e. 1,621 billion Yen was in the Governmental research institutes Figure 4.3.[22]

The impact of the initiatives by the government for increased co-operation of the universities with the industry grew rapidly from 1983, when the system of joint research was created by the Monbusho to provide encouragement in this regard (figure 4.4).[23]

22. *Ibid.*, p. 11.
23. *Source:* page 49, MONBUSHO.

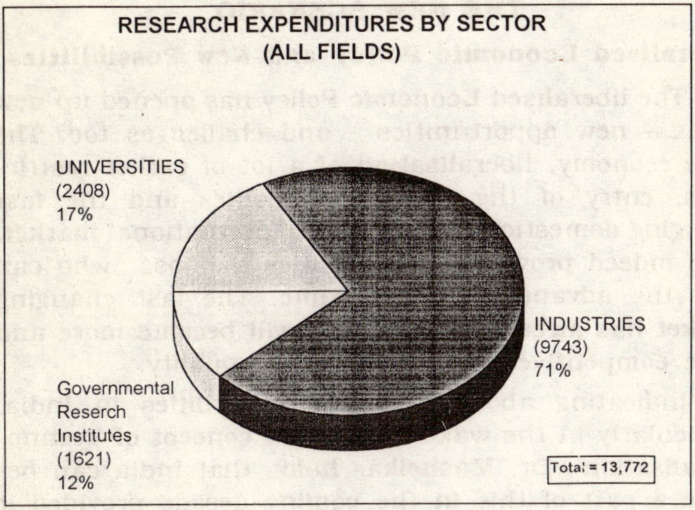

Figure - 4.3 [22]

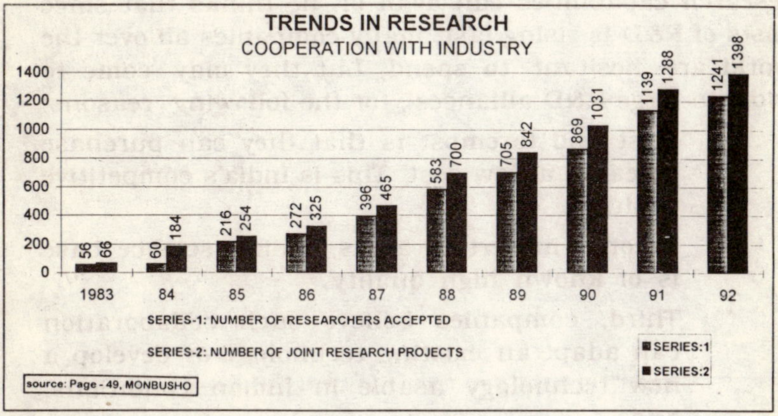

Figure - 4.4 [23]

Series 1 : Number of Researchers Accepted

Series 2 : Number of Joint Research Projects

Source : page-49, Monbusho

THE NEW SCENARIO

Liberalised Economic Policy and New Possibilities

The liberalised Economic Policy has opened up new vistas - new opportunities - and challenges too. The open economy, liberalisation of a lot of earlier restrictions, entry of the foreign companies and the fast changing domestic market into an international market, have indeed provided opportunities to those who can take the advantage of the same. The fast changing market has already become and will become more and more competitive both in price and quality.

Indicating about the new possibilities in India, particularly in the wake of the new concept of 'techno-globalisation', Dr. Mashelkar holds that India can become a part of this in the coming decade provided it understands the forces that are driving the globalisation of R&D. Talking about the opportunities that the Indian research capabilities can avail of, he thinks that since costs of R&D is rising fast, many companies all over the world are 'hesitant' to spend, but they may 'come to India to forge R&D alliances', for the following reasons:

* First and foremost is that they can purchase research at low cost. This is India's competitive position,
* Second, in certain areas, India's science base is of known high quality,
* Third, companies believe such collaboration can adapt an existing technology or develop a new technology usable in Indian conditions, and
* Fourth, economic reforms have changed the environment in which R&D institutes and industrial firms operate.

In fact, some collaborative research efforts have already started, e.g. the Ranbaxy-Eli Lily tie up, and many known companies are moving their R&D centres in India. Dr. Mashelkar strongly believes that "India can capitalise on this movement. He also thinks that India can use several different ways to form industrial R&D alliances making research a business."

Ostensibly, Indian industry has perhaps now no option, if it has to survive and do well in the midst of competition but to collaborate with the institutions and exploit their huge-reservoir of expertise and infrastructure facilities, to innovate and upgrade their products and compete with the products of foreign companies in price and quality, particularly in the international market.

In chapter one, it has been discussed how the institutions are facing unprecedented resource crunch and they too have now no option but to generate income through various means one of which is through interaction with the industry, and meet the rising costs of running the institutions. While fees of students have been and are being revised, but there is a limit of that for it is already felt that in a background of almost no revision of fees in the last about 20-30 years, upward revision has become rather a wave in which poor parents feel drowned. Institutions have therefore, to look for other means of income which should be stable, productive, innovative and service oriented.

Excepting a few well-known institutions of the country and a small number of the university departments, there is little interaction with the industry. The real income generated by the institutions which are already having reasonable industry interaction is also not adequate to take care of the rising costs of running the institution. In fact, such income alone cannot meet the rising costs. Even these institutions (IITS and some other Institutions) have planned to strengthen the industry interaction activities. While that will generate more income, optimal utilisation of the costly equipment and other facilities would also be ensured in that process. For them, it is a question of giving a boost to the already on-line activities.

How far Industry Interaction by Multi-Faculty University Possible

An oft heard question is how the multi-faculty university-institutions which have mostly the departments of humanities, social sciences and traditional sciences can gainfully interact with industry. Really speaking, they have no definite, no positive idea about how to go about in this direction. It is also possible that most of them are not fully aware of their strengths for they have not done any systematic survey or documentation in this regard. There would always be a number of teachers in every institution who would be doing some research projects funded by the government agencies. But they may not have explored the possibilities of interaction with the industry.

A large number of university-institutions have good physical facilities. How much of that are optimally utilised is now no secret. If interaction with industry picks up, the university-institutions will be able to generate income which now has to be a priority activity for them. That would also ensure optimal utilisation of the strengths that they have in their faculty, post-graduate students, and physical possibilities. The possibilities are enormous; it is a question of exploring and exploiting them and for that, the university-institutions have to go to the market to generate income.

HOW TO GO TO MARKET TO GENERATE INCOME

Essentials for Industry Interaction

Basic to all efforts in this process is a positive will on the part of the university-institution and the faculty, that besides their traditional function of teaching and research, they intend to interact with industry to solve industrial problems and other associated matters.

Every university-institution has certain strengths which however, vary from institution to institution. To move to the direction of initiating interaction with the industry and to sustain the same, there are certain essentials as given in Table 4.14 and Fig. 4.5.

Table 4.14
Essentials to Initiate and Sustain Interaction with Industry

Sequence	*Essentials*
One	To identify and develop out of the existing human resources and physical facilities for possible interaction with industry.
Two	To prepare a Document of capabilities containing all relevant information that a prospective client would look forward, e.g. expertise and facilities available in the institution.
Three	To frame Rules providing incentives to the faculty for consultancy work which should be unambiguously clear and simple, easy to follow and implement.
	To identify an authority for Consultancy Activities to work as interface between the institute-faculty and the industry as also

other external agencies.

Four — Once the Document is ready, the interface authority should survey the market with reference to the capabilities both local and national and decide priority steps for initiating interaction.

Five — Priority steps should decide strategies to market the capabilities.

Six — To build credibility of interaction and sustain the same through - quality, cost-effectiveness, confidentiality, readiness to accept penalty (in the event of failures on certain counts) and time frame to deliver goods

How to go to Market to Generate Income

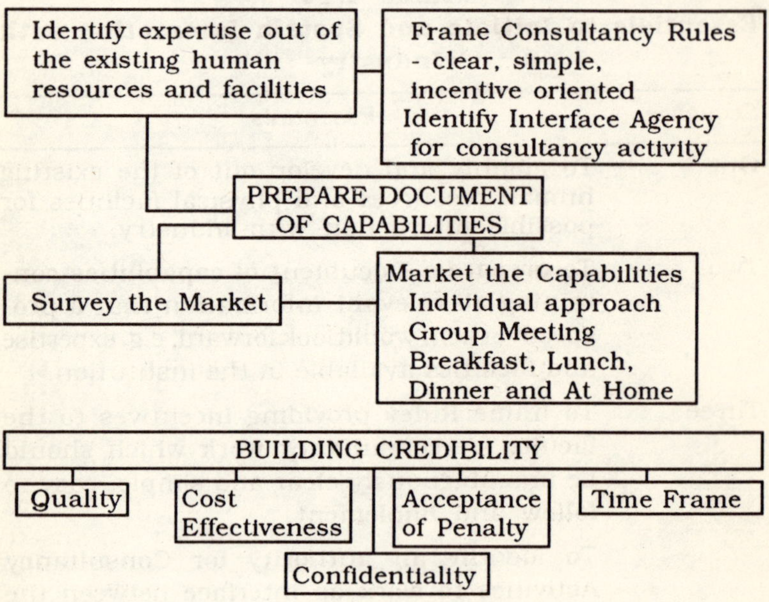

Fig. 4.5.

Development of Expertise

The first thing first. Basic to all efforts to move to the direction of interaction, is to identify experts for that purpose. Primarily, it is for the expertise that the industry would be interested for interaction. In view of this, the first requirement is to identify the faculty members in the various departments who have the potential to be consultants. While the faculty themselves are the best persons to specify their areas of expertise, broadly, consultancy could be for:

* product, process design/development,
* problem-solving in the specific areas of specialisation
* Retainership i.e. advising on a continuing basis,
* Testing and Evaluation, and
* Other areas.

It is important that each department/faculty also identifies the physical facilities that exist for consultancy work. Of course, for a specific work, some of the equipment and materials/consumable have to be procured through the consultancy project funds.

This information is needed to be provided in the Document of Capabilities which the industry should be able to use as the access instrument to the university system for the purpose of interaction. For some universities, strengths of the departments may need collaboration with colleges. In view of this, it is for the leadership to decide, keeping in view the strengths of the university departments alone, whether the strengths of the constituent and affiliated colleges be also included by involving them for interaction with the industry. However, there cannot be any hard and fast guideline for this as the position will be different in different universities, more particularly the local culture which is important.

Documentation of R&D Capabilities

Once the university has identified the expertise and the facilities for interaction with industry, it should prepare a document giving details of the expertise, e.g. names of the faculty their specialisation, major and significant work done and are being done by them, infrastructure facilities available for meaningful interaction with the industry, etc. Since the purpose of the document is to market the capabilities to the industry, if should be attractive and useful. It should reflect both the capabilities as well as interest of the university for effective and meaningful interaction with the industry.

Through the document, the university should also assure the industry of a smooth, time-bound and result-oriented approach for interaction. Information about the interface authority should also be given for initiating interaction. Precisely, it should look like a business document of the university and that it means business.

A note of precaution is necessary here. While the document will be to market the capabilities, it should be ensured beforehand that all that are assured in that will realy be available. For example, if a smooth and efficient interaction is assured, the industry should not find that procedural delays, indecisiveness, unresponsiveness are coming in the way. This is necessary to build confidence and credibility for a lasting partnership.

Framing Consultancy Rules

In the fast changing scenario, devoting time by the faculty from their primary duties of teaching and training for consultancy work of the industry cannot be called secondary although it is true that teaching-training is the basic function. It may be more appropriate to call participation in industry interaction as complimentary for through problem-solving, advising, product and process designing and developing, the faculty develops new knowledge and enhance expertise which would have positive impact on his basic function of teaching.

For the purpose of framing Rules for Consultancy Activities, the aspects as are mentioned in Table 4.15 should be included, besides any other aspect that the individual institution finds necessary:

Table 4.15

Aspects to be Covered while Framing Consultancy Rules

---

* Categories of Consultancy activities, e.g. Retainership, Design/Development, Problem-Solving, Testing and Evaluation etc.
* What should be the economics of the Consultancy Work in relation to use of infrastructural facilities, hiring of person for work, payments to be made and time, etc.
* Value of time of the Experts (i.e. Faculty), how should the cost be decided.
* Time that a faculty can devote for consultancy work;
* What responsibilities should not be taken in the work. Legal aspect — so as to avoid any responsibilities of the work by the faculty/ institution, e.g. to indemnify, etc.
* Financial benefits, i.e. annual limits, if any, for

income share of fees between individual and organisation, proportion, etc.

* How would accounting be done to protect the interests of the faculty and institution and at the same time conforming to Government Rules and Regulations.
* Some norms to be strictly followed particularly about time-frame and responsibility of completing the work.
* Confidentiality/secrecy, etc.

Interface Authority

Much of the leadership has to flow from the interface authority for he/she has to act as the first contact point both for a faculty willing to participate in the industry interaction, as also to the industry looking for interaction with the institution. It is crucially important to decide what attributes the person should have for this challenging work and by what names he/she should be called.

Ordinarily, the authority charged with the responsibilities that are being talked about, is called, in the Indian Institutes of Technology as Dean of Research and Development or Consultancy, or Industrial Research and Development. In some institutions, a Professor is charged with the responsibility for industry interaction. By whatever name called, currently in all institutions, the authority is a part-timer discharging the responsibilities which are so time consuming, onerous, arduous and challenging. It is a difficult job to interact and motivate the faculty for undertaking consultancy work and completing them in time. Nor is it easy to make sure that all rules and regulations are followed and accounts are correctly maintained to avoid consequential problems of audit. On the other side, talking to a variety of people from the industry who essentially are from different culture, and reaching acceptable terms to protect the best interests of the institution is equally demanding. Other important areas of her/his functions to ensure protection from all legal complications in the matters of intellectual property rights, patents, etc.

In the context of the need to act efficiently and aggressively so as to deliver the goods, concept of the University Company has been discussed in the next chapter. Wherever necessary and possible, Consortium of Colleges has also been discussed.

Surveying the Market and Marketing Capabilities

Once the University has identified its expertise and facilities, prepared the document of capabilities, appointed the Interface Authority, each department or a representative group of a number of departments, which could be clustered, should survey the market to sell the capabilities. For example, the Department of Management Studies with the Department of Economics and the Department of Psychology can together form a group and find out which are the organisations who could be their possible clients for interaction. In the case of a medium-size business house with their factories, consultancy activities in the areas of management, industrial psychology, economic studies and economic forecasting can be undertaken.

What is important at this stage is to identify possible clients with some basic data to find out which are the potential areas in an organisation where these departments can offer something. Such survey of markets can be local and regional to begin with, and later at national level, as experience and capabilities may command. Gradually, a data base should be created.

Confederation of Indian Industry (CII), Chamber of Commerce, Indian Chemical Manufacturers' Association (ICMA), etc. may be contacted for a list of companies in India.

Once the survey reports are available, the interface authority may then draw up a plan, in consultation with the Vice-Chancellor/Head of the institution, and invite the Managing Director or the General Manager for discussions. As a good strategy, it will be better if the invitation is for tea or at home, lunch or dinner This has to be decided keeping in view who is being invited and what is the potential of interaction in terms of magnitude. Two-three faculty members who are experts of the area of interest may also be invited for discussion.

Once the first discussion is found encouraging, further discussion may be held between the faculty members and the relevant industry group. However, the interface authority may have to monitor this till the matter reaches a stable position to take off. This may be necessary till the culture is fully imbedded into the system.

Building Credibility

Sustaining the interaction with the industry is at least as important as the beginning itself for the objective of making a beginning is never to have it as a one-time affair, but on a continuing basis. How to sustain the relationship is the question. In order to sustain it, the prerequisite is to build credibility of the university through interaction. Broadly, credibility depends on certain conditions being fulfilled as given in Table 4.16.

In the course of the meeting of the Vice-Chancellor/Head of the institution with the Managing Director or General Manager, it should appropriately be brought into the discussions about the various benefits of Industry from the interaction. Broadly, they are:

* Training of Technical Manpower,
* Solving Industry problems with University Expertise,
* University as a possible source of Information on Technological developments, latest trends in Research, etc., and library facilities.
* Utilising Research capabilities of University in implementation of short-term and long-term collaborative research programmes.

Table 4.16

Building and Sustaining Credibility of the University-Institutions for Industry

Conditions	*Reasons*
Quality	Here, quality means, the desired outputs of the research project. For obvious reasons, industry which funds the project would expect quality. It need hardly be justified that quality is the crucial aspect of the interaction.
Cost Effectiveness	For product, process, design/development, the industry would expect that cost effectiveness is kept in view so that they are able to compete in the national and international market. The element of cost-effectiveness is, there-

	fore, very important from the point of view of industry.
Confidentiality	Not infrequently, industry thinks that the academics do not attach much importance to the requirement of confidentiality of the work assigned to them. This is very important to the industry for if confidentiality is not maintained, that may ultimately affect and at times seriously, the prospect of marketing the product. Rightly therefore, industry would insist the academics to maintain confidentiality.
Time-Frame	If there is any one particular point over which industry feels disappointed and at times jittery, that is the time-frame to deliver the results of the consultancy work. This is the most common complaint. It is true that the academics have first to discharge their basic duties of teaching and some other organisational work and then complete the consultancy for which the time allowed is not always adequate. Yet, since time is the essence of business, time-frame has necessarily to be honoured and strictly adhered to.
Acceptance of Penalty	At times, industry think that when it pays for the services sometime at almost 'on demand' price, why should not the academics agree to a penalty clause in the event of failures. This is debatable. However, it will not be too long when this may be insisted by the industry.

Some Problems of Interaction

It is better to be aware that there are some problems of interaction with the industry. Efforts to overcome them can certainly improve the position. The problems that are known to be are:

* Faculty-industry isolation,
* Lack of awareness of capabilities and expertise of the faculty,
* Lack of awareness of problems and needs of Industry,
* Faculty options between sponsored research and consultancy for career advancement,
* Lack of faculty motivation due to operational constraints and inadequate financial incentives, and
* Industry reservations because of issues of secrecy, requirement of rigid time schedule, etc.

New Trends in University-Industry Interaction

For an effective, meaningful and lasting bond of interaction with the industry, certain steps are necessary. While there cannot be any exhaustive or final list for this purpose, the following are considered useful:

A. Strengthening Industry Involvement in Academic Programmes:

* Involvement of Industry Experts in academic Programmes,
* Greater support to cooperate Academic Programmes, and
* Liberal sponsorship of Projects at Masters and Ph.D. levels.

B. Providing Incentives for Faculty-Industry expert Exchange.

C. New Initiatives for continuing and Lasting Bond:

* Challenging Conusultancy Projects,
* Involving University/Faculty in Technology Sourcing, Selection, Absorption, Technology Development, Transfer and Forecasting, and
* Strong Industry Involvement in Planning and conduct of Academic and Continuing Education Programmes.

D. Industry Participation with University and Government Funding Agencies in Sponsored research in Emerging and Need-based Areas.

Industry Interaction with Multi-faculty Universities

Earlier, it has been mentioned about an oft raised question that how would a multi-faculty university be able to generate income through interaction with industry. It has also been discussed that every university has some strengths and therefore what is necessary is the positive will and a plan to exploit the strengths for interaction.

It may be interesting to examine what kind of interaction is possible in the case of a University which has the following strengths and clients within its given jurisdiction.

Strengths	*Possible clients*
Economics	* Steel Plant
Management	* Re-rolling Mills
Psychology	* Cement Factories
Physics	* Medium size Factories
Chemistry	* Medium size Workshops
Painting	* Municipal Corporations
Computer Science and Engineering	* Business Houses
Environmental Science and Engineering	* Institutions of various types and sizes
Metallurgy	* Life Insurance Corporation
Civil Engineering	
Mechanical Engineering	* Financial Institutions
Electrical Engineering	* Small Businesses

It may now be examined, what are the possibilities of interaction by each of the above departments for-generation of income. Really speaking, the possibilities are many. It is a question of initiative and drive. The possibilities for each department are mentioned, one after another in the order mentioned above.

POSSIBLE INTERACTION WITH INDUSTRY

ECONOMICS

AREAS OF INTERACTION

Studying and Analysing various economic aspects

eg.- Investment Vs. Returns
- Taxation - Income tax
  - Sales tax

-Excise Duty-Rule Application

-Feasibility Study

-Export-Import Rule application for better management and profit

CLIENTS

* Small to Medium level Factories
* Business Houses

MANAGEMENT

AREAS OF INTERACTION

* Advising to improve efficiency, to be cost-effective
* Studying and Advising on structure, Organisation and Staffing
* Staff Training and Appraisal etc.
* Management Audit
* Tools to reduce cost at various level
* Human Resource Development
* Business and Technology Management

CLIENTS

* Medium level-Factories
* Business Houses
* Institutions

PSYCHOLOGY

AREAS OF INTERACTION

* Industrial Psychology–Advising the Management **Interpersonal Dynamics**
* Counselling for
  - students
  - employees
  - before and after selection
* Organising short-term courses for employees for productivity

CLIENTS

* Factories
* Institutions
* LIC
* Banks
* Offices of other organisations

PHYSICS

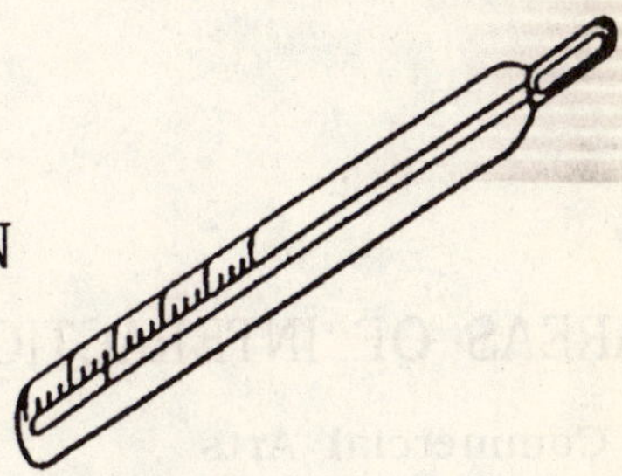

AREAS OF INTERACTION

* Development and Calibration of Instrument
* Training Teachers and Technicians in organisations/ factories for maintenance of equipment

CLIENTS

* Factories,
* Electronics
* Industry

CHEMISTRY

AREAS OF INTERACTION

Chemical and Metallurgical Environmental Problems

CLIENTS

Chemical and Metallurgical Industries

PAINTING (VISUAL ARTS)

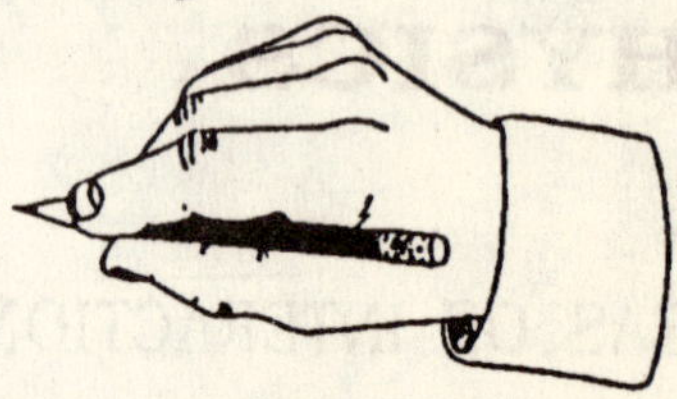

AREAS OF INTERACTION

* Commercial Arts Advertisement Posters, etc.

* Advising on Aesthetics and executing jobs for better environments and productivity

CLIENTS

* Business Houses
* Civic Bodies
* Factories

COMPUTER SCIENCE AND ENGINEERING

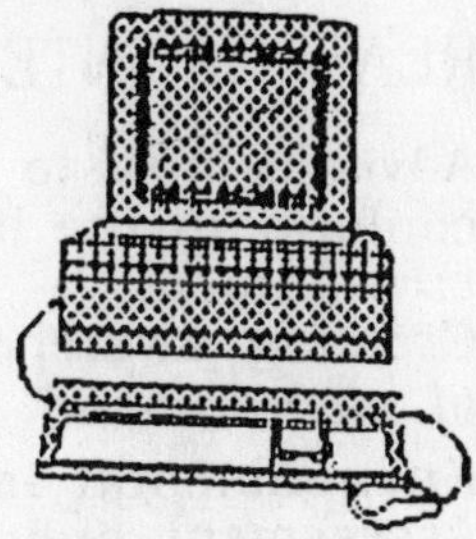

AREAS OF INTERACTION

* Software Development for Information Systems, Realtime Control etc.
* Computing Work/Facilities for Industries
* Development of Hardware & Software Tools for special applications
* Short-term Courses for:
  - Industry people
  - Bank personnel
  - Local people
  - Institutions
* Providing servicing facilities/contract for others

CLIENTS

* Factories
* Offices
* Banks
* Business Houses

ENVIRONMENTAL SCIENCE & ENGINEERING

AREAS OF INTERACTION

* Advising how to conform to the laws of environment
* Creating awareness of environment
* Environmental Impact Assessment and Environmental Audit
* Actual Implementation and monitoring of Govt. Regulations
* Testing Facilities

CLIENTS

* Factories before and after establishment
* Civic Authority

METALLURGY

AREAS OF INTERACTION

* Powder Metallurgy
* Melting and Casting
* Metal Refining and Alloying
* Welding and joining of Metals
* Heat Treatment
* Surface Engineering (Emerging Area)
* Metallic implant in Human Body
* Ferrites
* Energy Audit

CLIENTS

* Steel Plants
* Steel Plants
* Re-rolling Mills
* Big Workshops
* Heat Treatment Shops and Foundry

CIVIL ENGINEERING

AREAS OF INTERACTION

* Testing Facilities
* computer based structural design work, soil structure related problems
* Water resources development
* Hazard mitigation studies
* Construction related irrigation problems
* Rehabilitation and strengthening of structures
* Exploiting concrete Lab. facilities

CLIENTS

* Builders
* Housing Boards
* Cement Factories
* PWD-CPWD and Irrigation Depts.

MECHANICAL ENGINEERING

AREAS OF INTERACTION

* Production Planning
* Integrated manufacturing
* CNC Machines
* Quality Assurance and ISO 9000
* Specialised training programmes for Managers and Technical Staff

CLIENTS

* Factories
* Fabrication shops

ELECTRICAL ENGINEERING

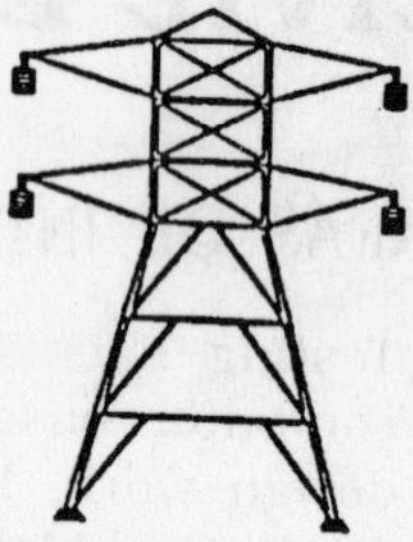

AREAS OF INTERACTION

* Power Generation & Distribution
* Planning and Operations of distribution grids
* Microprocessor Applications

CLIENTS

* State Electricity Boards
* Power Generation Units
* Electronics and Computers

ACTION PLAN TIME-FRAME

Undeniably, there is enormous scope for university-institution to generate income through interaction with the industry. It is really the question of will and a determination to make a beginning and sustain it. Making a beginning is very important.

In order to make a beginning, the University should move in a structured way. And for this, it is necessary to draw up a plan of action. The following time-frame Action Plan is suggested:

ACTION PLAN TIME FRAME MONTHS

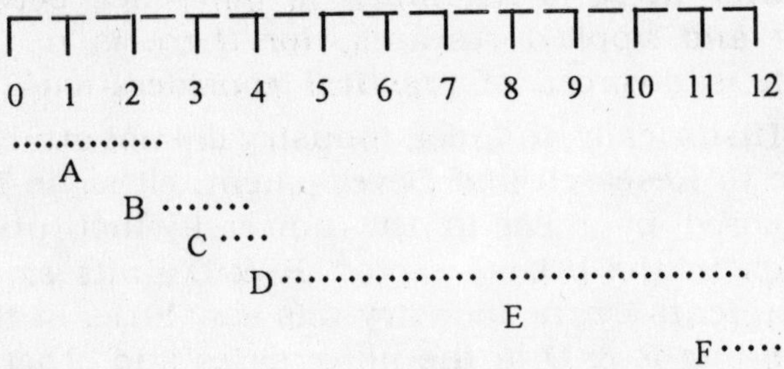

A. * Identification of Experts and Facilities in the University and Documentation thereof as a printed material.

   * Frame Consultancy Rules, if not already done.

B. Field Survey of Industries and other Organisations to identify as potential clients, by Experts.

C. First Invitation to the potential clients for establishing linkages.

D. Exchange of visits between University and Industry and framing of proposals.

E. Period to sort out teething problems including Review of actions taken.

F. Adjustment period for unforeseen reasons.

CONCLUSION

Fundamentally, all universities and other institutions of higher learning for whom teaching is the primary responsibility, also conduct some research - fundamental (basic) or applied or both - the magnitude of which may vary from institution to institution. Reasons for variations are primarily due to the priority, availability of researchers, suitable facilities and ultimately funds required for research. Many experts now feel that there is not much of difference between the basic and applied research, for there is no research which is divorced of practical considerations.,

Historically, in India, industry did not attach importance to Research and Development, either in-house or sponsored by them in the university-institutions. Although in the private sector, R & D units existed but investments by the industry was very little. In the name of funding R & D in the universities and other institutions of higher learning, it has been negligible. It is only a handful of universities and that too some departments of those universities and other Institutions like IITs and IISc that have industry sponsored research activities. Among the university. University of Roorkee, the Department of Chemical Technology, University of Bombay and the Anna Universities, are notable. Regional Colleges of Engineering and some other good colleges also have some interaction. However, in the real sense of R & D, the activity is very little. A considerable part of interaction in many institutions is for testing and evaluation.

In the context of the liberalized economy, there is no option for the private sector, but to be innovative and competitive and for that a partnership with the academics is a *sine-qua-non*. In 1992-93, R & D expenditure of the private sector was only 15%, the central government expenditure both by the various departments and the public sectors together was as high as 75.7%, the remaining 9.3% was in the state government sectors. As against this, the private sector in Japan spent 71% of the total national R & D expenditures.

Realizing that the R & D capabilities cannot be raised overnight, as rightly pointed out by Dr. Mashelkar, India should encash the current trend to forge R & D alliances with the multi-nationals, who are keen to come to India for collaborative R & D for the low-cost research in India, particularly because they are not willing to invest heavily at this stage in R & D activities.

However, Indian industry have also to build its own in-house R & D capabilities and in that direction also partnership with academics is a necessity. Academics have also not demonstrated their willingness and capabilities to the industry for smooth interaction. This, they have now to do in a structured and sustained manner to generate income much needed in the context of the resource crunch. The universities have to organise themselves to move in this direction and do all that are necessary to initiate and sustain interaction with the industry, as shown in Table 4.14. Figure 4.5 gives an over-view of what need to be done to move in the direction of university-industry interaction and how to build credibility so that interaction becomes sustainable. Table 4.16 spells out the various implications of the Figure 4.5.

It is only the individual university which is in the best position to find out what are its strengths and who could be its clients for interaction to generate income. However with a view to providing some recipes based on the likely strengths of a multi-faculty university and the possible clients within its jurisdiction, efforts have been made to indicate how interaction can be initiated and sustained and what are the requirements on both sides.

However, it has to be admitted that there is no short-cut to anything. It is only after moving to the right direction and passing through the processes that the desired results will be available. The suggested Action Plan should prove handy to the universities and all other institutions willing to go in for generation of income through interaction with the industry. By no means, the suggestions are complete or just the ones to fit all alike.

5

Interface Factor for Interaction with Industry

EXISTING MODEL

In the preceding chapter, importance of the interface factor has been emphasised, for it is indeed this factor which would play crucial role in the entire game of interaction with industry. The interface authority has to remain in constant touch with the faculty on one hand and the industry on the other hand. It calls for quality leadership with the requisite industry leaning, preferably with industry background.

Earlier in the preceding chapter, it has been discussed that only a few institutions are significantly involved in the industry-interaction activities and that in some other institutions interaction is mainly limited to testing and evaluation leaving a large number which have no industry interaction.

Traditionally, the interface authority in the IITs, IISc and the universities is called by different names. In IITs, it is generally called Dean, in the Indian Institute of Science (IISc), it is called 'Chairman, Centre for Scientific and Industrial Research'. In the University of Roorkee, it is called 'Dean, Research and Industrial Liaison'. However, the Department of Chemical Technology, University of Bombay, the Director himself looks after the consultancy activities. In the Anna University, it is again the 'Dean (Sponsored Research)'. Although the term sponsored research generally means the research projects sponsored by the government agencies, in the Anna University, this term includes consultancy activities as well. In all the universities in Maharahshtra, the Professor who looks after the consultancy activities is called 'Co-ordinator, University-Industry Interaction Cell'.

In other places, generally, the interface authority is called the Professor-in-Charge. In the Regional Engineering Colleges, it is the Principal himself who acts as interface authority. For obvious reasons, it is only when interaction is of sufficient magnitude that an independent authority is necessary.

In all the above institutions by whatever name it is called, the fact is that the interface authority is a part-time faculty. However, in the institutions where the activities are sizable, after sometime by default, the functions of the interface authority may precede over his teaching work, due to the pressure of work relating to consultancy activities.

In the emerging situation when the university has to generate more income, the universities will be required as time goes by, to undertake some commercial activities which they are not permitted to do so, as a non-profit making educational institution for they enjoy certain privileges granted by the Income Tax Authority which are subject to certain conditions.

Currently, the interface authority, irrespective of any name that he may be called by, is required to perform multifarious functions, some of which are listed as follows:

A. General

(i) Interacting with and motivating the faculty for undertaking consultancy work. In the process, at least in the cases of new faculty members, he has to suggest ways and means as to how to go about. It is time consuming, involve patience and understanding of the temperament of the faculty members that he interacts, with a definite purpose.

(ii) Updating the data of the experts and facilities for industry interaction and make sure that all relevant information is there for when industry would contact the interface authority, he should be able to discuss with full data in his command.

(iii) Answering various queries by the different industry even when some may not mean or lead to any interaction.

(iv) Guiding and helping the faculty members to prepare proposals to conform to the policies and rules of the university.

(v) Generally checking and forwarding the Consultancy proposals and subsequent queries and answers for them.

(vi) Administrative work for the staff that may work for him and ensure that services that they are expected to render are really given to make matters smooth and faculty members happy.

(vii) Attending to all legal and procedural work relating to intellectual property rights, patenting, and other work incidental to the consultancy activities which too are innumerous.

B. Fund Management

In addition to the work mentioned above, the work of fund management is a major responsibility for the Dean/Professor-in-Charge. Besides various implications, it also involves a good deal of knowledge in the matter of admissibility of expenditures which have to conform to the rules for audit purposes and these he has to be quite knowledgeable of. An alert mind is an asset to ensure timely receipt and recovery of funds from various organizations which by itself is an uphill task. Following are some of the important work involved in the funds management:

(i) Receipt of funds and examining the immediate, and time-to-time needs and plan for investment of idle funds in short-time deposits of various duration. An alert interface authority can earn good amount of interest, if planned well.

(ii) Monitoring the expenditures of all the consultancy work, ensuring correctness in them and in the accounting procedures and requirements so that subsequent problems are avoided.

(iii) Providing relevant data about funds to the higher authorities for various purposes including analysis as may be necessary from time to time.

NEEDS OF CHANGING TIME

It is time that the profile of the interface authority in the changing situation is drawn up, with due vision and care. The reality is that it is not practical that a faculty who has the basic responsibility of teaching would, in addition to that, be able to devote his full attention as interface authority particularly when greater attention and more time would now be necessary to achieve the objectives. Some faculty members, even if asked to devote full-time as the interface authority may not like to suspend his teaching and his own research work which is his real constituency, for he may think that over a period of 2-3 years, he may be out of circulation in his discipline and that he would not like to happen.

Meaningful, vibrating and sustained consultancy activities mean that the interface authority has the time and tools to identify and build a group of faculty to interact with the industry. In order to do this, he has to spend a good deal of time with the faculty and motivate them assuring all assistance needed for interaction purpose. Since industry will interact only when it finds potential in the faculty, quite a few attributes are prerequisites - one: that the faculty is able to *prima-facie* impress the industry about the deliverable, two: that there are reasonable infrastructure facilities in the university to carry out the consultancy work, three: that the various conditions of cost-effectiveness, time-frame, confidentiality, - acceptance of penalty etc. are at least reasonably assured.

For obvious reasons, the interface authority is the first contact point for consultancy activities. In the case of the faculty members who are already in the game and are known in the market, the contact may be direct. In all other cases, the first contact point will be the interface authority. In the process of involving more and more faculty, new faculty members would come in the picture and for them, it is necessary to provide guidance, which many a time, have to be in detail. This would demand more and more time. They would have many questions and all of them need be answered to their satisfaction.

Turning to the more difficult job of marketing the expertise and facilities to the industry, it really means many things including importantly the following:

(i) knowledge of the industry of various types and size and interest both at local regional and national levels,

(ii) in order to market the capabilities and facilities, repeated approach and at times changing of marketing strategy would be necessary for all industry may not appreciate at once the benefits of interaction or the capabilities of the university. Repeated talking and meeting would be a necessity which a faculty would find it difficult and may, at times, seem irritating and absurd to them to do this. The truth is that unless this is done, it would be difficult to increase consultancy activities. A professional can do this tactfully with the necessary marketing strategy. This would be more and more necessary in the days to come. Moreover, more and more universities would in future bid for consultancy work when to compete and win, these would be necessary,

(iii) pragmatically, despite all efforts, all assurances and all sincere steps, getting the work done in time may still not be, in many cases easy. Nevertheless, industry will always press the interface authority for timely completion of the work. It becomes very uncomfortable for the faculty interface authority to face such situation again and again in such cases. It is only a professional who can face such a situation and yet continue unaffected for he knows that he is paid for that, and

(iv) in order to ensure that the job is completed in time, the interface authority has almost to chase the consultant-faculty at regular intervals, ask for progress reports and do the overall monitoring. This requires tremendous patience and tact which is not easy for a faculty interface authority. Only a professional can do this.

In the changing situation, for handling the legal work, ensuring that all government and other relevant rules are followed, much more time than what is needed today would be a must. Precisely, there will be increasing pressure on the interface authority both by the faculty on one hand, and the university and industry on the other hand. Both the sides would expect smoothness and delivery of the goods and that too in time. Faculty would not like any 'irritants'. They would like clear rules and regulations which are implementable. They would also like the payment procedures to be smooth, less of taxation problems and without undue rigidity. Industry would expect everything to happen fast right from answering queries, initial negotiation, proposal and finding the results. Coming to the university, it would also like results. For a faculty-interface authority to do all these would be practically difficult.

UNDERTAKING COMMERCIAL ACTIVITIES

With the economic liberalisation, there are now openings for commercial activities which the universities must encash. For example, software development for domestic and international markets, product development, process and design can be sold to the Industry. Many university departments can develop marketable products, but they cannot be sold by the university directly. At present, it is not possible for universities as it is not permissible to indulge in such activities.

An objective analysis of the present structure and organization as also the various arrangements of the interface authority *vis-a-vis* the fast changing needs, definitely point out to seek an alternative model., The real question is what that alternative model could be. At this stage, it would be interesting and worthwhile to look into what the universities in U.K. did to boost their consultancy activities under pressure to generate income almost in similar situations that they faced in 1981.

CONCEPT AND MODEL OF UNIVERSITY COMPANY OF UK[1]

Years back, many universities in UK had realized that the university was not a business oriented group and therefore to expect that they would perform commercially in that direction so as to deliver the goods was not practical. It was also realized that for boosting income, some commercial activities were unavoidable and therefore there was a need to create an interface body of the university which would function as an independent professional body for commercial activities and would market the university expertise and facilities to the industry and other organisations inside and outside UK. It would also help the faculty to win contracts and complete consultancy activities. (For group activity it is called contract research and when it is an individual activity it is called consultancy). The company would also keep constant pressure on the faculty for timely completion of work.

Historically, many of todays University Company were originally established as Commercial Bureau which,

1. D.K. Ghosh, Concept of University Company: UK Story- Possibilities in the Indian Context, University News, AIU, May 22, 1993, New Delhi.

as time passed by, grew into regular University Company, wholly owned by the University.

Consequent to the pressure on the universities in UK, following the traumatic cuts in grants by the government and the mandate to explore all possible avenues to increase non-government income, many universities of the United Kingdom have established University Company as the interface body between the university and industry to boost and sustain contract research and consultancy work. In a number of universities in UK today, University Company system is functioning with full success.

STRUCTURE OF UNIVERSITY COMPANY

Generally, the structure of the University Company is that there is a Board of Directors with the Vice-Chancellor as the Chairman. In addition, a few faculty members are drawn from the university system and some from the industry and financial institutions. The Board meets at fixed intervals for policy decisions.

In Salford, it is called the Salford University Business Services Ltd. It is the most successful university based company in UK with an annual turnover of over £ 11 million. It has even associated companies including one with the City Council of Salford. All told, the turnover is of £ 23 million per annum.

Much of the success of the University Company depends on the Managing Director or General Manager of the Company. An ideal incumbent is he who has strong industry background with good academic achievements. A combination of this with teaching or research experience in a university always helps for successful performance and delivering the goods.

OBJECTIVES OF THE UNIVERSITY COMPANY

Broadly, objectives of the University Company are as follows:

* To undertake commercial activities otherwise not possible by, University directly.
* To perform along commercial lines with an outsider inducted as Manager or Managing Director with strong industrial background.
* To free Faculty from various formalities and act as interface between University and Industry.
* To act as the first contact point for external enquiries and develop contacts between faculty and industry.
* To transfer the profits to the University which is a non-profit making body.

MODEL ORGANIZATION

The model organisation of the University Company in UK is generally as follows:

* Contacts Group,
* European Office,
* Business Development Section,
* Finance Section,
* Technology Transfer Section, and
* Support Structure:
  - Central Services
  - Finance Section

Contacts Group

The contact group performs very important areas

which are essential to present and future activities of contract research of the University. In particular:

* it aims at protecting and increasing academic and financial interest and maximize long-term academic and commercial benefits, and
* advices and offers direct support services in negotiating contract research and consultancy activities.

Another important area where this group operates is to introduce funding opportunities to areas of the university where potential has not been maximized and to promote cost-effective collaborative research and consultancy work.

European Office

The Universities all over Europe have opportunities for contract research. They are however required to win through bids and are therefore competitive, which requires the universities to have separate Office:

* to ensure that the university gains maximum advantage from European Community initiatives,
* to co-ordinate the University's European activities with special focus on collaborative research, and
* to assist academics at all stages of a Project from bid preparations contract negotiations to the total contract management.

Business Development Section

Basic to the various responsibilities of the University Company, Business Development Section is the most important section which aims at:

* Developing new contacts and sources of funding, particularly from industry through marketing of University Research Expertise and a Programme of Industrial visits to assess corporate research needs, and
* Planning dissemination of a range of research funding opportunities and other research programme information to increase contact bids and income.

Added to the above responsibilities which involve a large number of associated questions and solutions the Business Development Section also does the following:

Manages all personnel related work, university's performance related pay scheme and appraisal system. This includes reception, Central Secretarial support and other office services.

These may not appear to be significant, but in reality they are important for if these are taken care of well, the faculty is comfortable to do a lot for they are not required to face at times irritating situations of mundane matters.

Finance Section

The Finance Section has its own importance for after all it is for money that all the activities are undertaken. Unless the finance aspect is managed well and accounting is done properly and on time; consequential problems would lead to a number of unhappy situations. Another important work is tax management and getting the accounts audited by the statutory auditors.

In addition, the section also does the following

important jobs:

* Managing all legal affairs when inventions are to be exploited, designs, software and know-how and marketing of inventions to potential licences, and
* Negotiating licence terms and royalty levels with licencees and monitors the performance of the licencees.

Technology Transfer

This is yet another area where specialised knowledge and experience is needed. When the University Company handles the technology transfer, it does so with professional skill. Precisely, it aims at:

* protecting valuable ideas and from legal and copyright complications,
* managing exploitation of inventions, designs, software and know-how, including pattented material, intellectual property rights protection, and
* advising to explore the option for exploration.

Besides the various responsibilities of the University Company mentioned above, it also publishes monthly Newsletter and offering follow up advice and assistance to staff.

Coming to the question of the overall performance of the University Companies in UK, the achievements could be measured as follows:

* Income of Contract Research and Consultancy increased upto three times,
* Larger number of faculty involved - increased by a factor of three, and

* Visible credibility in Government, industry and society at large.

CONCEPT OF CONSORTIUM OF COLLEGES

Over 80% of the higher education enrolment is in the colleges affiliated to the universities. In terms of the number of colleges, it is more than 8000 having over... Teachers. However, a large number of the colleges are non-viable, having enrolment less than 400. In any case, the number of viable colleges is not small. Many of such colleges have quality teachers and good facilities. It is necessary to find out alternative to the concept of 'University Company' for although the concept of the University Company is basically meant for the University itself, it is quite open and possible to bring the colleges within the purview of the company functioning. However, in reality, it may not, for practical reasons of organisational limitations, cover the colleges and even if it does, colleges may sometime or other find themselves neglected.

Fundamentally, the concept of University Company is to ensure optimal utilisation of the expertise and facilities in all the institutions - be it a University or a College, for interaction with Industry and thereby while institutions will generate income, industry will benefit through the former's expertise and facilities.

POSSIBILITIES FOR COLLEGES

The recipes given in the chapter four can be explored by the colleges as well, including colleges for humanities, science and social sciences and art. It is a question of taking initiative and drive.

It is necessary that the colleges particularly the good ones and big ones including some Polytechnics should be organised first for the purpose of interaction with industry. It would be an advantage to involve Engineering Colleges in this effort. In some States, there is a large number of Engineering Colleges and Polytechnics. Among the various States, four have the largest number of colleges and polytechnics at different levels—postgraduate, degree and diploma, approved by the All-India Council for Technical Education (AICTE), as shown in the following Table 5.1.

Table 5.1

State	*Number of Colleges approved by AICTE*			
	Post-Graduate	*Under-Graduate*	*Diploma*	*Total*
1. Karnataka	26 (22.41)	97 (19.28)	263 (20.00)	386 (19.96)
2. Maharashtra	13 (11.21)	124 (24.65)	214 (16.27)	351 (18.15)
3. Tamil Nadu	12 (10.34)	79 (15.71}	150 (11.41)	241 (12.46)
4. Uttar Pradesh	10 (8.62)	25 (4.97)	133 (10.11)	168 (8.69)
	61 (52.58)	325 (64.61)	760 (57.79)	1146 (59.26)
Total Number in India	116	503	1315	1934

Source: Pages 177-78, ISTE Handbook - 1995-96.
Percentages in parenthesis is in relation to the total in the country.

It is clear from the above table that out of 1934 Engineering Colleges and Polytechnics all over the country:

Karnataka has	19.96%
Maharashtra has	18.15%
Tamil Nadu has	12.46%, and
Uttar Pradesh has	8.69%

While a large number of the institutions are poorly funded and ill-equipped, many of them have very good staff and facilities. And there is no denying the fact that these facilities are not optimally utilised particularly in terms of marketing them to the industry. However, as we know some of these institutions already have some interaction with industry, but that again is not upto the optimal level. Many of these institutions carry out testing activities which though is a source of income, does not contribute to any innovative activity.

Besides the Engineering Colleges and Polytechnics, there are a number of colleges all over the country for Science, Commerce and Humanities which have quality teachers and good facilities for interaction with the Industry, business houses, Municipal Corporations, financial institutions, etc. For them too, the recipes given in the chapter four may apply. To repeat what has been said before, is that it is a question of will, plan and drive.

CONSORTIUM OF COLLEGES AS ALTERNATIVE TO UNIVERSITY COMPANY

With the background that has been provided and the fact that a large number of engineering colleges, polytechnics and colleges of science, commerce and humanities, have a large number of experts and good facilities to interact with the industry effectively and meaningfully for generation of income, there is a need to create a structure which should be able to:

* continuously interact with the industry around and receive feed back from them about the performance of the students which the institutions should analyse for corrections. This particularly applies to engineering colleges and polytechnics and colleges for science and commerce also;
* devise a mechanism through which needs of the industry, business houses, financial institutions, as also their futuristic suggestions are seriously examined and considered to update the curriculum. (This can well be done by involving industry representatives on the relevant committees and getting them to lecture from time to time to the students, and at seminars, with the teachers); and
* aggresively interact with the industry for marketing the expertise and facilities of the institutions which, on one hand, would generate income both of the teachers and the institutions, and on the other hand, industry will be benefitted of the innovative ideas and facilities of the institutions for better productivity.

For abvious reasons, the structure of the University Company cannot be adopted even with minor adjustment for any individual college, howsoever big that may be. However, to serve the purposes of the University Company, the concept of a Consortium of Colleges seems possible. A number of Colleges, say 15-20, may come together, which have good staff and facilities and have definite mission to interact with industry, and form a Consortium which may be housed in one of the buildings of members of the Consortium. A possible model could be as given in Table 5.2 and Figure 5.1.

Table 5.2
Possible Model of Consortium of Colleges

Title: (Name of place) Consortium of Colleges

	Constitution
President (One)	One of the Principals or Chairman/President of one of Trusts/societies of these colleges as may be decided, may be elected as the President.
Vice-Presidents (Two)	Two Principals of Colleges elected/selected by rotation.
Members (Six)	Two Teachers by rotation from colleges, Three Industry Representatives, One Nominee of the President.
Secretary	A whole-time Manager with industry background having some academic work/interest.

The Secretary will be a whole-time paid Officer of the Consortium, appointed on contract for result-oriented activities.

POSSIBILITIES IN THE INDIAN CONTEXT

With the passage of time and the pressure of the resource crunch, the Universities of UK which generally were rather conservative (in the sense of accepting business oriented approach), accepted and developed the concept of University Company and found it in reality a boon to boost the income generation.

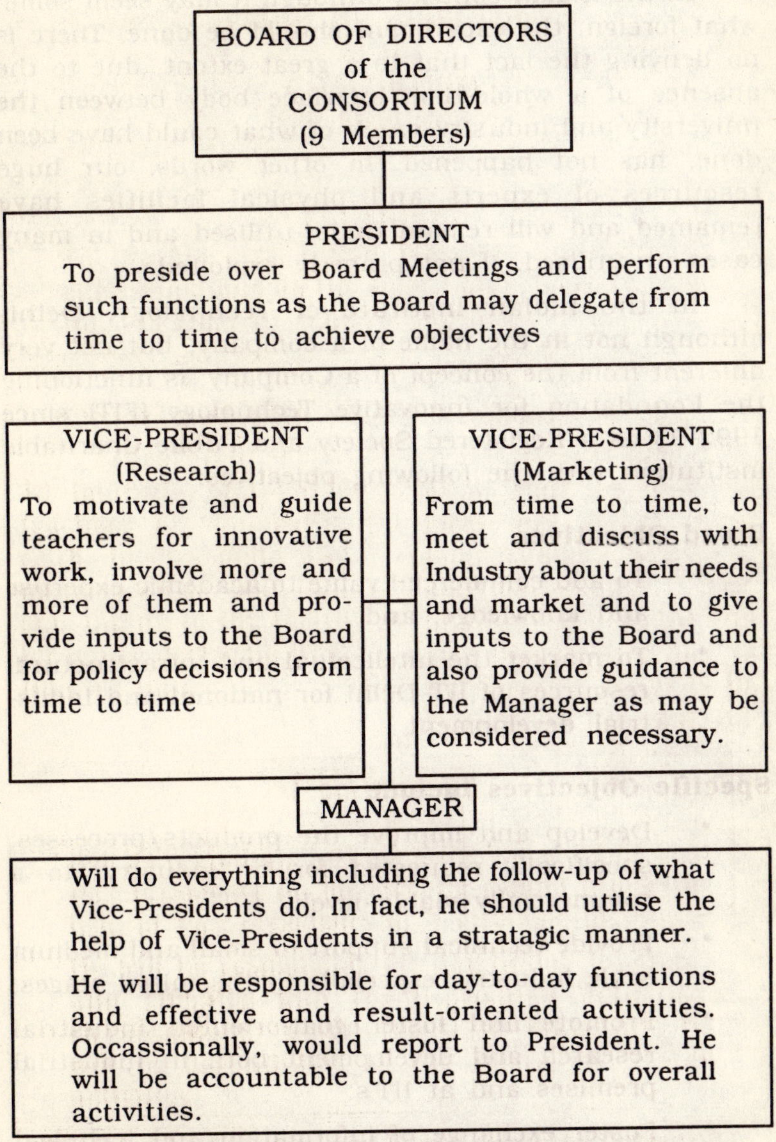

Fig. 5.1. The Structure and Functions of the Consortium

In the Indian context, although it may seem somewhat foreign, the experiment should be done. There is no denying the fact that to a great extent, due to the absence of a whole-time interface body between the university and industry much of what could have been done, has not happened. In other words, our huge resources of experts and physical facilities have remained and will remain under-utilised and in many cases un-utilised, if not properly exploited.

In the Indian Institute of Technology, Delhi, although not in the name of a company, but not very different from the concept of a Company, is functioning the Foundation for Innovative Technology (FIT) since 1992-93 as a Registered Society and Public Charitable institution with the following objectives:

Broad Objectives

* To add commercial value to academic expertise and knowledge; and
* To market the intellectual and infrastructural resources of IIT Delhi for national and industrial development.

Specific Objectives include

* Develop and improve the products/processes, specifically requested for by industry, to a commercially viable level;
* Provide technical support to small and medium scale industry, especially in the initial stages;
* Promote and foster goal-oriented industrial research and development both in industrial premises and at IIT's;
* Foster exchange of information and technical

experts between IIT's and Industry, to work in generic areas of interest; and

* Extend the infrastructure and expertise at IIT's for advanced/refresher training of the personnel from industry and/or entrepreneurs.

It is necessary to clarify that the idea of the University Company or the Consortium of Colleges is not to do away with the existing position of Dean or Chairman or Co-ordinator or Professor-in-Charge for Consultancy activities. What is intended is that the current positions should remain but be generally limited to provide academic direction to the faculty and the policy of the university with regard to the consultancy activities and motivate them to achieve the objectives.

CONCLUSION

Undeniably, in a fast changing situation when the universities and colleges will be required to generate income through consultancy activities, the existing model cannot achieve the objectives, particularly the part-time arrangement of looking after the work by a faculty.

For vibrating consultancy activities, the interface authority has necessarily to be aggressive and for that, there appears to be no option but to hire a professional who would be the Managing Director of the Company or the Manager of the Consortium concept.

However, a senior Professor should continue to be there to provide guidance and policy directions in the matter of consultancy work.

For a variety of reasons, the present interface arrangements for the purpose of industry-interaction to achieve all that are desired through interaction cannot, to be practical, be achieved. First, the current part-time of a Dean or Professor-in-Charge arrangement will do justice to none - neither to the faculty member who is charged with the responsibilities nor to the institution to deliver the goods. Second, the back-up support to the Dean is not geared to handle the matters when the Dean is a part-timer. Third, the Dean being basically an academic is hardly expected to be knowledgeable in legal and many governmental rules and regulations. Fourth, in the new situation, the interface authority would be required to be more mobile, free from the normal hesitation to approach, negotiate, re-negotiate, aggressively market the capabilities and be business-like, and Fifth, the current structure does not permit commercial activities which would be necessary in the new situation.

In order to meet all the needs of tomorrow, it would be beneficial to the university to have University Company, along the lines of the universities in the United Kingdom and the Consortium of Colleges for viable colleges.

6

Conclusions

RESOURCE CRUNCH - A GLOBAL PHENOMENON

Consequences of the Second World War had made new impact in the socio-economic scenario all over the world. Education, particularly higher education in science and technology, was recognized as the most important factor both for economic prosperity through industrial development as also for superiority of powers over others. The process of development started from thereafter. In the higher education sector, the 'development' resulted in expansion to meet demands of the growing population from 1960s. This, together with the increasing and pressing demand of other social sectors, led to constant rise in public expenditure. Resultantly, a slowing down trend of the earlier expansion was noticed from the later-half of 1970s, and from 1980s crunch appeared with full visibility. Public funding declined in many countries like Japan, U.K., France, and USA.

The resource crunch announced in 1981 for the universities in UK is widely known, for that created serious disturbances in the university system leading to such unprecedented problems that some of them even faced the threat of 'bankruptcy' and they considered the situation 'traumatic'. This forced the universities to take steps to be cost-effctive and more efficient. They took initiatives to generate additional income mainly through more and more contract research and consultancy.

India was no exception either in respect of expansion or the resource crunch. With only 25 universities including 'deemed universities' in 1947-48, the number rose to 93 by 1970-71 and over 200 by now. Although universities in India have never been funded well, save exceptions and save the central universities and institutions of national importance like IITs, the real crunch has come now to all alike including these institutions. In fact, these institutions (Central universities and IITs) feel the crunch more for they were generally funded well in the past.

In the other developing countries, except China and South Korea, public expenditure on education has declined (Table 1.2). The resource crunch that the various developing countries are facing have been shown in the Table 1.3. Resultantly, the universities had to undertake plans and programmes to reduce expenditure and generate income as given in Table 1.4. This makes it abundantly clear that the universities have taken actions from the normal step of raising fees to undertaking of commercial activities.

Precisely,universities of both - the developed and the developing countries - have been facing the crunch. This has forced the universities to try to learn to be cost-effective, efficient and to go for sustained generation of income through various means, importantly, by reducing expenditure and tapping various sources for resource generation. For the universities, balancing the budget is a big question.

In India, inadequate funding has led to mounting

deficits and in some cases, for years together deficits continue. The causes of deficits as identified in a study by AIU are as follows:

(i) inadequate grants,

(ii) inefficiency in the distribution of funds,

(iii) rigidity in the method of funding,

(iv) adhocism in budgetary allocation by the State Governments, and

(v) financial mismanagement by universities.

Now there is no option to the universities but to accept the mandate to generate income, and following are the means for that:

(i) To rejuvenate the management and make it efficient and promising.

(ii) To reduce expenditure as far as possible.

(iii) To arrest the growing expenditure on as many counts as possible.

(iv) To generate income by:

(a) boosting the existing sources, and

(b) tapping new sources.

Justice Punnayya Committee, appointed by the University Grants Commission, has also recommended various measures to generate income mainly by raising various fees - tuition, hostel, etc. It has also strongly recommended to generate income through university-industry interaction. The Punnayya Committee has strongly recommended that the universities should generate at least 15% of the total recurring expenditure at the end of five years and at least 25% by the end of ten years. To achieve this target, it has recommended that the universities must draw up specific plans and programmes. The real question is how to go about?

For the purpose of generation of income, the universities have to go in that direction in a structured manner so that the income generation could be sustained.

In a scenario where most of the universities have deficits and some have deficits for years together, how would they move from that position to an additional income of 15% in relation to the total expenditures when expenditures are constantly rising? Salary bills alone accounts for 60 to 70 per cent expenditure. In the case of the universities which are already in the deficit trap, the priority task is to bail them out of that position for which it is only the lump-sum payment of grants that can save them. How far the governments would come to the rescue of these universities is anybody's guess. But it is also true that unless the government first bails out to start anew, on a clean slate, with the mandate to generate income, it will be impossible for the universities to meet the crisis.

In the given situation, the crisis can be met with determination and a well structured plan. But how to go about is the real question.

THE LEADERSHIP FACTOR

Basic to all plans to · travel to the routes for resource generation, is the crucial question of the leadership for it is directly related to conceiving vision, developing missions and motivating his people for successful organization of efforts to achieve the objectives with speed, efficiency and cost-effectiveness for these are, in the changing situation, important factors to be successful.

In an institution like a university where democratic structure is predominent and the most important constituents of the system are teachers and students, the job of the Vice-Chancellor is more difficult and onerous. Yet, it is the Vice-Chancellor who has to, with his leadership quality, carry the teachers and students with him in all his efforts to implement all his plans and programmes in the interest of the university. All efforts to balance the budget and to generate income must necessarily be done in a structured manner to make it sustainable.

VISION AND MISSIONS

Fundamental to all structured efforts to achieve objectives, is a vision statement which really means a dream of future of the university. In other words, vision is what the university wants it to be in future. And this dream could be anything that the management conceives for betterment of the university. For example, even though the university is financially in good health, it may decide that:

* it should be ahead of time than others in the field through reengineering,
* it should make improvements in some other areas to increase efficiency,
* it should close down some of its activities, which are no longer too relevant and likely to lose relevance in near future, and
* it should introduce new areas which have greater relevance in the changing scenario.

However, when the university is in a debt trap, what kind of vision statement it could be. It is really for the management to conceive, but in such a situation, the Vision Statement could be to achieve the following:

Vision		*Time Frame*
Finance		
Deficit to Surplus	:	3 years
Teaching and Research		
Making Teaching more relevant and Research current	:	2 years
Administration		
A Responsive and Efficient Management	:	1 year
Reputation		
A Better Image Projection	:	1 year

It is important that for a sustainable and balanced vision, in a situation of debt trap, not only that the financial position has to be improved and steps taken in that direction, other aspects which would help sustain the basic efforts should also be taken into consideration. In this case, they are: making teaching more relevant and research current; a responsive and efficient management; and finally, a better image projection.

THE CRUCIAL FACTOR

Team building is the crucial factor to achieve the vision and to implement the Missions without which the objectives are not likely to be achieved. Here too, the leadership factor will play the role to build the team that he needs to achieve the Vision Statement.

In order to build the team, the leader has to carry with him the constituents of the system i.e. faculty, students and staff. Although the Total Quality Management (TQM) concept of bottom-up approach can he applied, but pragmatically that may not work in the existing situation till the concept is understood across the organization. The head of the university i.e. the Vice-Chancellor or the Director of the Institute or the Principal of the college has to plan how best he should ensure that the message trickles down the line. For this, he has to plan out, hold discussions with his senior colleagues and move in the right direction. It would always be advantageous if the Vision Statement is properly spelt out in the form of a document to enable one and all to understand the 'why'. Efforts should be made to see that there is no scope to misinterpret the Vision Statement.

THE MISSIONS

It is only with dedicated Missions that the Vision can be achieved. The three 'Musts' for successful missions, according to Peter Drucker, are crucial. They are: Opportunities, Competence and Commitment. For obvious reasons, each of the three independently and together is important and therefore it should be ensured that they are there with the university.

STRATEGIES OF MISSIONS

For a structured plan to achieve the Vision, it is necessary to develop Missions. As the next step, it is necessary to design strategies to fulfill the set Missions. 'Strategy' which was basically borrowed from the military speaks as why each time to fulfill a Mission, strategies are necessary. Without strategy, there is no success. Strategies really decide the details how to meet success. For example, to fulfill the twin Missions—

(i) Reduction and Arresting of Expenditure, and *(ii)* Generation of Additional Income, Table 2.2, spells out the details how the Missions can be fulfilled. Development of perfect strategies is therefore of great importance and significance. If the strategies are developed well, chances of success are more.

FROM DEFICIT TO SURPLUS

Money saved is money generated. Therefore, reduction of expenditures and arresting the growth of expenditures ultimately lead to implied income generation and additionally, steps towards cost-effectiveness.

Besides effecting economy and thereby reducing expenditure in many possible areas, one important area which is accepted by all is deployment of minimum manpower. This is so for two reasons - one: to achieve cost-effectiveness and two: optimal utilisation of the staff help improve work culture and raise efficiency for idle staff pollutes the work environment and culture.

Broadly, the same principles apply to all efforts to arrest the growth of expenditure in selected areas. Efficient use of the facilities can certainly lead to arresting growth of expenditures e.g. electricity consumption, use of telephones, transport, stationary etc. What is really needed is a definite plan which is pursued vigorously and continuously, not half-heartedly and not just once or twice. To move from deficit to surplus, while savings definitely help in this direction, it is really the generation of non-government income that is crucial through various efforts e.g. sponsored research, alumni association, continuing education programme, revision of fees, investments to earn more interest and the much talked about university-industry interaction. These have all been discussed later in this chapter also.

MAKING TEACHING MORE RELEVANT AND RESEARCH CURRENT

It is expected that any academic institution would, in addition to the routine teaching, undertake research—both-basic, to make a good base of research strength, and applied, to generate income, and to extend the benefit of expertise and facilities to the society at large, mainly through the industry.

Strategies for the twin Missions of the Vision statement to make teaching more relevant and teaching more current, are also basically two. One: to involve industry/employers in a feed back system to make course-contents meaningful and teaching relevant, and two : to continue to promote basic research and motivate the faculty for applied research with the industry/ business houses.

While fund is a must for carrying out research, it is not the only parameter to ensure good result of research. Examples of the research work in the universities in the United Kingdom given in the chapter two clearly tell us that with less money, best results were given, and with much more money, not so high level of result could be given. Precisely, along with money, other factors are important e.g. level of researchers, facilities for research, areas of research etc.

RESPONSIVE AND EFFICIENT MANAGEMENT

In today's context, 'management' plays crucial role in all efforts be it reduction of expenditures, generation of income or providing of environment conducive to teaching and research. Unless the management is imaginative, responsive and trained to meet the various needs of the organization which is basically of teachers and students, there would be irritating problems to achieve the Vision Statement and fulfill the Missions. In view of this, it is necessary to involve the staff members in the policy planning to share responsibilities and also enjoy the achievements of the goals. In order to raise the level of efficiency, professional training is a must. This should be continuously done and exposures to good system, good culture, need also be provided.

BETTER IMAGE PROJECTION

Traditionally, very little attention is given to image building of any institution. Generally, it is taken for granted that since the purpose of an institute is to teach and train students, it is bound to have good impact in the society and that is enough. While it is true that the basic activity is certainly noble and fundamental to the existence, survival and development of the modern society, it must be remembered that in the changing scenario of competition to attract quality teachers, bright students and seeking to raise funds from industry, projection of the right and good image is a *sine-qua-non*.

Broadly, there are two factors of image building and projection, as given in the Figure 2.7. They are: internal image factors and external image factors. The various areas of image building, correction and projection are the following:

* reputation of overall teaching,
* reputation of research activities,
* reputation of discipline,
* reputation of teachers,
* reputation of students,
* reputation of management, and

* reputation of participation in social activities.

GENERATION OF INCOME

Broadly, for the purpose of generation of non-government income, following are the sources viz.:

* Sponsored Research Projects,
* Continuing Education Programme (CEP),
* Alumni Association,
* Fees - Tuition, Hostel etc.,
* Investments - short-term and long-term, and
* Interaction with Industry.

Sponsored Research Projects

Unlike consultancy activities through industry-interaction, there is no direct income from the Sponsored Research Frojects. But there is hidden income from the Sponsored Research Projects, particularly when there is a number of Projects in the university. The benefits of undertaking sponsored research projects are quite a few; they are:

* through the creation and acquisition of a number of facilities during the period the project work is done, the university benefits by such facilities after the projects are closed. If properly utilised, the university can save on equipment and at times consumables, which would ultimately save some money of the university which otherwise would have been required to spend for teaching/research purposes,
* the overhead charges of 15% may mean sizable income if there are a number of such projects in a particular university. Even if part of this

income is earmarked for updating the infrastructure facilities, there would be some flow of income through this channel, and

* through investments of the project funds which are not needed immediately for short-term duration, some income generation is always possible, but for that an alert and calculative mind is necessary. In fact, a suitable mechanism is needed.

For achieving what have been mentioned above, it is necessary that a common interface authority should be there, without which it would not be possible to achieve the objective fully.

Initiatives for Sponsored Research

With a view to providing opportunities to the universities and colleges, various departments of the Central Government and State Governments have been providing funds. During the Seventh Five Year Plan, the funds provided was Rs. 297.75 crores, which works out to Rs. 59.50 lakhs per year. During the Seventh Five Year Plan, the universities and colleges together bagged projects to the extent of 31.67% of the total amount of Rs. 297.75 crores. This, however, does not include the five IITs and IISc who bagged 21.64%. As against this, the research institutes bagged 34.72%.

During the Seventh Plan period, in terms of the number of universities and colleges which bagged sponsored projects, it was 132 out of 146. But in the case of colleges, as against 6942 in 1989-90, only 299 colleges could bag projects. There were about 2 lakhs, of teachers in the colleges. This certainly presents a disappointing picture. However, it is no surprise for, firstly a large number of colleges are not viable and secondly, the trend and motivation for undertaking research in the colleges is hardly any.

After the Seventh Five Year Plan which ended in 1989-90, the years 1990-91 and 1991-92 were the annual plan periods. The Eighth Five Year Plan actually started from 1992-93.

The Table 3.2 shows a growing trend of undertaking more projects, and investments of larger amount of money by the Goverrnment. In 1990-91 alone 1225 projects were approved as against 5314 in the Seventh Five Year Plan period.

The average annual investments by the various governments for R&D support during the Seventh Five Year Plan was Rs. 59.50 lakhs. As against this, investments in 1990-91 alone was Rs. 99.47 crores. Although in 1991-92, there was a slight fall in the investment, but in 1992-93, it rose to Rs.104.51 lakhs. In 1993-94, it was over 174 crores.

Table 3.2 shows that as against 1225 projects in 1990-91, in the year 1992-93, there were 1420. In 1991-92, there was a drop in the number of projects to 1149 and as such, the cost (Rs. 85.16 crores) was also less. When looked at these figures in relation to the figures of the Seventh Plan, the position was satisfactory. But keeping in view the inflation factors and the need to promote more research work, higher investments is called for.

International Scenario

An international comparison of research expenditures in the universities of five developed countries - Japan, USA, UK, Germany and France, given in Table 3.5, reveals that USA spent the highest (4540) billion Yen). Although Japan was next to USA, but it was far behind it, for it spent only 1140 billion Yen. In the case of UK, France and Germany, the expenditure-range was between 580 and 780 billion Yen.

For 1993, the Government of Japan earmarked 73.6 billion Yen for the various projects as given in Table 3.6. This includes 3.9 billion Yen for overseas scientific research which was for 'survey or research conducted abroad'. This was perhaps for exploring possibilities of investments for expansion programmes outside Japan. Such activities are strategically important for long-term targets.

Table 3.7 shows the trends of research grants paid by the Ministry of Education. Science and Culture (MONBUSHO). In terms of the billion Yen, in 1983, the total research grants paid by MONBUSHO was 39.5 billion Yen which rose to 73.6 billion Yen in 1993. Although the increase over 11 years does not appear to be significant, it was really good increase considering the fact that the rate of inflation has been minimum in Japan.

Continuing Education Programme

For a variety of reasons, Continuing Education Programme (CEP) can prove to be a stable and good source of income provided they are organised in a structured manner and after necessary assessment of the needs in and around the locality and region.

Besides the income generation through the Continuing Education Programme, there are quite a few benefits as mentioned in the Chapter three. For the purpose of organising the Continuing Education Programme in a structured and sustainable manner, the following would be necessary:

* Conceive programmes which in the context of the current liberalisation, would be of interest to the industry and other organizations to get their staff trained.
* Fix target groups and sell the idea particularly benefits of training: prepare simple but attractive brochure and mail them to the target groups. Additionally, personal contact over telephone will help.
* Prepare an estimate for a minimum number of trainees to ensure cost-effectiveness and about thirty per cent saving for the institution after meeting all expenses. Greater care should be taken fixing the fees that the trainees should pay, keeping in view all expenses, e.g. space, facilities, printing, postage, stationery, telephones, transport, honorarium to experts (internal and external) and some remuneration to staff members, and a saving of about 30% for the institution.
* Finalise list of experts and facilities and their availability and fix dates.
* In case the training programme is of a longer duration, say more than 3 to 5 days, provide opportunities and facilities to avoid boredom by arranging visits, entertainment programmes etc.
* Depending on the type of programme, visits to relevant places and discussions with different groups would be beneficial.

To achieve success, the following points should be borne in mind:

* Identification of target groups and conceiving

the right kind of programmes - by all departments,

* Number of trainees that will be cost-effective,
* Maximum number that should be limited to, for effective training programme,
* Which period(s) of the year would suit the organizations to spare their staff members for training, and
* Organizations which should first be approached and the target groups.

Alumni Association

Every university and every college has, over the years, educated and trained a large number of students and in the case of some universities and colleges, many of such students are doing well both in the country and abroad. In any case, there would always be at least some students of every university/college who are doing well in some profession or other. It is necessary to locate and involve them through the creation of an Alumni Association, in the developmental activities of their alma-mater. However, this should be done with care. Some hints about this have been given in the chapter three.

How universities in USA involve the alumni have also been narrated in the chapter three and it is because of the continuous involvement of the alumni by the universities that most of the universities in USA have been able to create sizable endowment funds with their contributions.

Income through Fees

Undeniably, the universities and colleges need to

raise tuition and other fees, for there has hardly been any revision in the last 20-30 years. However, in doing so, three guiding principles should be followed:

* there should be a gradual, rather than abrupt rise in fees,
* the fees should be related to the market value of the programmes. Even there could be a differential fee between urban and rural areas keeping in view the economic conditions of the parents, and
* reasonable and smooth facilities of loans and freeships for poor and meritorious must be provided. Justice Punnayya Committee, while recommending for upward revision of fees, has also emphasised the need of providing freeships and loans to the students.

Income through other Sources

(a) Renting out of facilities: Besides the conventional sources of income, depending upon the facilities that the universities have, there can be generation of income through renting out of facilities such as use of equipments of the departments at such hours when they are not needed for teaching purposes. Similarly, facilities of space and equipments in the Gymkhana may also be rented out.

By way of extending library facilities to the external persons, the universities can also generate some income. However, care should be taken to see that the establishment cost is much less than the earnings through such source.

(b) Long-term - Short-term Investments: Income through interest of investments is a potential source for

generation of income. While universities must be earning some interest, an alert and knowledgeable person who can get funds in time and can plan out the spendings and is also knowledgeable of the various investment opportunities *vis-a-vis* the rules of investments required to be followed by them, can get more interest than are currentiv being earned.

(c) Sale/Lease out of Land: Another non-conventional suggestion for generation of income is to sell/lease out of unusable land with the permission of the Government. Many universities and colleges have vast lands not required in the foreseeable future. In fact, protecting the land and keeping it free from encroachment itself is a problem of the management. If such land is leased out, or sold out with the permission of the Government, without affecting the aesthetic aspect of the campus, that will help create an Endowment Fund for the university and would, over the years, contribute to the running cost or to meet some developmental needs of the university.

(d) Donations: Although for making donations to the universities, the Government has now provided exemptions to the donors to the extent of 100% and another 25% for funding approved research projects, it is a matter of attracting and persuading the potential donors who expect approach by those who need funds. For this, strategic marketing by the university is necessary and for doing that, again it is the leadership factor that will play the crucial role.

Why University-Industry Interaction

Over the years, much has been said, debated and written about the university-industry interaction. Yet, little precious has taken place. While quite a few reasons could be listed out for this, one important reason is the lack of appreciation of the underlying benefits which cut across the society. When somebody talks of motivating people to go in for interaction with industry, mostly it is mistaken to be a pressure to generate income for the university. Income is in fact just one aspect only, albeit important. The fact, which generally does not come under focus is that primarily it is for national development, and not merely for generating income, that meaningful and effective interaction between the academics and industry is necessary.

In an industrial survey in USA, it has been found that university research contributes to the advance of industrial development. Theoretically, what is true in USAR in this regard is true elsewhere also in so far as the valuable contributions of the academics to the industry is concerned.

Admittedly, in the process and through university-industry interaction, all sectors are benefited. While industry benefits more, university too gains for, besides the achievement of contributions to the industrial development of the nation and the monetary benefit attached to that, in the process, the individuals involved in the research activities and application thereof, continuously develop their capabilities which, in turn, help in further research and of course teaching. In the developed countries, companies spend about 10% of their revenues on R & D. It is estimated that a Company like the Toyota spends about US$ 5 billion which is about three times of our national budget on technology.

National R&D Expenditure

Of the total national R & D expenditure of

Rs. 5141.64 crores in 1992-93, the Central Government spent as high as 64.3% and the share of the State Governments was 9.4%. Thus the governmental share (Central and State together) was 73.7%. Investments by industry in R & D has hardly been anything worth-mentioning. It has also not spent in in any significant order on R & D through universities by way of interaction. Industry spent only 15%. as against 71% by the industry in Janan. According to an editorial of the Times of India (Bombay - March 17, 1995), only 12 companies had approached the Department of Scientific and Industrial Research "to take advantage" of the 125 per cent tax deduction on investments in research and development and that is 'truly shocking.' Apparently, it is not a question of funds needed for investments in research, but a question of priority that the companies decide. For example, as the editorial points out the 'industry spends a mere 0.6. per cent of its sales turnover on R & D, against six to seven per cent on advertising and marketing and 0.5 to 2 per cent on entertainment'. This certainly points out to the apathy of the industry for R & D aspect.

The editorial rightly concludes that 'if Indian business has to become globally competitive and stand on its own feet, however, it has to invest in technology development at home as well as encourage whatever indigenous effort is already going on. This calls for an improved interface between business the government and R&D community'.

As regards the public sector, expenditure on R & D during 1992-93 was 11.4%, the major sectors involved in R & D activities being defence production and supplies, space, heavy industry, petroleum and natural gas, steel, telecommunications, chemicals and petrochemicals, atomic energy and electronics. Table 4.5

shows the percentage share by the public sector in national R & D over a period of 11 years. In terms of percentage, it has remained the same, for in 1980-81, it was 11.4% (Rs. 86.37 crores) and it remained the same in 1992-93 although in terms of money, it rose to Rs. 586.7 crores. In between 1981-82 and 1991-92, the percentage share was less.

International Scenario

In 1990, in relation to the GNP, the entire world average of R & D expenditure was Rs.2.55% improving from 1.85% in 1980 and 2.22% in 1985. In that year, (1990), the developed countries spent 2.92 on R & D as percentage of GNP., while it was only 0.64 in the case of developing countries in that year. However, in the case of developing countries, there was marginal increase for in 1980 it was 0.52%, and in 1985 - 0.54%. In 1990, USA alone spent 43.4% of the world R & D expenditure of 452.6 billion US$ as against only 23.2% by the whole of Europe. The share of the entire Asia was only 20.2% while the former USSR spent 12.3%. The remaining was in Africa - 0.2% and 0.7% in Oceania.

In UK, consequent to the cuts in the university grants on an average 17% imposed by the Thatcher government in 1981, the universities had to initiate various steps to boost university-industry interaction as a result of which, their income through interaction raised from 535 million pounds in 1985-86 to 762 million pounds in 1989-90.

In Japan, recognising the growing importance in Science and Technology, the Ministry of Education, Science and Culture (MONBUSHO) conduct 5 various programmes "to encourage increased cooperation between the universities and industry" as shown in Table

4.13. National Research expenditure in Japan in 1993 was 13,772 billion Yen of which 71% i.e. 9,743 billion yen was shared by the industry, 17% i.e. 2,408 billion Yen research expenditure was in the universities and the remaining 12%, i.e. 1,621 billion yen was in the Governmental research institutes (Figure 4.3).

It is interesting that even in 1983, university-industry co-operation was minimal, but increased phenomenally by 1992. Fifty six researchers were accepted and 66 joint research projects materialised in 1983. The corresponding figures for 1992 were 1241 and 1398 respectively.

Although late we are, nevertheless it is time that the university-industry interaction should be accepted in the right meaning and spirit and a partnership should be forged with mutual cooperation. This is all the more necessary because of the liberalised economic policies and the new possibilities.

The new possibilities in the fast changing globalized scenario is, as Dr. R.A. Mashelkar holds, lies in the concept of "techno-globalization", in which he thinks "India can become a part of this in the coming decade provided it understands the forces that are driving the globalization of R & D".

Multi-faculty University-Industry Interaction

Rather frequently, a question is raised whether the multi-faculty universities which are having mostly the departments of humanities, social sciences and not engineering, and similarly the colleges, would be able to have any meaningful interaction with industry. The short answer to this is 'yes'. However, it depends on the initiative, drive and capabilities that may be developed and organised for this purpose. Although a large number of universities and colleges have good facilities, little interaction has taken place. It is true that it has to be a two-way traffic between the academics and industry, but the fact remains that there has been a general lack of initiatives on the part of the universities and colleges.

How to go for Interaction

There are certain essentials for industry interaction and six such essentials have been mentioned in Table 4.14. Briefly, they are: to identify and develop expertise and facilities, to prepare document of capabilities, to frame consultancy rules, to survey the market, to market capabilities and finally to build and sustain the interaction. The Figure 4.5 shows how these steps are connected with each other.

Developing the expertise is really the first step. The university has first to identify the faculty members in the various departments who have the potential to be consultants, broadly for the following purposes:

* product, process design/development,
* problem-solving in the specific areas of specialisation,
* retainership i.e. advising on a continuing basis,
* testing and Evaluation, and
* other areas.

After the experts are identified, it is important that the document of capabilities has to be prepared giving details of the strengths of the departments and specializations for possibile interaction with the industry so that while marketing the capabilities, this document can be handed over to the industry. It is also important that the university assures the industry through the document, a smooth, time-bound and result-oriented approach for interaction. Information for the interface authority should also be given for initiating interaction. In short, it should look like a business document of the university, that it means business.

It is essential to frame consultancy rules and to appoint an effective interface authority who should function as the leader to motivate the faculty and work as interface between university and industry and who will also ensure that the interaction is meaningful and smooth.

Surveying the market and marketing the capabilities are important matters which have to be organised by the interface authority. What is important is to identify the possible clients with some basic data to find out which are the potential areas in an organization where the departments with their expertise and facilities can offer something. Creating a data-base is a "Must" to sustain interaction. Collaboration with Confederation of Indian Industry (CII), Chamber of Commerce, Indian Chemical Manufacturers' Association (ICMA), etc. would prove of great help in this direction.

In a university where.the universitv-industry interaction is yet to take off, it would be desirable that the interface authority should involve the Vice-Chancellor/ Head of the Institute for a fruitful discussion. This can be done over a cup of tea or at home, lunch or dinner. This has to be decided keeping in view who is to be invited and what is the potential of interaction in terms of money and work.

Building credibility and sustaning the interaction with the industry is very important and for that the conditions given in Table 4.16 should be borne in mind. Broadly, they are: Quality, cost-effectiveness, confidentiality, time-frame and not infrequently, acceptance of penalty in the event of failures on the part of the university.

There is nothing that does not have some problems. Similarly there are certain problems in the way of the faculty-industry interaction e.g., faculty-industry isolation, lack of awareness of capabilities and expertise of faculty as also of problems and needs of industry by the faculty, faculty options between sponsored research and consultancy for career advancement, lack of faculty motivation due to operational constraints and inadequate financial incentives and finally the industry reservations because of issues of secrecy, requirement of rigid time schedule etc. Most of these problems can, however, be solved with the cooperation and a positive will to do that. These have been discussed elaborately in the chapter four.

How a multi-faculty university can go for interaction has been discussed in the chapter four, with recipes for various departments. It is believed that if steps are taken with a dedicated will, and missionary zeal to initiate interaction with industry, much can be achieved.

In order to achieve this, action plan time-frame over a period of 12 months, mentioned in the chapter four should be of help. The suggested action plan should prove to be handy to the universities and all other institutions willing to go in for generation of income through interaction with the industry. In any case, the suggestions are not exhaustive, for no suggestion can be complete. These are only the suggested lines for those who wish to go for interaction.

Interface Factor

Earlier in the book, at more than one place, importance of the interface facilities has been mentioned for effective and meaningful interaction with industry. It is important to ensure that the interface authority is the right person for he has to be in constant touch with the faculty and interact with industry every now and then. This calls for quality leadership with the requisite industry-leaning, preferably with industry background.

Generally, the interface authority in the IITs and the University of Roorkee is called the Dean. In the Indian Institute of Science (IISc), it is called 'Chairman, Centre for Scientific and Industrial Research'. In most of the universities, there is an independent interface authority which is generally called Professor-in-charge. By whatever name it is called, the fact is that the interface authority is a part-time faculty whether it is in IITs, IISc or universities. In the fast changing scenario, when the interface authority has to devote more time, work aggressively with the industry and pursue the activities vigorously it is necessary that he should be a whole-time person. The interface authority is required to perform multifarious functions, some of which are listed in the chapter five including the fund management.

For a meaningful, vibrating and sustained consultancy activities and also to undertake some commercial activities, as is the demand of the changing time, it is necessary to understand the needs of the changing time. The needs include updated knowledge of industries of various types and sizes, going and meeting the industry again and again for marketing purposes, vigorously pursuing with the faculty to complete consultancy jobs and also to motivate those who are not yet in the consultancy activities. Legal implications in the changing environment is another important aspect which the interface authority has necessarily to know. In fact, he is also to educate all the faculty with the various provisions of laws particularly relating to intellectual property rights, patenting etc.

CONCEPT OF UNIVERSITY COMPANY OF UK

The concept and model of University Company of UK, which has been working successfully in a number of universities there, need to be experimented in the Indian context. The structure and organization of the company would take care of the various problems that one hears not infrequently from the faculty members. As a company, it would also be able to undertake commercial activities and that is a need in the .changing time which a university under the existing laws, cannot do so.

POSSIBILITIES FOR COLLEGES

The recipes that have been given in the chapter four for the universities of multi-faculty characters are also suitable for the colleges for humanities, science, social sciences and art, besides engineering colleges.

The concept of the university company can very well be adopted by a group of 10 to 15 colleges, which may include one or two engineering colleges and perhaps polytechnics and a company can be formed. To achieve the same objectives as in the case of University Company, basically meant for the Universities, the benefits of Consortium of Colleges as alternative for colleges have been mentioned in the chapter five. A Model of Consortium of Colleges, its structure and functions have also been given in the chapter five.

Finally, it is a matter of will, leadership and organization that alone can bring success. There is really no short-cut for generation of income.

Index